A
George Jean Nathan
Reader

A
George Jean Nathan
Reader

Selected and Edited

by A. L. Lazarus

Rutherford • Madison • Teaneck
Fairleigh Dickinson University Press
London and Toronto: Associated University Presses

Associated University Presses
440 Forsgate Drive
Cranbury, NJ 08512

Associated University Presses
25 Sicilian Avenue
London WC1A 2QH, England

Associated University Presses
P.O. Box 488, Port Credit
Mississauga, Ontario
Canada L5G 4M2

The paper used in this publication meets the requirements
of the American National Standard for Permanence of Paper
for Printed Library Materials Z39.48-1984.

Library of Congress Cataloging-in-Publication Data

Nathan, George Jean, 1882–1958.
  [Essays. Selections]
  A George Jean Nathan reader / selected and edited by A.L. Lazarus.
  p.   cm.
  Includes selected letters.
  Bibliography: p.
  ISBN 0-8386-3369-2 (alk. paper)
  I. Lazarus, Arnold Leslie.   II. Nathan, George Jean, 1882–1958.
Correspondence.   Selections.   1989.   III. Title.
PS3527.A72A6   1990
818'.5209—dc20   88-45873
                                                                      CIP

PRINTED IN THE UNITED STATES OF AMERICA

Contents

Preface (By Three of Nathan's Contemporaries)

Critic's View of a Critic

John Mason Brown (1900–1968)

Pasted in the back of my copy of George Jean Nathan's *The Critic and the Drama* I find, to my surprise, a review of it which I wrote for the *Harvard Crimson* in 1922. I was 22, George 40. I did not get to know him until eight years later, when a book of mine appeared that included a chapter on Nathan that mixed thistles and roses. . . . Of course, I had followed him in print for years, with the wonder, the delighted shock, and the admiration that all of us who were young then felt as we gobbled up his audacities in *Smart Set, The American Mercury,* and in books. Of course, too, I had come to recognize him as the landmark he was at first nights, to watch for his disdainful exits at the ends of many second acts and, if near enough, to steal glances at his remarkably handsome, haughty, and expressive face, on which reviews blistering or favorable seemed to be written. . . .

One meeting (a summit for me) occurred during the intermission of some forgotten opening in the fall of 1930. He came up to me in the lobby, as trim a figure as a fencing master[1] with his cigarette holder jauntily aslant, and his dark eyes sparkling with amusement at what he properly guessed was my embarrassment. After introducing himself, he made it clear that he, the wizard of the verbal cactus, had not been scratched by my thistles.

In the years that followed I saw a good deal of George, at and away from the theatre. I saw him quietly at my home. I saw him at stormy meetings of the Critics Circle when at times he behaved like a spoiled child. I saw him at late afternoon gatherings at Twenty-One. . . . And I had many treasured stag evenings at Lüchow's or at The Colony with him, Brooks Atkinson, and John Anderson, at which George officiated as the most gracious and spoiling of hosts.

I must have noticed as the years slipped by that his curly dark hair was

---

From *The New York Times* (13 April, 1958), Drama section, p. 3.

whitening. . . . But for me his eyes, his face, his smile, and his laugh never lost their youth. Though he was 74 when I last saw him, he did not seem old to me, and he never will. He will always remain . . . as young as he was when I first met him, as young as when I first read him, as young as he continues to be in print.

His books, not all of the more than forty he published but most of them, are spread across two shelves in my study, and I am amazed at their vitality every time I turn to them. They have different titles—some as misleading in their solemnity as *Encyclopedia of the Theatre* or *Since Ibsen;* some masquerading as routine reference works under the name of *Theatre Book of the Year;* and others as tempting in their ingenuity as *The House of Satan* and *The World in Falseface*. But all of them are alike in their gleeful irreverence; all are battles in the same campaign against mediocrity; and all could with equal accuracy be known (to choose again from the Nathan shelves) as either *The Autobiography of an Attitude* or *Mr. George Jean Nathan Presents.*

Reviewers, as a whole, only cover performances; George Nathan, as a critic, gave them. He was a dazzling showman, and what he wrote was often more entertaining than what he wrote about. He would have been the first to admit that he had in him a touch of charlatanism that he thought any first-rater had to have to get his message across.

George, like his Katzenjammer brother H. L. Mencken, delighted upsetting any boat with a false dignitary aboard. He rejoiced in the mucker pose, loved to shock the conventional, and never tired of keeping his thumb to his nose. His was the most sizable snicker-see as far as was known to American dramatic criticism. This man, who wielded it ruthlessly and joyously, was blessed with a mind of exceptional alertness. . . . He may often have chosen to have bad manners but he seldom failed to have good taste.

George's prowess at attack has caused many people to think of him only as a destructive critic, forgetting how much there was that needed to be destroyed and how constructive was the service he performed in destroying what he did. If he had not possessed that unusual skill, the standards of the American theatre would not be what they are today, and the excellence he championed would not be taken for granted.

George loved the theatre as few have, and he fought valiantly for the recognition of such dramatists as Eugene O'Neill, Sean O'Casey, and William Saroyan.[2] . . . George also loved life, beauty, laughter, pleasure; and he trumpeted his hedonism. . . . "Beauty," he once wrote, "makes idiots sad as it makes wise men merry."

---

1. At Cornell, Nathan had been captain of the varsity fencing team.
2. See "Profiles of Playwrights" below.

Account Closed

Brooks Atkinson (1894–1983)

. . . As a critic he [George Jean Nathan] was in the tradition of two men he thoroughly admired—Shaw and [James] Huneker, whose salty comments appeared successively in many newspapers and magazines. George liked Shaw's egotistical jeers at stuffiness and cant in the theatre. He liked Huneker's enthusiasm for European art and thought. Having spent a year of [pre]graduate study in the University of Bologna, and having traveled in Europe, he had an extensive background of his own, and he knew how provincial and pallid American art was at the turn of the century.

When he and Mencken took over *Smart Set* in 1914 (certainly the most unlikely magazine to leave a mark on American culture) they tossed decorum out of the office window and applied the bastinado to decorum wherever they found it. They belabored all kinds of sacred cows—not only in literature but in public morals and university education. "Herr Professor" became an opprobrious epithet.

With the First World War shaking America out of its provincialism, the time was ripe for a cultural upheaval. Thousands of people who were amused by Nathan and Mencken also believed in the fundamental common sense of what they were writing. It was the most stimulating unsettling and salutary period of the century in America.

Since creative writers take first rank in any culture. O'Neill must be regarded as the father of modern American drama. For he wrote the first serious plays that have to be taken seriously. But it is a fortunate thing for him and for the American theatre that he had a prophet who could prepare an audience. Before O'Neill was generally known, Nathan had published some of his short plays in *Smart Set*. When his first full-length play, *Beyond the Horizon,* was produced on Broadway in 1920 O'Neill already had a powerful friend in court who not only recognized his genius but understood the broad significance to the theatre and culture of what he was writing. When the time came, the iconoclast became the herald. Nathan's impact on the American theatre when it was coming of age was invaluable. He stood for excellence.

As a hedonist, he eliminated politics from his category of adult subjects. "I decline to pollute my mind with such obscenities," he said. But this article in his credo prevented him from participating in the America that began with the Depression. A political revolution equivalent to his cultural revolution changed the social values of the American civilization, but he remained aloof. He was not sour. He simply was not interested.

From *The New York Times* (27 April, 1958), Drama section, p. 1.

Although his later writing lacked the cocky joyousness of his *Smart Set* and *Mercury* days, his iconoclastic point of view never changed. Nor did he. His hair turned white. But he was still the trim immaculate slender man of the world who dressed with elegance, patronized the best restaurants, and lived in the same apartment.[1] Apparently it had not been tidied up for thirty-five years.

When he suspected that a bore was testing his defenses, he could have a forbidding exterior. But he was a cheerful man with a soft voice, the manners of a gentleman, and the convivial loyalties of a comrade.

---

1. The Royalton, 44 West 44th Street, New York City

George Jean Nathan

H. L. Mencken (1880–1956)

One thinks of Gordon Craig,[1] not as a jester, but as a very serious and even solemn fellow. For a dozen years past, all the more sober dramatic critics of America have approached him with the utmost politeness, and to the gushing old maids and autointoxicated professors of the Drama League of America he has stood for the last word in theatrical æstheticism. Moreover, a good deal of this veneration has been deserved, for Craig has done excellent work in the theatre, and is a man of much force and ingenuity and no little originality. Nevertheless, there must be some flavor of low, bar-room wit in him, some echo of Sir Toby Belch and the *Captain of Köpenick*,[2] for a year or so ago he shook up his admirers with a joke most foul. Need I say that I refer to the notorious Nathan affair? Imagine the scene: the campus Archers and Walkleys in ponderous conclave, perhaps preparing their monthly cablegram of devotion to Maeterlinck. Arrives now a messenger with dreadful news. Gordon Craig, from his far-off Italian retreat, has issued a bull praising Nathan! Which Nathan? George Jean, of course. What! The *Smart Set* scaramouche, the ribald fellow, the raffish mocker, with his praise of Florenz Ziegfeld, his naughty enthusiasm for pretty legs, his contumacious scoffing at Brieux,[3] Belasco, Augustus Thomas, Mrs. Fiske?[4] Aye; even so. And what has Craig to say of him? . . . In brief, that he is the *only* American dramatic critic worth reading, that he knows far more about the theatre than all the honorary pallbearers of criticism rolled together, that he is immeasurably

---

From *Prejudices, First Series* (New York: Knopf, 1919), pp. 208-23. When Mencken published this essay, Nathan was only twenty-seven years old.

the superior, in learning, in sense, in shrewdness, in candor, in plausibility, in skill at writing. . . .

What Craig, an intelligent man, discovered was his [Nathan's] extraordinary capacity for differentiating between sham and reality, his catholic freedom from formulæ and prejudice, his astonishing acquaintance with the literature of the theatre, his firm grounding in æsthetic theory—above all, his capacity for making what he writes interesting, his uncommon craftsmanship. This craftsmanship had already got him a large audience; he had been for half a dozen years, indeed, one of the most widely read of American dramatic critics. . . .

Nathan ardently champions such diverse men as Avery Hopwood, Florenz Ziegfeld, Lord Dunsany, Ferenc Molnar, and Gerhart Hauptmann, all of whom have one thing in common: They are full of ideas and know their trade. In Europe, of course, there are many more such men than in America, and some of the least of them are almost as good as our best. That is why Nathan is forever advocating the presentation of their works—not because he favors foreignness for its own sake but because it is so often accompanied by sound achievement and by stimulating example to our own artists. . . .

Nathan does not denounce melodrama with a black cap upon his head, painfully demonstrating its inferiority to the drama of Ibsen and Euripides; he simply sits down and writes a little melodrama [*Bottoms Up,* 1917] so extravagantly ludicrous that the whole genre collapses.

He is intensely interested in [originality] of whatever sort, if it be only free from sham. Such experimentalists as Max Reinhardt, George Bernard Shaw . . . such divergent originals as Dunsany, George M. Cohan, and Arthur Schnitzler have enlisted his partisanship. He saw something new to our theatre in the farce of Avery Hopwood before anyone else saw it; he at once rescued what was sound in the Little Theatre movement [e.g., Eugene O'Neill] from mere attitudinizing and pseudo-intellectuality. . . .

He saw at once the high merit of Ibsen as a dramatic craftsman and welcomed him as a reformer of dramatic technique, but he also saw how platitudinous was the ideational content of the plays and announced the fact in terms highly offensive to the Ibsenites. But the Ibsenites have vanished, and Nathan remains . . .

Nathan has made it [drama criticism] amusing, stimulating, challenging—even, at times, startling. And to this business, [more often than not] artfully concealed, he has brought a sound and thorough acquaintance with the [critical] work of pioneers Lessing, Schlegel, Hazlitt, *et al.,* and an even wider acquaintance with every nook and corner of the current theatrical scene across the water. And to discharge this extraordinarily copious information he has [sometimes] hauled and battered the English language into new and astounding forms. When English has failed he has helped it out with French, German, Italian, American, Swedish, Russian . . . algebraic symbols, musical notations, and signs of the Zodiac. This manner is of course not without its perils. A man so inordinately articulate is bound to succumb, now and then, to the seductions of mere virtuosity. The average critic of the drama does well if he gets a single new and racy phrase into an essay. Nathan does well if he dilutes his inventions with enough commonplaces to enable the average reader to understand his discourse at all. . . . He carries his avoidance of the cliché to the length of an *idée fixe*. It would be difficult to find, in all his books, a dozen of the rubber stamps of criticism. . . . At best this incessant flight from the obvious makes for an arresting style, a procession of fantastic and pungent neologisms—in brief, for Nathanism.

---

1. Edward Gordon Craig (1872–1966). English critic and producer; son of the actress Ellen Terry. See his letter to Nathan, p. 199.
2. Satirical anti-Nazi play by Carl Zuckmayer (1896–1977)
3. Brieux, Belasco, Archer, Walkley, Maeterlinck, Thomas, et al., see Glossary.
4. But Nathan later praised Mrs. Fiske in *Since Ibsen* (New York: Knopf, 1933), p. 146.

Acknowledgments

For gracious encouragement or substantive help, or both, I am indebted to the following: Julie Haydon (Mrs. George Jean Nathan); Thomas Yoseloff and the George Jean Nathan Estate; Julien Yoseloff, Director, Associated University Presses; Lauren Lepow, Managing Editor, Associated University Presses; Nancy Kennedy, copy editor; Donald Eddy, Curator of the Nathan Collection, Cornell University; Jean Preston, Curator of Manuscripts, Library of Princeton University; Donald Gallup, Beinecke Library of Americana, Yale University; Averill Kadis and Neil Jordahl, The Mencken Collection, Enoch Pratt Free Library, Baltimore, Maryland; Ellen Dunlap, Humanities Research Center, University of Texas, Austin; Lois Szladits, Curator of the Berg Collection, New York Public Library; Diane Haskell, the Newberry Library, Chicago; Saundra Taylor, the Lilly Library, Bloomington, Indiana; Anne Laskey and Laura Kusler, Academy of Motion Picture Arts & Sciences; D. C. Weber, Special Collections, Stanford University Library; JoAnne Hamlin, Reference Librarian, University of California, Santa Barbara; Betty Trammell, Periodicals Archivist, University of California, Santa Barbara; Faith Behrens and Myra Nichols, Goleta, California, Public Library; Katherine Helsell, Sunnyvale, California; Virginia Bidgood, Santa Ynez, California; Nina Krilanovich, Santa Barbara, California; Rachel Silva, Marblehead, Massachusetts; Dianne Runnels, Minneapolis, Minnesota; Karie Friedman, Urbana, Illinois; Paul Rieder, production editor; Keo Felker Lazarus, Santa Barbara, California; and Brynne Lazarus, Sunnyvale, California.

For permission to reprint selections and photographs under copyright I acknowledge with thanks the co-operation of the following: Mrs. George Jean Nathan, Mr. Thomas Yoseloff, the Nathan Estate, and Fairleigh Dickinson University Press for all the selections not otherwise specified below; Mr. R. A. Boose, Chairman, Fitzgerald Literary Trustees, for F. Scott Fitzgerald's letter of December, 1923, to Bernard Vaughan and for the photograph of Scott and Zelda from Zelda Fitzgerald's Scrapbook in the Library of Princeton University; Condé Nast Publications for Nathan's "Lillian Gish" from *Vanity Fair* (November 1931); Cornell University and Donald Eddy, Curator of the Nathan Collection, for all the extant Nathan correspondence not otherwise specified here; *Esquire* for excerpts from Nathan's "The Happiest Days of H. L. Mencken" (October

7

1957) and the Fitzgerald portion of Nathan's "Memories of Fitzgerald, Lewis, and Dreiser" (October 1958); Lillian Gish and James Frasher for the photograph of Miss Gish facing page 254 in *The Movies, Mr. Griffith and Me* (published 1969 by Prentice-Hall; rights now controlled by the authors); Harcourt Brace Jovanovich for Nathan's essays "Best Place to Work" and "Country Life in New York" (published 1941 by Reynal and Hitchcock; rights now controlled by Harcourt Brace Jovanovich); *New York Times* for John Mason Brown's "Critic's View of a Critic" (13 April 1958) and for Brooks Atkinson's "Account Closed" (27 April 1958); The Eugene O'Neill Literary Trustees, Yale University, for O'Neill's letter of 14 June 1926 to Isaac Goldberg; Pratt Library, Baltimore Maryland, and the trustees of the Mencken Literary Estate, for Nathan's letters to H. L. Mencken's brother August; Pennsylvania University Press for Theodore Dreiser's letter of 7 August 1932 to Nathan, from Robert Elias, ed., *Letters of Theodore Dreiser: a Selection* (University of Pennsylvania Press, 1959) also from the same book Dreiser's letters to Nathan, 19 September 1932 and 17 April 1933; The Library of Princeton University for Nathan's letter of 14 November 1919 to F. Scott Fitzgerald from Scrapbook #1, and for Zelda Fitzgerald's letter of fall, 1930 from The Fitzgerald Papers, Box 41, folder 62; Random House for H. L. Mencken's "George Jean Nathan," *Prejudices, First Series* (Knopf, 1919; rights now controlled by Random House); Simon & Schuster for the photograph of Gordon Craig facing page 169 in Isaac Goldberg's *The Theatre of George Jean Nathan* (1926); Van Pelt Library of the University of Pennsylvania for the photograph of Theodore Dreiser (*circa* 1900) from The Dreiser Collection of the Van Pelt Library Special Collections; and Thomas Yoseloff for all the photographs not otherwise specified above.

Introduction

George Jean Nathan was born in Fort Wayne, Indiana, on 14 February 1882. His well-to-do parents and other relatives helped to propel him early into prominence. His own talents and quality of mind, along with a cosmopolitan education, propelled him into brilliance as a critic of drama.

George's father, Charles Narét-Nathan, originally from Alsace-Lorraine, was a graduate of Heidelberg University, a practical linguist, and a world traveler. He was also a successful investor. He owned the Perét Vineyard of France and a coffee plantation near Bahia, Brazil. He had spent eight years in Brazil, six in Argentina, three in China, and two in India. George's Uncle Paul Nathan was a professor of history at the University of Brussels.

George's mother, Ella Nördlinger Nathan, was born in Fort Wayne. Her parents had come from Nördlinger, and her mother, Hannah Myorson, were among the first settlers of Fort Wayne, when it was still Indiana Territory. They had emigrated in a covered wagon from Chambersburg, Pennsylvania, their first stop in America. Grandfather Nördlinger, a leading frontier trader, became the prime mover in developing Fort Wayne as one of the largest trading posts in the Midwest. (Some members of the family, when writing their name, dropped the umlaut from Nördlinger, preferring Nordlinger or, as a phonetic compromise, Nirdlinger.)

George's mother was educated at St. Mary's Convent Academy in nearby Notre Dame. (Here she befriended Ella Quinlan, who was to marry the actor James O'Neill and become the mother of Eugene O'Neill.) Ella Nathan's Catholicism apparently had little effect on George; he remained an agnostic for most of his life like his friend Eugene O'Neill. But in 1955, when Goerge married the actress Julie Haydon, he converted to Catholicism.

Growing up in an affluent household, George was exposed to highly qualified tutors. He studied several languages, took piano lessons, and read avidly, especially history and literature, including drama.

In 1888, when George was six years old, the family moved to Cleveland. Here George's Uncle Fred Nördlinger-Nixon managed playhouses for a Cleveland and Philadelphia syndicate. Because of this connection, at least in part, George and his parents attended many a play during the 1880s and most of the 1890s. At the age of ten George met Sarah Bernhardt when she was a house guest at Uncle Nixon's. She placed on his finger a souvenir ring, which he wore for several years.

From time to time, during these same years, George spent several summers in Europe with his father, who was engaged in international business transactions. For some of the regular school sessions, after these sojourns, the precocious young man was enrolled as a special student at the University of Bologna (1897–98), at the University of Paris (1898), and at Heidelberg University (1899). At the age of sixteen, while he was a student in Paris, he wrote the essay "Love: a Scientific Analysis."[1]

Back home in 1900, at the age of eighteen, George entered Cornell University, from which he was graduated in 1904, the year his father died and his mother moved to Philadelphia. At Cornell, George excelled in his courses, mainly literature, and he became editor of the *Cornell Daily Sun* and the *Cornell Widow*. He also won prizes, including a gold medal, for his main extracurricular activity—fencing, no doubt influenced by his experience at Heidelberg.

In 1905, with the help of another uncle—Charles Nordlinger, drama critic of the *New York Herald*—George got a job as a cub reporter on the *Herald* at a salary of $15 a week. He also sold feature articles to the *Sunday Herald*.

The following year, when he was twenty-four, he was hired as the drama critic of *The Bohemian* magazine by Lynn Wright, a fellow alumnus from Cornell. Two years later Nathan achieved national visibility when *Harper's Weekly* began publishing his play reviews on a regular basis.

Meanwhile at such fashionable restaurants as Delmonico's and Lüchow's Nathan fraternized with many a celebrity of the New York world of theatre, music, journalism, and publishing—among them, Samuel Knopf (Alfred's father), Victor Herbert, H. N. McClure, David Belasco, Marie Dressler, Diamond Jim Brady, and the talented James Huneker ("Lord Jim"), one of Nathan's idols among the critics. At Lüchow's or the Hofbräuhaus, Nathan may well have brushed shoulders with H. L. Mencken, but their first formal meeting occurred in the offices of *Smart Set* magazine in the summer of 1908.

Here, while Mencken was appointed literary editor, Nathan was appointed drama critic. The Editor-in-Chief was Willard Wright, a self-driven dynamo who was also turning out best-selling detective stories under the pen-name of "S. S. Van Dine." In 1914, when Wright became incapacitated by illness, he recommended to *Smart Set*'s owner, E. F. Warner, that "a first-rate successor as editor would be George Jean Nathan." Warner acquiesced. He approached Nathan with an offer, but according to Burton Rascoe, Nathan agreed to accept only on condition that Henry Mencken be appointed co-editor. (*Smart Set Anthology*. New York: Reynal and Hitchcock, 1934. p. xxxiii). By the terms of the ensuing contract, Nathan was to manage the office in New York, while Mencken was to commute from Baltimore "at least once a month."

Under the aegis of Nathan and Mencken the *Smart Set* enjoyed even more enthusiastic acceptance than ever before, especially among the literati. *Smart Set* published first pieces by writers who were to become the stars of the 1920s and 1930s. For example, it published Eugene O'Neill's one-act plays "The Long Voyage Home" in 1917 and in 1918, "Ile" and "The Moon of the Caribbees." James Joyce's *Dubliner* stories "The Boarding House" and "A Little Cloud" appeared first in *Smart Set,* as did F. Scott Fitzgerald's one-act play "The Debutante" and Somerset Maugham's story "Miss Thompson," source of the subsequent film *Rain.* But in 1923, beset by Warner's financial difficulties, the magazine folded. Even before then, however, Nathan and Mencken had become disenchanted in their relations with Warner.

Early the next year Nathan and Mencken persuaded their friend Alfred Knopf and his father, who had published several of their books, to underwrite a new magazine, *The American Mercury,* with Nathan and Mencken as co-editors and part owners. But little more than a year later, the two editors had a falling out. Nathan wanted the magazine to emphasize literature, the theatre, and the arts (he had persuaded the recalcitrant Mencken to publish O'Neill's play *All God's Chillun Got Wings* with its white protagonist and her black husband); while Mencken, gravitating toward the ambience of *The Nation* preferred emphasizing social and political issues. On 8 November 1924, Nathan submitted to Alfred Knopf a letter of resignation, which became effective 1 February 1925. Knopf accepted regretfully but persuaded Nathan to continue contributing drama reviews. This Nathan did for five years. Although he insisted that he and Mencken were still friends, the rift deepened, especially on Mencken's side.

Nathan did not lack for publishing outlets. Aside from his books, which kept appearing annually under the Knopf imprint (over forty between 1913 and 1951), he could hardly keep up with the demand for his reviews from such magazines as *Vanity Fair, Saturday Review, Scribner's, Esquire,* and *Newsweek*—to say nothing of his own new magazine *The American Spectator,* which in 1932 he founded with Ernest Boyd, James Branch Cabell, Theodore Dreiser, and Eugene O'Neill. But *The Spectator,* too, was short-lived, folding in 1935.

During the Depression of the early 1930s, although some movie houses survived by giving away dishware, legitimate theatres were hard hit. Certain theatre managers, looking for a scapegoat, blamed the empty seats on the caustic reviews of George Jean Nathan. In his reviews Nathan had indeed castigated mercilessly where no mercy was due, for he conscientiously sought to raise the standards of American theatre fare. In

March, 1932, a theatre manager by the name of M. L. Erlanger, in collusion with a congressman, William Sirovich, threatened to serve Nathan and other "offensive critics" with subpoenas to appear before a Congressional committee (harbinger of the House Committee on Un-American Activities). Nathan refused to kowtow, of course, and the incident blew over as a mere threat. Nathan knew how to deal with such Philistines, having defended in court, during the previous year, his friend O'Neill on unjustified charges of plagiarism.

Not long after Nathan arrived in New York he moved, from a series of random roosts, to the Royalton Apartments, 44 West 44th Street, across from the Algonquin Hotel. At the Royalton his book-lined rooms remained his life-long residence and the rendezvous for several of the beautiful women whose friendship he cultivated before his marriage. He remained a bachelor for fifty years, however, a state he celebrated in one of his informal essays.

Among the most beautiful and talented of his female friends was the actress Lillian Gish. Born in Springfield, Ohio, in 1896, a descendant of President Zachary Taylor, she was fourteen years younger than Nathan. She had acted on the stage since the age of five, and on stage and screen since she was nineteen. Nathan may have seen her as early as 1915, when she was a member of the cast of D. W. Griffith's film *Birth of a Nation*. No doubt, Nathan saw her in a number of her many performances during the 1920s, including those in the MGM films *La Bohème* (1926), *Annie Laurie* (1927), and *The Enemy* (1928). At the Booth Theatre, in 1930, she played Helena in Chekov's *Uncle Vanya,* the role that elicited Nathan's *Vanity Fair* rave review in which he described her smile as "a bit of happiness trembling on a bed of death," imagery uncannily prophetic of her subsequent stage role as Camille. For eight years during the late 1920s and early 1930s it was assumed that Nathan and Miss Gish were engaged; indeed, the relationship had all the earmarks of a courtship. He squired her to play openings (mixing business with pleasure), restaurants, concerts, and stage parties. In New York, at least, they were usually chaperoned by Lillian's sister Dorothy or by the sisters' mother or both. (For mere intimacies, Nathan indulged himself with non-intellectual chorus girls.) During the summer of 1929 Nathan and Miss Gish were guests of Eugene O'Neill and his wife Carlotta at "Le Plessis," the O'Neills' chateau in France. Although Miss Gish admired Nathan, she repeatedly turned down his marriage proposals. Nor did she marry anyone else, so deeply committed was she to her career on stage and screen. In her autobiography (*The Movies, Mr. Griffith, and Me,* Englewood Cliffs, N.J.: Prentice-Hall, 1969, pp. 338–39) she wrote, "I will always be grateful to George for sharing with me his knowledge of drama, good food, and wine. . . . Through him I came to know all the interesting writers and artists of the 20s and 30s . . . . He introduced me to Scott and Zelda Fitzgerald,[2] Theodore Dreiser, Sinclair Lewis, Sherwood Anderson, James Branch Cabell,[3] Eugene O'Neill. It was a great privilege to listen to the most exciting minds of our time. . . . And I will always be grateful that I did not marry George and spoil his life."

Nathan never quite got over his unrequited love for Lillian Gish, although much later in life, he married another actress. He first met Julie Haydon at rehearsals of Tennessee Williams' play *The Glass Menagerie* at the Chicago Civic Theatre in December, 1944. Nathan had been invited by producers Eddie Dowling and Margo Jones to make suggestions before launching the premiere production. (One of Nathan's contributions, at first reluctantly accepted by Williams, was the drunkard cameo at the beginning of Scene IV.) Miss Haydon, although twenty-eight years younger than Nathan, was no novice; she had many stage credits, and she was an avid reader of drama criticism, including Nathan's. Already an admirer from afar, she now became "quite fond of him" according to Tennessee Williams's *Memoirs,* (New York: Doubleday, 1975, pp. 81–82.) But for more than ten years before her marriage to Nathan (the knot tied on a Caribbean cruise liner on 19 June 1955) she was to win many another credit for stellar performances in such plays as *The Cocktail Party, The Seagull, Major Barbara, Man and Superman, The Barretts of Wimpole Street,* and *A Streetcar Named Desire.* During several of those performances the mutual respect between actress and critic grew and deepened.

Meanwhile Nathan kept publishing books and reviews, and—what has not been generally known before now, before recent releases of certain correspondence—he not only encouraged but also materially helped several playwrights he strongly believed in. For example, Nathan encouraged O'Neill, for whom he served as a kind of father-confessor, as reflected in O'Neill's many letters to him. Nathan also encouraged William Saroyan and Arthur Miller. He especially admired Sean O'Casey and did more than anyone else to get his plays produced in New York. Scores of Nathan's letters to O'Casey (in the Nathan Collection at Cornell University's Olin Library) reveal that for more than two years Nathan hounded the Broadway producer John Williams to take on O'Casey's *Within the Gates.* That play was ultimately produced at the National Theatre in October 1934, with the virginal Lillian Gish playing the role of the prostitute.

During the late 1940s and early 1950s, as if in sympathetic suffering with his former colleague Mencken, who had suffered a stroke, Nathan battled similarly debilitating illnesses, mostly related to an increasingly persistent arteriosclerosis. But whereas Mencken never fully recovered and required the almost constant attention of his solicitous brother August Mencken, Nathan recovered enough between bouts to take cruises (his favorite ship was the Grace Line's *Santa Rosa*) and to accept a doctor of letters degree from Indiana University. "You may now address me as Herr Doktor," he wrote to August Mencken in July 1953. "You should see my robe. Lillian Russell would have died of envy."

In his letter of 17 January 1956, Nathan said, "Dear August: I understand from Alfred [Knopf] that he has told you both the reason for my long silence. No sooner was I out of the hospital [after a minor stroke] than I was rushed to the Harkness Medical Center for emergency hernia surgery. . . . It has been a hell of a time for me. . . . My wife has nursed me day and night." On 29 January 1956, the day Mencken died, Nathan wrote to August: "The Associated Press has just called me (Sunday, 1:45 p.m.) to tell me the sad news. . . . My heart is as heavy as yours."

Little more than two years later, on 8 April 1958, Nathan suffered his severest stroke. Despite his essential agnosticism he requested Catholic last rites. At 12:15 a.m. he died in the arms of Julie Haydon. *New York Times* obituary essays by Brooks Atkinson and by John Mason Brown, among others, observed that George Jean Nathan's passing marked the close of an unprecedented era not only of dramatic criticism but also— through Nathan's criticism—an improvement in American drama itself.

So much for matters biographical. Now for highlights of the main text.

---

1. A copy of this bumptious essay appears in Isaac Goldberg, *The Theatre of George Jean Nathan* (New York: Simon & Schuster, 1926), pp. 253–62.
2. The tactful Miss Gish made no mention of Nathan's flirtation with Mrs. Fitzgerald.
3. Miss Gish is said to have inspired the Helen in Cabell's novel *Jurgen* (1919).

Personal and Informal Essays

These are an undiluted delight. They compete in originality and humor with those of G. K. Chesterton, especially the essay "On Moviegoing."

Profiles of Players

Aside from individual profiles of certain players, Nathan makes informative comments, in other contexts, on scores of actors and actresses, both his contemporaries and those of the past. He pays homage to Joseph Jefferson for a long-lived role as Rip Van Winkle; similarly to James O'Neill (father of Eugene) for a long-lived role as the Count of Monte Cristo. But William Gillette is dismissed as a "mere trickster of acting."

Not surprisingly Nathan nominates Eleonora Duse and Sarah Bernhardt as the "superstars" of their times—Duse especially for her high quality of mind, mind which "controlled her body" rather than the other way around: "She was sensitive to every turn of dramatic writing." Above all, he observes, she had early on mastered the art of understatement. In contrast, Nathan gives Maude Adams short shrift as too much a slave of overstatement and of her directors (including David Belasco) in the Frohman Syndicate. Nathan regrets her failure to demonstrate a mind of her own. He perhaps unfairly ignores her triumph in the role of Peter Pan.

Nathan praises Walter Hampden's imaginative handling of the role of Cyrano de Bergerac but uses him as a kind of stick with which to beat John Barrymore, whose Hamlet is condemned as "cold" and as a mere "shadowgraph of audience expectations."

The Lunts (Alfred and Lynne) fare much better, especially for their performances in S. N. Behrman's adaptation of Giraudoux's *Amphitryon 38*. So does Lillian Gish, whom Nathan virtually apotheosizes for her Duse-like understatement, her acting "as if behind a veil of chiffon."

To Katharine Cornell, Nathan gives kudos for her performance as Juliet (in *Romeo and Juliet*), as Joan (in Shaw's *Joan of Arc*), as Elizabeth (in *The Barretts of Wimpole Street*), and as Iris March (in *The Green Hat*). Nathan also awards high marks to Maurice Evans and John Gielgud for their performances—albeit sometimes "too intellectual and fastidious"—in the plays of Shakespeare. But lest readers jump to the conclusion that Nathan is interested only in the so-called legitimate theatre, he praises certain popular entertainers who seem endowed with intelligence and imagination. He praises Beatrice Lillie, for example, as "pretty hot stuff" whether for her performances in London music halls, in Tony Pastor's New York night clubs, or in the Follies of the "artistic" Mr. Ziegfeld.

But Nathan reserves his highest homage for Helen Hayes. In "Helen Hayes and Her Rivals" the longest and the most detailed of his profiles of players, he proclaims her "the best actress in the American theatre." He substantiates this claim with critical analyses of her most memorable roles. Among runners-up to Hayes, he nominates Katharine Cornell, Lynne Fontanne, Jane Cowl, Ethel Barrymore, and—"closest contender"—Judith Anderson.

Profiles of Playwrights

Among Continental and British playwrights, Nathan specifies what he admires and does not admire in August Strindberg, Edmond Rostand, Arthur Schnitzler, Luigi Pirandello, Ferenc Molnar, and Jean Giraudoux—each of these in separate essays; and, in other contexts, Henrik Ibsen, Anton Chekhov, Gerhart Hauptman, and Jean Anouilh. Unfortunately, he damns Maurice Maeterlinck with faint praise. Nathan also points out what he admires and does not admire in such British playwrights as Sean O'Casey, Lord Dunsany, Oscar Wilde, James M. Barrie, Arthur Pinero,

Henry Arthur Jones, Christopher Fry, and John Galsworthy. In a penetrating essay on George Bernard Shaw, Nathan "makes bold to predict" that long after Shaw may be forgotten for his satire and iconoclastic wit, he will be cherished for the tender love scenes in *Candida, The Doctor's Dilemma, The Devil's Disciple, Capatin Brassbound's Conversion,* and— above all—*Caesar and Cleopatra.*

American Playwrights

Nathan discusses in detail the plays of Clifford Odets, Maxwell Anderson, S. N. Behrman, Lillian Hellman, Susan Glaspell, Tennessee Williams, and William Saroyan. He deals perhaps too harshly with Odets, faults Williams for a "distorted" treatment of matters sexual, and teases Anderson for versifying "where there is in the subject, e.g., garbage, really no poetry." Here Nathan's theory about what is and what is not a subject for poetry remains at best controversial. And in his adverse criticism of Odets and Williams one infers Nathan's political conservatism and prejudicial distaste for homosexuals. Nathan reserves his unqualified kudos for S. N. Behrman (a graduate of George Pierce Baker's Harvard Workshop 47) and for Lillian Hellman. To Hellman, Nathan awards the highest accolades.

Eugene O'Neill

To Eugene O'Neill, his protegé and lifelong friend, who in numerous letters regarded Nathan a kind of father confessor, Nathan devotes the longest and most analytic profile, partly in response to short-sighted criticism by the British critic Eric Bentley. Here, in chronological order (from 1913 and beyond—into the manuscripts of *A Moon for the Misbegotten* and *A Touch of the Poet*) Nathan examines each play briefly but knowlingly for its strengths and weaknesses, along with evidences of the influence, on O'Neill, of Nietzsche's *Thus Spake Zarathustra* and Maxim Gorki's *The Lower Depths.*

Fianlly, in various contexts, no playwright (and no critic) in the history of the theatre—from its Greek beginnings up to Nathan's times—whether a master or an also-ran, escapes at least a stroke of Nathan's brush.

Writers Other Than Playwrights

As co-editor of *Smart Set,* a magazine popular enough among the literati to attract manuscript submissions from not only the established but also the ambitious young unknowns, Nathan accepted and published the tyro James Joyce's stories "The Boarding House" and "A Little Cloud," which would later appear in the celebrated collection *Dubliners*. In *Smart Set,* too, Nathan published Somerset Maugham's story "Miss Thompson," which would later be adapted to the movie *Rain;* stories and articles by Theodore Dreiser; and the first stories and a one-act play by the then unheard of F. Scott Fitzgerald. Nathan and co-editor Mencken disagreed on their assessment of submissions by Max Beerbohm, with Mencken probably closer to the mark in praising the work of that British caricaturist. As the glossary at the end of the reader shows, the well-read and cosmopolitan Nathan discusses writers too numerous to mention here. But he devotes specific profiles to Scott and Zelda Fitzgerald, Somerset Maugham, Gertrude Stein, T. S. Eliot, H. L. Mencken, Theodore Dreiser, and Sinclair Lewis.

From the Fitzgerald profile (also from the Fitzgerald letters) we learn that although Nathan himself imbibed cocktails in moderation, he regrets that the Fitzgeralds indulge in all too many "booze binges," but is nonetheless one of the first to send congratulations on *The Great Gatsby.* Scott's proposal to Nathan to enter a partnership in opening an alcoholic roadhouse on Long Island falls through. Both in the profile and in the letters, Scott's wife, Zelda, is revealed as much more talented than is generally realized.

On Gertrude Stein, Nathan dumps a delightful spoof, out-Steining her with the Bronx cheer "Sell a cellar, door a cellar, adore a door . . ." He adds, "There will always be critics who mistake the *tour de force* for some strange and inscrutable kind of wayward genius."

T. S. Eliot receives Nathan's due praise, albeit with a slap on the wrist for "boring prolixity"—for failing to cut and condense.

The Mencken profile reveals that writer as a lovable hypochondriac. The profile of Dreiser also reveals an equally lovable person but much too generous in the appraisal of fellow writers. Dreiser tends to crown with the accolade "genius" writers whom Nathan and Mencken have not even heard of. In the same profile, Dreiser is portrayed as an indefatigable workhorse in the face of heart-breaking hardships.

Finally, in this section, the most surprising and amusing profile—a veritable little masterpiece deserving perennial anthologizing—remains Nathans portrayal of a rarely revealed side of Sinclair Lewis. Lewis was apparently addicted to giving parties for editors and reviewers as soon as one of his forthcoming books was in press. To let the invitees know what that book would be about, he would assume the role of the protagonist, ranting long eccentric speeches. As Mencken observed, each encounter of this kind with "Red Lewis" was worth much more than the gratis price of admission.

Directors and Producers

As reflected in several sections of the reader, Nathan was closely acquainted with several, and distantly acquainted with many, American and European directors and producers of his time—among them, Gordon Craig ("genius of set design"); George M. Cohan; Robert Edmond Jones; John Williams (the New York producer of several O'Neill plays); Eddie Dowling and Margo Jones (producers of plays starring Julie Haydon, who would become Mrs. George Jean Nathan); Kenneth Magowan (when he was associated with the Provincetown Playhouse); and Guthrie McClintic (in whose honor the Guthrie Theatre of Minneapolis would be named). Among the New York producers with whom Nathan was "unavoidably" acquainted were the Shuberts (Jacob and Lee) and the whole family of Selwyns (Archibald, Edgar, and Ruth). The Selwyns often courted Nathan sycophantically, once going so far as to have delivered to him a seat reservation encased in sterling silver.

The New York producer most frequently mentioned by Nathan was Charles Frohman (boss of the Frohmann Syndicate). Although Nathan regarded Frohman's manipulation of American performers and bookings reprehensible (as did Minnie Maddern Fiske and her husband, Harrison Fiske, editor of the *New York Dramatic Mirror*), Nathan conceded that Frohman was almost always on target in recognizing the first-rate plays, playwrights, and players that had to be imported, in large measure, from across the Atlantic Ocean. Nathan also applauded Frohman for persuading the Syndicate stockholders to produce the then controversial plays of Ibsen—this before Frohman went down, in 1915, on the *Lusitania*.

Nathan's acquaintances among British and European directors included the Frenchman Georges Pitoëff; the successors of Sean O'Casey at the Abbey Theatre, Dublin; and the founders of the Moscow Art Theatre, albeit from afar, Constantin Stanislavsky and Vladimir Danchenko. Nathan dismisses Danchenko as "second-rate," but praises Stanislavsky and the "Stanislavsky Method," which echoes the advice in Lessing's *Hamburgische Dramaturgie*. For Reinhardt, who had immigrated from Germany to New York, Nathan reserves superlatives: "the most talented director and producer in the world theatre."

Through his nine years' close friendship with Lillian Gish, Nathan became acquainted with several movie directors and producers, most of whom were his seniors. In various contexts, he alludes, for example, to the achievements and innovations, in silent films, of D. W. Griffith and the latter's associate Eric von Stroheim. No document has as yet been found to let us know whether Nathan shared O'Neill's enthusiasm for the new "talkies." But Nathan does assign to movies in general an aesthetic position below that of "the living drama." ("Critical Convictions.")

In the profile of Florenz Ziegfeld, Nathan argues that the producer of the celebrated annual Follies should be placed several cuts above John Murray Anderson and the Minsky brothers. "Ziegfeld was an artist—not just a showman." Nathan is "not beguiled by" Winthrop Ames and only grudgingly acknowledges George Abbott's supremacy as a director and producer of comedy—"but only comedy."

Somewhat disappointing is Nathan's half-hearted recognition of the achievments of David Belasco (the "Bishop of Broadway"). Had Nathan lived longer, he might have re-examined his niggardly assessment of the director and author of the *Girl of the Golden West,* which inspired Puccini's opera *La Fanciulla del West*.

On Playwriting

Commenting (in "Literature and Drama" and in "Intelligence and the Drama") on novelists who fail as playwrights, Nathan pinpoints certain distinctions between drama and fiction: "The novelist peoples the imagination with ghosts; the dramatist peoples the eye and ear with living, moving forms and voices." In other words, successful playwrights treat the spectator's eye to an immediate camera, the frames or building-blocks of drama consisting more of scene and action than of theme, except as implied.

Aside from commenting *obiter dicta* on various schools and persuasions (for example, expressionism. commedia dell'arte, etc.) and on the challenges and pitfalls of various types of plays, Nathan devotes a separate essay to each of the following types: melodramas, adaptations, and biographicals. He judges the biographical the easiest to write (although elsewhere he makes a similar claim for melodrama), and adaptations the most challenging. Contrary to most received prejudices, he does not consider all melodramas categorically beneath notice, noting that Shakespeare's *Macbeth* remains one of the greatest of all melodramas. Elsewhere, Nathan reiterates that the melodrama is a good type of play for novices to cut their teeth on.

He observes that one's good work will be far outweighed by the bad ("Myself") but he rejects the notion that a playwright must write some bad plays before writing a good one. He cites, among those who "did not know about this," Shakespeare, Strindberg, Ibsen, Pirandello, Hauptmann O'Casey, and O'Neill. But tyro playwrights may well protest, "We can't all be geniuses!" Besides, Shakespeare scholars agree that a few of the Bard's early plays do remain comparatively inferior.

Nathan also reminds prospective playwrights that 95 percent of plays that achieve long runs on Broadway have so-called happy endings. He thus implicitly approves of one of Hollywood's inveterate axioms. He also applauds in principle Hollywood's cutting-room floors. Repeatedly he emphasizes the need for cutting and telescoping, ("Leave something to the intelligence of the audience!") He regrets that certain cutting went neglected in the plays of even such Nobel laureates as T. S. Eliot and Eugene O'Neill.

Nathan regards *plot* as a necessity that playwrights may dispense with if they are prepared (like Shaw, Wilde, and Saroyan) to compensate for its absence with extraordinary wit, originality, and a sense of humanity ("Critical Convictions"). Repeatedly he stresses the importance of the playwright's tuning in to the human heart: "The highest aim of drama," he says in "Intelligence and the Drama," "is to prove something not to the human head but to the human heart." When the playwright sets himself to the actual business of writing "he must leave his intelligence off stage." Yet paradoxically, Nathan deplores "dramatic ideas that fall into the hands of incompetent writers" ("Critical Convictions"). As an example of one such idea, he cites "the Negro's ironic position in the atmospheres of two different civilizations." Unwittingly Nathan thus anticipates "Cry Freedom," a screenplay produced after his time.

First-rate playwrights, he observes further, concentrate on characterization and conflict (even in melodrama) rather than on theme, lest their plays end up as mere propaganda ("Mark of the First-Rate Playwright").

Finally, writers of any genre, he observes, need not deceive themselves that they need a special place to work. One may write creatively even amid the hurly-burly of a metropolis like New York City ("Best Place to Work").

On Acting

"Acting," observes Nathan, "is the world's only profession in which a person is loudly applauded at the end of his day's work for drawing down a higher financial reward than he often deserves" ("Critical Convictions"). In this observation, Nathan is of course exaggerating, at least as regards salaries for acting on the so-called legitimate stage. The financial rewards of box-office favorites from Hollywood (for example, Lillian Gish and John Barrymore) remain a different matter.

With a few exceptions (including make-up artists' and wardrobe personnel's improvisations on non-black Uncle Toms, short-nosed Cyranos, and about-to-be transvestite Charley's Aunts) nobody dare pontificate on what an actor or actress should look like to begin with in order to create a convincing illusion of reality. Almost any good performer—regardless of native physical characteristics—can create an illusion of physical reality. But a performer cannot successfully express on stage an "emotion he or she does not really feel" ("Critical Convictions"). In expressing emotions, moreover, good actors under-emote—they resist "hamming it up," as Stanislavsky and Lessing have written. Among the great performers who have demonstrated such restraint—by using natural voice and gestures effectively—Nathan cites Eleonora Duse and Helen Hayes.

Literary Criticism and Reviewing

Distinguishing between literary criticism and reviewing, Nathan concedes that some newspaper reviews can be "sagacious and helpful" but in the end cannot compete at least in purpose with literary criticism, "the afterthoughts of reviewing." Authentic criticism focuses on and analyzes the more significant aspects of a play and its performers, he concludes. This view may seem prejudicial, if not snobbish. He also regrets that the large numbers of newspaper reviews, for the most part negative when honest, give "the" theater as a whole a bad reputation. In his essay "Destructive Criticism," he observes that the honest *coup de grâce* demands "an exhaustive knowledge of the subject under the microscope, an original and analytic turn of mind, and power over words." Most newspaper reviewing, he says, is not dishonest; it is merely "disqualified."

Early on, one of Nathan's idols among "authentic" critics is James Huneker ("Lord Jim"), an accomplished composer and the author of *Painted Veils,* a *roman à clef,* which evaluates his contemporaries. Of George Bernard Shaw, Nathan says, in "Critical Convictions," "a better critic of the drama never lived." Throughout his lifetime, Nathan's bible on dramatic criticism remained Lessing's *Hamburgische Dramaturgie,* which he had studied at Heidelberg. Among his contemporaries, a British critic with whom he disagreed, especially in regard to certain plays by O'Neill, was the eminent Eric Bentley.

Selected Letters

The letters included in the reader have been selected to reinforce points made in the essays and to illuminate events mentioned in the profiles— especially the profiles of H. L. Mencken, Eugene O'Neill, Theodore Dreiser, and the F. Scott Fitzgeralds. Most of Nathan's letters have yet to be located and collected, but his few letters here, along with the many letters by others to him, constitute a rich cache. They afford glimpses of a George Jean Nathan that O'Neill calls "warm and friendly and human, where I half expected an aloof and caustic intelligence," as he wrote to Isaac Goldberg on 4 June 1926.

Reading between the lines of Gordon Craig's first letter to Nathan (9 January 1916) one gleans intimations of Nathan's growing reputation, in England and beyond, as an important critic. And in the Nathan-O'Casey correspondence, one learns of Nathan's admiration for, and attempts to bring, O'Casey's play *Within the Gates* to New York.

In other letters, one learns that Nathan was a friend of Harold Ross, editor of *The New Yorker,* and of the critic Joseph Wood Krutch. One also gets further glimpses of Nathan as an all too human (and somewhat chauvinistic) person: "The Critics' Circle party this year was the best so far; nobody got home before 9 a.m.. . . . Joe [Krutch] and I sang to the accompaniment of a hurdy-gurdy played by a couple of cops . . . and we picked up two beautiful girls" (Nathan to Sean O'Casey, 14 May 1939).

In several of Nathan's letters to H. L. Mencken and his brother August, the reader can vicariously experience both the humorous and the poignant moments in the Nathan-Mencken relationship—also the relationship between Nathan and Theodore Dreiser, who early on resigned from the editorial consortium that was to preside over *The American Spectator* (Dreiser to Nathan, 7 October 1933). In one of Nathan's brief letters to August Mencken, between December 1948 and August 1953 and intended to be shared with the ailing brother Henry, one learns that the publisher Alfred Knopf, a mutual friend and benefactor of Nathan and Mencken, is vacationing in the West via a pack trip, "having purchased [expensive] equipment, including a purple rosette for the donkey's behind" (3 October 1951).

Among Nathan's protégés who write to ask for editorial advice or to express gratitude for help and encouragement is the young F. Scott Fitzgerald. In accepting for *Smart Set* Fitzgerald's short story "Dalrymple Goes Wrong" (November 1919), Nathan writes "You have a decidedly uncommon gift for light dialogue." And Zelda Fitzgerald's letter (ca. 1930) to her husband, who was out of town, reveals Nathan as a party-giver, serving his favorite cocktails and playing Tin Pan Alley songs (e.g., "Cuddle Up a Little Closer") on the piano in his apartment at the Royalton.

Finally, the richest cache of letters, fortunately preserved in the George Jean Nathan Collection at Cornell University, his alma mater, remains the O'Neill correspondence. The letters from O'Neill (May 1919 to October 1943) preserve a record of the warm friendship, discussions of dramaturgy in general and certain of O'Neill's plays in particular, evidences of Nathan's contributions to O'Neill's development as a playwright, and O'Neill's frequent expressions of gratitude. Here are some key excerpts: "My sincerest gratitude . . . encouraging boost to my spirits," (4 November 1919). "I am glad that *Beyond the Horizon* pleased its godfather" (March 12, 1920). "Your criticism [of *Anna Christie*] certainly probes a vital spot" (1 February 1921). Please do come [to Provincetown] . . . I'd like to hear what you feel is wrong [in *The Fountain*] and whether you detect any false spots" (2 January 1922). "It is hard to say how deeply grateful I have been ever since you read the play [*Strange Interlude*] to know your high opinion of it" (16 June 1927). "No need to say how grateful I will be for your help in this affair" [in which O'Neill is being unjustifiably sued for plagiarism] (31 August 1929). "It was grand to have you here [the O'Neills' chateau in France] and it was grand to get to know Lillian [Gish]. She is simple and charming and I sure admire her. Carlotta [O'Neill's third wife] aussi!" (31 August 1929). " The Nobel caught me with my pants down . . . I had absolutely no thought of it this year [1936] . . . had it all doped out that a Frenchman was due, Gide or Valéry . . . Thank you for all your encouragement has meant to me and my work . . . Again, all gratitude, Friend—Gene." (November 1936). "I've just finished [reading your new book] *The Morning After the First Night*. The amazing thing, looking back over all your critical books, is that you never let yourself let down; each book has the same vital integrity, wit, clear vision, zest and love for the theatre" (7 February 1938).

The Glossary

George Jean Nathan's erudition dazzles. More learned than even the proverbial Renaissance man who took all knowledge for his field, Nathan had more fields and more ages to ransack—and ransack them he does, not only in literature and theatre but also in history, philosophy, the sciences, music, and the other fine arts. In his essay "Intelligence and the Drama," for example, he does not merely refer in passing to Mozart but to details of *Don Giovanni;* not just to Wagner but to details of *Siegfried* and *Tännhauser;* not just to Bellini but to details of the *Madonna and Child;* not just to Raphael but to details of the *Victory of Leo IV;* not just to Tintoretto but to details of the *Adam and Eve*.

In short, to avoid a plethora of footnotes—also to avoid insulting any reader's intelligence—the editor of the reader has appended a glossary which attempts to identify all the persons, places, plays, books, periodicals, aesthetic terms and movements mentioned or alluded to by Nathan. But a reading of the glossary alone (as a ruse to bypass the main text) can yield only the raw beginnings of a liberal education.

A
George Jean Nathan
Reader

Personal and Informal Essays

Myself

What manner of organism am I? What are my fundamental habits of thought, my tastes, prejudices, predilections, eccentricities—in short, my pitch and tone? The topic does not at all interest me personally, since the attributes in question have been imbedded in me for too many years and, even were I to wish it, it is now too late for them to undergo any change. But it may possibly interest the customers of my critical performances, who, it seems to me, have a right to know the nature of the creature whose opinions, sometimes perhaps very peculiar, they have been buying, inner-sight unseen, for so unbelievable, if gratifying, a stretch of time.

I am, it may be confided at the outset, in many respects the average man—if I do not unduly flatter myself. What has periodically been written about me to the contrary, though sweet in intention, I do not believe. Though I may have had more experience in various directions than the average brother, it has not much profited or elevated me to any essential way and I remain, for better or worse, largely the original package. That is to say, while my personal philosophy and ideas, such as they are, may differ markedly from the communal norm, their mouthpiece is by habit and in practice at bottom a conventional member of human society. He respects now and then against his cynical, better judgment, the time-honored and accepted precepts and, though he sometimes slips from grace, he does his damnedest to live up to them. He hopes that by and large, whatever his pleasant, happy and contenting departures from what is generally approved, he nevertheless still is what the gods, in their more worldly and rational moments, describe as decent.

Though in no respect sentimentally inclined, your subject does not subscribe to the theory, so popular with the adolescent Strindbergs, that any degree of sentiment is incompatible with a majestic brain and that the man who goes so far as even to allow that a field flower is a rather pretty thing or that a girl with a straight nose and soft hair merits a look is *ipso facto* one with a mind not be trusted by simon-pure intellects.

From *The Theatre Book of the Year, 1949–1950* (New York: Knopf, 1950), foreword.

Indignation is as foreign to my system as piety or self-satisfaction. That is, indignation toward others, though when the situation warrants, it would seem that my dander rises over stupidity, incompetence, and vainglory. What indignation there may be in my chemical composition otherwise is directed rather toward myself and is inspired by the consciousness that, despite certain gifts which I feel are in me, I am not a lot better than I factually am. I have, I think, improved in performance as the years have traveled on, but there is, I am fully aware, a heap of room left and though people are occasionally kind enough to contradict me, I am not so chipper as I once was, for all some seeming external evidence to the contrary. I work as hard as ever I did, or at least I think I do, but I sometimes say to myself that, since I have already done what I consider to be my share, I am foolish to do so and not take life a little easier. But I don't listen to myself and grunt and groan and plod on nevertheless.

The reason, I daresay, is that, being a writer, I cannot, like Trigorin, help myself and, since there does not seem to be much chance in my lifetime of anyone instituting a Writers Anonymous, I despair of a cure. As Osbert Sitwell explains the agonizing malady, "An author can never take a holiday. It is impossible for him to become another sort of person; he must absorb and reflect and observe the whole time . . . Even while he is asleep, the writer's subconscious mind is always busily occupied in preparing various ideas to lay before him when he wakes." I shall not be so hypocritical as to say that it is a bore, but it is pretty close to one. The head buzzes with all kinds of what seem transiently to be ideas; a hundred tosses on the pillow eventually give birth to some word to replace the arid one which has been set down in the daylight chore; the old, unbeatable urge to say one's say on paper hastens the breakfast coffee. And to what end—aside from a momentary stimulation, an evanescent smugness—God alone knows.

Since, in the very nature of the critical profession, one is faced with bad work out of all proportion to good, it is not possible for the practitioner to erase from his reader's mind the impression that he is a chronic grumbler or, worse, one who seeks to lift himself to a bogus eminence by demolishing the performances of others. The impression is understandable, but there is no way to prevent it. That is, there is no way to prevent it save one were willing to indulge in equivoque, in false generosity, or in language tricked to make palatable unpalatable fact. I have never been able to persuade myself that contemptible work merits any such strain and courtesy, and as a consequence there are undoubtedly some, indeed perhaps many, who believe that I take a mean delight in what they choose to call destructive criticism.

Though, of course, it is easier, as every critic comes to learn, to write an interesting detractory review than an interesting favorable one, I would be only too happy to exert myself in the latter direction night after night were the occasions to justify it. But it need hardly be mentioned that the great majority of them unfortunately do no such thing, and detraction is consequently the only honest course left open. There is, however, a saving and salving personal reflection. If, after more than forty years in practice, such a wealth of detraction were not proved by time to have been sound, I would have lost all my readers long before this, and not only all my readers but all the many editors who in that protracted period have bought my opinions for good money. It is this thought that consoles me when frequently those opinions are taken icily to task by others.

I read now and then that I have offended this or that complainant by what he terms my air of infallibility. If ever I have given any such impression I assure you that it has been very far from intentional and must have been the result of a deplorable, slipshod manner of expression. Never for a moment have I ever regarded myself as infallible. I have in my day negotiated some of the handsomest bloomers on record, and in all probability will accomplish more of an even greater beauty. I have also, however, in that same period made some admirable guesses, and I am not loath to admit it. But, though I think that by this time I have learned my job about as well as ever I shall be able to learn it, I no more look upon myself as being always right than I look upon any other man in a like way. My average has not been so bad; in fact, it has been pretty good, if I say so myself; but there nevertheless are on the library shelves some thirty-five or more volumes in which my mistakes are embalmed for posterity.

I have mentioned the subject of my prejudices and predilections. I should like to be able to say that I am completely free from bias on both counts, but I fear that I cannot. I have an open mind, in a manner of speaking, but it has been open for so long now that some bugs have flown in through the doors and windows. Among these insects are, in the first category, a hostility toward the pretentiousness that invest the writings of men who mistake an excessive ambition for high competence; a prejudice against playwrights who seek to palliate their emotional immaturity with anonymous injections of the borrowed mature thought of others; a distaste for the kind of dramatic cynicism born of obviously limited experience; and an acute disrelish of popgun revolutionaries, dewy sentimentalists, one-cake-soapbox philosophers, commerical uplifters, and greasepaint mentalities in general.

But some butterflies have flown in also and in that category are a cordiality toward the daring young fellows who, whether successfully or not, try honestly to express the plays that are in them without regard for the scholastic injunctions of the standpatters; a warm friendliness toward skeptics of the accepted, popular points of view; an affection for men who do not subscribe to the theory that drama is not literature and who do subscribe to the beauty of language and the surge and burst of the poetic line; a hospitality toward the unstrained simplicity that so often is just around the corner from profundity and much nearer to it than the strained complexity which frequently passes in the drama for loftly thought; and a respect for any head that has in it, besides a brain, a little of the wayward music that colors and enlivens life.

There are, as everyone knows, no morals in art, but art and hack work are two different things, and I cannot get steamed up, like many of my colleagues, when censorship, albeit intrinsically imbecile, has at some piece of junk on the score of its alleged immorality. Suppression of such rubbish, whether on one ground or another, seems to me to be a desirable thing and, if there is no other way to get the business done than through its morals, I say go ahead, and with my blessing. The notion that if one gives an inch to censorship, it will take a mile is not inevitably true; and those who believe it, would do well to look up the records of the last American theatrical century. I am constitutionally opposed to censorship *per se,* but I am not so silly as to believe that if it intermittently descends upon such guano as *Sex, Pleasure Man,* and the like it will in due and bumptious course seek also to outlaw *Oedipus Rex* and *Measure for Measure*. This is not to say that at times it has not gone too far and has made itself ridiculous; but in the whole history of our theatre's last one hundred years, I can find no more than two plays out of many thousands which in any critical sense have suffered unjustly and, of the two, one was soon given a clean bill of health by the courts and reproduced. Nor in that same history can I find a single instance where, if one of the censored junkpots had not been interfered with, its continued life would in any degree have profited the stage. Foul claptrap belongs in the garbage can, and I cannot see that it matters who puts it there, whether it be censors, police, critics, or the theatre's customers themselves. The people who make it their profession to boil against any and all censorship on any and all occasions impress me as being more than merely obtuse. They lose the battle by sniping with bean-shooters.

What is hailed in the Broadway theatre as success frequently to my way of looking at things is contemptible failure. A successful play, it seems, is not necessarily one of quality but one, however seedy, that, like chewing-gum, hot dogs and Harry Truman, is endorsed by a sufficiently large number of people, many of them of doubtful taste and mentality, to make it a winner. Thus, there is no distinction between a mere box-office success like *Kiss and Tell* and a box-office plus critical and artistic success like *Strange Interlude*. Successes like *Abie's Irish Rose, White Cargo,* and *Junior Miss* are lumped under the same label with successes like *Rain, The Green Pastures,* and *Victoria Regina*. Intrinsic worth does not figure in Broadway's calculations; it is only money that counts—money, money, money, the golden god of tin minds.

It is accordingly often that plays Broadway sneers at as failures figure among the most reputable and respected plays in the theatre. It is a sorry critic, indeed, who would prefer, for example, a big Broadway success like *Edward, My Son* over a rank box-office failure like *A Highland Fling,* an acclaimed success like *John Loves Mary* over a quick failure like *A Sound of Hunting* or what Broadway labels a smash hit, like *The Happy Time,* over what it nominates an immediate dud, like *My Heart's in the Highlands, The Beautiful People,* or *Outrageous Fortune.* It has been that way for many years now. The money losers are worthless drama in the Broadway estimate; the money makers are masterpieces. Yet over the years compare, among scores of others, such stark failures as Birmingham's *General John Regan,* Duke's *The Man with a Load of Mischief,* O'Neill's *Marco Millions* and *The Fountain,* O'Casey's *The Plough and the Stars,* Porto-Riche's *L'Amoureuse,* and Johnston's *The Moon in the Yellow River* with such triumphant and blessed successes, such box-office record breakers, such Broadway endorsed jewels, as *Seventh Heaven, East Is West, Kiki, What a Life!, Room Service, Janie,* and *I Remember Mama.*

I must agree with Marcus Aurelius Antoninus. Said that stoic philosopher, reflecting on what so large a portion of mankind calls success: "Success, it stinks."

How Many Work Days in a Year?

How much does the poor working man, abused and oppressed by capital, actually work? Let us see.

There are 365 days in the year. Of these, 52 are Sundays. That leaves 313 days. Of these 52 are Saturdays or half-work days. Half of 52 is 26. That leaves 287 days. Of these, there are New Year's Day, Lincoln's Birthday, Washington's Birthday, Decoration Day, the Fourth of July, Labor Day, Columbus' Birthday, Thanksgiving Day and Christmas—all holidays, which leaves 278 days. In addition there are such State holidays as Arbor Day, such holidays as St. Patrick's Day and various religious holidays like Good Friday—an average of, let us say—to put it low—a half dozen. That leaves 272 days. The average human being, according to the best medical statistics available, is ill, taking one year with another, at least twelve days

From *The Autobiography of an Attitude,* (New York: Knopf, 1925), pp. 106–8, as abridged in A. L. Lazarus, ed., *The Indiana Experience* (Bloomington: Indiana University Press, 1977), p. 43.

each year, and is then unfit for work. That leaves 260 days. The average working man's vacation period amounts to two weeks or, less the two Sundays and two half-Saturdays already counted, eleven days. That leaves 249 days. A day contains 24 hours, eight of which are the union limit of labor. Eight is one-third of 24, hence the working man works for one third of 249 days. That is 83 days. On each of these 83 days he takes an hour off for lunch. Eighty-three hours amounts approximately to three and one-half days. That leaves 79½ days. Now, it is impossible for any human being to work continuously, without periodic rest, for seven hours. There must be time to stop for breath, to ease up the muscles, to take the crick out of one's back, to wait until one's helper is ready, to light one's pipe, to wipe the sweat from one's forehead—to do any number of such things. In a working period of seven hours, at least one hour is necessarily so wasted. That means, in 79½ days, 79½ hours—or approximately three and one-third days. That leaves approximately 76⅙ days. The average poor working man thus actually works just 76⅙ days out of the 365. When you have figured out the percentage, breathe a sympathetic sigh for him.

The Best Place to Work

Horace Greeley has been quoted as saying that he wrote the best editorials of his life while a circus parade, including two brass bands, three elephants, and a calliope, was passing under his windows in the old New York *Tribune* building. Being a gourmand of circus parades, I am afraid that I cannot hope to vie with the late Mr. Greeley's capacity for work, whether good or bad, on such gala occasions. Yet I think I can share his feeling and know what he meant, for of all the places best designed for work—at least to my peculiar way of looking at it—the alleged and generally condemned circus city of New York seems to me to be the pick.

It is now just thirty-four years since I first began to engage in the craft of belles-lettres in New York, and in that city—in fact, in the very heart and core of that city—and in that time I have written my twenty-seven books, fashioned millions of words into magazine articles, edited or assisted in the editing of half a dozen different periodicals, composed articles for encyclopedias, symposia, textbooks, anthologies, and God knows what else, syndicated for many years weekly dramatic critiques to newspapers all over the country, and otherwise pursued for better or worse the work in life which, also for better or worse, I have cut out for myself. What is

From *The Bachelor Life* (New York: Reynal and Hitchcock, 1941), pp. 220–31.

more—and this is the point—I have pursued it in perfect peace and entire comfort.

The notion that New York is a combination boiler factory and jazz palace running at full blast twenty-four hours a day, take it from one who has lived in it and worked in it these more than three decades, is a notion maintained chiefly by yokel visitors to the city who spend all of their time on top of busses or under tables, and by those more recent settlers in the city who are unable to get the nostalgic perfume of farm dung out of their nostrils and the soothing peace of loud frog croakings, horse whinnyings, goat gurglings, rooster crowings, shutter bangings, duck cacklings, tin-roof rattlings, tree creakings, and other such sweet melodies out of their ears. Not only may one find in the metropolis the composure and tran-quility necessary to literary labor but one may, too, find there a gratifying lack of all those distractions that tempt one from one's writing desk in the neighborhood of the sea, in the hills and the mountains, in the ambling green countryside, and in other such localities where nature lures the loafing and playing sense that is born deep in every man.

I have tried to work on Sea Island, off the coast of Georgia, that lovely and remote strip of ocean-bound land where my friend O'Neill long found himself able to work on his plays as he couldn't elsewhere in the world. But I wasn't able to. The broad, smooth, warm lazy beach and the blue sea were too inviting, and I couldn't resist them. And, even if I could have, the wash and surge of the waves, penetrating to my work table, would have hypnotized me out of concentration. I have tried to work in Switzerland, in the Alpland, but I also have been unable to. If I have not been out on climbs, I have been looking out of the window. I have tried to work in the cool, green English country, but I have ended up by walking in the irresistible fields and over the irresistible hills. And it has been the same, I have discovered, whenever I have left my quarters on the eleventh floor of a bachelor apartment in West Forty-fourth Street, New York.

In that apartment I have now lived for something more than twenty-five years, thus in all probability establishing a residential record for a New Yorker. It is a quiet, old-fashioned apartment, so quiet, indeed, that it is the marvel of my writing friends who, living in the country or elsewhere, have not believed it possible for anyone to find in New York an apartment that did not have the air of a continuous performance of *Feuersnot* adapted by George Antheil[1] to an orchestra composed wholly of tin pans, wash boilers, locomotive whistles, automobile sirens, and foghorns. A bay of three tall windows envelops my writing desk, and through them the sunlight, unimpeded by close, tall buildings, floods my study. What is more and what is better, there is no distracting temptation to look out of the windows, as all I can see if I do look out of them is the broad, flat gray roof of the Bar Association a couple of stories below. My rooms, furthermore, are situated between Forty-fourth and Forty-third Streets—the building is an arcade—and thus are spared the noises emanating directly from either thoroughfare. I challenge anyone to find a better place in which to work.

The theory that meditative literary work is impossible or next to impossible in New York must suffer the embarrassment of many contradictory statistics, if the theorists explore their prejudice. From Mark Twain to William Dean Howells, from David Graham Phillips to Theodore Dreiser, from Edith Wharton to Willa Cather, from Scott Fitzgerald to John Dos Passos, we have a record of writers who have been able to produce some of their best work in the midst of the metropolitan life. The best literary magazines are edited in the hurly-burly of New York, and in New York Elinor Wylie, Archibald MacLeish, Edna St. Vincent Millay, Stephen Vincent Benét, and other such poets have contrived to sing many of their sweetest songs. Hamlin Garland, Richard Harding Davis, O. Henry, and three-quarters of the present-day better American playwrights of the younger group, from S. N. Behrman to Clifford Odets, have done much of their best writing in New York. As have essayists and critics like John Macy, Joseph Wood Krutch, Lewis Mumford, and Ludwig Lewisohn; musicians and composers like Walter Damrosch, Henry Hadley, Ernest Schelling, Victor Herbert, Reginald DeKoven, Deems Taylor, Jerome Kern, et al.; anthropologists like Frank Boas and historians like James Truslow Adams.

A wide variety of writers like W. E. Woodward, Carl Sandburg, Carolyn Wells, Katharine Anthony, Mary Austin, Michael Gold, William Rose Benét, Ben Hecht, Ernest Boyd, Brian Hooker, Sherwood Anderson, Abraham Cahan, Robert Sherwood, Hendrik Willem Van Loon, Sinclair Lewis, Elmer Davis, Stanley Walker, Finley Peter Dunne, Montague Glass, Waldo Frank, Max Eastman, Hatch Hughes, George Philip Krapp, Don Marquis, Fannie Hurst, Edgar Lee Masters, James M. Cain, Carl Van Doren, Albert Shaw, Louis Untermeyer, Robert Underwood Johnson, Mark Van Doren, James Weldon Johnson, S. S. Van Dine, Stark Young, Herbert Asbury, and Clarence Day have arranged their diverse literary performances simultaneously in New York and in presumable comfort.

James Huneker thrived in New York; when in his later years he moved even a relatively short distance away, across the bridge to the ulterior reaches of Brooklyn, he confessed he could do little but guzzle beer and play Chopin. What he needed for critical inspiration was the stone and steel music of Manhattan. Since they left New York to work in remote places, such once-promising playwrights as Zoë Akins, Arthur Richman, Vincent Lawrence, and Maurine Watkins haven't written a single play that has ranked anywhere near their earlier efforts. Harry Leon Wilson, Gouverneur Morris, and the other writers of their generation who expatriated themselves from New York to California have done little after they sought the lazy land of sun and oranges. In New York there is the endless challenge to work, a constant current of electrical energy that penetrates into even the most quiet and secluded writing-room, an invisible but clearly felt flying flag to lead the spirit on.

It occasionally takes some resolution, of course, to resist the appeals that a city like New York makes to the lighter side of life. But one can more easily resist a plethora of diversion than a pittance of diversion. When one is conscious that within a stone's throw there is all the machinery of pleasure and gaiety that one might ask for, one doesn't particularly feel like asking for it. It isn't the temptation that is offered by the sporadic and isolated—often the rare—gaiety of the small town. It is the old story of the clerk in the candy store gagging at the sight of candy. Perhaps that was the metaphor behind Greeley's circus parade.

I often wonder if some of the writers who live in New York or have lived in New York and who have done a lot of their work there are entirely sincere and without posture when they subsequently claim that they can work well "anywhere but in New York," and that the muse starts to operate for them only when they are adjacent to an Ohio glue factory or residing at Provincetown in a shack that hasn't a bathroom.[2] That there are places other than New York where a writer can do his writing to his completest comfort and fullest satisfaction no one, certainly, will deny; there are unquestionably many such places. But the best place for any man's or woman's work is generally the place, whatever it is, where he has lived, lives, and has his home. And that place, for a New Yorker, is New York.

---

1. George Antheil (1900–59), iconoclastic American composer who in his first composition used cacophonous metal quasi-instruments. He was caricatured as Abe North in the Riviera beach scenes of F. Scott Fitzgerald's novel *Tender Is the Night* (1934).

2. An allusion to one of Eugene O'Neill's residences, which he shared with his second wife, Agnes Boulton, during the 1920s, before he moved to Brook Farm, Ridgefield, Connecticut.

Country Life in New York

Comes summer and the influx of city folk into bucolic New York reaches its height. The lure of the good old country brings in residents of such municipalities as Pugh's Corners, Connecticut, Five Forks, New York, and the like by the bus- and train-load. For it is in Manhattan that

---

From *The Bachelor Life* (New York: Reynal & Hitchcock, 1941), pp. 211–16

they can find all those attributes and delights of real country life which are denied them in their pastoral retreats.

The first joy of the thitherward rustics in New York lies in the good, honest country food which is to be found in abundance. Unable to get fresh corn, peas, string beans and other such vegetables at home, and forced to use the canned variety because all the fresh stuff is bought up by the New York markets, they here can revel in them to their hearts' content. Fresh and juicy meats, which are a rarity down on the farm, are the natural order of the day, and so is all the fresh fruit that is shot out of the hinterlands on express trains the moment it is picked.

Worn out by lack of sleep because of the loud noises made by birds, frogs and crickets, the country visitor to the city revels in the quiet and peace of hotel rooms, and soon discovers his health and mental well-being restored. For the first time in months, his slumbers are serene. He may sleep his fill, safe from dawn disturbances by crowing roosters and mooing cows, and safe as well from the early sunlight's intrusion through broken window shades and cracks in the wall.

The absence of mosquitoes is another source of comfort to him. If in his countryside he so much as pokes his head out of doors after dark, he will look like a violent case of measles, somewhat complicated with hives, the moment he draws it in again. But in the city no such agony awaits him. He may freely walk miles or sit outdoors for hours on end without a single bite. Nor is there the busy bee to buzz him and maybe painfully sting him into profuse cuss words.

The rural scenery of the city is still another bid drawing-card for the country boys and girls. Condemned for eleven months in the year to live in localities where most of the trees have been cut down to make room for farm land and where flowers are as rare as bathtubs, they find an especial thrill in the wooded parks and squares, in the real trees and blooms of Rockefeller Center, in the profusion of flowers in the windows and shops of the countless florists and in the blooms and blossoms in innumerable window-boxes along the streets and on the terraces of an endless number of apartment houses and hotels. The waterfalls which they behold in various restaurants, and the running streams and brooks which they encounter in some of the Italian spaghetti eating-places, similarly bring the feel of the real country to them, a feel which they seldom get where they came from.

The cool days and nights maneuvered through air-conditioners, re-frigerating devices, etc., are yet still another rustic feature that only the city can vouchsafe them. In what passes for the actual country, there is no escape from the hot days and hotter nights. But in the city the fresh, cool country breezes are the yokel visitor's gift at a mere button's press. If he wanders in the open, the backwoodsman may additionally get all the real country breezes, hitherto denied him and which he longs for, by sitting in one or another of the many roof gardens, or standing on the balcony of one of the many skyscrapers, or simply getting into a speeding taxicab or climbing atop a bus.

One of the theoretical contentments of living in the country is the rocking chair. A farmhouse porch and its inevitable rocking chair have long been hymned in fiction as the ultimate in physical ease and peace. But anyone who can discover a rocking chair in the rural regions that isn't lopsided or busted is worthy to have his statue placed in the world's Hall of Fame alongside those of Amerigo Vespucci, Balboa, and Stanley. In the city, on the contrary, country folk may have thousands of rockers in perfect condition and may rock and lull themselves into an authentic and ecstatic bucolic complacency.

And don't overlook the good old bucolic smells! Deep in the sticks, the good old bucolic smells that you read about are as hard to find as a copy of today's newspaper. Aside from the time-honored manure, whose rich fragrance is an acknowledged pleasure, there isn't a genuine country odor within sniffing distance. The flowers, as I have pointed out, are negligible; the trees, where they exist, have been so doused with insecticides and whitewash that all their olfactory delights have vanished; the droughts banish the smell of fresh earth; and about the only real rustic smell left is that provided by the garbage cans in the backyards.

In the city, however, you get the beautiful country smells by wholesale. The potted palms in even the cheapest hotel corridors give out a fragrance of foliage that comes as a godsend to the visiting farmers. The flowers in the little side vases in automobiles and taxicabs regale their famished nostrils. The fountains in parks and restaurants and plazas splash their dews on the grass below and enchant their senses. The trees in the side streets and elsewhere, left largely to their own devices, retain a leafy freshness. And the fresh, moist smell of earth fills the circumambient atmosphere in countless little back gardens, in many well-tended districts like Gramercy, Mount Morris, Madison Square and other such small parks,[1] in hundreds of shops where seeds and bulbs are for sale, in the thousands of markets and grocery stores with their loads of vegetables only recently pulled out of the still-clinging but here carefully sprinkled soil, and in even the five-and-ten stores where soil demonstrations are conducted on behalf of ambitious city gardeners by lovely and provocative salesgirls.

---

1. To say nothing of Central Park—Ed.

On Memorizing Historical Dates

Were I elected Chairman of the Board of Education in any municipality of this great Republic—which, in view of my lavish grade of intelligence, would obviously be most unlikely—the very first thing I should do would be to issue an order to school-teachers to desist from their present idiocy in cramming the heads of the young with dates. Of all the elements of so-called education, this is one of the most imbecile and useless, yet the practice keeps up simply because no one has ever had the good sense to call a halt to it, and the juvenile American cranium as a consequence is annually loaded up with a mass of figures which, if they are not promptly forgotten, not only serve no earthly purpose but occupy a cerebral space that might with immensely more profit be occupied by something else.

Speaking recently with a dozen or more youngsters of various sizes and ages and from various schools, I found that the date-stuffing business was still going on with even greater assiduity than in the days when I was a youngster and that their little heads were still being tortured with such absurd wastes of time as being asked to remember the date of the battle between Pisa and Lucca, the date of the birth of Gaius Lutatius Catulus, the dates of the institution of the League of Cambray and the Union of Kalmar, the date of Peter the Great's death, and the date of the ceding of Norway to Sweden. The attempt to convert the schoolboy mind into a calendar instead of into a thinking apparatus is nicely illustrated by such educational farce. What practical end it furthers or what good it does, the Lord alone knows, yet it persists simply out of tradition.

A knowledge of important dates in the world's history is, of course, valuable, but such dates are relatively few in number. Nine-tenths of the dates that youngsters are bidden to remember are of no value whatsoever to them in after life. Of what possible use is it, save in the case of the thirtieth-thousand boy who becomes in later life a school-master or historian of sorts, to know that the Peloponnesian War lasted from 431 B.C. to 404 B.C., that Albumazar was born in 805 A.D., that William of Orange embarked from Hellevoetsluis for England in 1688 and that Manuel I permitted the Crusaders under Conrad III and Louis VII to pass through his dominions in 1147? The answer, obviously, is that it is of utterly no use.

While it is meet to instruct children in the different historical periods and the more importatnt occurrences in those periods, that instruction would be vastly more satisfactory if the welter of particularized dates, relating to specific years, were abandoned and much more readily remembered and just as valuable dates by centuries or half-centuries substituted

From *The Intimate Notebooks of George Jean Nathan* (New York: Knopf, 1932), pp. 288–90.

in their stead. There are certain unavoidable exceptions, of course, but in the main the latter method would, I daresay, prove much more economical and profitable in the long run. It is sufficient—aye, more than sufficient— that a man know the general rather than the specific period of such events as the Wars of the Roses, the battle of Langside, the exploratory achievements of Magellan and the occurrence at Runnymede. If it ever becomes violently necessary for him to know the exact day, month, year and hour he can easily look it up in a book, but it will probably become that necessary not more than once in his life in order to settle some such very important and profound problem as to who will have to pay for the drinks.

The Old Police Gazette

The death, not long ago, of Richard K. Fox, editor and publisher of the *Police Gazette,* has brought one to ponder afresh on the persistent underestimation of the man that clung to him during his lifetime . . . Here in America, you will reflect, Fox and his journal were treated mainly as a joke: the two were summarily and idiotically condemned with the designation "barbershop." But the Europeans, the English in particular, were quick to see through the cheap mossback disesteem in which the man and his paper were held and to estimate the fellow in the terms of the peculiar genius that was his. Perhaps not more than two other men—Dana and Hearst—have exercised so profound an influence as Fox on the practical side of American journalism. This may seem superficially farfetched, but even a cursory survey of the man's philosophies and practices must convince the skeptic.

Often humorously described as "the paper that everybody read and nobody took," the *Police Gazette* was the first journal in the United States to treat of sports in such wise that the layman could understand what they were about. Fox's editorial plan, since imitated by every journal in America and Europe, changed the entire manner of this kind of reporting. The *Police Gazette,* further, was the first periodical to use a species of tinted paper that made reading easier on the eyes and that, from a commercial point of view, spectacularized the appearance of the paper and made it sell. Consider Fox's imitators in this direction: Bennett and his New York *Telegram,* Pulitzer and the sporting edition of his New York *Evening World,* Hearst and the late editions of the New York *Journal,* to mention only three, and all of these in a single city. There are hundreds of other imitations throughout America; there are two in London; there are two in Paris; there is one in Vienna; there are two in Berlin; there is one in Rome.

From *The Autobiography of an Attitude* (New York: Knopf, 1925), pp. 238–40.

Turn to the question of advertising. Fox was, during his life as he remains after his death, the only publisher in America who was not a hypocrite in this direction. He appreciated that the object of printing advertisements was, finally and simply, to make money—and he conducted himself accordingly. "Pay me what I charge and I'll print any dingblasted ad you give me." That was his intelligent attitude, and that was an attitude that he never changed. The bogus moral pose of his fellow publishers, he had no use for. "Ads", as he once eloquently put it, "aren't literature; they have nothing to do with the text of my *Gazette;* they are simply extra money in my pocket. Shoot!" The result was that the advertisements in the *Police Gazette* were the most interesting to be found anywhere in America . . .

Fox was, contrary to opinion in certain benighted quarters, an eminently moral man. Born in Belfast, Ireland, his early training was of a distinctly religious turn, and his career began on the staff of the Ulster *Banner,* a church publication. In all the years that he owned and edited the *Police Gazette,* he never once published, or permitted to be published therein, the photograph of any woman who was not pure. He would print pictures of women in tights—some of them almost nude—but never the picture of one who wasn't, so far as he knew, moral and virtuous. Well, never is perhaps stretching the thing a bit too far, for at one time, during his absence in Europe, a dozen or more pictures of dubious babies got into the *Gazette's* pages and contrived to cast suspicion on Fox's editorial integrity in this quarter. But those in the know never doubted that integrity for a moment, as his prompt dismissal of the guilty sub-editor, immediately upon his return from abroad left no further room for suspicion.

On Moviegoing

Whenever I go to the movies and wherever I sit, it always seems that the person sitting either next to me or directly behind me has a bad cold. This bad cold is invariably accompanied by an obbligato of sneezing which contrives to render either the side of my collar or the back of my hair so moist that I am contemplating taking a bath-towel along in the future. The person with the bad cold, furthermore, in nine cases out of ten appears to be convinced that any kind of candy, if only it be wrapped in paper which in the process of opening sounds like a Chinese New Year's celebration, is wonderful for colds. He seemingly is also persuaded that part of the cure consists either in crossing his legs so that one of his feet may handily

From *Encyclopedia of the Theatre* (New York: Knopf, 1940) pp. 266–71. Copyright renewed 1968 by Mrs. George Jean Nathan.

insert itself into your side trouser pocket or in pressing his knees hard against the back of your chair and periodically and suddenly pushing them so that you are propelled half-way out of your seat.

The moment I have at length accustomed myself to all this and prepared myself to give attention to the screen, an usher parades down the aisle and turns a bright pocket-flashlight into my eyes, blinding me for at least two minutes. He then also blinds everybody in my vicinity, after which he slowly walks up the aisle with his flashlight and blinds everybody else. He must consider this fun, as he keeps walking up and down the aisle at intervals of every seven or eight minutes doing the same thing, all under the innocent guise of determining what vacant seats there may be or pretending to watch out for someone who has perchance lit a cigarette.

Seated on the other side of me from the person with the cold or next to the sufferer behind me there is sure to be a very small boy. This small boy evidently comes to the movies for the sole purpose, if he is beside me, of tangling himself up in his seat like a pretzel and kicking my elbow off the arm of my chair or, if he is behind me, leaning over the back of my seat and breathing furiously in my ear. However, I can stand this, as I get a respite every three minutes when he goes out to the washroom.

All the people around me at a movie seem to be great conversationalists. Since I have never mastered the trick of dissociating what is coming in my left ear from what is coming in my right, I thus constantly am confused as to whether Mr. Clark Gable is telling Miss Carole Lombard that he loves her or whether it is all about what remarkable stockings he can get at Macy's for forty-nine cents. Not long ago I went to a Western picture and I could have sworn that it had to do with a cowboy whose Uncle Moe was having an awful time with his haberdashery store on Amsterdam Ave., whose cousin Minnie who lived in Paterson, New Jersey, had an ingrowing toe-nail, and who was thinking of spending his summer vacation in Atlantic City.

Adjacent to or in close juxtaposition to a movie theatre there always seems to be a nut shop, and no sound-track yet invented has succeeded in triumphing over it. These nut shops, judging from the deafening crackling noises emanating from their merchandise, must do an enormous business. Things have got to the point where you can tell the difference between a drawing-room comedy and a Western only by closely watching the clothes the actors have on. A short time ago I went to see what I thought was Tyrone Power in *Jesse James* and, blinded by the usher's flashlight, thought the gunfire in it pretty exciting, only to learn the next day that what I had been at was a Deanna Durbin picture.

In the winter season, I generally find an elderly lady in my proximity who wears at least six coats, to say nothing of enough scarves, mufflers and overshoes to stock an Army and Navy store. The old girl proceeds gradually to go through a strip-tease that begins at the first reel to the feature picture and isn't concluded until the Fitzpatrick travelogue comes on. During the strip-tease, she bangs you on the head a couple of times, one of her cast-aside coats tumbles over your eyes, another knocks off your glasses, a muffler brushes your hat off your lap, a scarf gets wound around your elbow, a rubber-shoe smears its mud all over your socks, and the old baby herself, when finally she sits down, sits down not in her seat but on top of you. By then the only thing left for you to see is the announcement of next week's picture and you can't even see that because now she has got up again, is standing half in front of you, and is taking off a seventh coat which she had previously overlooked.

A movie theatre also has a peculiar concept of ventilation. I suppose there are exceptions, but not in the case of the movie theatres I seem to go to. These theatres apparently work on two principles. Either they think that no ventilation at all is desirable, with the result that they smell like a Russian herring cannery, or they abruptly and simultaneously open a door out front and one back stage, with the result that you either get pneumonia or are blown slam-bang forward up against Edna May Oliver. (If it was Hedy Lamarr, it wouldn't be so bad, pneumonia or no pneumonia.) Certain other theatres which have been honored by my patronage steer a middle course. They have installed so-called fresh-air systems which always seem to be placed in such wise that they funnel the cold air directly down into your collar, with the result that after you have sat through a full-length feature you find yourself with a stiff neck, threatened sinus trouble, and backside chilblains.

Film houses with girl ushers present another embarrassment. Many of the girls aren't bad-looking and seem to be acutely aware of it. When you hand one your ticket stub, she looks you over in a rather coy, if theoretically impersonal, manner, winks her impression, if even remotely gratified, to her usher girl-friend, and escorts you to your seat with something of a saucy wave of the bustle. It thereupon suddenly in some strange way occurs to you that you will want something to eat before you go to bed that night, though you hitherto have never wanted anything to eat before going to bed, and you accordingly invite her to have a bit of supper with you. That is where the embarrassment enters. She can't. She is sorry, but she has a date. With whom? you indignantly demand. With her boy-friend, she replies. And who may your boy-friend be, my pigeon?, you blandly inquire. But even before she answers, you know. The boy-friend of every good-looking movie usher is invariably either the young man who presides over the candy-stand in the lobby or the resplendently uniformed beanpole whose post is near the ticket-window and whose duty it is to lie about plenty of good seats inside.

If you have ever tried the loges in the more elaborate movie theatres, I needn't tell you what you are up against. You pay double the regular admission fee for the hypothetical pleasure and comfort of seeing a picture in quiet and peace, and what do you get? To one side of you, you unfailingly get a man smoking a cigar evidently made of Port du Salut cheese wrapped in alpaca. To the other side, you regularly get a hand-holding couple who devote the evening to arguing where they are going and what the girl is or, more usually, is not willing to do when the show is over, the colloquy generally ending in a quarrel and the stumbling of the couple over you on the way out in the middle of the picture. And to the back of you, you are pretty certain to get someone who has evidently mistaken the loge for a bedroom at the Hotel Taft and who snores or grunts so loudly that you can't hear even Victor McLaglen.

But the little cinema art theatres present the most embarrasing problem of all. They are so small and the screen is so close to you that you can't tell whether it is Charles Boyer or yourself who is in bed with Danielle Darrieux.

On Love Letters

Every man should specify in a codicil to his last will and testament that under no circumstances are his letters, to whomsoever written during his life-time, to be published after his death. The only conceivable exceptions should be such vain fellows, of whom there are a few, as deliberately compose letters with an eye to their posthumous publication. These letters, of course, are not actually letters at all, but purposefully literary documents—posturing, insincere, and of the popinjay all compact. They are no more letters, properly speaking, than Grant's Tomb is a deviled ham sandwich. The letters written by other men are, however and nevertheless, generally equally unrevelatory so far as the men themselves are concerned. And where they do reveal the character and nature of their writers, they usually have so little claim to literary value, or any other sound value, that their publication disgraces the respective corpses. A man may tell the truth about himself and his acquaintances in a few letters during his life-time, but the letters he customarily writes illuminate him with a very dim honesty. For once he tells the truth about the way some man has swindled him, he fails ten times to tell the truth about the ways, he, in turn, swindled other men. For once he writes a letter saying what he actually thinks, he twenty times writes letters saying merely what he knows will please the recipients of those letters. A man's letters, in short, represent less himself than more or less necessary evasions of himself.

From *The Autobiography of an Attitude*, (New York: Knopf, 1925), pp. 45–46.

Even in the doodlish department of love-letter writing, a man's episto-
lary confections seldom have much sincerity. Where sincerity creeps in to
any considerable degree, the love-letter descends very largely to rubber-
stamp expressions and terms of endearment as old as John the Baptist,
and so is not worth publishing. A man generally writes his love-letters, if
he compromises his dignity so far as to write them at all, not for their truth,
but for their sound—and they hence give us very much less accurate news
of his character and nature than, say, his laundry bills. Now and again a
poet's love-letters are worth publication, yet this is not because they are
letters, but because they are literary compositions converted into letters
only by the grace of a postage stamp and the circumstance that some post-
office clerk has canceled it with some mush message as "Don't Forget
Ashtabula Old-Home Week."

Sex Mores

The historian who will set himself to chronicle the salient change in sex
morals that has come over the United States in these years of the Twentieth Century will be impressed by one or two phenomena that have been
omitted from various recent disquisitions on the subject. One of these is
the manner in which that change has affected the American social classes
of the second and even third level. That a looseness of sex morals is always
more or less a characteristic of the rich and leisurely class in any country
is, of course, sufficiently known. In any period this stratum of society is
found to suffer less than any other from moral infractions, and for obvious
reasons. In the first place, it is, by virtue of its position and affluence, able
to afford an indifference to the moral and ethical standards prevailing
among the less fortunate classes. In the second place, its manner of life is
conducive to lax moral standards. And in the third place, its opportunities
for pleasure, whether of a sexual nature or otherwise, are manifestly
greater than those of the classes that are poorer in the world's goods and
hence in leisure. So much is platitude. And platitude, too, is the fact that
the classes below this class must inevitably and arbitrarily obey a more
rigorous code whether they wish to or not, since they must conduct
themselves in such wise that the upper class, upon which they depend for
a livelihood, may, as the word goes, respect them. Whatever the character
of the boss, he expects his clerks to be abstemious, prudent, honorable
and moral. This is not so much hypocrisy on the employer's part as it is
sound business sense, and not only sound business policy but, on a wider

From *Land of the Pilgrims' Pride*, (New York: Knopf, 1927), pp. 1, 2, 5, 7–13, 16, 18–19.

basis, sound social policy. The king may have a dozen mistresses, but his chamberlain must be a respectable married man with one wife, ten children and a pew in the kirk. . . .

In America, as in every country under the sun, the so-called inferior classes imitate the upper classes in so far as they can. They imitate these upper classes in dress, in deportment, in pleasures, in thought and in every other way that they are, within the possibilities of their means, able to. In most countries, this cuckooing cannot go very far, since the lesser classes lack the necessary money and leisure. In America, however, the so-called middle class has, in the last fifteen years, acquired money and a consequent share of leisure in an unheard of and amazing degree. Today, it is the richest middle class in the world. And, as a result, it has been able to imitate the upper class of the country more closely than such an imitation has ever before been possible. Thus we find this middle class of Americans presently exhibiting an attitude toward sex morals largely of a piece with that exhibited by its superiors. The middle class I allude to is, plainly enough, that of the larger cities. If the middle classes of the rest of the country have not yet taken color from the former's changed attitude, they may be expected to do so in due time, as the hinterland, however independent of the cities it may be politically and alcoholically, is ever a vassal to the cities' dictate and prejudice in the matter of everything from radio music and moving pictures to store clothes and the philosophy of prophylactic sprays.

A second fact that will impress itself upon the historian of modern sex is the perhaps deplorable practicability of a moderate lack of chastity on the part of the present-day young woman. . . . Chastity alone is no longer the excellent bait that it once was. Other qualities are demanded in a woman, and are regarded as vastly more important, and are more efficient in roping and pulling in the marrying male. I do not mean to justify a young woman's looseness in sex morals; that is certainly far from my purpose; all that I wish to do is to point out, and perhaps even lament, the undeniable fact that the not too circumspect girl of today pretty generally gets a much better grade of husband for herself than the girl who obeys the injunction of Marie Lloyd's familiar music hall ditty[1] . . . .

Nothing is more clearly indicative of this change in sex morals which has come over the Anglo-American world than man's present attitude toward woman's virtue, already briefly alluded to. Up to comparatively recent years, the question of a woman's virtue was an even greater consideration on the part of the man contemplating marriage with her than her culinary skill, the cleanliness of her hair and her father's police record. The woman who had succumbed to some knave's wiles was not only sidestepped by the matrimonially inclined male, but was looked upon by other women as a creature headed for the eternal fires. She was, in a word, morally and socially *déclassée*. The novels and plays of the era invariably dealt with her in much the same manner, to wit, as one either to be scorned or pitied. Such was the situation up to within no more than ten or fifteen years ago. Then, suddenly, there came an abrupt change. Not only was comparative lack of virtue no longer held against a woman, it was actually looked on with favor and endorsed. So much so, indeed, that today things have come to such a point that the so-called virgin is actually a subject of esoteric mirth and jeer not only on the part of men but also on the part of women, and not only on the part of women, but, what is more, on the part of the unhappy creature herself. She is not proud of her virtue, as she once was, but actually ashamed of it.

Although it is commonly assumed that virtue was originally imposed upon women by men in order that the security, dignity and self-esteem of the latter might be duly safeguarded, it is much more likely that virtue was originally imposed upon women by women themselves, and for a simple reason. Virtue was woman's sole protection against other women. It was demanded by women of other women because their men, as they knew all too well, were ever fetched by the unvirtuous woman and were weaned from them by her. Fearing such competition, women took every means to stave it off and destroy it by announcing the obloquy that they would make and did make the unvirtuous woman suffer. Now, it has long been a characteristic of woman that she has feared her sisters' opinion and estimate of her more than those of men, and the stratagem enjoyed, accordingly, its reign of prosperity. But, gradually, that prosperity grew less and less. For women began to find that it was no longer possible to attach obloquy to sexual dereliction in the way that they had once seen successful in attaching it, since such dereliction has begun to take on a number of hitherto strange and disconcerting aspects which undermined and weakened the old stigma.

In the first place, there were ridiculous divorce laws that divorced, or at least separated, man and wife, while yet they did not actually divorce them. There were rulings as to various arbitrary periods, ranging up to three years, wherein the parties to the divorce, though they had already picked out their future mates, were forbidden to marry the latter. There were periods of from six months to a year that one of the parties had to spend in a certain State or otherwise endure until he or she obtained the desired release. There were utterly nonsensical barriers to marital dissolution that freed the parties yet didn't free them. The preponderant weight of public opinion was against all these legal devices. And, as a consequence, sexual dereliction by the separated parties with men and women denied legal union with them for the time being was quietly passed over. In the second place, obloquy is utterly ineffective and incapable of operation in the face of what is generally regarded as romance. Need I, at this tardy date, be guilty of observing again that the late war provided that romance, and in such bulk, in so far as the average man and woman were concerned, that all the old-maid moral opinion in the world was helpless against it? The girl whose affianced young man was about to go overseas, theoretically never to return, the nurse at the front with her charge apparently doomed to but a few more days of life, the lover on a fortnight's leave before going back into the slaughterhouse—the former order of stenciled morals disappeared in connection with such as these, and not only in the minds of those directly concerned but in the minds, or at least the ears, of understanding and sympathetic outsiders. The bands were playing; the flags were streaming; the cannon were rumbling; the Sunday-schools were given over to Red Cross workers, sock-knitters and recruiting officers; the organs were playing not "Nearer, My God, to Thee," but "If He Can Fight Like He Can Love, Good-night Germany!" With two million men jumping at one another's throats, the chastity of some girls in Shamokin, Pa. seemed a negligible affair. . . .

It is entertaining, incidentally, in the light of the present attitude of the community toward sex, to consider the position of the various States in the Union in the matter of bigamy. In Alabama, the penalty for bigamy is from two to five years in prison, the penalty for forgery being, in the court's power, twice as many years. In Arizona, one may get not more than ten years for bigamy, but four more years for simple perjury. In Arkansas, a bigamist can get off with a three years' sentence, where he may have to serve fifteen years for perjury or twenty-one years for robbery. The same relative schedule obtains in many other States. In Louisiana, a bigamist faces the possibility of only a year in jail and a small fine, where a thief may have to serve fourteen years. In Maryland, the bigamist may get off with eighteen months, the very lowest sentence in the entire higher criminal catalogue of the State. In Nebraska, he need, in the court's discretion, serve only a year; in North Carolina, possibly only four months; in North Dakota, Ohio and Oregon, only a year; in South Carolina, only half a year; and in numerous other States only a year. In Arkansas, on the other hand, the man who steals a mule may be fifteen years in the cooler and, in Texas, the stealing of a horse may bring a similar sentence. . . .

That modern literature (both book and periodical), drama and even the cinema, in addition to reflecting the sex nonchalance of the period, have also directly influenced that nonchalance is more or less apparent. Three-quarters of the fiction and plays and a recognizable share of motion pictures (for all we hear of censorship) presently view loose sex morals lightly or romantically; gone almost entirely is the former uncompromising, tragic approach to the subject. The wages of sin is no longer death, but a happy ending.[2]

---

1. Marie Lloyd (1870–1922), English music-hall artiste. The risqué song Nathan refers to began "Oh, Mr. Porter, whatever shall I do?"

2. Except for AIDS—Ed.

On Exercise

On an average of three times a week in the instance of oral communication and twice a week in the instance of the United States mails, I have lately been approached on the subject of why I do not go in for exercise. "The trouble with you," importune certain of my acquaintances—not my friends, who are more carefully selected on intelligence qualifications— "the trouble with you, my boy, is that you don't exercise enough!" The mails bring me the same information. Gymnasiums all over town, judging from the amount of "literature" I get from them, apparently employ special mailing clerks for the express purpose of looking out fearfully for my physical well-being. I have before me, as I make these notes, a typical circular. "Do you realize that you are all wrong and will go to pieces if you don't see to your condition?" it argues ominously. "What you need is exercise—every day—systematic exercise such as our trained instructors can map out for you and *make* you take even against your present foolish disinclination! Two hours a day in our gymnasium will make a new man of you! Get busy before it is too late!"

Toward these persons who are so solicitous of me and of my physical welfare, I generally conduct myself in a single manner and, I discover, with a single result. Whenever I meet a man who is enthusiastic about exercise I have an annoying habit of propounding a set question to him, and whenever I depart from the aforesaid man I invariably find that his answer to my question has been equally set. My question is as follows: "Just what is it that leads you to imagine that a lot of exercise is a good thing?" His answer, in turn, is as follows: "Look at animals; they all take a lot of exercise and they are wonderfully fit! Look at *me!* Don't *I* look the picture of health?"

Pursuing my researches, I have accordingly looked at animals, Englishmen and several hundred exercise fanatics and I have a report to make. The theory that animals spend most of their time exercising does not, I find, hold much water. The great majority of animals, as a matter of zoölogical record, take hardly any exercise at all. Furthermore, the particular species of animals that do go in for exercise are almost generally those with the shortest span of life. The tortoise, the laziest creature on earth,enjoys—according to Prof. Carl W. Newmann (*vide* the Leipzig *Illustrierte Zeitung*)—the greatest longevity, from 200 to 300 years. The elephant, a sluggish fellow if ever there was one, lives from 150 to 200 years. The swan, aristocratically languid, sometimes reaches the 102-year mark. The parrot among birds, and the most indolent of all the feathered

From *The Intimate Notebooks of George Jean Nathan* (New York: Knopf, 1932), pp. 311–17.

tribe, touches, like the tortoise, the 200- to 300-year limit. The rhinoceros, surely no relative of the late Mr. Walter Camp, lives from forty to fifty years and the crocodile touches forty. On the other hand, the statistical records inform us that such devotees of exercise as the dog die in from ten to fifteen years, the squirrel in from ten to twelve, the hare in from seven to eight, and the mouse in from three to four.

Descending the scale of animal life, we discover that the inert mussel often lives sixty or seventy years, while the lively fox kicks the bucket at an average of ten. The leech, which is about as active as a frozen water-tap, enjoys the world for twenty years, but the ant, that hardly ever stands still for a moment, goes to his Maker in less than half that time. The goose lives much longer than the eagle; the eider duck much longer than the crane or the woodpecker; and the ordinary quiescent sty pig longer than the overly active guinea-pig. And the beaver, one of the busiest animals, whose very name stands for exercise, lives just half as long as the lazy donkey. As for the busy little bee, it dies in six weeks, while the queen bee, taking life serenely the while the other damn fools hustle, lives from four to five years.

The second item in my report has to do with the exercise addict's theory that Englishmen generally appear to be in the pink of condition because of the great amount of exercise they take. It is the average American's notion that the middle-aged and older Englishman spends most of his time on the golf links, riding to hounds, playing cricket and whanging at tennis balls. I have spent parts of twenty-one different years in England; I know hundreds of Englishmen intimately; I have watched thousands of others whom I have not had the pleasure of meeting—and if they spend their time as the American imagines they do, they must do it either secretly or during the periods when I am out of their country. The English youth, like the youth of every land, goes in for exercise in one form of sport or another, but the middle-aged and most certainly the older Englishman spends considerably more time drinking whiskey and soda or quietly tending his little garden than he does hitting a golf ball or gesticulating with a tennis racquet. Although I am not given to facetiousness, I have a feeling that it is the whiskey and soda much more than the golf sticks or racquet that gives him that fine, ruddy, outdoor look and that glow of health. And it is the same, to an even greater degree, with the Englishman's neighbor, the Frenchman. The young Frenchman has lately got to be a hound for tennis, bicycling and cross-country hiking, but the older boys may still be found, as they have been found for scores upon scores of years, keeping a good physical trim by sitting for hours in front of cafés sipping Picon and occasionally varying the business by slowly getting up, stretching their legs and following some boulevard midinette.[1]

The third item in my report concerns the exercise addict's climacteric challenge: "Look at *me!* Don't *I* look the picture of health?" After looking at hundreds of such gentlemen I am prepared to admit that some of them do *look* the picture of health, but whether they honestly *feel* and *are* the picture of health is another matter. They may feel it for the immediate time being, as a man feels it after he has drunk five Popocatepetl cocktails—or, for that matter, one absinthe drip—but the doctors' memoranda often prove that, after the superficial glow and imitation health induced by a lot of exercise wear off, the gentlemen are anything but what they think they are. A vigorous body massage indulged in several times a day would impart the same lively blood circulation induced by athletic monkeyshines and the same superficial look of well-being, yet even the most rabid golfer or tennis zealot would admit that it wasn't a good thing. "But," proclaim all the latter, "it's the fresh air that does the trick!" They could get the same amount of fresh air, so far as that kind of argument goes, by taking their massages on the roof or out in the back yard.

Rex Beach once said that the man over thirty-five who goes in elaborately for exercise isn't really half so much interested in his health as in his looks. . . If he achieves a fresh complexion and keeps his waistline down, he is tickled to death—even if his heart or some other important item in his corpus suffers some damage. Vanity is at the bottom of much of the exercise indulged in by men after their youth is gone; the question of health is of second consideration. Golf, tennis and other such forms of physiological racketeering are largely to men what the widely used sunburn powder is to women.

The National Collegiate Athletic Association, of which Prof. F. W. Nicolson, of Wesleyan, is secretary, in convention, assembled not long ago broadcast to a surprised world a set of carefully arrived at statistics that should give the exercising gentry pause. While the gentry may, perhaps fairly, dismiss my own unprofessional animadversion as prejudiced, they will experience some trouble in dismissing as quickly the report made by the Association which, it might be fair to presume, would, if anything, be greatly prejudiced in favor of athletic exercise. Well, what do the figures compiled by this august body, through its investigators, show? They show, and conclusively, that—even among young men—college athletes die much sooner than boys who do not go in for athletics, that college men who take no exercise at all or at best very little—for example, the "grinds"—not only live longer but show a general average of health much higher than the other college boys, and that—in the general run—the fellow who sits quietly in a rocking chair, or even a stationary armchair, is better off all around than the one who cavorts on the gridiron, diamond or lake. The lowest mortality, the Association's statistics forcefully demonstrate, is indicated among the so-called honor students who leave athletics to the boneheads. The obvious corollary is that these students must also enjoy the best actual physical condition and health. They may not look so fit, but they *are* fitter. Not for the moment, perhaps, but for the long months and years that lie ahead of them.

The investigations of the National Collegiate Athletic Association were not confined to a few colleges, but were—as the Association's title implies—wide and comprehensive. Furthermore, its inquiry was supplemented by the collaborative investigations of the American Student Health Association and of the statistical chieftain of the Metropolitan Life Insurance Company. The job consumed three solid years and the resulting study represents the vital history of almost 40,000 graduates of various representative colleges and universities and of classes ranging over a period of thirty-five years. In the study is further represented the vital history of something like 5,000 athletes of various colleges and of something like 6,500 honor students during the same period. The statistics cover the time from graduation until a few years ago. And they prove, doubtless more pointedly than anything else, the futility and even danger of the unnatural strain that men impose upon themselves under the name of exercise and make appetizing to themselves with pretty names.

The chief burden of gathering these revelatory data fell upon the shoulders of the painstaking and proficient Dr. Louis I. Dublin, head statistician of the Metropolitan Life Insurance Company, a man who has given the general subject much study and whose admiration for exactness and literal fact is sufficiently known. Dr. Dublin reports, "At twenty-two, which is close to the average age of graduation, athletes are found to show an expectation of 45.56 additional years, that is, an even chance of reaching the age of 67.56 years. The showing of graduates generally betters this record by two months, but honor men, that is the scholars pure and simple, better the record of athletes, at the beginning of their adult lives by *more than two years*. These honor men, the Phi Beta Kappa group and the like, show an extraordinary longevity record—three and a half years better than for carefully selected insured lives and *one year better than for the best population group in the world, namely, New Zealanders!*"

"At thirty-two and later, much the same relations in statistics are found," Dr. Dublin proceeds. "At forty-two," he reports, "the record is not changed; the honor men still have a considerable edge on the athletes. At fifty-two, the record is the same; still the scholars have it all over the big muscle boys. And so it is, too," he concludes, "at sixty-five and beyond."

While I am addressing myself to the subject of exercise generally rather than to the specific case of college athletics, a further word on the latter may not be amiss. The latest bulletin published by the Carnegie Foundation on American college athletics contains much for the exercising dervishes to ponder. If, as the statistical bulletin in point shows—it is an imposing volume of more than 380 printed pages—strenuous exercise is often dangerous to youth, what must it be to men long past their youth? Surely the Carnegie Foundation's figures gathered by Howard J. Savage with the assistance of Dean F. Smiley, John T. McGovern and Harold W. Bentley, experienced men all, do not lie. This is no place to go into an extensive quotation of the presented facts, but the record of the burning out of high-school boys from indulgence in athletics, the record of serious injuries suffered by athletes (1320 cases in twenty-two colleges in a single year), the record of cases of impaired health and the record even of collapse and tragic death—such reading should make older men who presently disport themselves like youngsters pause and reflect.

That a mild amount of exercise—a very mild amount—may be good for a man, I am not fool enough to deny. But, as I see it, the average man gets enough of it during a day without thinking of it. Every man does a sufficient amount of exercising daily in the course of his routine amply to serve his purpose. He may not know it for exercise or call it exercise but it is exercise none the less. Such physical activity is enough for the well-being of any man. To ask him, after it, to go out and work himself half to death on a golf links or tennis court is merely to increase some doctor's holdings in Treasury 4¼'s.

---

1. midinette—a Parisian girl employed in the fashion industry.

Essays in Criticism

Criticism and Reviewing

When I speak separately of criticism and reviewing, I imply no lofty sniff at the latter. At its best—and there are in New York, Boston and one or two other cities reviewers as competent as you will find anywhere—it is frequently indistinguishable from what goes somewhat more elegantly by the name of dramatic criticism. These reviewers are critics in the honest sense and what they write of the theatre is at once often sagacious and helpful. But nevertheless, in the aggregate, reviewing as it is presently conducted by the newspapers, even at its best, is injurious to the theatre, and for a simple reason. Whereas crticism, which may roughly be defined as the after-thought of reviewing, may because of its more leisurely and withdrawn nature choose and select the more significant and important aspects of the theatre and drama for its analytical performances, and so immediately dismiss from its consideration most of the aspects of the theatre and drama that are beneath contempt, reviewing must because of its leaven of reportorial and news character embrace the theatre by and large. By virtue of this demand that is made upon it, it must, if it have any respect for itself, denounce and ridicule at least two-thirds of the plays shown in the theatre during any single season, as any single season that discloses a one-third share of reputable drama is obviously a season to be proclaimed from the mountain tops. Nor am I slighting the theatre, for any year that reveals, in literature, so much as a third of book produce of merit or that reveals, in music or painting or sculpture or anything else, a third measure of worth is a year to be shouted equally to the corners of the earth.

The theatre, however, is different from these other arts in that the good in it suffers from the bad in it. If fifty novels are denounced and made mock of and if fifty paintings are contemptuously dismissed as daubs, the more reputable publishing houses with their fifty-first, fifty-second and fifty-third good novels and the more reputable art galleries with their fifty-first, fifty-second and fifty-third good paintings still get the trade, and the

From *The Intimate Notebooks of George Jean Nathan* (New York: Knopf, 1932), pp. 138–42.

fifty bad novels and fifty bad paintings are not given a second thought. But, unlike publishing and the art gallery, the theatre's public is kin to the elephant that does not forget; it remembers and resents the theatre's trash. And, further, it is the idiosyncrasy of that public not to think of *a* theatre, as other publics think of *a* novel or *an* art gallery, but to lump good and bad together and to think of *the* theatre. All this may not sound very convincing when it is written upon paper and subsequently put into print, but it remains that every last reader will readily recognize the truth of it when he reflects on the attitude of those theatregoers with whom he happens to be acquainted. "I hear that the last two weeks' plays are rotten; the theatre is getting pretty sick"; "what's the use of going to the theatre; I read that there have been six flops in the last ten days"; "the new plays all seem to be duds; what's happened to the theatre?" Etc., etc. The reader's ears surely recognize the sound of such cavils. And it is thus that where one should properly encounter some such observation as, "I read, or see, or hear that six or eight or ten theatres have bad plays in them," one encounters the blanket implication that *the* theatre, that is, the theatre *in toto,* has gone to the dogs.

It is reviewing, as we currently observe it, that is largely responsible for confusing *the* theatre and separate and individual theatres in the public mind. And it is because of this confusion, induced not dishonestly but inevitably out of complete and admirable honesty, that the theatre in its best sweep has suffered. To argue that the comparatively few theatres that house good plays do not suffer is beside the immediate point, for it is not the financial aspect of the theatre of which we are speaking so much as the psychical attitude of the public toward the theatre. In other words, the theatre-mindedness of the public, the theatre-mindedness that brought the German theatre some years ago to the high peak it reached . . . the theatre-mindedness that England prospered by in the Nineteen-Hundreds and that America prospered by twenty and thirty years ago. It is this theatre-mindedness, this interest in and even enthusiasm for the theatre, that play reviewing as practised in America today has innocently debilitated and corrupted. Take the New York example. About fifty legitimate theatres of all kinds and varieties were in periodic operation during the past season. In those fifty theatres, there were shown something like one hundred and fifty productions, all duly reviewed in the newspapers. The great majority of these productions were completely devoid of critical merit and were undeserving of criticism. Criticism, in the separate sense in which I have employed the term, accordingly allowed them to pass unnoticed and to die in their tracks unmourned and promptly forgotten. But reviewing was willy-nilly forced by newspaper policy to recognize them, to comment at more or less length upon them, to emphasize their worthlessness in the public's mind, and to lament with loud groans, coincidentally, the dismalness which they contributed to the theatrical scene.

Reading thus week in and week out, with but occasional recess, of bad plays, dull plays, boresome plays, trashy plays, depressing plays, the public has gradually come to regard the theatre as an institution with a rather olidous air to it and has gradually had it dinned into its consciousness that what must so often be bad may very, very seldom be hoped to be any good. And, accordingly, its old theatre-mindedness has had a serious crimp put into it. What is needed to restore the old-theatre-mindedness is, I believe, a reconstitution of the methods of play reviewing. Let this play reviewing be as honest and as forthright as it in general presently is, but let there be a clear and unmistakable segregation of its various performances. Let it allow itself not to review *the* theatre in terms of trumpery productions of trumpery plays by trumpery entrepreneurs but *a* theatre here and *a* theatre there, as the situation may arise. Under the heading of *The Theatre,* or *The Play,* let it review such exhibits as *Mourning Becomes Electra, The Barretts of Wimpole Street, The Left Bank, The Moon in the Yellow River* and, say, a dozen or so other such worthy and relatively worthy productions in the course of a season. And let it have some such heading as *Not the Theatre,* or *The Rubbish Heap,* or *The Ashcan,* or something of the sort for the twaddle that the theatre-in-name-only annually, even in its most prosperous times, uncovers. Thus will *the* theatre and mere buildings temporarily housing so-called plays until they may be converted into Automats, garages and ten-cent dance halls and so pay a cent on the dollar to the gypped bondholders—thus will *the* theatre and such imitations be clearly dissociated in the public's mind.

The Theatre Is One of the World's Pleasures

The theatre, as I have said, is to me one of the world's pleasures. On such occasions as it devotes itself to fine art it is one of the world's genuine pleasures. On such occasions as it devotes itself instead to the spectacle of Dutch comedians alternately kicking each other in the *scrobiculus cordis* and falling violently upon their *amplitudina emphatica,* it is a pleasure no less, albeit of a meaner species. It is, of course, not to be denied that for one evening of real pleasure in the theatre one often has to undergo a number of profound tortures, but the same thing holds true of the aesthetic satisfaction to be derived in an art gallery, where bogus art is often no less relatively in evidence than in the theatre. One reads a dozen new books

From *The World in Falseface* (New York: Knopf, 1923) pp. xiv–xxi. Copyright renewed 1950 by George Jean Nathan.

before one encounters one that imparts a glow. One sits through a dozen new plays before one encounters a *White-Headed Boy,* or a *March Hares,* or a *pas seul* by George Bickel—and through nine or ten dozen before one encounters a *Caesar and Cleopatra.* To hold against the theatre on that score is to hold as well against most of the other sources of human gratification.

With all its faults, the theatre has amused and improved the spirit of man for centuries on end. Like the doll, it is the one toy that has outlived, and will continue to outlive, the horde of attacking years. It has now and then risen to greatness; it has now and then fallen to triviality—so have literature, and music, and sculpture, and painting. William Shakespeare and Owen Davis, Michelangelo and Paul Manship, Peter Paul Rubens and Penrhyn Stanlaws, Johann Sebastian Bach and Raymond Hubbell. There is no argument in contrasts; there are always contrasts. But aside from the question of the theatre's place in art, it remains that the theatre is good fun—and it is of good fun of one kind and another that I am, at the moment, speaking. My days are spent professionally in the channels of literature—my mornings with reading, my afternoons with writing. When evening comes, I am occasionally very glad to have done with literature. Dinner parties I can't abide; they bore me to death; I never accept an invitation to one if I can lie out of it. Drinking is amusing enough, but it is not easy to find sufficiently amusing persons to drink with. I am, furthermore, a bachelor and have no household duties to concern me, no wife to drive crazy, no offspring to play peek-a-boo with. Clubs no longer interest me. Every time I enter one, some terrible wet-blanket, preposterously overjoyed at seeing me again after so long an absence, rushes up to me, invites me to dinner on Wednesday at the other end of Long Island, and asks me to tell him confidentially if it is really true that Irene Castle is in love with her husband. I lost my taste for card playing some years ago; if I want to go to a supper party there are still four hours to kill; and the diversions that most persons favor in the intervening time do not especially quicken me. There is left, as Goethe agreed, the theatre. There is left, between the demi-tasse and the bedtime cigarette, this night *Romeo and Juliet,* that night Sam Bernard, this night *Electra,* that night Ann Pennington, this night a smash of beauty and that, a smash of slapsticks. A farce by the younger Guitry, an operetta from the Kärntner-Ring, a burlesque show down in Fourteenth Street, the monkeyshines of Robert B. Mantell, a Eugene O'Neill play, a touch of double meaning from Budapest, an unintentionally jocose English "society play," a tune by Oscar Straus, or Emmerich Kalmann or Victor Herbert, a Ziegfeld show, something by Dunsany or Synge or Rostand or Thoma, a revival of some excellent comedy or merely, perhaps, a trim ankle, a sudden, surprising, lightning flash of real poetry, a comedian with an allegorical nose—one pays one's money and takes one's choice. It is the grab-bag nature of the theatre that makes it what it is. It is not curiosity that takes me there, but hope. . . .

But all this has to do with the theatre merely as a diversion, and not as the peg for a writing-man on which to hang, as I have more or less hung, a career. Pleasure is one thing, serious work quite another thing. Well, let us see. The theatre, as I look at it, is one of the best subjects in the world from which to fashion a variegated assortment of predicates. It is almost impossible for the writer on politics to use politics as a hook whereon to hang his opinions, say, of music or cow diseases. The same thing holds true of writers on music itself, or painting, or architecture, or sports, or science, or archaeology, or economics, or religion, or almost anything else save books. The theatre, to the contrary, by the very nature of its diverse constituent elements and its peculiar ramifications, offers to the man who writes about it a hundred convenient opportunities to air his views *con sordini* on nearly everything under the sun, and what a writer craves are such opportunities. What is more, these digressions from the main theme are not, in dramatic and theatrical criticism, so patently or objectionably out of key as they would be in other forms of critical exposition. Furthermore, if Mr. H. G. Wells is justified in using the history of the whole world to work off his implied opinion of Lloyd George, I see no reason why objection should be made to me for using a single line in a play by Mr. Samuel Shipman to work off my opinion of unipolar induction, sex hygiene, the political situation in central Siam, or anything else.

For such meditations, the theatre provides an admirably provocative field. One of the best ideas I ever got for a digressive essay on humour came to me while I was watching the characters in a Strindberg play go crazy. The best essay on Shakespeare that I ever composed was inspired by a play written by the Hattons. My most valuable sardonic ideas on the labour problem came to me while a two hundred pound blonde in strip tights was being chased around the stage of a fifty-cent burlesque theatre by an Irish comedian, as the soundest theory I ever achieved on the flaw in Regulus' African campaign in the first Punic war was inspired by a shapely leg in a Gaiety show. This is why my critical writings deal at times with trivial and obscure plays and playwrights. The trivial is often the inspiration of something that is not trivial. Shakespeare so engrosses the mind that it cannot wander, cannot stray into other meadows. It is in the tensest moment of a Broadway crook play that one philosophizes upon the initiative and referendum, the life and habits of the bee, the condition of the babies in the southern provinces of Russia, the art of Henri Emmanuel Félix Phillippoteaux, and the battle of Bull Run.

I am, of course, not so vainglorious as to imply that what I personally am able to derive from the trivial is always unfortunately also not trivial; I address myself simply to the theory that is, at least in the instance of others more talented than I, sound enough. The common notion that only great art can inspire and produce great criticism does not entirely convince me. Great criticism often from little acorns grows. Dryden's "Defense of an Essay of Dramatic Poesy" grew out of a third-rate preface to his brother-in-law's[1] book of fourth-rate plays, as his "Of Heroic Plays" and "Defence of the Epilogue" grew out of Buckingham's inconsiderable *The Rehearsal.* Some of the greatest criticism in Lessing's *Hamburg Dramaturgy* grew out of completely negligible theatrical performances. Goethe wrote imperishable criticism that grew out of plays by Kotzebue, . . . and some of Zola's finest critical writing . . . was inspired, during the years of his service as dramatic critic, by the trifling exhibitions that he was forced to sit through. Some of Hazlitt's most pointed criticism in his celebrated *On the Comic Writers of the Last Century* was derived from such artistic immaterialities as Mrs. Centlivre, the actor Liston, and Cibber's feeble *Love in a Riddle,* together with such mediocrities in playwriting as Bickerstaff, Arthur Murphy, Mrs. Cowley, Charles Macklin and John O'Keefe. And half of George Bernard Shaw's admirable critical essays are founded upon such things as *Trilby, The Girl I Left Behind Me, The Sign of the Cross, The Colleen Bawn, True Blue, The Sin of St. Hulda, A Night Out, Under the Red Robe, The Sorrows of Satan, The White Heather, The Heart of Maryland*—plays by Sydney Grundy, Stanley Weyman, Marie Corelli, Herman Merivale, Paul Potter and David Belasco—French bedroom farces by Antony Mars, Drury Lane melodramas by Cecil Raleigh, and leg shows . . . A thousand trivialities are placed in the test tubes of aesthetics that a single piece of sound criticism may endure. Ten thousand unknown men die in battle that history shall record—and the human race take inspiration from—the name of a hill.

---

1. John Dryden (1631–1700), English poet and critic; Poet Laureate (1668–1700); his brother-in-law was Charles Howard, Earl of Carlisle.

Style

The common statement that a writer's style is a true reflection of the man, that his style is an outgrowth of his personality, is often absurd. The truth is that, in the case of many a writer, the personality is an outgrowth of the style. The writer creates a fictitious picture of himself as a man in his style and then takes color from his style by way of living up to the popular

---

From *The American Mercury* (December 1925), p. 492.

conception of him. Shaw is an excellent example. His style is of tele-graphic dynamite all compact: mentally aphrodisiac adjectives, meat-eating verbs, sequences that are tipsy with the wine of gaiety. The man himself is intrinsically exactly the opposite. Shaw, the man, is no more the blood-brother of the Shaw style than Cabell, the man, is the blood-brother of the Cabell style. Shaw's style is less a true reflection of Shaw as man than, let us say, of John Maynard Keynes as man. Shaw, however, wise showman that he is, has simply created himself in its own image. He has carefully evolved a completely alien and artificial style, set it up as a dummy, and then appropriated the dummy's trousers for himself.

Dreiser's style is Dreiser; Lewis' style is Lewis; Harold Bell Wright's style is Wright. But Lardner's style is not more Lardner, *Homo sapiens* and Great Neck householder, than Dunsany's style is Dunsany, *Homo sapiens* and Gargantuan oyster eater. The ivory elephant that the estim-able and realistic Lord wears on a black ribbon around his neck is a concession to his style, just as the open-collar shirt and tousled hair of Jack London were a concession to his. Style is less often the man than the concept of him he wishes his readers to have. The sentence structure, the sequences, the juxtapositions and the verbal trickeries and cadences of many men of letters are no more reflections of their inner beings than the roles most actors play are reflections of theirs.

The Mark of the First-Rate Playwright

It is the mark of the first-rate playwright that his attitude toward his dramatic themes is, for all his affection and sympathy, platonic. Unlike the second-rate playwright, who is ever passionately enamored of and men-tally seduced by his themes, this other remains superior to those themes that he concerns himself with and, while they move ahead in their dra-matic courses, stands aside and lets them pass by him in review to the accompaniment of his sympathetic yet critical snickers. The second-rate playwright cries out in his recognizably typical enthusiasm, "I've got a great idea for a play—if it be properly disparaged."

This is, of course, not necessarily to say that the first-rate playwright is insincere, or a mocker, or a wearer of the cap and bells. What he is is one in whom the creative and critical impulses run as twin streams, one gifted with the sophistication to doubt the verity of the strongest of his own passions and prejudices, and with the wisdom to appreciate that this very doubt will the better persuade his auditors of the approach to verity of these same passions and prejudices. He dramatizes exactly neither his

From *Materia Critica* (New York: Knopf, 1924), pp. 48–50.

passions and prejudices nor his skepticism of these passions and prejudices but rather the strip of philosophical no-man's-land that lies between.
He does not precisely disparage his thematic idea; he permits his idea
rather to disparage him, at least to a degree. For, being a first-rate man, he
has a first-rate man's distrust of himself and of even the best of his ideas
and philosophies. That distrust Shakespeare had, and Molière had, and
Ibsen had, and Porto-Riche and Shaw have now. The plays of these men
are in considerable part full of that distrust, and it is this distrust that has
given birth to a drama that is full, round and complete as opposed to the
profile drama of their lesser contemporaries.

One can add nothing to the great dramatists of self-distrust, for they
dramatize not only themselves and their own ideas but, ever skeptical,
they dramatize simultaneously and coincidently us and our opposing
ideas. These they fuse with their own, or, if they do not exactly fuse, at
least permit intermittently to invade. The great drama is not a one-man
drama but a two-man drama: a dramatization of me in terms of you. Or,
perhaps more accurately, a dramatization by one man of another man in
terms of a third man in whom are combined the skepticism of the first man
and the faith of the second. This, of course, sounds like a mere tricky way
of presenting the ancient platitude that a great play is simply a play that
sees all around a character and a theme, that exhibits all the phases and all
the sides. But there may be a trifle more to it. For if it were merely a case of
presenting all the sides of a theme, Galsworthy would be a greater dramatist than—to stick to contemporary dramatists—either Porto-Riche or
Shaw, which I privilege myself violently to doubt. There is something still
more to the notion. Galsworthy, for all his ability to see two sides of a
theme, cannot, like Porto-Riche and Shaw, see two sides of *himself.* There
lies the difference. He writes plays the way a very competent lawyer might
write them. Porto-Riche and Shaw, on the other hand, write plays the way
each would write them were each an entirely different man somehow
possessed of his own peculiar genius. These dramatists, like fine dramatists ever, are each of them Siamese twins of philosophy and philosophical
doubt bound together by the tissue of sardonic humor. Great drama is the
reflection of a great doubt in the heart and mind of a great, sad, happy man.
The drama of such a writer as Galsworthy is only the reflection of a great
faith in the heart and mind of a skeptic. The gulf is a wide one.

Literature and Drama

The contempt exhibited by literary men for drama on the ground that
drama, because of the intrinsic nature of the theatre, cannot be literature is

From *Art of the Night* (New York: Knopf, 1928), pp. 140–43.

analogous to a contempt that architects might affect for music on the ground that it cannot be made out of bricks. Aside from the painfully obvious fact that great drama actually is literature, and great literature, the literary gentlemen conveniently overlook the second and even more painfully obvious fact that the circumstance that drama may not necessarily be literature is no more valid criticism of it as art than the circumstance that literature need not necessarily be dramatic is valid criticism against literature as art.

Of all artists, literary men are the most self-sufficient, snobbish and, generally, the least catholic and critically sagacious. Whimsical fellows, they look scornfully upon a dramatist who must perforce resort to such ignoble and inartistic devices as the condensing of a character's lifetime into an arbitrary two hours while they themselves enjoy all of two hundred pages, which take two hours to read, for the same purpose. They laugh at the arbitrary demands of the stage in the matter of curtain falls, while they agreeably forget the arbitrary demands of the novel in the matter of chapters of similar necessary furloughs for the reading eye. They speak from a superior vantage point of bad actors, and overlook bad typesetters, bad proofreaders, bad binders. They think of theatre audiences, and double up as with colic; but they do not recall that nine out of every ten persons who read their own work are similar bounders and pickleheads.

This attitude toward the drama on the part of literary men may easily be explained. It derives from their own inability to write drama when they try their hands at it and a subsequent attempt to apologize to themselves for that failure with the reassuring remonstrance that drama must be a very low art form, else they would be able to master it. It seems to be the literary craftsman's idea that drama is child's play, something to be taken up, largely as a joke, when his own more serious important and difficult work is done. He does not realize that the two arts are as far apart as sculpture and painting. Thus, an Arnold Bennett observes loftily that any proficient *littérateur* can write a good play with one of his hands tied behind his back and his eyes blindfolded—and turns out such stuff as *Polite Farces, Cupid and Common Sense, What the Public Wants, The Honeymoon, Mr. Prohack, Sacred and Profane Love,* and *Milestones.* The best that Frank Harris can manage is a *Mr. and Mrs. Daventry,* which is to his literary canon what *Papa Loves Mama* is to *Andromache.* Huneker, a champion of literature at the expense of the poor drama, tried to write a play called *Chopin* with sad results, and Sinclair Lewis is the author of *Hobohemia* and another opus *City Hall,* which shall be enveloped in a polite silence. Dreiser would doubtless be loath to have anyone speak of his *Hand of the Potter* in the same breath with *Sister Carrie, Jennie Gerhardt* and other of his novels; and H. G. Wells is responsible in part for *The Wonderful Visit.* George Moore, a great scoffer at drama and one who has looked on it as being a piece with making mudpies, when he condescendingly tried his skill at it succeeded in producing only a *Coming of Gabrielle* and a *Strike at Arlingford*. Heinrich Mann's literary talent gives birth to a *Die Grosse Liebe;* and Gustav Frenssen's to a *Sönke Erichsen*. What Knut Hamsun's plays are like, I don't know; I haven't read them, but I heard that they are very bad. Henry James' attempt to make a play out of his novel *Daisy Miller* is still a dolorous memory, as is his *Guy Domville;* and Joseph Conrad's *One Day More* is, considering Conrad, pathetic. David Graham Phillips, after much sincere trying, could manage only *The Worth of a Woman;* and Hergesheimer, after two separate attempts, appears to have given up. The short comedies and farces of William Dean Howells are of puny dramatic merit; Bret Harte's *Two Men of Sandy Bar* is drivel; and Robert Louis Stevenson's and W. E. Henley's attempts, *Deacon Brodie* and *Admiral Guinea,* are equally drivel. No need to multiply the list; dozens upon dozens of additional instances will readily occur to you, both of yesterday and today. The legitimate exceptions are few. Galsworthy, for example, is by his own confession a dramatist first and a novelist second: the dramatic form is closest to his heart. So with Maugham, though his plays are far beneath the quality of his novels. Thomas Hardy tried to made a dramatization of his *Tess of the D'Urbervilles* and failed to make one that was anywhere nearly so good as the antecedent one made by a more experienced theatrician.

The difference between a novel and a drama is the difference between music read and music played. The novelist peoples the imagination with ghosts; the dramatist peoples the eye and ear with living, moving forms and voices. This difference the literary man turned playwright seldom perceives; and as a result the drama that he fashions often too greatly neglects the eye and ear in favor of an overtaxed (and undersupplied) theatrical imagination. I speak here, of course, of the literary man who approaches the dramatic form seriously and not merely as a means to hornswoggle the box-office out of a bit of change. In the average play of the literary man, one can, in one's mind's eye, see the book leaves turning with the movements of the stage characters. One feels that the characters are reading their lines rather than speaking them. The dramatic personages move less in terms of sentences than in terms of paragraphs. They are less types than typography. A shoemaker should stick to his last. The composer of *Parsifal* is ill at ease in *Religion und Kunst;* the painter of the *Cenacolo* is lost when he woos the art of the composer; the author of *Romeo and Juliet* sloshes around uncomfortably in Ben Jonson's sock and buskin[1]; the confector of the *Essays of Elia* brings down a deserved booing upon himself when he confects a *Mr. H.*[2]

Of the several recent instances of the condescension of literary men toward the drama that have come to my notice, none is more illuminating than that of the gifted Mr. Aldous Huxley. Mr. Huxley makes known his airy disdain in an essay called "Why I Do Not Go to the Theatre." The title, considering the ancient point of view which the essay sets forth, would be vastly more pat had the author omitted its first word. For the theatre which Mr. Huxley so contumeliously discourses upon obviously belongs to the early eighties.

Let us glance briefly at a few of our friend's antiquated opinions. First, that "the popular conventions are accepted in the theatre at their face value without any attempt to discover the psychological realities that lie behind them." Brushing aside as being too apparent contradictions of Mr. Huxley's horsehair-sofa viewpoint the plays of such present-day dramatists as Shaw, O'Casey, Toller, O'Neill, Pirandello and a score of others, let us sample the hollowness of his contention by descending to even the Broadway commercial drama of a recent year. I list herewith a number of plays that, during that season along in the New York theatre, turned the popular conventions inside out and at least tried to make the very attempt that Huxley denies is ever made: *The Home Towners, Sour Grapes, Sandalwood, The Captive, The Good Fellow, God Loves Us, Gentle Grafters, This Was a Man, The Constant Wife, The Silver Cord, Lady Alone, Inheritors, Mariners, Spread Eagle* and *The Second Man*. During the same period, there were produced on Broadway such equally controverting examples of modern drama as the *Naked* and *Right You Are* of Pirandello.

"There are only two kinds of love on the stage—the pure and impure," continues Huxley in defence of his non-theatre-going attitude. "No hint is ever dropped that in reality sacred and profane love are inextricably mixed together; it is never so much as whispered that there may be a great many varieties of both kinds." Need I bring to our friend's notice a hundred and one modern plays that must make his statement ring loudly with foolishness, such, for excample, as Porto-Riche's *L'Amoureuse,* certain of Arnold Bennett's later comedies, d'Annunzio's *La Città Morta,* Capus' *L'Oiseau Blessé* and *Les Passagères,* Strindberg's *The Dance of Death* and O'Neill's *Welded,* Sudermann's *Das Blumenboot,* Schnitzler's *Zwischenspiel* and *Der Ruf des Lebens,* and Lenormand's *Simoon*? "On the stage," concludes Huxley, "love is, moreover, always a function of the loved object, dependent exclusively on the blonde curls and the virtue of the heroine, the black shingle and the alluring impurity of the villainess. No allowance is ever made for the lover's state of mind and body. If there is one thing (on the other hand) that the novelist's exploration of reality has made abundantly clear, it is that love is, to a great extent, the product of the lover's imagination and desire and that it has comparatively little to do with the qualities of the beloved." It appears that Mr. Huxley is completely unaware of the multitude of plays like Schnitzler's *Countess Mitzi,* Sudermann's *The Three Heron Feathers,* Barker's *The Madras House,*

Strindberg's *To Damascus,* and the various Guitry and Dieudonné comedies, to mention only a few that come readily to mind.

---

1. Nathan faults Shakespeare for missing the mark achieved by Ben Jonson (1573–1637) in certain comedies ("sock") and certain tragedies ("buskin").
2. Mr. H . . . the critic William Hazlitt (1778–1830); Elia was the pen-name of Charles Lamb (1775–1834).

Melodrama

It is a convention of criticism that melodrama, even at its best, is somehow peculiarly one of the dramatic sub-arts and that it must accordingly be treated with proper condescension. If this be true, the reason for its truth eludes me. The only way in which I can figure out the senseless prejudice is to recall the persistent custom of affixing definite labels to everything and, once they are duly affixed, of basing criticism upon the labels instead of upon what is in the bottles. The word *melodrama* has fallen into disrepute simply because the English critics, abandoning its exact meaning, began carelessly to employ it some forty-odd years ago to designate any play that they like but felt they shouldn't like.

Today, the word is never used with literal accuracy, but is used indiscriminately to describe any theatrical exhibit that doesn't fall with a ready click into one or another of the standard pigeon-holes. A drama in which a revolver is fired thus automatically becomes a melodrama. So does a genre study in which one of the characters steals money, is caught in the act by a policeman and avoids arrest by jumping out of the first-floor window and breaking the pane. So does a comedy that contains a safe hidden in the wall. So does a tragedy in which a railroad express train is even casually mentioned. The monkeyshines performed with the label are endless.

The detractors of melodrama—still using the word as it is currently employed—apparently never stop to think that their derogatory designation fits many of the classics quite as closely as it fits the modern plays upon which they slap it. If a melodrama is a play in which action is more important than character, in which a character is influenced from without rather than from within, and in which emotions are played *fortissimo,* then *Electra* and *Seven Before Thebes* are melodramas. If a melodrama is a play in which lust, murder, revenge and physical action predominate, then *Macbeth* and *Hamlet* are melodramas. If a melodrama is a play in which a man, bent upon evil, disguises himself, enters a house, commits a murder, is confronted by a woman with an axe, jumps at her with his bloody sword

---

From *Land of the Pilgrim's Pride* (New York: Knopf, 1927), pp. 202–4.

and, upon her running away from him, chases her around until he catches up with her and runs her through the gizzard, then the *Choephoræ* of Æschylus is a melodrama. If a melodrama is a play in which a woman of criminal impulses meditates a Grand Guignol revenge and slowly puts it into execution, then the *Medea* of Euripides is a melodrama. And if a melodrama is a play in which high emotion dominates and controls rational thought, then the *Antigone* of Sophocles is ten times the melodrama that *Sherlock Holmes* is.

On Expressionism

For all their pretence to the contrary, elaborately enunciated tracts that seek to conceal a forthright knowledge of what they are talking about in a welter of terminology more suitably associated with architecture, bridge building, the navigation of sailing-vessels and the manufacture of steam pumps, it is quite clear that what appeals to our adolescent dramatists about expressionism is the ease with which it may be negotiated. Of all the forms of dramaturgy that have been devised in modern times, expressionism, together with its blood-brother, impressionism, is the simplest superficially to master, and it hence naturally has a strong appeal for those young men who wish to become playwrights without knowing how to write plays. Expressionism is, in essence, simply the emotional skeleton of a play, the scenario. It presents the outline of drama, substituting mere close-ups of faces for a near view of character and sudden, startling claps of thunder for the slowly gathering dramatic storm of human passions. The first essay that every schoolboy writes is always full of italics; they are his means of a forceful expression that eludes his unpractised pen. In the same way, expressionism is a convenient subterfuge for such talents as are unable to achieve the intricacies and profundities of dramatic writing. It is to dramatic strength of expression what cuss words are to an inarticulate man.

If there are mind and experience back of expressionism, we find the technique of expression subservient to that mind and experience and we get, accordingly, a measure of genuine strength and pulsating conviction. But the majority of the youngsters who lay hold of the dramatic form popularized by the Germans have neither mind nor experience, and consequently all that we get from their exhibits is the technical monkeyshine. Incapable of drawing character in its various detail, they foxily resort to

From *Art of the Night* (New York: Knopf, 1928), pp. 101–5. Copyright renewed 1955 by George Jean Nathan.

faking it by throwing into relief only its highlights, wrapping themselves the while in the comfortable, protected cloak of the expressionistic theory and pretending that their abandonment of that detail is deliberate, when anyone with half an eye can see quite clearly that the abandonment is due simply to the fact that they can't help it. Unable, further, painstakingly to unfold a drama in all its devious complexity and to tell a story in a more conventional and vastly more difficult manner, they resort to the new formula with avidity, since it offers them the very convenient and lazy means of getting an effect by telling the plot of a play theatrically without writing the play dramatically. The theory that expressionism's value lies in its power of suggestion, that it gives to the audience untessellated tiles and materials wherewith the audience may fashion the drama into a complete mosaic for itself and with its own imagination, is buncombe pure and simple. It does nothing of the kind. An audience gets from expressionism exactly what expressionism shows it on the stage; it gets three times more, as a matter of fact, from the actually much more suggestive and inferential drama of standard form.

Almost anyone with a slight facility in the way of literary composition can write an expressionistic play, and one just as good as most of those our young men are turning out with such rabbit-like fecundity. The unhindered fluidity of the technique, the dismissal of the unities, the cinema-like hop, skip and jump, the absurd ease with which characters may be brought on and shooed off, the need only to indicate character superficially and the privilege to allow character to be identified in an entirely external manner and by such external means as manifold shifts of environment and inter-mittent comments by a mob of supers—these make the writing of ex-pressionistic drama even less difficult than the writing of music-show librettos, in which some slight degree of consanguinity with the actual world must be preserved. A George Kaiser and an Ernst Toller employ expressionism because it is a natural channel for, and even a natural outgrowth of, certain of their dramatic themes and ideas. No other form would serve as so apt a funnel for those themes and ideas. Our young men, on the other hand, lay hold of the technique as a quick-change vaudeville artist lays hold of a dickey with a diamond stud painted on it and a dress suit that can be jumped into from the back. It permits them easily to give a show. It is a ready-to-hand method for them to parade as dramatists. Its eye-holding hocus-pocus, its off-stage jazz noises and its revue-like shift-ing of sets and pulling back and forth of curtains throw the audience off the scent and conceal the fact that they have nothing to say. Nothing? Well, perhaps that is going a bit too far. The young men usually have some such colossal thing to say as (a) that New York is a Juggernaut that consumes youthful dreams; (b) that modern business is a Moloch; or (c) that the syncopated gin life of today is bad for young girls. These great ideas that would cause them to be booted out instanter by any half-sober magazine editor to whom they submitted short stories containing them and that would go to make plays that would never get a reading from any manager, they set forth in terms of a set of scenery that looks like a waffle-iron and in the staccato form of tabloid newspaper headlines and thereafter posture themselves as very intellectual fellows. What they are are dramatic frauds.

The Biographical Play

Of all plays, the so-called biographical one is undoubtedly the easiest to write. Consider, for example, the following scene from a famous play:

Enter Jean Jacques Rousseau.

Rousseau. I am deeply grieved, Madame—*(he recognizes Thérèse Le Vasseur with a start)*. Mon Dieu! You, Thérèse, here!

Thérèse. Ah, Jean Jacques, I could not die until I had your forgiveness. Do not turn away from me—bear with me one small moment—only say that you will forgive me, and I can rest in peace.

Rousseau. Why did you come here?

Thérèse. I could not stay away from you and my children. The longing for the sight of them was killing me. I knew no moment's peace after the mad act I was guilty of—in leaving you. Not an hour had I departed ere repentance set in. Even then I would have come back, but I did not know how. My sin was great, and my punishment has been greater; it has been one, long, long mental agony.

Rousseau. Why did you go away?

Thérèse. Did you not know why?

Rousseau. No; it was ever a mystery to me.

Thérèse. I went out of love for you. Ah, do not look at me in that reproachful way! I loved you dearly, and I grew to doubt you. I thought you false and deceitful to me; that your love was given to another, and, in my sore jealousy, I listened to the temptings of the man who whispered of revenge. But it was not so—tell me it was not so, Jean!

Rousseau. Can you ask me that, knowing me as you did then, and as you must have known me since? I was not false to you in word, in thought, or in deed, Thérèse.

Thérèse. I know it now, mon cher, but I was mad. I could not have committed the act save in madness. Say, mon Jean Jacques, that you will forget all and forgive me!

Rousseau. I cannot forget—I have forgiven already.

You recognize it immediately, if a bit vaguely. One of the greatest successes the theatre has ever known. But you cannot recall its title? I supply it: *East Lynne*. I have quoted the old lulu word for word and have

From *The World in Falseface* (New York: Knopf, 1923), pp. 80–83. Copyright renewed 1950 by George Jean Nathan.

merely renamed Archibald Carlyle Jean Jacques Rousseau and Lady Isabel Thérèse Le Vasseur. The dialogue fits the lives of R and his mistress-wife quite as snugly and accurately as is the general case in biographical plays. And the same thing may be done just as simply, effectively and no doubt as profitably, with *The Lady of Lyons* by calling Claude Melnotte Verlaine; with *Camille,* by calling Marguerite Gautier Madame Rachel and renaming Armand after one of her more persistent and devoted lovers; and with *Up in Mabel's Room,* by naming the central male character King Edward VII, late Prince of Wales.

Adaptations

Despite the not uncommon assumption that approximnately all that is necessary to the adaptation of the Continental play is to set the second-act clock back six hours, take out the bedstead and cast Mr. John Barrymore for the husband instead of the lover, it is reversely true that this business of adaptation calls for the highest playwriting sagacity and talent. And it is equally true, by reason of this, that not more than one such adaptation in every twenty-five is worth a hoot; and true, further, that what holds for American-made adaptations holds equally of the attempts at adaptation made by the English, the Germans, the Austrians, and the French.

It is, with reservations, almost as difficult to translate a play from one language into another, and from the viewpoint of one people into that of another, and from the favor of one nation into the prejudice of another nation, as it is to write the play in the first place. A careful scrutiny of the statistics of the world's theatre for the last ten years discovers astonishingly few adaptations that, whether from the artistic or even the commercial orthodoxy, have been fully successful. And the figures seem all the more surprising when one observes the very large proportion of failure in the matter of the adaptation of plays which even in their original form would appear to have been automatically preadapted, and easily to have been made ready for an alien audience by a mere scratch or two of the pen. . . .

There is surely something more than mere theatre chance behind the fact that ten more or less celebrated Continental plays failed in quick succession in their adapted form when brought to the American stage, several years ago, by the late Charles Frohman. For all Mr. Belasco's exceptional astuteness as a showman, the *Fable of the Wolf (The Phantom Rival)* and *The Lilly* baffled his most shrewdly selected translators. In France, Synge's *Playboy* (adapted by Maurice Bourgeois for the Théâtre

From *Comedians All* (New York: Knopf, 1919), pp. 29–35.

de l'Oeuvre in the Antoine), Wedekind's *Awakening of Spring* (adapted by Robert d'Humières), Moody's *Great Divide* (adapted by the Cazamians), Pinero's *House in Order* (adapted by Bazalgette and Bienstock), to say nothing of Shaw's *You Never Can Tell* and *Mrs. Warren* . . . Scores of other such interesting plays have regularly gone astray . . . plays beyond and above those of Hauptmann, Schnitzler, Guimèra, Molnar, Guitry, Björnson, Sudermann, *et al.*

When an adapted play fails, whether in this country or in England or on the Continent, it is the habitual critical pastime to lay blame for the demise not upon the adaptation, but upon the original play; the blame usually taking flower in the theory that the theme and development of the original are alien to the philosophy, taste and whim of the national audience immediately concerned. In the majority of cases, this is, of course, a mere braying, a wiggling of ears. When a respectable piece of dramatic writing fails in adaptation, the philosophy, taste and whim of the alien audience are often less at fault than the philosophy, taste and whim of the adaptor. For example, the failure in American of the Hungarian Imre Földes's *Hallo,* adapted by Mr. George Broadhurst as *Over the Phone,* and without exception laid by the critics to the difference in moral attitude on the part of Viennese and American audiences, was actually due not to the difference in moral attitude on the part of Viennese and American audiences, but to the difference in moral attitude on the part of the original author of the play and the adaptor. How in God's name the difference in sex-morals attitude 'twixt the European and American audiences could be brought forward as an argument to account for the local failure of the play when the adaptor by deleting the adultery motif and substituting therefor a kiss motif had completely removed any preliminary ground for this difference in sex-morals attitude, is pretty hard to understand. The failure of the play was due, not to the fact that an American audience is unsympathetic to casual adultery, but, very simply, to the fact that the adaptor believed an American audience was unsympathetic to casual adultery. The effect and the result were precisely the effect and the result that would automatically be achieved were *Peg o' My Heart* to be adapted for French audiences by, say, Pierre Veber and Maurice Rémon and were the MM. Veber and Rémon to think to enchant their Gallic public by deleting the artless innocence of the heroine and making her, instead, a *fille de joie*.

If Granville-Barker were entrusted with the job of bringing Albrecht Dürer's painting of the *Adoration of the Trinity* to London from Vienna, it is reasonable to suppose that he would exercise the greatest care in transit to see that no nicks got into it. But when Granville-Barker is entrusted with the job of bringing Arthur Schnitzler's word-painting of *Anatol* to London from Vienna, what does he do? He does exactly what nine-tenths of the adaptors do when a work of art is given into their care. He nicks it up with his own petty morals and petty prejudices until little more remains of the original than the frame. . . .

The trouble with the majority of adaptors, wherever one finds them, is a very simple trouble: they imagine that adaptation consists primarily in adapting an alien play to the different taste of a local audience, where, in reality, adaptation should consist rather in adapting the different taste of a local audience to the alien play.

The Mystery Story

The mystery story is a form of diversion that appeals to highly intelligent men and to morons. It jumps the wide gulf with the pole of rational paradox. It is the middle mind alone that does not care for the mystery tale and that sneers at it contemptuously. The greatest scientist living has declared that the mystery story provides his favorite form of light amusement, and a certain manufacturer of a commodity that took William Jennings Bryan's place as the chief source of American jokes has made the same declaration. Between the right wing of intelligence and the left wing of ignorance we find the layer of humanity that is neither sufficiently educated nor sufficiently uneducated properly to relish the mystery story. In this layer we observe the class that affects keenly to enjoy dialectics in the theatre, that goes into giddy raptures over the tremendous genius of some moving-picture producer, that professes to be warmed by the tonal monkeyshines of Schönberg, and that stands in open-mouthed awe every other Tuesday when an art gallery displays the latest importation of modern art from Tzpzyzpk, Hungary, or Kvalzvalokovitch, Russia. The mystery story succeeds in the theatre, when it is dramatized with any degree of skill, because the theatre culls its patrons chiefly from the intelligentsia and the half-wits, the latter, of course, being in the overwhelming majority.

Negroes in American Drama

Up to eight or nine years ago, [1915–16] it is doubtful if, in the entire range of the American drama, there was to be found a single authentic Negro character.[1] The Negro of drama was then either of the white wool wig and kidney-pain species, given to excessive hobbling, many a "Yas,

---

From *Materia Critica* (New York: Knopf, 1924) p. 140.
From *Materia Critica* (New York: Knopf, 1924), pp. 186–87.

yas, massa, I's a-comin'," and a comic line on his every exit, or of the species that was essentially a mere blacked-up Caucasian minstrel end man in a cutaway coat three sizes too large for him and a snowy toupé who was rather dubiously transformed into a dramatic character by giving him one scene in which he taught little Frieda and Otto how to say their prayers and another in which he apologetically shuffled into his master's library when the mortgage on the latter's old Southern estate was about to be foreclosed by the Northern villain and, with tears in his eyes and a quiver in his voice, informed him that, come what might, he would stick to him until he was daid. The moment a Negro character appeared in the drama one knew for a certainty that the last act would either show him happily dancing a *pas seul* in the background when Miss Sally eventually fell into the marital embrace of Lieut. Jack Terhune, U.S.A., or tremblingly awaiting his doom at the end of a clothesline held by half a dozen supers dressed up in Ku Klux regalia.

It is further doubtful if up to eight or nine years ago there was on the American stage a single Negro character under fifty years of age. In the dramatic credo of the antecedent epoch it was an invariable doctrine that no Negro existed who did not have white hair and the misery in his back, and who had not been in the employ of the same family since boyhood. Those stage Ethiops were a peculiar lot, as far removed from the American Negro of actuality as the *raisonneurs* of Galsworthy are removed from the *raisonneurs* of Viennese musical comedy. Now and again a playwright would come along and try to break from the established tradition, but the best he seemed to be able to negotiate was, as in Edward Sheldon's case, a burnt-cork Sardou, or, in Thomas Dixon's, a melodramatic dummy who served as the fox in a chase by a number of white supers decked out in bed-sheets.

---

1. According to Arthur and Barbara Gelb (in *O'Neill*, [New York: Harper & Row, 1962], p. 445), O'Neill's *The Emperor Jones* (1920) provided the first major role for a Negro, Brutus Jones, in American drama. The actor Charles Gilpin was replaced in 1921 by Paul Robeson.

Intelligence and the Drama

Although we live in the enlightened years of the Twentieth Century, the talk of intelligence in the theatre continues. We hear still of "intelligent drama" on the one hand and plays that "insult the intelligence" on the other. The whole canon of dramatic criticism in the last thirty years, indeed, appears to rest snootily on the premise that the virtue of drama is

---

From *The American Mercury* (December 1925), pp. 500–512.

predicated on this intelligence, and that, save drama possess it and, possessing it, gratify intelligence in turn, the aforesaid drama may be dismissed from serious consideration without further ado.

Just how this notion of the consanguinity of intelligence and drama first got bruited about, one has trouble in ascertaining, for if intelligence were the chief desideratum in drama and if all the plays written in the world today were chock full of it from beginning to end, there wouldn't be a single theatre between here and the island of Amorgopula that could pay its rent next Saturday night. But, of course, everyone except most dramatic critics knows perfectly well that the last thing necessary and valuable to drama is intelligence, and so the theatre prospers today as it has never before. . . . Intelligence is no more relevantly a part of drama than it is of music, painting, sculpture, hooch dancing, six-day bicycle racing or any other art or diversion; it is a tremendous handicap rather than a magnificent asset. The drama is not the place for intelligence but only for a deft and superficially deceptive counterfeit of intelligence. To speak disparagingly, therefore, of drama that insults the intelligence is to speak disparagingly of graphic art that insults the intelligence and to complain of, say Veronese's *St Anthony Preaching to the Fishes* that it is of absolutely no worth because any man who thought he could accomplish anything by addressing lake trout on the subject of Holy Writ was a damned fool.

All fine art, in fact, not only insults the intelligence; it deliberately spits in the eye of intelligence. The ennobling tragedies of Shakespeare ask us to believe in ghosts and witches; and the great drama of Ibsen asks us to believe that the world is savagely cruel to a woman who has violated the Seventh Commandment, that dishonesty must inevitably turn upon its practitioner and smite him with a blow from which he cannot recover, that a syphilitic is doomed to end his days as a lunatic, and that, symbolism or no symbolism, when amorous old gentlemen afflicted with vertigo fall off the tops of towers, the young folk standing down below hear a harp recital going on in the air. Mozart, in *Don Giovanni,* asks us to believe that a woman who could express herself in the harmonic beauty of a "Non ti fider, O misera" might be thought insane; and Wagner asks us to believe, in *Lohengrin,* that a *swan* can pull a boat; in *Tannhäuser,* that if a man speaks of physical love in high terms all the women will promptly leave the room; and, in *Siegfried,* that a sword can split an anvil in two and that birds can speak excellent German. Bellini, in the *Madonna, Child and Six Saints,* asks us to believe that an angel views the spectacle of a naked man with a puritanical Methodist concern; Raphael, in the *Victory of Leo IV at Ostia,* asks us to believe that soldiers are constantly mindful of the picturesqueness of their poses in the heat of battle; and Tintoretto asks us, in *Adam and Eve,* to believe that Adam looked like Bernarr Macfadden. To speak of intelligent art, which is to say, to demand that overpowering beauty be coincidently rational, is to speak of an intelligent Grand Canyon or an intelligent Granada or Lombard Plain; and the demand that moonlight and the summer stars satisfy the philosophical doctrines of Spinoza, William Lloyd Garrison and Herbert Croly.

In drama, a forthright metaphysic spells certain disaster. Nothing is so corruptive of drama as hard logic. What the drama calls for is not mental intelligence, but only emotional intelligence. No matter how poorly the characters of drama reason, the demands of drama are fully satisfied so long as their emotions are, or at least seem to be, reasonable. A great dramatic character may have the mind of an alley-cat or a congressman, but so long as his emotions are rational and logical, as long as he feels convincingly, so long as he doesn't become angry when someone hands him an excellent cigar or doesn't fall in love with a woman who is too fat, he may continue to be a great dramatic character. Macbeth is a simpleton, but his emotions are those of a great man; hence he is a great dramatic character. And it is the same with most of the other great characters of drama. It is almost impossible to imagine a fine play built around, say, Kant or Hegel as a philosopher. The theatre has no call for such heroes. Its heroes must think with their hearts and feel with their minds. (Bahr's *The Master,* on a not important dramatic level, may in this regard nevertheless be offered as supplementary reading.) To build a play around Kant or Hegel and hope to keep even the most intelligent theatrical audience in the world in its seats after nine o'clock, one would inevitably have to make up either Immanuel or Georg Wilhelm to look like John Drew, have him crawl under Fifi's bed when her husband unexpectedly came back from Detroit, and introduce a scene in the second act in which he eluded the Scotland Yard detectives by hiding in the cuckoo clock.

Fine drama, as a matter of fact, generally insults the intelligence, as the phrase goes, vastly more than gimcrack drama. *Hamlet* frequently impresses the logical mind as mere gorgeously beautiful drivel, where some such twentieth-rate piece of work as *They Knew What They Wanted* satisfies the rational sense more or less completely. Great art is as irrational as great music. It is mad with its own loveliness. Æschylus and Richard Strauss are beer-brothers under their skins; the *Eumenides* is as drunk with the dazzling beauty of æsthetic scapulimancy on the one hand as *Also Sprach Zarathustra* is on the other. If you are looking for sense, go to the plays of Channing Pollock and the songs of Irving Berlin.

And so we come to Shaw's dramatic gigolo, Eugène Brieux.[1] Brieux's chief fault as a dramatist is his intelligence, or, more accurately, his dervish-like belief that what he knows constitutes intelligence and his passion for inculcating it in his plays. Take the average Brieux play, cut out the names of its leading characters, run the text together, borrow an ice-water pitcher, and you have a first-class lyceum bureau lecture for use at the Town Hall. The flame of intelligent nonsense is never—or, at least, very seldom—present in his work, as it is present in the work of such greatly more intelligent men as, for instance, his god-father, Shaw. He seizes upon an available theme for a good play and then proceeds painstakingly to think it right out of the theatre. Where a competent and persuasive dramatist would take the same theme and carefully drain from it every vestige of vagrant beauty and every trace of human charm and boil it down to its elemental and vastly depressing syllogistic bones. He seems to be of the theory that drama is designed to prove something to the human head, unaware completely that the highest aim of drama is rather to prove something only to the human heart. He burns with the fervor of a shyster lawyer; like a movie comedian he is not content to be what he is— in this case, a writer of plays—but must needs also be regarded by the world beyond the theatre as a thinker. It is thus that he goes about composing his plays with his eye ever set upon convincing by stark logic, whereas the eye of the real dramatist is ever set upon convincing by beautifully embellished equivocation. For in the theatre we believe not so much what may be true as what may be merely plausible. The logic of heredity, let us say, as we get it in some such drama as Brieux's *The Escape* is never one-tenth so effective in the theatre as the romantic sophistry of heredity as we get it in a Rostand's *L'Aiglon*.

There is no man so stupid, in point of fact, as the intelligent dramatist who carries his intelligence full-fledged over into his plays. His intelligence is of very great service to him before he proceeds to the actual writing of his plays, since it tells him what he should not write and since it further safeguards him from writing the kind of plays that men less intelligent than himself write; but when he sets himself to the actual business of writing, he must leave his intelligence off stage and permit it simply to criticize confidentially from time to time the charming holiday from sound intelligence that is giving a show out on the stage. To the Polichinelle secret, Brieux is seldom privy, and as a result his plays generally disclose themselves to be masses of platitudes, since by the time almost any philosophic idea finds its way into the theatre it is, by the intrinsic nature of the theatre, already a great-grandfather. Brieux, however, constantly bemuses himself with the theory that because he has thought of something for the first time, it is therefore of a revolutionary newness and must so impress others; and his plays, as a consequence, generally take on the aspect of so many rush telegrams, delivered by a breathless messenger-boy, which contain information that the recipient has read in day before yesterday's newspaper, and not been the least interested in. Once in his life, Brieux forgot himself and wrote an excellent comedy, *Les Hannetons*. Once again, he partly forgot himself and came near writing a very good play, *Le Trois Filles de M. Dupont*. But for most of the rest of his life he has been writing such things as *La Robe Rouge, La Femme Seule* and *L'Avocat* which turn their stages into lecture platforms, Hyde Park soap-boxes and street-corner cart-tails, and their auditors into somnambulists groping their way to the exits.

The last named play has been shown in America recently by Mr. Belasco under the title of *Accused*. In a brochure published in commemoration of the great event, Mr. Belasco delivers himself of the following illuminating syllogism: "France, always conservative in her recognition of talent until talent is proved beyond question, has awarded M. Eugène Brieux two of the world's *supreme* honors—the decoration of the Legion of Honor and admittance to the ranks of the Forty Immortals of the Académie Française[2] . . . so it is no exaggeration to describe M. Brieux as the foremost contemporary author of his country, *if not the world*." To which a dozen French, German and English dramatists—to limit Mr. Belasco's contemporary authors to the drama alone—must kneel, cross themselves, and join Toto, the Hippodrome clown, in saying Amen.

---

1. Eugène Brieux (1858–1932), French playwright concerned with social problems. He was, of course, overvalued by Shaw and Belasco.
2. See glossary.

Destructive Criticism

Of the numerous and fecund fallacies concerned with criticism, doubtless the most unremittingly *enceinte* is that which holds it a vastly more easy business to blame than to praise. "Any fool can find fault" has been the cornerstone of protestant retaliation to so-called destructive criticism for something over two centuries. Upon it have been reared the most sardonic animadversions of the Balzacs, Landors, Coleridges, Shelleys, Addisons, Lambs, Drydens and Disraelis, the very acuteness and hence longevity of whose destructive criticism of destructive criticism might possibly suggest to the more waggish logician that the exceptionally gifted disparager in point—by proving both what they set out to prove and, automatically, the reverse—swung the punitive cowhide so far around their heads that it nipped their own ears.

That any fool can find fault is, of course, perfectly true. But that any fool can find fault accurately, soundly and searchingly is a horse of another color. So to find fault calls upon and commands a decidedly uncommon talent. And so, above this, to find fault with such a fault-finder calls upon and commands—as the history of destructive criticism emphatically

---

From *Comedians All* (New York: Knopf, 1919), pp. 13–17.

proves—a down-right genius. Any picturesque but empty dodo like the late Nat Goodwin can toss off a four-pound five-dollar book finding fault with everything from the criticism of Dr. Johnson to Edna Goodrich's mother, but it takes the talent of a William Archer to find searching fault even with a single one of Brunetière's dramatic theories, and the genius of a Bernard Shaw to find sound fault with what seemed to be the searching fault that William Archer found.

The extraororinarily capric quality of the mass of journalistic criticism in America is due, not as is generally maintained, to the desire of its writers to please by indiscriminate praise, but to the utter incapacity on the part of these writers to dispraise. In the theatrical criticism that appears in the native morning newspapers, the omnipresent note of eulogy is attributable less to the commentator's wish to eulogize than to the recognized fact that, given less than an hour in which to confect an estimate of a play, gush is immensely more simple of negotiation than diatribe. Every critical writer knows well the truth of this. When he is lazy, he writes praise; only when his mind is alert and eager does he feel himself capable of fault-finding. The art of the careful, honest and demolishing *coup de grâce* is an art calling, firstly, for an exhaustive knowledge of the subject under the microscope, secondly, for an original and sharply inventive analytical turn of mind, and thirdly, for a wit and power over words that shall make them whiz through the printed page. The art of the equally careful and honest hip-hooray, even at its highest, on the other hand, calls upon at least the first two of these attributes in considerably less degree.

That the art of penetrating fault-finding—or "destructive criticism," as the misnomer has it—is a grant denied the considerable majority of our journalistic luminaries may be clearly discerned not only in the lavish bravos and vivas already mentioned as constituting the bulk of the daily reviews, but —better still—in the retrospective and more carefully pondered weekly reviews of reviews published in the Sunday editions. In these latter reviews one regularly observes a brave effort at qualification of the morning-after doxologies and joss-burnings, a sincere and upright attempt to expose holes. But what the sum? Generally little more than a faint barking of amiable dachshunds suddenly disguised as ferocious bloodhounds—with Eliza already twenty miles away. The notion that this daily journalistic criticism is dishonest—a theory cherished by most playwrights who compose dramas in which the heroine, when the detective's back is turned, cleverly substitutes a railroad time-table for the warrant for her lover's arrest, and by most actors whose eyes have been alleged by the critic for the *Mercure de Hoboken* to be not quite so dreamy as Chauncey Olcott's, or Louis Mann's—this notion is absurd. The American journalistic criticism, whether morning or evening, is, save in a few notorious instances, not dishonest; it is, save in a few equally notorious instances, merely disqualified. It is disqualified because it honestly assays, when the occasion honestly presents itself, to write razor-keen destructive criticism and finds itself, because of the supreme difficulty of the job and its own dialectical shortcomings, sorely confounded. Its toe, eager, well-aimed and valiant, is poised trembling abaft the breeches, yet condemned by inhibitory tendons to lift gingerly and rest content merely to flick a bit of lint off the coat-tail.

Critical Convictions

To speak of impersonal criticism is as ridiculous as to speak of impersonal drama, impersonal music, impersonal painting, or impersonal reaction to alcoholic liquor. There is no such thing. There is only live criticism and dead criticism. To speak of even the latter as impersonal is to confuse criticism with its practising corpse.

The younger the critic, the more he is fetched by mere theme. If the theme, in his eyes, is an important one, that is, one that deals with matters of immediate public concern, treatment takes second or even third place with him. It is thus that any play, however otherwise defective, which treats of something in the popular consciousness of the moment usually receives his hearty endorsement not only as a play of weight but as one of considerable artistic merit as well.

Patriotism is the enemy of sound criticism. It is thus that three-quarters of the criticism generally written in wartime never survives the armistice.

What the actress as woman is off the stage reflects itself for better or worse, whatever the nature of the role, when she is on. This may sound nonsensical, but it somehow seems to be true.

What it proves critically I wouldn't know, but the fact remains that in fifty years of the American stage only one out of the many plays that have shown a small, illuminated railroad train moving by night across the backdrop has been a failure. That one was *Fulton of Oak Falls*, which achieved a run of but thirty-seven performances. The rest have made lots of money.

"A good play enacted by competent principals," one of my colleagues has written, "can easily survive an ineffective bit by an untalented bit player." Not always so easily. I have seen an otherwise very competently acted *The Weavers* go completely to pieces on the shoals of its child Mielchen.

The vogue of the short skirt is one of the severest trials that actresses have ever been made to suffer.

From *The Theatre Book of the Year, 1946–47* (New York: Knopf, 1947), pp. 177–86.

The notion, favorite of women and effeminate actors, that the critics, being for the most part not overly blessed by nature, are enviously contemptuous of handsome actors is far from the fact. Every handsome actor on the modern stage, with but one exception that I can think of, has been given a happy deal by the critics. The exception was Lou Tellegen, who was such a bad actor that the critics, for all the good will in the world, could not help themselves. Henry Dixey, Richard Bennett as a young man, George Alexander, William Faversham, James O'Neill, E. H. Sothern, Kyrle Bellew, James Carew, James K. Hackett, Charles Cherry, Hamilton Revelle, Harry Davenport, Vincent Serrano, Frederic De Belleville, Henry Miller, Herbert Standing, William Courtenay, Edgar Selwyn, Harry Woodruff, John Barrymore—these and others of the pictorially elect have literally been made by their friendly, ugly brothers, the critics.

There are actors, whatever their share of talent, who find audiences prejudiced against them from the start. Let an actor be too precise and glossy in his dress, like the late Robert Hilliard, or move about with a too severely erect posture, like the late Tellegen aforesaid, or steal a glance at the ladies out front so much as once, like the late Lowell Sherman, or be or do any such trivial thing and he is doomed.

I not long ago read this, from the pen of one of my colleagues: "He (the playwright) hasn't learned the most elementary principle of dramatic construction, which is that you cannot have a good person evilly put upon without making his persecutors pay for their crimes." Hardly elementary, my dear Watson, except in the case of box-office dramaturgy. Examples: Strindberg's *The Father,* Becque's *The Ravens,* Galsworthy's *Justice,* among many others.

Criticism as the adventures of a soul among masterpieces is an ideal. Criticism is most often bound to be the misadventures of a soul among gimcracks.

The critic who can remain absolutely honest in his appraisal of an exceptionally pretty actress is either a genius or a fool.

"There are," I once observed, "critics who are less interested in the impression a play makes upon them than in the impression they make upon the play." But do not jump to too sarcastic conclusions. Shaw was one such, and a better critic of the drama never lived.

Whatever the faults of much of contemporary drama it at least has avoided one of the weaknesses of much of contemporary literature. The latter, especially where it is the product of the younger practitioners, seems often to be ridden by the notion that there is something strangely virile and impressive in sexual intercourse conducted *al fresco.* The drama, even when written by the younger playwrights, generally refrains from any such undergraduate nonsense and keeps it indoors, where it belongs. The anatomical romance hypothetically implicit in bramble-bush, hillside, sleeping-bag and other such extramural discomforts, however starlit, is considerably less the material for serious fiction or drama than for farce, good and loud. Nature, as the saying goes, may be wonderful, but—.

Acting is the world's only profession in which a person is loudly applauded at the end of his day's work for drawing down a higher financial reward than he often deserves.

What of the American playwriting gods of the drama critics of yesterday? What is their standing today? Augustus Thomas, Edward Sheldon, Charles Klein, Eugene Walter, George Broadhurst? Let us take time out for laughter.

It is a pity that so many valid dramatic ideas seem to fall into the hands of incompetent playwrights. The waste is sad to contemplate. The idea in *South Pacific,* which a few seasons ago ran for only five performances, for one example, was much too good to lose: the Negro's ironic position in the atmosphere of two different civilizations. And over the years there have been many others, light and serious, in such failures as *The Man Who Ate the Popomack,* treating of the influence of odors on human society; *The Upstart,* dealing with the final inefficacy of mere speech, however eloquent; etc., etc. A catalogue of all the tasty ideas that have been quickly buried in the storehouse for lack of skillful treatment would fill a book.

To critics who write praisefully of an actor having "felt" his role, let us commend Coquelin's retort to Madame Ristori's insistence that the actor cannot express on the stage an emotion that he does not really feel. "Yes, madame," observed Coquelin, "but you often die."

Thinking of illustrious French theatrical figures of the past, much of the wisdom which they otherwise contributed to the dramatic record is today found to be not only hollow but quite foolish. For example:

    a. "A meditative being may not enter into any dramatic combination."—Paul Bourget. Hamlet, Brand, and half a hundred others make mock of the criticism.

    b. "As romantic situations are always very special, the more you make use of them in plays the more you decrease general interest." —Brunetière. *Camille, Cyrano de Bergerac,* and half a hundred others are observed thumbing their noses.

    c. "It is permissible to make a mistake in the details of the execution of a play, but it is not permissible to make a mistake . . . in facts." —Alexandre Dumas, fils. *Vide* the dramas of Shakespeare and Bernard Shaw.

    d. "A playwright must write many bad plays before he can make a good one."—Houssaye. Shakespeare, Strindberg, Ibsen, Björnson, Heijermans, Hofmannsthal, Pirandello, Hauptmann, O'Casey, O'Neill, among various others, didn't somehow seem to know this.

e. "The dignity of tragedy demands some grand state interest, or some passion nobler than love."—Corneille. As, for example, *Romeo and Juliet.*

f. "The tragic author admits atrocious crime, conspiracy, murder, parricide, regicide, and so on. Comedy, less audacious, never goes beyond the conventional because its pictures are drawn from conventional manners."—Beaumarchais. *Arsenic and Old Lace,* for one example out of many.

The worst of all bores encountered by a dramatic critic is the one who approaches him after the first act and asks him what he thinks of the play. My own usual retort to any such jackass is to inquire of him in turn what he thinks of a dinner after the oysters.

In real life any woman who sought to express her rapt interest in a man's words by blinking her eyes throughout his conversation would be put down by him as a transparent idiot. On the stage she is customarily regarded by the reviewers as either a delightful ingénue with a very promising future or as an actress of more mature years who has remarkably retained her youthfulness and girlish charm.

The old schoolroom saying that genius is the capacity for taking infinite pains calls for revaluation. It is mere talent, rather, which demands that capacity. I must have looked up again the stories of some hundred acknowledged geniuses from Aristophanes to Shakespeare and Bernard Shaw, along with the sculptors, painters and composers, and much of the greatest of their work seems to have been the result of no particular overassiduity or headaches.

So many of the well-made plays of the past, notably those of Pinero and his school, give one the impression of nothing so much as well prepared dinners served with paper napkins.

The majority of our popular playwrights seem to have as their worshipful credo the old German saying, "Beautiful is youth; it never comes again." Youth to their way of thinking and writing is the desideratum above all desiderata, and their plays are full of wistful elderly creatures who yearn for its recapture and blissful return. What, one meditates in one's later years, if it did return? Gradually, as one slid back over the years, one would lose the proud and secure place one had made for one's self in the world; one would lose the happy job that has gone hand in hand with it; one would lose all the good and trusted friends whom one had gathered in the fuller years of one's life; and worse still and more awful to contemplate, if the metamorphosis were extreme, one would wind up again having to drink milk!

On that day when an audience, as in the theatre, interrupts the progress of a film with periodic applause and remains at the end to cheer the screen play and players, I will be persuaded to believe that the moving pictures can approach the effectiveness of the living drama.

The word "charm" is usually as critically obnoxious to me as the words "glamour" and "authority," but I am afraid I shall have to fall back on it, since that is just what I am going to talk about. So: the one commodity lacking in the greater proportion of our current actresses is charm. And sadly, because most other things considered and duly allowed for, an actress without that attribute is much like a pickpocket with it. We have all kinds of actresses with talent; we have all kinds who can do their jobs well and some who can do them beautifully; we have expert technicians and very satisfactory minor players and all of that. But among the lot there are not in the present years more than a handful who have in them that rare quality that, like a prehensile mist, steals over the footlights and gathers men into its warm embrace. Without descending to the ungentlemanliness of mentioning the few actresses, young and not so young, who possess it and thus wounding the plurality who do not, I can at this moment think of only two older actresses who are blessed with the property, and only two in the middle bracket, and only two in the younger. Which amounts to just a paltry, if welcome, six out of many hundreds. Some of these others have what is known as sex appeal (a phrase also obnoxious to me—at least, I should say, literarily); some are endowed with looks; some are among the leaders in their acting age groups. But without charm they are, if the truth were told, even for a good half of the Critics' Circle little more than proficient hams.

The fact remains that there is not a single leading actor on the contemporary American stage with a speaking voice that one affectionately remembers. There is not one with the dry and wonderful impressive voice of a William Gillette, or one with the grand romantic tones of a William Faversham or one with the smooth finish of a John Drew, or one with the rare gentleness of a Bruce McRea, or one with the crackle and fire of an Arnold Daly, or one with the halting charm of an early William Courtenay, or one with the winning inner smile of a Leo Ditrichstein, or one with the summer thunder of a Henry Miller, or one with the silken challenge of a Kyrle Bellew, or one with the quiet style of a Guy Standing, or one with the soft ease of a Frank Worthing or an E. S. Willard.

While plot as plot is the chief concern of our amateurs, box-office hacks and deficient literary and dramatic practitioners generally, and while I myself am perfectly willing to leave plot to admirers of detective stories, murder melodramas and other such diversions of the emotionally un-washed, it nevertheless paradoxically strikes me that the fear of plot, instilled in them by literary and drama critics, has dulled the plays of a number of our younger and more ambitious playwrights. Afraid of plot lest they be superiorly relegated by these critics to the company of mere pulp writers, they hit it over the head, whenever it pops up in their plays, with wisecracks, satirical spoofs, heavy witticisms and similar self-criticism. (The consequence is usually plays not only without sufficiently satisfactory wit, but also without original viewpoint to make one remit the absence of plot.)

The difference between an actress like Elizabeth Bergner and one like, say, Ethel Barrymore is the difference between a minute chemical analysis of a cocoanut pie and the cocoanut pie itself.

A novelist may introduce his hero in any manner whatsoever with no worry over his readers. A dramatist, on the other hand, must often arbitrarily take his audiences into concerned consideration. To give just one example out of many, it would be next to impossible for a playwright to introduce his hero by having him rush onto the stage with the words, "Quick! There's not a moment to lose!" Since his hero in all likelihood would be cast with a more or less prominent actor he would have to figure on the audience applause which would greet his first entrance and which would hold up the stage and make the speech ridiculous. The laugh which would inevitably follow would obviously ruin not only the moment but the action immediately following.

It is generally overlooked by historians of the theatre that variety theatres in their earlier day were shunned by respectable women as if they were so many houses of ill-fame. It was Tony Pastor who rid them of their prejudice, not by changing materially the form of stage entertainment but by bringing them into his theatre with prizes of half-barrels of flour, half-tons of coal, and fancy dress patterns. The erstwhile aloof girls flocked to his playhouse in droves and his theatre soon became so packed with them that he had to add extra chairs to accommodate the overflow.

It significantly remains that ninety-five per cent of the fifty straight plays that have achieved the longest runs in our modern American theatre have had so-called happy endings.

The American passion for short sentences has gone to such an extreme that any sentence containing more than ten or twelve words is regarded not only as a literary affectation but as so extraordinarily involved that it is almost impossible to disentangle it.

The spectacle of a college professor-critic trying to be one of the boys has always been one of the most diverting acts on the bill of our national vaudeville. But it has seldom since been so amusing as the performance of the late Prof. Brander Matthews. Not only did he come out on the critical stage in a red undershirt and baggy pants and proclaim the Irish comedian, Ned Harrigan, a blood-brother to Molière but, before the stomps and whistles ended, sprang this personal nifty: "An American professor of dramatic literature, whenever he came to discuss the lyrical burlesques of Aristophanes, was in the habit of sending his whole class to Weber and Fields that his students might see for themselves the nearest modern analogy to the robust fancies of the great Greek humorist."

The villains in the old-time melodramas were almost always identified as such on the score of their superior diction. There seldom was a dyed-in-the-wool scoundrel in those shows who didn't speak English impeccably—and whose trousers, incidentally, weren't just a shade too short.

There is much bosh about this or that Hamlet actor, whatever his other virtues, not looking like Hamlet. A number of the critics have recently been saying it again about Maurice Evans. Aside from one or two faint and debatable clues, Shakespeare gives us very little idea of what Hamlet really looked like. so who knows for certain? Hamlet's looks amount in the end very largely only to the particular prejudice of his beholder. Anyway, if the player is a good one, what matter.? Where is the stage Juliet who ever looked fully like the Juliet of our imaginations? Or, God knows, the Cleopatra, Ariel, or Titania? Or even the Julius Caesar or Marc Antony? Few actors ever look exactly like the characters we are requested to imagine them to be. The only characters, indeed, who uniformly look like the actors playing them are Uncle Tom, Topsy, Charley's aunt, Mrs. Malaprop, and Cinderella's stepsisters.

Despite the common directorial belief, little is so ruinous to the effect of an actress's performance, save in farce and certain comedy, as too much vitality. The best actresses are those who silently and inwardly suggest it. The worst are those who physically demonstrate it. The great Eleonora Duse in all the thirty-odd years I beheld her in various roles in different corners of Europe and America never for a moment allowed her audiences to feel that she had just eaten a large Porterhouse steak and was rarin' to go. There was about her always, even in her earlier and more vigorous years, the faint suggestion that she was not physically quite up to snuff. The Katina Paxinou, on the other hand, habitually have at their customers with so much energy that, if Joe Louis were out front, he'd swoon.

It is said that the trouble with many of the newer playwrights is that they have not learned the business of sound play construction and that, as a consequence, their plays, even when possessed of intermittent merits, miss fire. This, in many instances, is sheer critical twaddle. The real trouble with the playwrights is not that they have not mastered the dramaturgical technique but that, even were they to be veritable hounds at it, their mental, spiritual, emotional and imaginative quotient is woefully deficient. It is, of course, perfectly true that a knowledge of technique is valuable, but that it is a prime essential is far from true. Genius, or merely an unusual talent, may be ignorant of it or may loftily wave it aside and nonetheless produce plays of worth. Gorki's admittedly best play is almost amateurish technically, at least in the sense that the critics understand the word. Most of Shaw's plays would have been marked C-minus by dramaturgical professors of the George Pierce Baker school. As a matter of record, Maurine Watkins' admirable satirical farce, *Chicago,* which subsequently proved a great success in the theatre, was so marked by Baker when the author, a member of his class, submitted it to him for his criticism. Wedekind's best play is a technical botch, and so, to the pundits of his day, was Georg Kaiser's. And Strindberg's *The Dream Play* originally had the critics yelling for mama. . . . Saroyan is a particular goat of the technical assayers. If only he obeyed the dramatic rules, they say, his plays would be what they should be. As Bobby Clark exclaimed in *All Men Are Alike,* Oh, balderdash! If Saroyan wrote his plays according to the stricter dramaturgical formula they would be unspeakably bad. One of their greatest virtues is their very neglect of that formula. Those who believe the opposite are those who insist that poetry is not poetry unless it rhymes. Some of the very worst plays in the theatre of the last ten years have been technically perfect. And some of the very best have been as technically imperfect as Shakespeare's *King Lear* and *A Midsummer Night's Dream.*

When ever a musical show of the past is revived, the critics are pretty sure to write that one of its greatest assets is the evocation in an audience of the nostalgic mood. This, I believe, is only partly true. What is also evoked, particularly by the lovely old songs, is the antonym of nostalgia. Fond melody does not make one think tenderly alone of what has been and is gone. It also sometimes makes one think of what may come in one's life, of sentimental dream and hope, and of wished-for illusion and flowered horizon.

Profiles of Players

Joseph Jefferson (1829–1905)

The posse of ambitious players who optimistically installed themselves in the municipal dramatic hot-spot as a repertory project[1] opened up shop with a revised version of Joseph Jefferson's famous meal-ticket[2] and with one Bourneuf in Joe's old role. I confess that I approached the occasion full of prejudice. Since this is obviously a shameful condition in any critic, I ask the reader either to stop reading at this point or, if he finds himself unable to resist the allure of my prose, to proceed at his own risk and doubtless to his own annoyance.

Rip is one of the most engaging of American legends, and whatever the version or whoever the actor, is bound to exercise at least a measure of its spell over an auditor. And here once again, despite miserable staging and direction, it did so. But while in this projection it may have been accepted with some favor by members of the more recent generation, it failed to enchant this older boy as it did in those distant days when Joe was in command of it.

It isn't that Jefferson was any giant as an actor. Far from it. He was, in fact, rather an ordinary one, one whose range was notoriously limited and whose eminence was predicated largely on this single role. His performance as Bob Acres in *The Rivals,* his second most popular role, was a negligible one. But as Rip he triumphed for almost half a century and anyone who saw him can not see any other actor in the part without wincing. There have been actors like that, actors whose personality, voice and manner, whatever the volume of their talents, have so stamped certain roles that the latter become forevermore part and parcel of them and in which subsequent actors seem to be gross intruders. James A. Herne in *Shore Acres,* William Gillette in *Sherlock Holmes,* and Kyrle Bellew in *Raffles* so closely identified the parts with themselves that, if one were to view any other actor, however able, in them, one would be sorely disquieted. And so, too, was it in the instances of James O'Neill and *Monte Cristo;* Denman Thompson and *The Old Homestead;* David Warfield and *The Music Master;* and George M. Cohan and any of his plays.

It was thus that, watching Bourneuf in Jefferson's shoes, I condoned my

From *The Theatre Book of the Year, 1947–48* (New York: Knopf, 1948), pp. 37–39.

prejudice by recalling Hazlitt's words: "No wise man can have a contempt for the prejudices of others; and he should even stand in a certain awe of his own, as if they were aged parents or monitors. They may in the end prove wiser than he." Be that as it may, Bourneuf simply was not on that stage so far as I was concerned. The years swept back their curtain and, for me, it was Joe who was giving his grand old performance in my memory. There, as a youngster, I saw him again in all his long, lean lovableness and with all that odd, cajoling croak in his voice. There I saw him making off from his testy wife like a household dog half-sad to be driven from surroundings that, though intolerable, yet remained home. There I saw him waking from his long sleep in clothes absurdly tattered, raising himself with those familiar Jeffersonian rheumatic calisthenics to his crooked height and squinting in disbelief at the Hudson gleaming below him. And there still I saw him, bewhiskered and betalcumed like some starved Dutch Edmond Dantes, stumbling back to his charged fireside. What Bourneuf was like all this while, I do not know and do not much care to know. He may have been a good Rip or a poor one. Let the younger generation decide for themselves. But my prejudice played another Rip in his stead. I wasn't a critic that evening; I was the boy who had seen Joe Jefferson a dozen or more times in bygone Cleveland and Philadelphia, and that boy was not to be disturbed for a minute by anyone else in Joe's place. . . .

There were some added things I missed in the production. All the modern scenic improvements could not make up for that wonderful old scene in the Catskills—at least it seemed wonderful then—with the stage crammed with great trees and such a wealth of carpenter work on the mound on which Rip slept as under today's prices would bankrupt half the producers on Broadway. Maybe my imagination is not what it used to be, but I also missed the warming old Dutch atmosphere that hovered over the stage in the early and late scenes. And I most certainly missed that thrilling old spectacle of the brown dwarfs with the thunder of their bowling balls so loud and detonating that it used to knock me out of my seat onto my best matinée knickerbockers.

---

1. City Center Repertory Players, 15 July 1947, and 15 performances thereafter.
2. *Rip Van Winkle*, revival of a play that melodramatist Dion Boucicault adapted from Washington Irving's story.

William Gillette (1885–1937)

Sitting before the performances of Mr. William Gillette in such concoctions of arch nonsense as *The Dream Maker*, one is reminded again of

---

From *The World in Falseface* (New York: Knopf, 1923), pp. 69–71. Copyright renewed 1950 by George Jean Nathan.

the great charm that so often reposes in what is, critically, bad acting. This Gillette, by any sound standard, is a mere trickster of acting; it is perhaps not too much to say that, as an actor, he is to his craft, what O. Henry was to his; yet there are surely few to deny that, for all his low estate as an histrionic artist, he is one of the most thoroughly watchable and engaging performers on our stage. And what is the secret of the paradox? The secret, very simply, is that bad acting often enchants by virtue of its very artlessness, where highly proficient acting leaves one cold. Acting that lacks sound artistic design is, in this, much like some ugly old easy chair. It has much of the cozy warmth, comfortableness, ease and agreeable friendliness that a beautiful, stiff Sheraton lacks.

If acting is an art at all, it is the baby art. And, like a baby, sophistication is, or should be, relevantly a stranger to it. Acting that is polished to the last degree is like a butler—distinguishedly lifeless. Mankind is itself a bad and fitful actor. Imitations of mankind upon the stage should have all of mankind's flaws, weaknesses, crudities and mistakes. Gillette commits a hundred sins against histrionic art in every one of his performances. Walter Hampden, to take a single example, commits not a tenth that number. Yet Gillette is ten times as pleasant an actor to watch. He is as charming in his imperfections as the dancing of a little girl of six. His monotonous voice has thrice the captivating quality of the fluid voice of a dozen Russ Whytals; his single awkward gesture six times the eloquence of the studied gestures of all the John Masons who ever tortured the public eye.

Gillette, however, is not the only bad actor whose very badness is refractorily fascinating. Cyril Keightly is another; Eric Maturin (whom we haven't laid eyes on since *Mid-Channel*) is another; and Reginald Barlow is still another. Dismiss from your thought, please, any notion that what I am writing here is an attempt at left-handed smartness. I mean seriously that these men are exceptionally effective actors because of their artistic guilt rather than in spite of it. They are, from the standpoint of penetrating criticism, not ranking actors, but they are actors who get illusion out of one as colleagues twice as proficient cannot. Where an artistically cruder actor than Lowell Sherman; yet where, in certain roles, one more peculiarly productive of results? Or, again, take such performers as Charles Cherry, Harry Mestayer, John Miltern, Kenneth Douglas, John Westley, James Rennie and Frank Sheridan. Surely it would be a school-boy of a critic who would be so rash as to say that any of these are first-rate actors or—some of them—even second-rate actors.

Eleonora Duse (1858?–1924)

Duse was the super-star of the theatre not because she did not look her age, not because her fingers happened to be long and tapering, not because her voice was what it was, not because newspaper interviewers bored the life out of her and she had the good sense to keep away from them, not because of anything to do with her soul, not because she built around her a romantic legend, not because she preferred to stay at home and keep to herself (this the "mystery" which they speak of) instead of hanging around the Algonquin Hotel at lunch and taking part in Equity Ball pageants—but, very simply, because she worked at her art as no other actress save Bernhardt worked in her time. She was gifted with the great sense always to play under a role and lift it up to the heights instead of playing down upon it from above—as most of her colleagues in histrionism are accustomed to do. Her mind was naturally sensitive to every turn of dramatic writing and, finally, unlike the overwhelming majority of actresses, she made her body the tool of that mind instead of making the mind the tool of her body. She acted from the head down, not from the feet up. Her body was eloquent because her legs had less to do with manipulating it and guiding it than did her brain. She was the magnificent, the peerless creature of the theatre—even if she didn't look younger than Baby Peggy, even if her hands were, after all, just hands, and even if her voice, as a voice, didn't move one any more electrically than did the voice of Ethel Barrymore.

Where Bernhardt gained every one of her greatest acting effects by a maximum of means, Duse achieved hers with a minimum. Hers was an economy not elsewhere seen in the theatre of her period. She acted the way Joseph Conrad writes, with the brilliance born of an imaginative, coherent and exact parsimony. Nothing was wasted. But as the years sapped from her some of her earlier vigor, she came to resort to a series of admirable tricks—but mere tricks withal—to further her performances and get the effects that in the years before she was wont to achieve by sounder and subtler means. These tricks, such as the nervous, staccato cutting-in on speeches, the holding up of a speech by way of gathering breath and the then sudden propulsion of the lines, the preparation for a speech by weaving its pattern in the air with the hands—these and the like were tokens of an ageing actress, an actress still radiant but moving on swiftly toward the sunset whose light already fell upon her, an actress who felt the need of props for a great but age-ridden mastery of her craft.

Duse, parenthetically, had that one thing that every great actress has had, has and must have—something that may idiotically be described as a

From *Materia Critica* (New York: Knopf, 1924), pp. 166–69.

sad arm: that line of the arm that, when extended from the shoulder, has about it something of melancholy. The extended right arm of Eleonora Duse had in it all the tears of *Tristan and Isolde*.

It is a peculiarity of the critical estimate of Duse that she is generally agreed to have been the greatest actress of her day by two sets of critics who, oddly, arrive at this estimate with arguments and reasons that are diametrically opposed. I privilege myself the suspicion that this is why Duse is called the "mystery woman." She is a mystery because she is the only actress of our time who has been eulogized by half of the critics for one thing and by the other half for the exact opposite of the same thing. I have in mind specifically her performances of the mother in Gallarati-Scotti's pious claptrap, *Cosi Sia*. In London, when she last performed the role at the New Oxford, she played it in the spirit of a tigress who, suddenly wakened from sleep, snaps out a flaming snarl of defiance. This mood of defiance gave way in turn to an impassioned, nay almost a frenzied, faith, a sullen stubbornness, a burst of heartrending appeal and, finally, a despairful agony of self-immolation. The London critics (and later, the New York critics) hailed the performance as the acme of intelligent and acute interpretation and Duse as the peerless actress of the stage. In New York, when she performed the same role at the Century, she played it in the spirit of an imperturbably sexagenarian who accepts her mission coolly, calmly. This mood of resignation gave way in turn to a resigned, nay almost a melancholy, faith, a complacent sweetness, a passive acceptance of abuse and, finally, a welcome and highly comfortable surrender to fate.

Maude Adams (1872–1953)

In the criticism of Miss Maude Adams, it has become a kind of *lex non scripta* that one must ever be exceeding chivalrous and speak nothing that is not good. Miss Adams occupies in the theatre the place that a wife occupies in the home: no matter how tired one becomes of her, no matter how much one becomes irritated, with the passing of time, by her eccentricities and her mannerisms, it is a law of social conduct that one keep up a show of loving her and refrain from saying aught ill for the public ear. Miss Adams and the tradition associated with her name have these many years succeeded in making a gentleman even of me.

I have known all along, of course, that she is a pretty poor actress as

From *Mr. George Jean Nathan Presents* (New York: Knopf, 1917), pp. 82–84. Copyright renewed 1944 by George Jean Nathan.

leading actresses go, and all along I have felt uncomfortable, as have many others, when she has spoiled so many truly beautiful lines by accompanying them with that peculiar neck-twist, that little semi-upper-cut gesture and other such idiosyncrasies of hers. But, following the ritual, I have regularly maintained a polite silence and have, with the rest of them, professed to be enthralled by the "dauntless frailty," the "brave wistfulness," the "odd, half-strangled utterance," the "throwing up of the head with that half-defiant gesture" and all the other of Miss Adams' attributes, qualities and trickeries. And what is more, so insistent is the thing, I am not even now going to write the truth about the lady. For what the use? After all, there is something rather fine about her, if not as an artist, at least as an institution of our theatre. Her name and position, in these days of a stage so promiscuously adorned with boudoir alumnæ and Wall Street ingénues, are of a pretty dignity. To her ears, the tin-din of Broadway seems not to have penetrated. She has played and played only, during the real years of her career, the plays of fine artists. From all the cheapness, all the shoddy press-agency, all the trashy appurtenances of the show-shop, she has firmly and consistently drawn aside her skirts. And in a theatre from which, by Sunday night "benefits," actors' dancing clubs, syndicated beauty-talks and Red Cross balls, all remoteness and illusion have been made to vanish, such a figure as this—one of the few, few figures it has—cannot but be regarded with respect and held high in esteem. And I am not sure but what, after all, criticism may not fairly be conscious of such items, however seemingly foreign their nature.

It is this Maude Adams, I suppose, rather than the Maude Adams we watch play before us, that makes such as I eager to fib eloquently in her behalf as an actress. And for one, I am glad to be a party to the polite misdemeanor.

Barrie's *A Kiss for Cinderella,* Miss Adams's 1917 offering, though not without its several typical Barrie conceits and lovely touches, fails to arouse my enthusiasms.[1] On all sides I have read and heard tell of its "unalloyed charm," its "gently pathetic fancy," its "heart-warmed, moist-eyed delicacy," its "wistful loveliness" and all its winsome et ceteras, but I am unpersuaded. At no point save in its first act does it approach to the stature of Miss [Eleanor] Gates' *Poor Little Rich Girl,* which it in content closely resembles. Much of it is of an aridity difficult to reconcile with the name of its author and in the matter of imagination generally it is not only beneath the Gates' play but beneath Paul Apel's *Hans Sonnenstösser's Trip to Hell,* a play of fabric similar to the *Poor Little Rich Girl* which was done abroad at an earlier date. The general effect of the Barrie play is of flat near-beer. The Barrie imagination has here taken flight as without a propeller. There is a loud inaugural buzz of engines, the beginning of a graceful mount, a wild indirection, a looping of loops, a sudden stopping—with the moon still a million miles away.

1. Nathan apparently chooses to say nothing here about Maude Adams's performance in Barrie's *Peter Pan* (1904). In another essay on Maude Adams, Nathan writes, "Charles Frohman [the syndicate manager] through his deft hocus-pocus managed to have her accepted by the public as genuinely important . . . Not one thing that Maude Adams did, did she without Frohman's say-so." (From *The Morning After the First Night* [New York: Knopf, 1938], p. 87. Copyright renewed 1965 by Mrs. George Jean Nathan.

Walter Hampden (1879–1955)

. . . And then came another expensive circular, followed by another and followed in turn by still another, announcing that Mr. Hampden was to do Cyrano. I may, under the circumstances, be forgiven for having pictured a Cyrano who would have all the poetic fire of a Sapolio rhyme, all the powerful sweep of a whisk-broom, all the heroic magnificence and purple gesture of—but enough of simile. Thus prejudiced—but fortifying myself against a too great prejudice by another perusal of the encomiastic circulars—I went to the theatre. And in that theatre I saw the Cyrano of all our finest fancies, the Cyrano that Mansfield failed to convey even to the impressionable and easy young man that was I at the time, a Cyrano stepped brilliantly, dazzlingly, out of the heart and pages of Rostand—a Cyrano, in short, that came as close to the ideal Cyrano as closeness well can come. Where was the college grind, the still minuet body that vainly, humorously, essayed to swing itself into the waltz measures of great poetic dramatic literature, the forum reader in whose mouth moon-bathed verse became so much dialectics—where was this Hampden of the years before in this Hampden who, there before us, was a truly gusty, a truly moving, a truly flashing, lazing and radiant romantic actor? There was no sign of him, not a trace. In his place was the Hampden of all the Horsecough and Hamilton and Towse ecstasies and eulogies, the mythical Hampden suddenly come to dramatic life. The expensive circulars had found truth at the end of a long road of their wholly absurd, if honest and well-meant, exaggerations. Hampden was at last an actor. And this Cyrano of his is one of the most completely meritorious performances that an actor of his time and my own has contributed to the American theatre.

Yet, even in the instance of this excellent performance of the Rostand masterpiece, the old low comedy note was not lacking from the comments of the Hampden Social and Marching Club. In a number of cases, the

From *Materia Critica* (New York: Knopf, 1924), pp. 173–75.

encompassing eulogies were so excessively horticultural that the falling petals covered the ground for miles 'round. Some of the choicest of these associated petals may be found in Mr. Hamilton's preface to Brian Hooker's praiseworthy transposition of the *Cyrano* text into English, heaving a grandmotherly sigh for the days when the Rostand play was new—"the brave days, indeed, when the world was not yet out of joint," the good Hamilton continues thus: "It was the time of the Spanish-American war, a knightly contest for a noble cause, in which we were fighting against gentlemen, not Germans!" One may readily enough allow with Colonel Hamilton that we Americans in the Spanish-American war were fighting against gentlemen but, in view of the fact that the odds in advance were something like one thousand to one in favor of us Americans, one may privilege one's self some speculation as to the opinion that the Spaniards hold in the matter.

John Barrymore (1882–1942)

I take it that there is no longer much question that the proficient modern actor of Hamlet is he who acts the role not with his own intelligence but with the intelligence of his audience. In plainer words, that Hamlet is, figuratively speaking, no longer so much an actor's role as an audience's role, and that the best actor of that role is he who creates the role less than he mirrors the modern audience's creation of it. Forbes-Robertson is a master in this; and Leiber, though conceding vastly more to himself as an actor, is similarly a captain of the stratagem. Barrymore comes to us with the same trick, and manages it admirably. His Hamlet is a calm, cool dramatic critic in the robes of the role; it is an analytical and synthetic shadowgraph of its audience's reactions; it is—and this is where it properly excels—a mere scenario of its emotional implications. Yet it is not, for all its undeniably sound plan and sagacious preparation, entirely successful. I am not persuaded that Barrymore's critically exact approach to the role, with its obvious wealth of study, scrupulously meticulous voice cultivation and intensive training in gesture, movement and facial play, has not deadened to a degree the human warmth that might have been projected from a less strainfully perfect preliminary self-instruction and artistic castigation. Barrymore's Hamlet is critically so precise that it is at times histrionically defective. It gets across perfectly to all the professional dramatic critics in the audience, but I doubt that it gets across quite so effectively to those whom acting must more speciously and fully inflame if

From *Materia Critica* (New York: Knopf, 1924), pp. 178–80.

they are to be brought to an understanding and appreciation of the role with which that acting is concerned. I thus join in the praise of Barrymore, but with certain misgivings. His Hamlet, like a diamond, is glittering, vari-colored, brilliant—but cold, intensely cold. We get from it the reflected rays of intelligence, but never—or at best rarely—the rays of heat. It is, this Hamlet, a dazzling and intricate piece of machinery, put together with a fine proficiency and revolving with a perfect rhythm, yet condemned by its very nature to serve as a cooling electric fan. There is in it breath—vigorous, consistent, sweeping—but it is not the breath of life. It is all that it was mathematically and validly designed to be: that is at once its tribute and its detraction.

Shaw said of Forbes-Robertson's Hamlet: "He plays as Shakespeare should be played, on the line and to the line, with the utterance and acting simultaneous, inseparable and in fact identical. Not for a moment is he solemnly conscious of Shakespeare's reputation or of Hamlet's mo-mentousness in literary history: on the contrary, he delivers us from all these boredoms. . . ." Barrymore's utterance and acting are not always identical: one detects a self-consciousness of the importance of great occasion, of the austerity and traditions of the role. He goes at the role as a brave and gallant soldier goes into battle: with flags flying in his Sem Benelli heart and with Richard's shining sword raised courageously aloft—but with just a trace of very human timidity and fear holding him in. He is glamorous; he is percipient; he is sound in apprehension; he is eminently praiseworthy—but he is not the complete Hamlet.

Alfred Lunt (1893–1977) and Lynn Fontanne (1887–1983)

It was a lucky day for the Theatre Guild when Eugene O'Neill first communicated to its board of directors the news of the advent in the southmost reaches of Georgia of Prof. Orville P. Mosedinck. This Prof. Mosedinck, O'Neill discovered, was a hypnotist extraordinaire; nothing like him, said O'Neill, had ever been seen anywhere; his powers were magic itself. "Get into touch with him at once," O'Neill urged. "He may, if he sufficiently exerts himself, be able to hypnotize a few good actors into the Guild service. He may, indeed, if you give him enough rope, even succeed in at last hypnotizing a good play into your hands."

The rest, of course, is history. Although the Prof.'s hypnotic virtuosity

From *Encyclopedia of the Theatre* (New York: Knopf, 1940), pp. 240–43. Copyright renewed 1968 by Mrs. George Jean Nathan.

does not seem to have worked so well in the case of plays, his great feat in persuading the Lunts, while under the influence, to ally themselves with the Guild is commonly appreciated. (There is no truth in the scandalous rumor that, in order to persuade the Lunts, the Guild directorate had to supplement the illustrious Prof.'s efforts with several gallons of vodka and a variety of hypodermic needles.) The credit is entirely, wholly and completely Prof. Orville P. Mosedinck's. If it had not been for him, the Guild would still be going around with even more holes in its socks than it already has. For it is a well-known fact that, after it has annually put on its customary play by a Hollywood movie scenario writer, its customary feeble little gesture in Left Wing drama, its dramatization of some rococo novel, and its proud revelation of the first work of some Grade-C genius, it is the Lunts who have had to come to its rescue and make up enough of the deficit at least to pay for the postage stamps on the press department's bulletins telling how good the Guild used to be.

The two life-savers, Alf and wife, never more valiantly performed their services on behalf of the sorely stricken Guild than in the instance of S. N. Behrman's adaptation of Giraudoux's *Amphitryon 38*. As the Jupiter who is sufficiently Latin to appreciate the Italian proverb that angels may be all right in their place but not in bed and who craves for a change in the person of the mortal Alkmena, Lunt employed that oddly cajoling voice of his, which always suggests a throat lozenge mocking a tenor, to admirable dry comedy effect. And as the married morsel whom he covets, Miss Fontanne stooged it handsomely for him throughout the evening. The play itself was slight stuff but it provided a sufficient share of agreeable and witty boulevard entertainment, all the more welcome in a season that seemed to promise so much and that, at least in its earlier phases, for the most part haplessly resolved itself into a series of such denicotinized dramatic cheroots as the hitherto applaudable Maxwell Anderson's three-decker combination of ham, cheese and boloney that with infinitely more relevance might have been called *The Dog-Wagon* and Rachel Crothers' fossilized fable of the separated married couple reunited by their child and attemptedly given a touch of modernity by making the wife guilty of Buchmanism instead of adultery. Into such a scene *Amphitryon 38* came as comparative manna. Liberally and wisely deleted of its verbose philosophical disquisitions and converted by Behrman into livelier theatrical material through a shrewd suppression of its original bookish flavor, its retelling of the familiar legend in terms of Sacha Guitry crossed with a little Shaw was to be recommended to all such theatregoers, Guild and otherwise, as were beginning to become discouraged over the thought that the season would be devoted largely to proving that wit and humor were lost to dead-pan greasepaint literature which distils the emotions of the witless with flash-backs, showing dejected old folk in their happy, picknicking youth and with close-ups and long-shots[1] of disconsolate intellectuals searching for their souls . . .

---

1. See, in glossary, D. W. Griffith.

Lillian Gish (b. 1896)

That she is one of the few real actresses that the films have brought forth, either here or abroad, is pretty well agreed upon by the majority of the critics. But it seems to me that, though the fact is taken for granted, the reasons for her eminence have in but small and misty part been set into print . . . The girl is superior to her medium . . . The particular genius of Lillian Gish lies in making the definite charmingly indefinite. Her technique consists in thinking out a characterization directly and concretely and then executing it in terms of semi-vague suggestions . . . The smile of the Gish girl is a bit of happiness trembling on a bed of death; the tears of the Gish girl are the tears that old Johann Strauss wrote into the rosemary of his waltzes. The whole secret of the young woman's remarkably effective acting rests, as I have observed, in her carefully devised and skilfully negotiated technique of playing always, as it were, behind a veil of silver chiffon . . . She is always present, she always dominates the scene, yet one feels somehow that she is ever just out of sight around the corner. One never feels that one is seeing her entirely. There is ever something pleasantly, alluringly missing, as there is always in the case of women who are truly "acting artists."

Katharine Cornell (1893–1974)

A scrutiny of her [Katharine Cornell's] major performances on the local stage results in the following estimates. In *A Bill of Divorcement,* in one of her earliest performances, she presented herself, in the not very difficult role of a young girl who finds herself the center of a disordered household, as an attractive and competent ingénue, little more. Various novices since, Margaret Sullavan, Sylvia Sidney and Barbara Robbins, for instance, have done every bit as well—some of them, indeed, better—in roles somewhat more trying. In the other two Clemence Dane plays, *Will Shakespeare* and

---

From *Vanity Fair* (November 1931), p. 32.

From *The Theatre of the Moment* (New York: Knopf, 1936), pp. 71–75. Copyright renewed 1964 by Mrs. George Jean Nathan).

The Way Things Happen, she gave what were mainly routine and orthodox performances. In the former, a physical awkwardness, due to the unaccustomed costumerie of her role, added to her embarrassment; and, in the latter, a tendency to work an arbitrary tragic tone into her voice, whatever the immediate nature of the situation, contributed to critical nose-scratching. In *The Enchanted Cottage,* the Barrie play written by Pinero, she had one of those sweet-sweet roles that offer less challenge to acting than to look and personality and managed to do pretty well by it. In *Casanova,* in the second-grade part of a lady of station who is not averse to a loose wink now and then, she wisely centered her efforts largely on the pictorial side and succeeded, with the aid of handsome costumes and efficient stage lighting, in projecting a very fetching picture. In *The Outsider,* a *Barretts of Wimpole Street* plot in which the invalid heroine is cured by faith and a handsome medico instead of by love and a handsome poet, she first caught the attention of the more acute critics with a performance that combined tenderness with strength and resolution with beauty, though the role, imbedded in hokum, was anything but onerous, as other occupants of it have sufficiently attested.

In the melodramatic and somewhat unintentionally humorous *Tiger Cats,* a dose of Scandinavian Minsky, she found herself in the position of a Metro-Goldwyn lion growling majestically in behalf of a pie farce; though she acted sincerely, even desperately, the dialogue constantly sneaked up behind her and tied tin cans to her art. And the same thing was true, though to a considerably less embarrassing extent, in *The Letter.* . . .

In *The Green Hat,* in the Laura Jean Libbey role of Iris March, the Ostermoor romancer, she was first-rate. Considering the awkwardness of the material, her performance in lifting a servant-girl heroine into some faint semblance of romantic dignity (grease-paint dignity, that is) was all the more critically interesting. In *The Age of Innocence,* she was entirely charming in a role artfully manufactured for nostalgic reaction and, in addition, her physical comportment began to take on a considerable ease and grace. . . . As the heroine of Shaw's *Candida* . . . she turned in a really excellent performance—delicate in its strength and lovely in its manner.

Coming down to more recent years, we find Miss Cornell at her best as Elizabeth Barrett, in *The Barretts of Wimpole Street,* a truly admirable performance in every detail, and doubtless too familiar to most readers to call for amplified comment. Her Lucrèce, in the Obey play of that name, was a sorry botch and proved, if nothing else, that, like the majority of our younger American players, she is sadly deficient in the art of pantomime. In *Alien Corn,* a trashy script about gamy doings in a Western college town, she comported herself, as in *Tiger Cats* and *The Letter,* with so overly tragic an air and so monotonously dirge-like a speaking voice that the impression, considering the play, was of a lady embalmer having breakfast with Mr. Samuel Shipman. In *Flowers of the Forest,* in the role of a woman whose lover calls to her from beyond the grave, she gave a smooth but undistinguished performance of an undistinguished part. Uncertain direction in this instance was doubtless responsible for her somewhat undue repression which, as the evening ran its course, became naturally confused in the audience's mind with histrionic inertness. Her recent Juliet, widely acclaimed by the younger reviewers as the top Juliet of all time, or at least from 1608 to 1935, inclusive, seemed to one older critic happy enough on its pictorial side but otherwise largely technicalized and calculated out of emotion, and in the aggregate rather chill. We come to *Saint Joan,* her latest offering.

That our theatrical critics go to, as well as come away from, Miss Cornell's various exhibits heavily prejudiced in her favor and ready and eager to give her the benefit of every doubt has been pretty clear for some time now. What is more, it is understandable, for in recent years she has become the one actress in our theatre who, in everything that she does, shows a high pride in the theatre as an institution.

Beatrice Lillie (b. 1898?)

The old contention that the English are deficient in a sense of humor finds some support in the circumstance that they do not sufficiently appreciate their own best musical show comédienne, Beatrice Lillie. Just a year ago, in fact, they so loftily refrained from being amused by her that the show she was in went soon into the discard. It has remained for us loafers over here to size her up for her own great humorous worth and to reward her with the diamonds she so richly deserves.

The Lillie was lately on American view again in a Noël Coward revue called *Set To Music*. Inasmuch as the revue without her would have been something more than feeble, Mr. Coward should chip in handsomely on those diamonds. For it is she who took its indifferent materials and with her own genius for healthy low comedy converted them into merry and bouncing sport. When she laid hold of some such overly familiar victual as a travesty of a fashionable charity pageant, it became in her hands a fresh and rip-roaring feast. When she tackled the old Russian spy hoopdedoodle, it turned into the tastiest kind of buffoonery. When she went into the *marron* about the bored actress haughtily spurning her admirer's jewels, the while she manages to keep them securely in her fist, she made the

From *Encyclopedia of the Theatre* (New York: Knopf, 1940), pp. 236–37. Copyright renewed 1968 by Mrs. George Jean Nathan).

whole business just about as gala as even the frostiest-faced critic might have wished. She is, it seems, one of the few persons in the entertainment world who doesn't need material with which to work. She can apparently make it up as she goes along. With one dart of her eye she can spare a skit writer a dozen lines; with one little affectionate pat on her rear and one little vocal squeak she can save the management royalties on the most desired blackout sketch. The girl is, in short, pretty hot stuff.

Helen Hayes (b. 1900) and Her Rivals

She hasn't, in the popularly accepted sense, looks; she lacks that theoretically necessary star acting attribute, height; she is wholly deficient in that quality which Hollywood calls glamor; her voice, by any old histrionic standard, is a small one; in her own person she is without what the critics call authority; she has a face that looks far from being a likely mirror of either the tragic or comic mask; and she is the best actress in the American theatre.

She has breasted other hurdles. Her well-meaning if somewhat too confiding mother publishes a book[1] about her which makes her out to be a not always entirely loyal party in the matter of traffic with friends and associates and often, to boot, something of a wilful and irritating person. Her otherwise charming husband, Charles MacArthur, encourages her into fruitless quarrels with the drama critics which she, as a dutiful wife, acrimoniously pursues. She every now and then speaks out in public on subjects removed from her own province, and gets her foot into it. She lends herself to advertising a commercial product on the radio. She fervently endorses bad plays written by persons close to her as pearls of dramatic art. Her publicity photographs would make Florenz Ziegfeld turn over in his grave. And yet, in addition to being the best actress on the American stage, she is peculiarly the most romantic and—to borrow that profaned Hollywood term—glamorous.

Ladies and gentlemen, Miss Helen Hayes.

Only a very expert actress could have made out of the dubious stage materials that are this Helen Hayes the leader of her gender in her profession. It is that expert actress who has acceptably metamorphosed a diminutive woman into the royal Mary of Scotland, who has vividly turned the forty-year-old mother of two children successively into a child of eighteen, the tremulous girl-wife of Prince Albert and the obese, seventy-eight-year-old Queen Victoria, who has been now and convincingly a

From *The Entertainment of a Nation* (New York: Knopf, 1942), pp. 95–98.

Viennese *madel* and then and equally convincingly a young girl of Dixie, a
Scottish spinster, and the dreamed Cleopatra of Bernard Shaw. It is this
expert actress, more, who has with equal skill at times played everything
from Shakespeare to Molnár, from Barrie to George Abbott, from farce-
comedy to melodrama and blank verse. Her recent appearance as Viola in
Twelfth Night only again emphasizes the fact that if there is a better and
more versatile and more audience-warming actress in our theatre she must
be hiding not only her light but herself under a bushel.

It isn't, surely, that Helen Hayes has not sometimes failed. Her attempt
at Portia was far from successful and her sortie into the Irish drama of
Liam O'Flaherty was more than unfortunate for her. But it isn't that way
generally. Even when she has appeared in such dreadful rubbish as *Ladies
and Gentlemen,* which in all likelihood would have dismayed the courage
of almost any actress, she has emerged with some honor to herself. She
can usually further glorify a genuinely fine play; she can add lustre and
interest to a middling one; she can even make superficially possible, at
least while she is on the stage, a trashy one. She has proved that.

There are various things that have contributed to her rank, her box-office
popularity, and her position in the theatrical community. Although, in that
book about her, her mother, Catherine Hayes Brown, takes considerable
credit for having picked some of her earlier plays, it is pretty hard to
believe that it hasn't been Helen Hayes herself who, since that period in
her career, has exercised a generally shrewd personal judgment. Such slips
in that judgment as the aforementioned *Ladies and Gentlemen,* for instance, are understandable, since the play was written in part by Charles
MacArthur, her husband, and since their marriage has been and is well-
known to be a love-match. But aside from such mistakes, deliberate
though in all probability they have been, her knowledge of her own script
needs most often has been accurate.

She has also been wise in her selection of managements, a matter in
which certain of her rivals have not always shared her wisdom. Furthermore, the theatre being her religion, she has seen to it that the plays in
which she appears, irrespective of their critical quality, have always the
best supporting casts and the best productions possible. She doesn't allow
her audiences to be cheated, whether in New York or in any thitherward
city. She has become her own trade-mark.

There is still another reason, and one that accounts in great part for the
affectionate regard in which the public holds her. I once expressed it thus,
and I express it so again:

There is something about Helen Hayes that most of our other actresses
of her age and experience—indeed, of even more than her age and experience—completely miss. It may be an inner warm womanliness; it may be a
dramatic heart beating in a theatrical mind; it may be that little-girl spirit

that has ever been a vital asset to the world's best actresses of whatever vintage; it may be a natural and ex officio sincerity that siphons itself into her stage person; it may be any one of ten or a dozen things. That it is, above them all, a genuine acting talent we of course know. But it is these other qualities, too, that must surely and so brilliantly differentiate and distinguish her from the rank and file of director puppets, greasepaint crooners, big chest-tone purveyors and superficially competent old war-horses of all ages who often drive us out into the cold alley to warm up.

Who are Helen Hayes' chief rivals for first acting honors? The one most often mentioned in this connection is Katharine Cornell, but there are others: Lynn Fontanne, Ina Claire, Judith Anderson, Jane Cowl, Laurette Taylor, Ethel Barrymore, Grace George. Let us consider them.

Katharine Cornell, personally an infinitely more romantic figure of a woman, has many performances to her considerable credit, but most of them are much the same performance. For in the general run of things Miss Cornell offers less a characterization of a role than she offers herself. Most of the roles she plays are less different characters, whatever the dramatist and the program may seek to suggest, than they are Katharine Cornell in different situations and different costumes. Always an attractive stage figure, possessed of a fine and indubitably effective voice and with admirable carriage and poise, it nevertheless remains for the record that, whereas Helen Hayes definitely characterizes her various roles, Miss Cornell simply recharacterizes the fundamentally unvarying Katharine Cornell. It remains primarily Katharine Cornell as everything from Lucrece to Joan of Arc from Elizabeth Barrett to Juliet, from Candida and Iris March and Jennifer Dubedat to Casanova's temptress and on through the heroines of *Age of Innocence, Flowers Of the Forest, Alien Corn* and the rest. The Malay princess of *The Wingless Victory* is as surely Katharine Cornell in dark brown greasepaint and with bangles rattling from her wrists as the heroine of *The Letter* is the same Katharine Cornell in lighter makeup and minus the bangles. Miss Cornell, in short, is a first-rate actress of a single role. That one role she plays beautifully. But one role hardly constitutes a critical career.

Lynn Fontanne is a meritorious comédienne and in this category merits all the applause she regularly gets. But, although her performance in a more serious dramatic role in *There Shall Be No Night* was an excellent one, her adventures into a field removed from comedy, while not altogether negligible, have been not too happy. O'Neill's *Strange Interlude,* Chekhov's *The Sea Gull* and Dostoievski's *The Brothers Karamazov,* among others, have clearly betrayed her shortcomings. It is as a comédienne that she shines, and as a comédienne she is uniformly delightful. But there, unlike Miss Hayes, she seems for the major part to be pigeonholed.

As a comédienne, Ina Claire is and for some time has been Miss

Fontanne's superior; in this restricted field she is the most proficient actress in our theatre—her most recent performance in *The Talley Method* again attested to the fact; but, like Miss Fontanne, the same pigeonhole confines her.

Ethel Barrymore, Laurette Taylor, Grace George, and even Jane Cowl are of the somewhat older acting order. All have now and again acquitted themselves handsomely—Miss Cowl's Juliet is accepted by many, including myself, as the best we have had in the American theatre of our time— but none of them, I believe, is today entirely the actress she once was, and none of them, as we view the scene today, is Helen Hayes' transcendress. Miss Barrymore knows all the tricks of the trade and surely, as late as *Whiteoaks* and *The Corn Is Green,* has made grand use of all of them; more, she miraculously retains much of that charm that made her, in her younger days, the toast of the town. But though she periodically comes through with a gleam of the old glory, the career which started out and for some time continued to be so rich in brilliant promise has latterly and gradually seemed to fade with the evening star.

Miss Taylor, once one of the loveliest of the younger actresses of her day, suffered something of an eclipse in her later years, largely because of a misguided selection of second-rate plays, and most recently seems to have condemned herself to obvious so-called character roles. Miss Cowl has done little in the last half dozen years, and that little with none of the flash and fire of her yesterdays. Miss George is an excellent comédienne who runs Miss Claire a photo-finish for top honors, but save for a very good performance of the beset spinster in the melodrama, *Kind Lady,* has not indicated overly much in later years in the way of straight dramatic acting, or at least what is commonly understood by that term.

There remains Judith Anderson, who, to this mind, is in this day and year Helen Hayes' closest contender. Although she has got her full share of favorable critical notices, it seems to me that Miss Anderson has never quite received the general respect for her talents that is her due. In no role that she has played—and the roles have been exceeding various—has she failed to do herself justice. Her mother of Christ two seasons ago was a gently beautiful a performance as our stage has seen. Her mother of Hamlet was superior Shakespearean acting. And from the far day of *The Dove* and *Behold, the Bridegroom* down through Pirandello and O'Neill (her performance in *Strange Interlude,* incidentally, cruelly showed up the deficiencies of Lynn Fontanne's) and on through such things as *Firebird, Come Of Age* and *The Old Maid* she has suggested in each instance her unusual imagination, her very considerable resource, and her genuine playing gift. If she ever has given a really poor performance, I have not seen it—and I have seen her in all the roles she has played since first she came into our theatre.

Just what it is that has kept real recognition from her, I do not know. Perhaps her protracted excursions to Hollywood have hurt her with the theatrical public, perhaps not. But whatever it is—it may be poor management, faulty consistent build-up, or something of that sort—it has to an appreciable degree denied her the public standing which her gifts have amply demonstrated she deserves.

Nevertheless, all things considered, the sheer black and white record as it stands gives the ballot, after a deep bow to Miss Anderson, to Helen Hayes. She has come a long way from the baby actress in a Lew Fields show of thirty-odd long years ago to the Viola of *Twelfth Night*. Nor has she trodden the easy path to fame. She has taken chances and failed. She has taken even more chances and succeeded. As always, from the very first, she has flown her theatre's flag high, and proudly, and challengingly. Her artistry has triumphed over great physical handicaps; she has created beauty out of what was not beauty; she has ridden the hard and rocky road to eminence in her profession. It has been said of her by experienced men of that profession that she knows more about acting in her little finger than most of her sisters know in their whole hands. I don't know about that. But summing it all up and giving several of those sisters of hers their full due, nevertheless maybe they are right about her. They seem to be. Or at least she persuades me that they are, and that is all I happen to be here concerned with.

So, gentlemen, on your feet!

---

1. Catherine Hayes Brown, *Letters to Mary* (New York: Random House, 1940).

Maurice Evans (b. 1901)

Reading Maurice Evans' pronouncement in advance of the opening of *Henry IV (Part 1)* that he would portray Falstaff "as a gentleman and not as a bloated old drunk," one was seized with misgivings. One had the fear that he and Miss Webster, his director, had perchance lately come upon James Branch Cabell's admirable essay in defence of the plump knight that showed him in actuality to have been no mere roisterer, lecher, and tosspot but a man of many heroic qualities, a fellow of high and proud record, and a fine gallant withal. One had the further fear that they might have allowed too much research to go to their actor and director heads, that long

---

From *Encyclopedia of the Theatre* (New York: Knopf, 1940), pp. 121–23. Copyright renewed 1968 by Mrs. George Jean Nathan).

delving o' nights might have entertained them with the merit of the idea that Falstaff should be played with an alleviating recollection of the libels that were originally charged to have been visited upon him and with various palliative intimations that the old souse possessed, hidden deep within him, traces of the more or less estimable historical personages from whom he was drawn: John Oldcastle, the holy martyr Cobham, and John Fastolfe himself. And one was particularly gripped by the fear that all this, together with the modern actor and director passion for new interpretations willy-nilly—a passion that has given us everything from Ophelias who comport themselves like medieval Eva Tanguays to, in London recently, Malvolios who suggest impersonations of Ibsen by Leslie Henson—would lead to offering us a Falstaff that might conceivably be the flesh but surely neither the fowl nor good red *marinierte* herring of Shakespeare's design and intention.

Up then, went the curtain at the St. James and proved our trepidations wholly groundless. For all Evans' pranky prefatory bulletin, Falstaff relievingly remained Shakespeare's own creation. Neither scholastic nor mummer freakishness had been permitted to work its vain whim upon him, and in the actor's shrewd and comprehending hands he lurched over the footlights not only for the every last, true ounce of his classic self but with an amiable clarity and beaming self-criticism that many actors who previously have battened on him have denied him. Under the Webster guidance, the brilliance of Evans in the role proceeded not from an obvious, periodic emphasis of the wisdom, the fundamental wit, the pervading humanity, and the healthy regard for self-interest, self-comfort and self-satisfaction that are imbedded in the character of the tun-bellied sot, but from the gradual internal establishment of those qualities and their confluence with the vapors of sack and rolling of ribald guts. The portrait was hardly that of gentleman rather than that of a venerable stew, but it may at least be said for Evans' publicity preamble that it was what Shakespeare undoubtedly meant it to be: the portrait of one who was once a gentleman cajolingly vindicating his decline from grace with a boozy, contemptuous, and convincing hedonistic philosophy. It is to Evans' credit, and to Miss Webster's, that they didn't permit their portrait to go any farther than that. For foolishly to make this Falstaff a gentleman of the moment would even more foolishly be to make at least one of the indubitable gentlemen who surrounded him and mocked him as a bounder. Which, in turn, would be to make the whole thing burlesque.

It is a double pleasure to American critics to see Evans, with his continuing excellent performances, reap from them his increasingly condign rewards. It is a double pleasure, I say, because aside from his professional merits, he has conducted himself while amongst us with a decency, modesty, reserve, affection, and good-feeling indicated in the instance of very few English actors who come over here. Too many of these others, talented though they are, arrive with an ill-concealed condescension (God alone being able to figure out how come), publicly play and personally conduct themselves as if they were doing the United States an unheard-of favor, and duly depart jingling our gold in their jeans the while they sniffishly derogate the theatre and the audiences that magnanimously gave it to them. Evans isn't any such mackerel. He is giving the American theatre the best that is in him; he shows frankly that he is tickled to death that the American theatre likes him; and we gladly give him back what he well deserves.

John Gielgud (b. 1904)

The so-called intellectual actors who assay Hamlet customarily make the humorous error of confusing imperturbation with intelligence. It seems to be their conviction that they can best persuade their audiences of their intelligence in the handling of the role by playing it in an emotionally *piano* manner, elaborately abjuring any show of passion and sedulously repressing any manifestations of physical excitement. In other words, they hope to heighten the effect of intellectuality by the simple process of playing down all emotionalism. That intelligence and intellectuality, save in the case of men slightly unsure of themselves who ceremoniously take refuge inside their stuffed shirts, often expand themselves in a white and dazzling heat, they are seemingly, being posturers and blockheads, unaware.

John Gielgud, one of the several darlings of the London theatre public, has recently shown us his particular idea of the Dane. His idea, it turns out, is a Hamlet for the most part so factitiously "intellectualized" out of its dramatic flame and fire and so full of a variety of interpretations (all as intellectual as hell) that Hamlet seems to be a completely different character at intervals of about every twenty minutes.* It is as if Fregoli were giving, one after the other, a series of imitations of half dozen or more actors who have variously played the role. In addition, Gielgud's delicate mannerisms and fastidious graces gave the exhibit the air of a Noël Coward drawing-room version of the tragedy. Along toward ten

From *The Morning After the First Night* (New York: Knopf, 1938), pp. 92–93. Copyright renewed 1965 by Mrs. George Jean Nathan).

*"I fear I am an inveterate ham and shall never be the conscientious interpreter of Shakespeare that I should like to be."—John Gielgud, in "John Gielgud's Hamlet, A Record of Performance," by Rosamond Gilder.—Nathan's note.

o'clock I could not resist the feeling that at any moment his Hamlet might be expected petulantly to stamp his foot, smash a vase and thereupon to sit furiously down and play the piano. There can be little fault found with his clear-voiced recital of the role, but as to his acting of it, that is a different matter. His weakness and treble vacillation are not Hamlet's but his own.

Profiles of Playwrights

August Strindberg (1849–1912)

It seems to be the opinion of some of my colleagues that the play[1], written in 1887, has dated—the implication being that drama in the aggregate has made tremendous advances in the intervening years. If it has, they have apparently been going to theatres that do not send me [tickets for] reviewing-seats or have been reading plays in Arabic, Lettish and Punjabi, languages beyond my grasp. No one will of course deny that many admirable plays have been written since Strindberg's time, but if there has been a better one of its kind since *The Father,* the aforesaid colleagues must have dreamed it up in their sleep. . . . In its almost every detail—psychological, psychopathic, dialogic, dramaturgical (I will not lengthen the list; it already sounds like a Gilbert and Sullivan lyric) *The Father* remains more modern than any of the numerous later ones it inspired; and not only more modern, but in all respects infinitely superior. When anyone says it has dated he probably means to say less that it has dated as a drama than that it has dated in a Broadway theatrical sense, which makes no decent critical sense. . . .

What makes *The Father* appear old-fashioned to the reviewers in question, to give them the benefit of the doubt, is doubtless not so much the play itself as the stage direction and performance, which are of a kind that would make something of [Jean Giraudoux's] *The Mad Woman of Chaillot* seem as out-of-date, stale and tedious as [Bulwer Lytton's] *The Lady of Lyons.* If anyone can think of an actor less suited than Raymond Massey to the intensely emotional role of the husband driven to insanity by his wife's taunts as to the paternity of their daughter, it must be Ivor Novello or Zero Mostel.

Mr. Massey's claim to acceptable acting has rested largely on his portrayal of the Emancipator in Robert Sherwood's *Abe Lincoln in Illinois.* Since not even a bad actor has failed in the role of Lincoln from the remote days of Hal Reid melodrama to Drinkwater and beyond and since the main requirements for an impressive interpretation of the role seem to be simply an actor's lanky height, an awkward gait, a face with little or no change in

From *The Theatre Book of the Year 1949–50* (New York: Knopf, 1950), pp. 95–100.

expression, and a dry, even voice, the range of Mr. Massey's art may be suspected. Venturing to play Strindberg's tortured protagonist, he accordingly falls back upon such a repertoire of grimaces, chokings, sputterings, howls and moans that the effect is of the late Willie Howard acting all the roles in Gorki's *The Lower Depths* at one and the same time.

As the wife bent on her mate's destruction, Mady Christians is still playing *I Remember Grandma,* albeit with alternating overtones of Theda Bara and Mae West. . . .

John D. Seymour,[2] on the other hand, has seemingly concluded with some positiveness that the doctor was written by Pinero as the companion role to Cayley Drummie in *The Second Mrs. Tanqueray,* despite the fact that he indulges in such bourgeois pronunciations as "histry," "captin," and "minerology." Only the novice Grace Kelly, convincing as the daughter, relieves the stage from the air of a minor hinterland stock company on one of its off days.

To conclude the obituary, the direction is additionally of a kind that throws the two principal characters up against each other's teeth in the scenes of fierce challenge and defiance and that, when the distraught husband is called upon to grab up and heave a lamp at his spouse in an abutting room, it causes him to aim it with cautious economy into the arms of a convenient stagehand who thereupon, while the spouse lets out a yell, in the interests of realism obligingly rattles a crashbox full of glass hazelnuts.

The Strindberg influence hitherto mentioned is no more clearly to be perceived than in the instance of the central woman characters in many of our later plays. Without any trace of the master's mind and talent, their creators, however, have succeeded only in presenting us with mental diseases in skirts minus any intelligible diagnosis, the consequence being a stage strewn with females. or heroines as the misnomer goes, who, having none of Strindberg's genius in their composition, have simply contaminated it with their arbitrary viruses. But Strindberg or no Strindberg, we seem to have a drama today often either intentionally or unintentionally so schizophrenicly misogynous[3] that one is sometimes tempted to go to a pig slaughterhouse for sentimental relief. In all the sixty-odd plays of the previous theatrical season, for example, there were three and only three heroines that any man with an educated taste in women would for a moment have considered worth his personal attention and interest. . . . The rest were largely the sort that the above-mentioned connoisseur would in real life have run from as from the pox, or in even the better cases would not have invited out to so much as a dish of Boston scrod. Though it is true that the exceptional roles were played by attractive and appealing actresses, I am not, I hope, one to confuse the player with the part, even though the job may sometimes be a bit difficult. It is character I am thinking of, and it is the heroine characters I have in mind when I make the sweeping statement, which will probably bring in the usual number of letters arguing that it is difference in tastes that makes horse races, all of which communications I shall, as heretofore, turn over for reply to my friends among the sports writers.

The newspapers and magazines have lately been printing an advertisement of a novel[4] by Philip Van Doren Stern in which the author's description of his heroine is quoted as follows:

> I remember Lola with all my senses. I see her, sun-dappled and shimmering, as she emerges from our secret forest pool; I recall the fresh, clean-washed odor of her skin; I taste once more her soft, sweet, clinging mouth; I hear the deep-throated sound of her laughter as she throws back her head and lets her long hair stream out in the mountain wind; I feel her warm, supple body close to me—and my arms long to hold her again. She was glorious. When she walked into a room even where she was unknown, men and women stopped talking to look at her. She did not even have to speak to exert her magnetism. She radiated it as naturally as a candle sends out light and heat.

When I speak of heroines, I obviously do not mean any such technicolor nonesuch who, if she ever possibly existed, even in the person of Lola Montez, outside the romantic fevers of moron kings, movie scenario writers, and novelists with an eye to *Forever Amber* profits, would have bored the pants back onto any man with an ounce of experience, humor, and common sense. The kind of heroine I refer to is the womanly simple, easily intelligent, smilingly comprehending, and physically passable girl of reasonable years with some appeal to the imagination, with a potential gift for companionship, and with at least a share of serenity, fancy, humility, and her own teeth. But that kind, in any shape or color, was as scarce in the last season's drama as literate fancy, good writing, and other such desirable qualities, and in its stead we got so-called heroines who were just about as desirable in turn as so many uncooked fish.

Please do not gather from this that I am arguing for a return of the nonsensically romantic heroines of the plays of other generations, though I confess that even they were a deal more acceptable than the dressed-up gallstones that so often pass for heroines in these theatrical years. The old-time princesses bathed in gelatine moonlight and babbled their undying love into the ears of English actors with all the reciprocal ardor of kippers; the dear little slaveys with the souls of angels and the pride of duchesses, the abused girls who remained pure and innocent despite pasts that stretched from the Boar's Head inn to Damascus—such and their sisters may have induced impolite chuckles in many of us. But in their unintentional absurdity they were still at bottom the stuff that heroines are made of and infinitely more appetizing than the clinical females we are nowadays asked to swallow as tonics. Look over last season's plays and get a whiff of them: the self-sanctified cheaters, the idealistic crackpots, the saintly alcoholics, the blonde social significancers, the psychopathic icebergs, the philosophical trollops, and the patient, plodding, and noble wives who haven't washed their hair for a month. Not to mention the sophisticated hard-bitten divorcées stylishly mouthing fourth-rate Oscar Wilde, the visionary French bobby-soxers sacrificing their virtue to intellectual movie actors, the Hollywood round-heels agonized by their husbands' infidelities, the money-digging tramps presented as lovable characters on the score of their wise-cracking talents, and all the dismal, drivelling, and dreary rest.

Even most of the musicals presently give us heroines with all the charm of corned beef. Except for the gentle, inarticulately loyal and delicately imagined Tonkinese girl in *South Pacific*, who figures in a minor role at that, there has not been a single heroine with any more claim on the sentimental imagination than a typhoid carrier, and if the musical shows do not give us heroines to make us sigh and blubber into our beer where are we going to hope to find them? But instead of providing us with creatures wrapped in moonbeams and roses they banish the springtime dream with a procession of wenches who in actual life would make a man yell for the police. One show offers us a heroine with such a nasty temper and disposition as would have scared the life out of Wedekind. Another has a heroine who badgers her husband for numberless years and, in final atonement, breaks into a repentant song with such vehemence that the performance is interrupted by the brightening barking of mutts out on the street. Yet another is supposed to enchant our imaginations with a heroine so dumb that it is evidently her sole emotion to wear her bridal dress in Central Park, and another still asks us to accept as a heroine, though admirably acted, a twangy Arkansas yodel whose mother was evidently alarmed in childbirth by Eva Tanguay.

We do not ask for the impossible. All we ask for, in both plays and musicals, are heroines who will have some of the attributes and qualities of heroines and not those generally associated in our minds with female revivalists, female politicians, female bass singers and, unjustly, female dogs.

---

1. *The Father,* next to *Miss Julie* (1888), Strindberg's best known play. Nathan attended the New York opening at the Cort Theatre on 16 November 1949. The play ran for sixty-nine consecutive performances. Its cast included, besides Raymond Massey as Captain Adolf, the daughter, Grace Kelly (1929–1982), who in 1956 would become the Princes of Monaco.

2. In *The Father* Seymour played the role of Dr. Oestermark.

3. "Misogynous, to be sure," writes Harry Carlson, ed. *Strindberg: Five Plays* (Berkeley: University of California Press, 1983, p. 2), "but also high priest and prophet of the Eternal Feminine." Still, most of Strindberg's plays derogate women and portray men as women's victims, as is Captain Adolf in *The Father.* Some of Strindberg's women suffer ambivalent love/hate feelings, as does Miss Julie, who says she hates men "most of the time. But sometimes, when the weakness comes, when passion burns—Oh, God, will the fire never die out?"

4. *Lola* (New York, Rinehart, 1949).

George Bernard Shaw (1856–1950)

"Shaw will live for the excellence and magnetism of his love scenes," says a character (Nathan's mouthpiece) in Nathan's only novel, *Monks Are Monks* (1929). The mouthpiece goes on to say: "The plays of Shaw, all of them, age badly. The one and only thing that today seems fresh and vital about them and that will probably still seem fresh and vital in future years is their love element, that is, their sentimental passages and their love scenes. I begin to believe that Shaw's plays will live, if at all, for just two reasons: first, purely as curiosities of the Twentieth Century dialectic drama, much as the plays of, say, Alfred de Vigny, equally regardless of lasting merit, persist as curiosities of Nineteenth Century romantic drama, as those of Steele or Rowe persist as curiosities of Eighteenth Century machinal drama, or as those of some writer like Chapman persist as curiosities of Seventeenth Century historical; and secondly, and much more likely, for the enduring excellence and fine magnetism of their love scenes. As plays, most of them will be as dead as door-nails, but as curios and symbols of a specific period they may conceivably remain as piquant as so many horsehair sofas, cigar-store Indians and Nathaniel P. Willis. Only their sentimental scenes will remain ever-green, and if they are revived for our grandchildren, save as dusty freaks, it will be their senti-mental scenes and their sentimental scenes alone that will still bequeath a semblance of life to them.

"Shaw would doubtless be disgusted to conceive of himself as being remembered by future generations not as a thinker and an idea-fountain but as a lover, yet that is the way I feel pretty sure he will be remembered. For the truth is that as thinker, at least so far as the drama is concerned, he doesn't grade so very much higher than his pet, Brieux, while as a lover, or at least as a writer of tremulant *violinata* dramatic scenes, he stands head and shoulders above every other Anglo-Saxon writing plays in our time. Shaw is the great lover in modern Anglo-Saxon dramatic literature. And long after his plays have been smiled out of countenance for the staleness and platitudinousness of their philosophical japery, their sentimental pas-sages will still retain the power to charm and move and pleasurably enrapture theatre audiences.

"Already this early the elaborate medical strictures of *The Doctor's Dilemma* have taken on a cobwebbed air and ring excessively flat. But the sentimental passages of the play are as fascinating and valid as they were twenty years ago. Shaw, the lover, the sentimentalist, lives where Shaw, the jester, the transient bubble-pricker, lies on the theatrical death-bed. It is the Shaw of Dubedat and Mrs. Dubedat in their enchanted moments,

From *Monks Are Monks* (New York: Knopf, 1929), pp. 134–41.

not the Shaw of Cullen, Ridgeon, Walpole and Bonington in their sardonic moments, who holds the interest of latter-day audiences. It is Shaw speaking through the mouth of the dying Louis, his wife's arms holding him tenderly close, that audiences remember, not the Shaw of ancient medical gags and pathological wheezes. 'Then you must always wear beautiful dresses and splendid magic jewels. Think of all the wonderful pictures I shall never paint. . . . Well, you must be transfigured with all the beauty of those pictures. Men must get such dreams from seeing you as they never could get from any daubing with paints and brushes. Painters must paint you as they never painted any mortal woman before. There must be a great tradition of beauty, a great atmosphere of wonder and romance. That is what men must always think of when they think of me. That is the sort of immortality I want. There are lots of things you don't understand that every woman in the street understands, but you can understand that and do it as nobody else can. Promise me that immortality. Promise me you will not make a little hell of crêpe and crying and undertaker's horrors and withering flowers and all that vulgar rubbish . . . I'm in Heaven, immortal in the heart of my beautiful Jennifer!'

"And what continues similarly to linger in the memory in the instance of the other Shaw plays? Is it the comic opera paradoxes of *Captain Brassbound's Conversion* or such passages as Brassbound's proposal of marriage to Cicely—and the end with Cicely in strange ecstasy crying, 'Oh farewell. With my heart's deepest feeling, farewell, farewell,' and Brassbound, 'With my heart's noblest honor and triumph farewell!' Above the labored irony of *The Devil's Disciple* is not the element in the play that persists in the recollection the charming sentimental counterpoint of Judith and Richard, in particular that in the third act? It is pretty well agreed by all critics, even those given to a superior admiration of Shaw's satirical, humorous and social purgative gifts, that the particular play of his which in all likelihood has about it the greatest promise of enduring life is *Candida*—and *Candida* is surely chiefly noteworthy for the depth and beauty of its sentiment. If there is a finer sentimental play in the whole range of modern drama, its name is a stranger to me. Consider, for example, the rich tenderness of such speeches as Morell's 'You are my wife, my mother, my sisters; you are the sum of all loving care to me,' and Candida's to Marchbanks at the play's conclusion, the one beginning, 'Now I want you to look at this boy here—my boy—spoiled from his cradle.' Or Morell's, spoken with proud humility, 'I have nothing to offer you but my strength for your defence, my honesty of purpose for your surety, my ability and industry for your livelihood, and my authority and position for your dignity. That is all it becomes a man to offer a woman.' Or Candida's, 'And you, Eugene? What do you offer?'—with the poet's passionate,, 'My weakness! My desolation! My heart's need!' There's writing for you! . . . And what of Caesar's magnificent parting from Cleopatra with its, 'Come, Cleopatra: Forgive me and bid me farewell, and I will send you a man. Roman from head to heel and Roman of the noblest; not old and ripe for the knife, not lean in the arms and cold in the heart, not hiding a bald head under his conqueror's laurels, not stooped with the weight of the world on his shoulders, but brisk and fresh, strong and young, hoping in the morning, fighting in the day, and revelling in the evening. Will you take such an one in exchange for Caesar?' And then the palpitating little one's 'His name, his name?', and Caesar's quiet, 'Shall it be Mark Antony?' Or of Julia in *The Philanderer* and her 'I am too miserable to argue—to think. I only know that I love you'? Or of Bashville's speeches to Lydia? What will be left in days to come—what, indeed, is left now—of such a play as, say, *Mrs. Warren's Profession* save the madam's alcoholic 'story of her life'?

"It is a poor critic who can't see under the top layers of the superficial Shavian bellicosity and detect there the really great sentimentalist, a sentimentalist of purest dye yet blessed with the faculty of making commonplace sentiment take on an air of dignity and poetry and beauty. That Shaw is, for all his pretence to the contrary, a sentimental man at heart is easily to be discovered from even a cursory study of his writings. This pretence of his is successful in fooling only such persons as take too seriously such of his obviously posturing and forced animadversions on the discomforts of the divine passion as Tanner's, 'I got up a love affair with her, and we met one night in the garden and walked about very uncomfortably with our arms around one another,' etc., and the *Back to Methuselah* maiden's reprise, 'Do you suppose I can spend centuries . . . lying about with your arms round me, which is really neither comfortable nor convenient'—or the same character's 'We used to think it would be nice to sleep in one another's arms, but we never could go to sleep because our weight stopped our circulations just above the elbows.' But these nose-fingerings are not the man, for the man himself is a romantic of romantics in his soul and as greatly given to gyneolatry and a faith in Strephon and Chloe, for all his attempt to conceal the fact, as any James M. Barrie or A. A. Milne. No man,' he says through Tanner, 'is a match for a woman, except with a poker and a pair of hob-nailed boots. Not always even then.' One cannot, true enough, always justly judge and appraise the men behind the dramatist from the speeches he puts into the mouths of his male characters, for he often uses those characters to hide his ingrained attitude and point of view and to give a show in which he makes himself appear in other than his true philosophical and personal light. But one can generally pretty well judge the man behind the playwright from the speeches he puts into the mouths of his woman characters, for then he is more greatly off guard and betrays himself. It is significant to note, in this regard, the speeches that Shaw gives to his women. What his women say so *amorosamente,* so tenderly, so feelingly and so convincingly is what he himself thinketh in his heart. And the poet that lies in that heart is the Shaw that will live long after the philosophical gag-man that lies in his head will have gone to his Maker."

Oscar Wilde (1854–1900)

I wish that some appropriate person would investigate and report to me why the epigram is so generally viewed as the arch-criminal of literature. For a reason that I have never been able to make out, even the best and most intelligent epigram is looked down on as being frivolous, flippant, and all too easy. Though it may be quoted for years on end and as wise as it is witty, it is still regarded as a black sheep, unworthy of the respect of any mentality duly appreciative of such more copious literary forms as the *Congressional Record* and the cerebral ensembles of Walter B. Pitkin.

The revival of *Lady Windermere's Fan* brings up the matter anew. As Shaw observed in his review of another of Wilde's plays, "He has the property of making his critics dull. They laugh angrily at his epigrams, like a child who is coaxed into being amused in the very act of setting up a yell of rage and agony. They protest that the trick is obvious, and that such epigrams can be turned out by the score by anyone lightminded enough to condescend to such frivolity. As far as I can ascertain, I am the only person in London who cannot sit down and write an Oscar Wilde play at will. The fact that his plays, though apparently lucrative, remain unique under these circumstances says much for the self-denial of our scribes." That was written more than fifty years ago and it is even truer today than it was then. Nor is it familiarity with the epigrams that has bred contempt; the contempt would be there even were they fresh out of the bottle. Nor, furthermore, is the contempt longer confined to the critics, who usually are blamed for everything; often justly. The attitude is pretty general, like that toward the epigram's illegitimate cousin, the pun, which, however amusing, is similarly always good for a lofty and disgusted grunt.

Again, one speculates, why? Take at random a few Wilde samples:

"The truths of metaphysics are the truths of masks." It took Brieux a whole two and a half hour play *(La Foi)* to say much the same thing, and not half so sharply.

"The history of woman is the history of the worst form of tyranny the world has ever known: the tyranny of the weak over the strong. It is the

---

From *The Theatre Book of the Year, 1946–47* (New York: Knopf, 1947), pp. 115-18.

only tyranny that lasts." The major part of the great Strindberg's dramatic canon was devoted to proving just that.

"Cynicism is merely the art of seeing things as they are instead of as they ought to be." Here, in little, is, among other things, a critical appraisal of much of the classic Russian drama.[1]

"The tragedy of old age is not that one is old but that one is young." Bataille consumed almost three hours to say the same thing in his admired *L'Homme à la Rose*.

"Ideals are dangerous things. Realities are better. They wound, but they are better." Yet Ibsen's *Brand,* Echegaray's *Folly or Saintliness,* Hartleben's *Rose Monday,* and many other such dramas enuciating the idea at great length are highly esteemed.

Along with the epigram, Wilde's sincerity, or rather alleged lack of it, is another favorite disparagement on the part of his critics. When they speak of sincerity, they obviously speak of it according to their own personal standards, not Oscar's. Oscar, for all his occasional self-mockery, was perfectly sincere in following his own lights, peculiarly colored though they were. When at odd times he was guilty of what seemed to be insincerity, it was only obliquely to ridicule the dull sincerity of others. The man's whole life, save in one or two instances, was a testimonial to his sincerity, such as it was. But since wit is so often regarded by the witless as a mark of insincerity—as Shaw, whose sincerity has been raised to a point of obstreperousness, has also discovered to his amusement—Oscar has been tagged with the label.

In what he said, Wilde was for the most part absolutely honest, even though his honesty was difficult of appreciation by men philosophically and emotionally alien to his point of view. In what he did, except in a couple of theatrical instances, he was equally honest; and one of the exceptions concerns *Lady Windermere's Fan*. In that case he dishonestly allowed himself to be influenced commercially in changing his play, though the meritorious critic, P. P. Howe, thinks otherwise and allows it was Wilde's utter disinterest in so-called "good" women that made it all a matter of indifference to him. This, however, seems to be straining a point for the defense. As originally written the important scene read as follows: Windermere *(calling after Lady W.)* "Margaret! Margaret! *(A pause)* My God! What shall I do? I dare not tell her what this woman is. The shame would kill her. . . ." To make things safer at the box-office, the line was altered to "My God! What shall I do? I dare not tell her that this woman is—her *Mother!*" The change was a concession to cautiously cheap, popular playwriting, and Wilde should have been ashamed of himself. (The present revival properly goes back to the line as first written.) His critics are further in the habit of waxing sarcastic over the fabricated nature of his plots. But, as Howe points out, Wilde is at one with Mr. Bayes of *The*

Rehearsal in saying, "What the devil is a plot good for but to bring in fine things?" The plot of *Lady Windermere's Fan,* for just one example, is little more than Bertha M. Clay[2] dressed in silk. But what matter? The plots of some of the best plays in dramatic history are even worse.

It was not plot that interested Wilde, or that should interest any critic not given to an admiration of detective fiction and other such juvenile diversions. It was style and at style, as a decoration, he excelled. "In all the unimportant matters," he declared without paradox, "sincerity, not style, is the essential." And his style in his dramatic time was an unrivaled as it is in ours. His sense of word and phrase and sentence is almost perfect. "Words," he said, "have not merely music as sweet as that of viol and lute, color as rich and vivid as any that makes lovely for us the canvas of the Venetian[3] or the Spaniard,[4] and plastic form no less sure and certain than that which reveals itself in marble or in bronze, but thought and passion and spirituality are theirs also—are theirs, indeed, alone."

In short, go listen to *Lady Windermere.* Creak sometimes in its rococo tracks as it may, it is still a toothsome play of escape—escape from the flat, humdrum, untutored and inanimate writing of so many of the plays we encounter today.

---

1. For example, Chekhov's *Uncle Vanya* (1899)
2. Bertha M. Clay, pen name of the English novelist Charlotte Braeme (1836–1884)
3. For example, Tintoretto (1518–1594)
4. For example, Goya (1746–1828)

James M. Barrie (1860–1937)

The chronic sentimentality of James Matthew Barrie finds its most brilliant illustration in the play called *What Every Woman Knows.* In the character of Maggie Wylie, Barrie presents his idea of a shrewd, discerning and canny little Scot female who, by a sedulous exercise of her qualities of understanding, observation and wit, manages to hold her husband after a long, hard battle not only with a woman rival but with the obtuse fellow himself. Dodge after dodge, wile after wile, tear after tear this Maggie is brought of apparent necessity to indulge in that the man of her heart may not wander from her. Time and again the odds seem against her, odds too heavy for her to surmount. And on each occasion Barrie comes to her rescue with some sort of impassionable device. What he contrives in sum to present, accordingly, is a character who is ever mindful that she is a

From *Art of the Night* (New York: Knopf, 1928), pp. 153–55. Copyright renewed 1955 by George Jean Nathan.

stage actress and who, for all her alleged and heavily insisted upon canniness, is very little the shrewd woman out of life and actuality that Barrie would have us believe her to be. There was a simple and very natural and most efficacious way for Maggie Wylie to hold her husband, and that way was to have a baby. But that would have been the way of a real Maggie Wylie, and Barrie was, as always, concerned only with a stage character.

The sentimentality of Barrie is, of course, an old story. With great skill, he permits nothing to stand in the way of it—not life, not reality, none of the hard truths of the world. His characters are for the most part marionettes with human hearts, but with heads filled only with sawdust and good theatrical dialogue. His talent consists in making an audience centre its entire attention upon these arbitrarily inserted hearts and thus making it unconscious of the complete absence of rationality in the characters. The technique of such a dramatist as Shaw is just the opposite; he cleverly distracts attention from his characters' lack of emotion, and so avoids commercial theatrical disaster, by making an audience centre its entire attention upon what the characters are thinking. Barrie's success as a popular playwright is due to his cunning in presenting sentimentality in relatively new stage terms. He lays hold of ancient sugars and molds them into novel and pretty candies. It is this trick that deceives all his audiences and most of his critics. They mistake for sound sentiment what is merely a statement of commonplace theatrical sentiment in an ingeniously fresh theatrical manner.

Edmond Rostand (1864–1918) and Arthur Schnitzler (1862–1931)

La Dernière Comédie de Don Rostand—I allude, obviously enough, to *La Dernière Nuit de Don Juan,*[1] a play profoundly born, profoundly wise, and profoundly beautiful. Three times in nine months I have read it, and three times, intoxicated by its beauty, I have found myself periodically raising my eyes from the manuscript and pausing to address to myself a glowing critical soliloquy. For here are the laughter and tears of genius woven into a great happy ache—a super-Schnitzlerian[2] tapestry shot through with the brilliant threads of fancy, poetry and sardonic pathos. For here are literature and drama inextricably intertwined: a masterpiece of the modern theatre.

Like fine drama of its kind ever, there is something remote about the play. You make to touch it with your fingers, and it is not there. It is a

From *The World in Falseface* (New York: Knopf, 1923), pp. 113–17. Copyright renewed 1950 by George Jean Nathan.

mood on the wind, springtime melting into summer and fading into autumn in the span of a moment. From the time its Don Juan re-climbs the steps of Hell to enjoy his respite in the world of women—repeating with each upward step the name of Ninon . . . Laura . . . Armande . . . Jeanne—to the time the devil metes out to him his ironic punishment as the reincarnation of Punchinello in a traveling marionette show—from beginning to end it is as present, and yet as elusive, as the memory of a forgotten tune. Its episodes are a succession of dramatic jewels.

Where Molière's *Le Festin de Pierre* ends, Rostand's work begins. (The prologue has been reconstructed from the author's notes, and is only an outline.) The play carries its central character through scene after scene of wit, charm and tender derisory philosophy. Beside it, all the Don Juan plays[3] ever written, from Zamora's to Grabbe's, and from Molière's to Tellez's and those of the modern continental comedy school of Hans Otto, von Schmitz and Thaddeus Rittner, take on a varying sense of imaginative pallor. Rostand's is an infinitely impudent, infinitely dreamful, infinitely delicate Don Juan."I am of another essence than your Doctor Faust[4] who wished nothing better than a litte German girl," he boasts;—"A town of love has watched my natal day; my dying day should see a town of love. Only one epitaph is fitting for Don Juan: "He was born at Seville and died at Venice!" he dreams;—"I have traveled everywhere, like a fairy tale," and his words are fragile and far away . . . Rostand's Don Juan is at once a wit, a philosopher and a child. "One is burned when one has said 'I love you.'" he reminds Punch. "Then how is it done?" asks Punch. "By nudging her? By making eyes?" "That is too stupid; 'tis too carp-like," replies Don Juan. "How should I look?" then Punch. "Like a chasm," replies Don Juan.

Here is Rostand's indomitable Aiglon,[5] grown mature, and off the field of Mars and in the court of Venus: "I am a monster with a soul, a wild-beast archangel, who has preserved, in his fall, his wing." Here is Rostand's Chantecler[6] in doublet and hose: "I am the nostalgia of all. There is no work—despite your hissing, oh ancient adder—no virtue, no science and no faith which does not regret it is not I." "What," asks the devil, "will remain of that?" And Rostand's Cyrano with the small nose answers, "That which remains of Alexander's ashes, and knows that it was Alexander!"

For sheer poetic loveliness there are a half dozen scenes in the play that are not surpassed in modern dramatic literature. Of these all, most noteworthy perhaps is the scene wherein the devil tears into as many small pieces the list of Don Juan's one thousand and three conquests and sends them, like snow, out upon the moonlit bosom of the Adriatic, there each suddenly to be transformed into a gondola bearing the spirit of the woman whose name was written thereon. I say most noteworthy, and promptly doubt my words. For even finer is the ensuing scene wherein the thousand

shadows of silver blue mount silently the stairway to challenge and tor-
ment Don Juan's memory of them—he cannot penetrate their masks, their
masks of what passed for love, and blindly, desperately, he searches face
upon face—it is . . . it is . . . it is—to the curtain fall. And finer, more
beautifully imagined still, are the scenes wherein the shadows slowly,
derisively, yet tenderly, strip Don Juan of his amorous gasconade and
wherein Don Juan, at the devil's bidding, collects in a frail chalice the
frozen tear-drop that each shadow wears, like a jewel, in the corner of her
mask—tears the devil, peering through an enormous lens, then ironically
analyses.

The life of the theatre lies in plays like this. For one such, a thousand
deadly evenings are gladly endurable. Such episodes as that of the secret
tear, the only one the devil may not touch, the tear of pity for Don Juan;
such profound mockery as the paint and canvas hell to which the still
strutting Don Juan is in the end consigned; such humour as lies in Don
Juan's pathetic serenity before the cavalcade of his shadow loves, and such
poetry as lies in the one white fragment of the torn list—these are the stuff
of a glorified and imperishable theatre.

---

1. *The Last Night of Don Juan* was published posthumously in 1921. Rostand remains
better known for his play *Cyrano de Bergerac* (1897).

2. Pertaining to Arthur Schnitzler (1862–1931), Viennese playwright; author of *Anatol*
(1898), among several other plays dealing with sophisticated urban marriage.

3. Don Juan, the Spanish playboy, has provided the theme of scores of plays, novels, and
poems. Best known are Lord Byron's *Don Juan* (1819–24) and George Bernard Shaw's "Don
Juan in Hell" scene in *Man and Superman* (1905). Nathan refers to Molière's *Dom Juan ou
Le Festin de Pierre* (1665). Nathan also alludes to a number of other, less well-known, writers
including Antonio de Zamora (1664?–1728?), author of *El Tenorio* (1714): Christian Grabbe
(1801–1836), author of *Don Juan und Faust* (1829); and Gabriel Tellez (1570?–1648?), author
of *El Burlador* [Playboy] *de Sevilla* (1620).

4. Dr. Faustus, in return for unholy wish-fulfillments, sells his soul to the Devil in the
poetic drama *Faust, Part I* (1805) and *Part II* (1832) by Johann Wolfgang von Goethe (1749–
1832). The "little German girl" was Gretchen (Margaret).

5. Aiglon (Eaglet) was the nickname of Napoleon Bonaparte's son, about whom Rostand
wrote the six-act play *L'Aiglon* (1900). In 1904 Sarah Bernhardt played the role of the young
man.

6. Chantecler is the protagonist in Rostand's allegorical play *Chantecler* (1910).

Luigi Pirandello (1867–1936)

Pirandello came into the modern Italian drama at a time when it was
suffering, in one direction, from an infection of French boulevard comedy

---

From *The Intimate Notebooks of George Jean Nathan* (New York: Knopf, 1932), pp. 263–
65.

anemia and, in the other, from an attempt to imitate Vesuvius in a constant state of eruption. At one end there were slightly more psychologized parrotings of the connubial and adulterous comedies of the Paris boudoir school and, at the other, dramas so turbulent with emotionalism that the Italian beaux had to run out constantly and revive their fair companions with lily cups full of aromatic spirits of ammonia. Into this situation stalked the eminent Luigi of Girgenti, fingering his nose not only at all these dull Gallic paraphrases and equally dull emotional explosions, but also at all the intermittent futuristic monkeyshines and so-called grotesques with which the younger crowd of playwrights were absurdly assaying to butter their little reputations.

Into a drama that was approximately as satisfactory as finding out about the weather from an elevator boy, came Pirandello with a new and valuable technique, a head that buzzed with ideas on subjects other than those that materialize solely in conjunction with chaises-longues and mattresses, and a skill in dramatic dialectic that had not been matched in his day. For a while, audiences did not know what to make of him. Long used to easily assimilable theatre spectacles wherein sculptors, finding that their beloveds had betrayed them, smashed the statues of the latter to smithereens; wherein painters, upon learning similar lamentable tidings, slashed their masterpieces on the eve of being awarded the grand prix; and wherein peasant girls murdered the rich padrones responsible for their illegitimate birth—all to the accompaniment of much telling of beads and kneelings before the shrine of the Virgin—these audiences had a time of it trying to figure out what Pirandello was up to. In his plays, the characters didn't ominously finger daggers, didn't passionately yell themselves hoarse at second act curtains, didn't choke one another half to death in the name of love, and didn't spill gallons of tears and every few minutes dolefully exclaim, "Oh, Mother of Sorrows, I know you are listening to me even though I speak to you like a poor woman!" Instead, they simply stood around quietly, meditatively stroking their chins and informing each other politely that no one really knew what he was talking about.

Naturally enough, what with the absence of daggers, demolished statues and roadside shrines, the Italian audiences were puzzled, and not only puzzled but disgruntled. What kind of drama was this? they wished to know. Go to a theatre and sit around for three hours while a lot of characters, without choking anybody even once, endlessly discussed one another's inability to think clearly and accurately, to distinguish between the real and the unreal, or even to recognize one's own mother-in-law unless she carried a sandwich-board announcing her identity—not on your life! It was all right to be asked, "Who was that lady I saw you with last night?" and to reply, "That was no lady, that was my wife." But to hear the question, "Who was that lady I saw you with last night?" and get the reply, "That was no lady, that was the metaphysical illusion of a woman who, while not a lady, was neither a wife but only a psychical simulacrum of a wife-lady"—that was enough promptly to boost business in the café next door.

It took some years, as I have said, for such theatre audiences to get the hang of Pirandello. But, once they got the hang, they began to see in him the most notable personage that their drama had produced in modern times. American audiences, save on such occasions as his plays are "adapted" into their easy comprehension, are still largely where Italian audiences were a decade and more ago. His dramatic imagination is still a little too wily for them; his plays are still what they—bookworms of E. Phillips Oppenheim, Ursula Parrott, Warwick Deeping and Dr. Joseph Collins—are condescendingly fond of calling "library plays." But for the minority of theatregoers who relish a display of philosophical nimbleness combined with an uncommon dramatic ingenuity, Pirandello is one of the few intelligently diverting playwrights to be encountered on the present-day stage.

Ferenc Molnar (1878–1952)

The popular conception of Ferenc Molnar in this country is of a persistently sardonic, and even iconoclastic, fellow who views the world mainly with a dubious half-closed left eye and who, for all his periods of warm sympathy and gracious concern, is yet at bottom at once a skeptic and cynic. The true Molnar is nothing of the sort. He is, in simple, a sentimentalist who shrewdly masks his sentimentality—a sentimentality almost of a piece with that, say, of a J. Hartley Manners—with a but half-believed in, yet extremely dexterous and most persuasive, derisory humor. It is Molnar's inherent and incorruptible literary-dramatic talent, automatically working its will upon him whether he wishes it or not, that conceals the personal and psychic peculiarities of the man himself.

This, as I put it on paper, sounds somewhat absurd, but a study of Molnar's work and a knowledge of the man lead me to believe that it isn't very far from the truth. Of all the plays he has ever written, but two—one a long one and the other a negligible one-acter—are not intrinsically as sweetly sentimental as any *Peg O' My Heart* or *Daddy Longlegs*. (I omit such a play as *Der Herr Verteidiger* which is plainly just a try for box-office money with thief and detective whang-doodle.) Aside from *The Devil* and the one-acter alluded to—"The Actress" is its title, unless memory betrays me—the bulk of the gifted Hungarian's writing for the

From *Materia Critica* (New York: Knopf, 1924), pp. 91–94.

theatre is, upon plumbing, found to be evening music sung in broad daylight: a serenade at high noon. Consider, for all the illusory counterpoint of cynicism, such as his leading plays as *Liliom, The Fable of the Wolf* (locally known as *The Phantom Rival*), *The Swan, The Guardsman* and *Heavenly and Earthly Love*. The impulse in each case (less, perhaps, in *The Guardsman* than in the instance of the others) is a frank and unabashed sentiment that hovers very closely about the borderland of sentimentality. *Liliom,* generally looked on as being inspired by a greater skepticism and irony than any of the other plays cited, was actually inspired by remorse for these qualities. It is, in a word, its author's apologia for a directly antecedent cynicism, as he himself has freely and with intimate detail confessed to his friends. "What is the theme of *Liliom* as you see it?" they asked of him one day not long ago. And before he replied they gave vent to their own views of the theme: its fantastic quasi-Nietzschean[1] doctrine, its hint at irreligion, its incredulity before the common concept of life, its dissent, its demur and its mockery. "You found all these in my play?" put in Molnar. "Excellent! They are admirable dramatic qualities; *Liliom,* with them, is not a bad idea at all. I am glad that you found them in it. Only I did not put them in!" "Then what is the idea that you did put in?" they wanted to know. "The idea of *Liliom,* as I wrote it, is simply this," he answered. "If a man is loved by a woman, and has a baby by her, his life may be said to be complete. That is all there is to it."

This preamble is only by way of speculating upon the surprise of the American critics when, encountering a play like Molnar's *Fashions for Men,* they find themselves confounded by its to them unwontedly sentimental nature. This, they say, is a Molnar they have never known and have not anticipated. Yet such a play is obviously Molnar through and through—the real and the typical Molnar. It is,true enough, more transparently sentimental than some of his other plays, but the formula is in the main that which bears the Molnar trademark and should be immediately recognizable. Where *Liliom* deals with the doctrine of resistance, *Fashions for Men* deals with the doctrine of non-resistance; but the point of view that Molnar brings to bear upon both is at bottom and in the end much the same. In both, sentiment triumphs over a realistic philosophy; in both, the tear of Molnar mingles with the smile of the world. *Liliom* is a sentimental defense of an apology for hardness; *Fashions for Men* a hard defense of an apology for sentiment. The drama of Molnar, in a word, is the drama of spiritual osteopathy.

---

1. Friedrich Nietzsche (1844–1900), the German philosopher, in *Thus Spake Zarathustra* and other books, rejected Christ in favor of "Superman." Nietzsche (along with Strindberg) influenced several of Eugene O'Neill's plays. See, further, *Also Sprach Zarathustra* in glossary.

Sean O'Casey (1880–1964)

Sean O'Casey's *Juno and the Paycock* is noteworthy for two very good instances of character drawing, for its measure of warm and comprehending humor, for its curiously effective handling, in a suspensive manner, of the character of the son of the Boyle household who has betrayed a fellow patriot, and for a brief flash of moving drama, toward the end of the play, in the boy's death at the hands of his colleagues' avengers. It is deficient in the trick of so assembling these virtues that the whole shall produce a play as meritorious as its component parts.[1]

The price of O'Casey's imperfect maneuvering of his materials is, after the evening has passed its middle mark, tedium. Everything is on the stage to make a consistently holding play, but the materials are like a troop of fully armed soldiers whose commander is down with the measles and who accordingly hang around, their rifles cocked, waiting vainly for orders to move forward. Time and again, the smell of approaching drama is in the air and the nose sniffs in eager anticipation only to be disappointed. The first act proceeds smoothly and amusingly, centred as it is upon the character of the lying, bragging, lovable loafer, Boyle, quondam sailor on a coal-barge that never got further than Liverpool, but in his own tireless imagination and gabble a sea-dog among sea-dogs. The colloquies between Boyle and his bootlicking neighbor, Joxer Daly, are as diverting as anything you'll find in the playhouse at the moment. But once the flush of this initial act is over, O'Casey's fancy and dexterity give out, and, after a half-hour more, his play drops with an audible bump.

The failure of O'Casey to master his materials is readily discernible in the length to which he goes to conceal his dramatic nervousness in heavy exaggeration of dramatic and comic episode. Not only does he so overdo the burlesque song renditions of his characters in the second act and the tragic melodrama of his last act that these portions of his play lack all conviction, but, to boot, he so segregates comedy and drama that one kills the effect of the other. His second act is almost entirely in the low comedy vein and his third act, cut off from the other as with a meat axe, piles tragedy upon tragedy so exaggeratedly that it would take a professional pallbearer to profess any show of sympathy over his characters' plight. The impression is of a man stopping suddenly short in the midst of a comic story to tell the plot of *Œdipus Rex*. Tragedy, to be convincing, must mount cumulatively and slowly; O'Casey directs it in the tempo of a rapid succession of unanticipated fire alarms. Within the space of a comparatively few minutes, he betrays his young heroine and gives her an

---

From *Art of the Night* (New York: Knopf, 1928), pp. 185–93. Copyright renewed 1955 by George Jean Nathan.

illegitimate baby, causes her lover to swindle the family out of a rightful inheritance and run off to England, brings the son of the household to be shot to death in a gutter, separates husband and wife, desolates the home of his protagonists to the extent of removing its last chair, gives his central character delirium tremens, induces the young man who has planned to marry the daughter to sneak away, and suggests that the cause of Irish freedom is up a tree. His traffic in tragedy reminds one, indeed, of nothing so much as the familiar smoking-car story about the sorely harassed parent whose steadily augmenting family woes are brought to a climax by his small son Abie's unhousebroken deportment and who, at his wits' end, is informed by an old gentleman seated back of him in the day-coach that, unless he mend his Abie's ways at once, the old gentleman will make trouble for him.

In his later *The Plough and the Stars,* on the other hand, O'Casey has produced a piece of work not less full of defective detail than his *Juno and the Paycock* but, for all that, a drama excellent in its characterizations, rich in an irony that reaches the heights of cruelty, and paradoxically powerful in lasting impression. Three or four of the episodes have the stamp of unmistakable dramatic genius; quietly as a cannon on rubber tires O'Casey rolls them toward the footlights and suddenly thunders them into the startled consciousness of his audience. As a surgical picture of the Irish, I know of nothing in drama or literature that comes anywhere near this play. That the Irish merely gave vent to catcalls and eggs when it was shown in Dublin is surprising; that they didn't bomb the theatre is even more surprising. O'Casey takes his people, themselves, their ambitions, their dreams, their pretences and their innermost philosophies, and doesn't leave a green thread in their chemises when he gets through. His clinical portrait is the most vicious thing in modern dramatic literature, but the viciousness is that of a deep understanding, a profoundly critical love and a prophylactic hairbrush swatting a turned-up child. His play is long, too long. As in *Juno and the Paycock,* he doesn't seem to know exactly when to let go. The technique in both plays is much the same, although it is exaggerated in the one under immediate discussion. O'Casey busies himself leisurely with character for the first thirty-five minutes of each act, and then suddenly in the last five minutes recalls, that, after all, a drama should have at least a little drama in it and belatedly dramatizes in a few moments the ambling antecedent business. The break is not too well dovetailed. The effect is of a Dutch concert disconcertingly interrupted by a pistol shot. Again, as in *Juno and the Paycock,* the dramatist piles on the final woe to such an extent that a measure of persuasiveness is deleted from his work. His wholesale murder, sudden death and general desolation are Shakespearian in every way but the compensatory one of great poetry. The stage at the conclusion of his tragedy resembles nothing so much as the floor of a slaughter-house. Those characters who haven't been shot and killed are either dead of tuberculosis, insane, in the last stages of alcoholism or being led off the stage for no good purpose. Still again, as in the other play, *The Plough and the Stars* overdoes to the point of irritation the vaudeville trick of repeating a word or phrase for humorous ends. It was Pinero who once pointed out the limit to which this device could prosperously be used, and then topped it by one. O'Casey tries to top it by ten or fifteen, and naturally fails. He also goes in once again for the mispronunciation of words by way of getting a cheap laugh, as in the instance of *chaos* in *Juno*—and he repeats and repeats. But—when the play is over, the effect the playwright has set himself to get is as peculiarly and bafflingly there as the hair in your nose. You carry with you out of the theatre a merciless, yet sympathetic, vision of Ireland and its youngsters in grown-old bodies. You feel the utter futility of a people and a purpose, the tragic ridiculousness of a nation of eternal children playing politics with loud nursery rattles and playing soldier with pop-guns. You look upon this picture of the Irish by an Irishman, one of the most articulate fellows on the Emerald Isle, and you smile and wince at the same time.

There isn't a character in O'Casey's gallery that isn't well-drawn. Some are superbly drawn. There is, for example, the carpenter Fluther, the alternately genial and bellicose souse who is constantly swearing off the stuff for good and who is as sharply perceived a study of an Irishman, down to the smallest detail of thought and act, as the drama has given us. There is the little old querulous Irishman, Peter Flynn, proud as a peacock over marching in meaningless parades in elaborate and meaningless regalia. There is the young Irish liberal and dreamer, constantly mouthing an ill assimilated amount of sociological information; there are, in sharp, brief little strokes, portraits of Irish women and of Irish ballyhoos and of English militia men. Some of the episodes, as I have said, have the vital smash of kindly gunpowder: the scene at the saloon bar with Irishmen getting indignantly cockeyed while, outside the place and as counterpoint to the bibbing inside, other Irishmen, equally indignant, are haranguing their fellow countrymen to defend their immemorial rights with their eternal souls; the climax to the second act wherein, the political indignation reaching its zenith, one of the Irishmen lets off his accumulated martial steam by fighting another Irishman, both of them drunk, for an insult offered by the latter to an Irish prostitute's virtue, and then goes off with the woman for the night; the richly comical yet searching episode[2] in the following act in which, with Dublin strewn with English bullets and Irishmen dying on every hand, the women make the practical best of the situation, news arriving of the pillaging of shops and stores, by taking a baby carriage, previously the subject of acrimonious dispute among them, and with true sisterly concurrence hustling off to load it with pink lingerie, white shoes, parlor lamps and other treasures out of demolished show-windows; and the final moment of the play wherein two English petty officers, with the results of carnage all about them, quietly observe that it is five o'clock and settle down to drink the tea that has been set out by an Irishwoman for her soldier husband dying somewhere in the gutter below the tenement.

---

1. With characteristic integrity Nathan points out shortcomings in these plays, which he otherwise admires. As reflected in the Nathan/O'Casey correspondence, Nathan championed O'Casey and worked successfully to get his plays produced in New York.
2. See *Episode* in glossary.

Jean Giraudoux (1882–1944)

Like any other panhandler beseeching a nickel for a cup of coffee, the theatre reviewer these days presents the pitiful spectacle of trooping up and down Broadway night after night begging for a nickel's worth of wit, and when once in a great while some producer comes along and generously drops it into his cup he so overglows with gratitude that one would think the nickel's worth was a million dollars. It is thus that when even a fifty-one-year-old play like *Caesar and Cleopatra* or a fifty-three-year-old one like *The Devil's Disciple* is revived and allows him to chuckle over lines already long and perfectly familiar to him, he comes near to growing tipsy with delight, and that when something like Giraudoux's *The Madwoman Of Chaillot* or even his relatively inferior *Intermezzo,* now renamed *The Enchanted,* comes his way, he acts as if some archangel had rescued him from dying of thirst on a desert. And little wonder. Unless they revive Wilde or Shaw, dig something occasionally out of the French market, or happen to find John van Druten in good working trim, wit in these later seasons has been as scarce on our American stage as it is in our American diplomacy, and to find even a relieving trace of it the reviewer perforce has had to consort with one or another of the more worldly and recherché bartenders. For what he gets instead, and has to be content with in our current dramatic theatre, is often at best the flip insult that is made to pass for wit by the device of placing it in the mouths of fashionably dressed women or wisecracks counterfeited as polite drollery by having them spoken by actors without Brooklyn accents.

From *The Theatre Book of the Year 1949–1950* (New York: Knopf, 1950), pp. 183–85.

The Enchanted, which frequently suggests Chesteron's *Magic,* is nothing particularly remarkable as a play, at least as we get it in the Valency adaptation. It seems often to be confused and muddled, and its fantasy about a young French school-teacher who communes with ghosts in her effort to learn the secret of the dead and with the hoped for knowledge bring happiness to the living sometimes gets out of clear hand and resembles an ill-orchestrated mixture of parts of such plays as *Death Takes A Holiday,* von Hofmannsthal's *Death And The Fool,* etc. Giraudoux himself, indeed, did not appear to be too certain of its independence and substantially, as his own modest title for it hints, since an intermezzo is defined as a short dramatic entertainment between the acts of a play. But he apparently knew, nevertheless, how to make the interlude, however thematically cloudy, entertaining, and that was to light it up not only with verbal wit but with wit of imagination; and it is these qualities that, let academic criticism go hang, make it on the whole a quite delightful pastime.

There are many gleams that penetrate and illuminate the script's fog: the juggling, like Chesteron, with paradox; the flashes of intelligent sentiment opposing theoretical logic; the routing of realistic approach with unsophisticated yet plausible argument; and so on. And there are several scenes of jolly invention: the two executioners who baffle a government official absolutely positive that there can be only one; the solemn bureaucratic attempts to exorcise spirits from the small town and to preserve the normal order which exorcises the people's happiness; and the weights and measures clerk who proves that romance may lie in the commonplace and routine.

I quote, in illustration of Giraudoux's amusing technique in combining satire with fantasy, a single colloquy. The pompous government inspector, determined that the ghost seen by the heroine must be laid for once and all, is explaining to the mayor what might happen were France to be invaded by the spirit world:

> *Inspector.* Do you realize what it would mean to France if the inhabitants of the other world were permitted to colonize this district? I say nothing of their influence on the local community, which is already mad. But take notice that these ghosts would not be aliens. They would be natives of France, and therefore entitled to all the rights and privileges of citizens, including the right to vote. And when you stop to think that the dead of this district outnumber the living in an astronomical proportion, you begin to see what the consequence might be. Within five years, with perfect legality, they could capture any electoral post in the nation. The President of the Republic would be a ghost, the Prime Minister a ghost, the members of the high court, all ghosts.
> *Mayor.* You think we would notice any difference?

Eugene O'Neill (1888–1953)

With the appearance of *The Iceman Cometh,* our theatre has become dramatically alive again. It makes most of the plays of other American playwrights produced during the more than twelve-year period of O'Neill's absence look comparatively like so much damp tissue paper. In it there is an understanding of the deeper elements of human nature, a comprehension of the confused instincts that make up the life of mortals, and an evocation of pity for the tortured existence of dazed mankind that not merely most but all of those plays in combination have not faintly suggested. It is, in short, one of the best of its author's works and one that again firmly secures his position not only as the first of American dramatists but, with Shaw and O'Casey, one of the three really distinguished among the world's living.

These, I appreciate, are big words and probably contributive to the suspicion that their inditer has forgone his old phyrronism. They are also doubtless obnoxious and challenging to such persons as either resent what seems to be extravagant praise at the expense of other playwrights or are constitutionally averse to superlatives of any kind and ready to throw off their coats if anyone has the gall to say even that Bach was the greatest composer who ever lived or that horseradish sauce is the best of all things to go with boiled beef. But the words, I believe, are none the less in good order. If they are not and if the play is not what I think it is, I am prepared to atone for my ignorance by presenting gratis to anyone who can offer convincing contrary evidence the complete bound works of all our American playwrights from Bronson Howard through Charles Klein, David Belasco and Augustus Thomas down to the geniuses responsible for *Joan of Lorraine, Another Part of the Forest, Dream Girl,* and *Maid in the Ozarks.*

Laying hold of an assortment of social outcasts quartered in a disreputable saloon on the fringe of New York in the year 1912 and introducing into their drunken semblance of contentful hope an allegory in the shape of a Werlean traveling salesman, O'Neill distils from them, slowly but inexorably, the tragedy that is death in life. Superficially at times suggesting a cross between Gorki's *The Lower Depths* and Saroyan's *The Time of Your Life,* let alone Ibsen's *The Wild Duck,* the play with its author's uncommon dramaturgical skill gradually weaves its various vagrant threads into a solid thematic pattern and in the end achieves a purge and mood of compassion that mark it apart from the bulk of contemporary drama. There are repetitions in the middle sections which O'Neill has deemed

From *The Theatre Book of the Year 1946–1947* (New York: Knopf, 1947), pp. 93–111.

necessary to the impact of the play but which in this opinion might be got rid of with no loss. There is also still an excess of profanity, for all the author's liberal cutting, which becomes disturbing to any ear that gags at such overemphasis. And since the uncut version of *Hamlet,* which is a good play too, can be played in its entirety in little more than three and a half hours, the longer running time of *The Iceman Cometh* may seem to some, and quite rightly, not only superfluous but a little pretentious. Yet small matter. In the whole history of drama there has been only one really perfect tragedy—incidentally, one one-third as long—and, while this of O'Neill's is scarcely to be compared with it, it still rises far above its possible errors.

With a few nimble strokes, O'Neill pictures vividly the innards of even the least of his variegated characters, from the one-time circus grifter to the one-time police lieutenant, from the quondam boss of a Negro gambling den to the erstwhile Boer War correspondent, and from the night and day bartenders and the wreck of a college graduate to the former editor of anarchist magazines and the old captain once in the British armed services. Only in the characters of his three street-walkers does he work rather obviously; truthfully, perhaps, but in a theatrically routine manner. Yet in his major figures, Slade, the one-time Syndicalist-anarchist, Hickey, the hardware salesman, Hope, the proprietor of the saloon, etc., the hand is as steady and sure as ever.

The long monologue, only now and then momentarily interrupted, wherein toward the drama's conclusion the salesman relates the relief from himself secured by the murder of his wife, is one of the most impressive pieces of writing in contemporary dramatic literature: emotionally searching and definitely moving. The relations of Slade and the young man with memory of his betrayed mother on his agonized conscience are maneuvered with high suspensive dexterity, even if at one or two points to the hypercritical slightly overplanted. The dialogue throughout is driving; there is robust humor to alleviate the atmospheric sordidness; and out of the whole emerges in no small degree the profound essence of authentic tragedy.

In the author's own analysis of his play, as he has confided it to me, the dominant intention has been a study in the workings of strange friendship. That intention, it is not to be gainsaid, has been fully realized. But as I read the script and see it in stage action it seems to me that, far above and beyond it, there rises the theme of the tragedy which lies in bogus self-substantiation and the transient, pitiable satisfaction which it bequeaths. That, however, is the play's virtue: to different men it may convey different things. But to all with any emotional understanding and to all with any appreciation of the drama it must convey the satisfaction of a theatre that, if only for a short while, has again come into its rightful own.

In a setting by Robert Edmond Jones which catches perfectly the atmosphere of the play and with lighting that alternately gives the stage and groupings the effect of Daumier and George Bellows, Eddie Dowling, with many acceptable critical suggestions from the author, has accomplished an impressive example of direction. In only two or three details has he missed, and the fault in those cases was scarcely his. O'Neill's men's toilet to the far left of the stage with the "This Is It" sign is gratuitous, since it is strangely, even phenomenally, never once used by any of the hard-drinking denizens of the saloon and since it thus serves no purpose and is simply a gesture in juvenile waggery. Dowling's idea that it be given some small justification by installing Hugo Kalmar, the drooling anarchist editor, in it at one point and having him declaim his parrot lines from its interior—an excellent comedy touch that would have suited the action with no slightest violation of the text—was vetoed by O'Neill. The play's ending, which presently goes a little flat, might also, as Dowling wished, have been inspirited if, as counterpoint to Slade's final "Be God, I'm the only real convert to death Hickey made here; from the bottom of my coward's heart I mean that now!," the drunken singing and wild pounding on the table by the assembled, happily unredeemed bibuli had not been cut by the author and had been moved a bit forward from its place in the original script. And if the director had been allowed to lend a greater touch of his familiar "mood" staging to the play, which he was not, the spirit of the drama would have been materially aided.

O'Neill is the only dramatist in the history of the American theatre who has achieved real world status. His plays have been produced in most of the civilized countries of the globe; he has been awarded the Nobel prize for the body of his work; he has been the subject of critical discussion in South America, England, Germany, France, Italy, Greece, Russia, the Scandinavian lands, the Balkans, Australia, Japan and China. Almost as much has been written about him as about one-half all the living playwrights rolled together. Only Shaw has consumed more space.

In the United States, South America, France, Italy, Russia, the Scandinavian countries, Rumania, Greece, Australia, Japan and China, the critical attitude toward him in the main has been extremely favorable. In Germany, when criticism was operating freely, it was, with a few exceptions, highly appreciative. In England alone has there most often been either a lukewarm or chilly attitude toward him.

Here in America his preëminence as the first dramatist of his nation is taken by the great majority of the critics for granted. Now and again a small voice from the sidelines lifts itself in contradiction and puts in some peculiar nomination for the honor, but in the aggregate his position is unchallenged. In France, where his plays have had their chief hearing at the hands of Pitoëff, all save one or two of the recognized critics have been impressed. In Russia, praise of him has been pretty uniform, and understandably, since his dramatic philosophy and usual attitude toward his subject matter find a sympathetic echo in the Slav temperament. In Italy, those of his plays that have been shown have fared well at most critical hands; his *Days without End,* which strikes a Catholic note, has received the Church's imprimatur and has been produced under the auspices of the Vatican. South America has paid him homage. Sweden has acclaimed him, and so has the theatre of Norway. Various of his plays have proved successes, both popular and critical, in Rumania; and Hungary, though to a lesser degree, has received him with hospitality. German critics, save in the few instances noted, have in the past treated him with respect, and in Japan and China the younger element, which alone is interested dramatically in the outside world, regards him, along with Shaw, as the most important of the Western playwrights.

On the other hand, though he has intermittently been accepted in England and even treated with considerable esteem by men of letters like Spender, *et al.,* the general run of drama criticism has frequently shown misgivings about him. In some cases indeed, the misgivings have been accompanied by lofty derision.

For an example of the English attitude, we may turn to Eric Bentley and his recent observations in *The Playwright as Thinker.* I quote four typical samples:

    a. "Among the untragic tragedians the most spectacular is Eugene O'Neill. At everything in the theatre except being tragic and being comic he is a success . . . . Tragedy is transported to the intense inane . . . . The tension that is missing in his work is inner tension."

    b. "O'Neill has not as yet been able adequately to represent the bourgeois world as the nightmare which in the twentieth century it became, though his portraits of neurosis and decay are a labored and overconscious striving in that direction. O'Neill's more powerful, *unconsciously* symbolic tendency was to flee the bourgeois world, not like Wedekind by standing it on its head, but trying to deny its existence, by proclaiming exclusive reality for the eternal. It was O'Neill himself who stood on his head."

    c. "T. S. Eliot's 'conception' (in *The Family Reunion*) is clear, noble, and mature . . . . O'Neill's 'conception' (in *Mourning Becomes Electra*) is rude, simple-minded, gaga."

    d. "Where Wedekind seems silly and turns out on further inspection to be profound, O'Neill seems profound and turns out on further inspection to be silly . . . . O'Neill has yet to show us he has a mind. So far he has only been earnest after the fashion of the popular pulpit or of professors who write on the romance of reality. Precisely because he pretends to be too much, he attains too little. He is false, and he is false in a particularly unpleasant way. His art is *faux-bon*. The 'good, clean fun' of a Hitchcock movie is better."

Since every critic has a right to his opinion, and in view of the differences thereof which have been O'Neill's portion, I (now that he has reappeared with *The Iceman Cometh* as a produced dramatist) venture my own on the plays which he has contributed to the stage since first he began to function. In chronological compositional order, herewith the plays and the present commentator's views on them *in piccolo:*

1913–14. "Thirst" and four other one-act plays. Wholly negligible and plainly the work of a novice.

1914. "Bound East for Cardiff." The first of his sea plays and the first indication of a significant new dramatic talent. A striking performance containing the seed of its author's future mental cast.

1916. "Before Breakfast." A trifle. Little in it to encourage the critical hopes found in "Bound East for Cardiff."

1917. "In the Zone," "Ile," "The Long Voyage Home," "The Moon of the Caribbees." The hopes were here reinforced in this rounding out of the cycle of short sea plays. "In the Zone" is the weakest of the four, melodramatically effective but built around an all too obvious theatrical device. "Ile" and "The Long Voyage Home," however, show an advance in character portrayal, thematic feel, and dramaturgical expertness. "The Moon of the Caribbees," the best of the four plays, is remarkable for the dramatic capturing of a mood and its projection. It remains one of the few genuinely important one-act plays in American dramatic literature.

1918. "The Rope," *Beyond the Horizon,* "The Dreamy Kid," "Where the Cross Is Made." "The Rope" is an only fair excursion into psychopathic melodrama. *Beyond the Horizon,* his first full-length play (there were two or three written in his nonage which he destroyed and of which no traces remain), may be said to have influenced perceptibly the course of American drama. Its honest realism filtered through a poetic impulse came as a revelation to a stage chiefly given over, at its serious best, to rhinestone imagination and, at its worst, to vacuity illuminated by Broadway lamplight. While here and there suggesting a certain infirmity in dramaturgy, it betokened clearly the more finished work that was to come. "The Dreamy Kid" was and is a distinctly minor effort, and of no consequence. "Where the Cross is Made," the germ of the later full-length play *Gold* was and remains a fabricated one-acter partly redeemed by a potentially serviceable thematic idea.

1919. *Chris, The Straw.* Produced briefly in Philadelphia and withdrawn, *Chris* was a crude attempt at the play *Anna Christie,* into which it was subsequently developed. *The Straw,* in its treatment of tuberculosis, is an unusual achievement of a difficult dramatic problem. Its emotional orchestration is one of O'Neill's best accomplishments.

1920. *Gold, Anna Christie, The Emperor Jones, Diff'rent. Gold,* though possessing several unmistakable virtues, fails in its entirety because of intermittent aberrant planning and uncertain playwrighting. *Anna Christie* is a new and forceful handling of a familiar theme, deep in its characterizations, driving in its firm composition, and etched with real observation and understanding. *The Emperor Jones* is a masterpiece of its kind. Its cumulative dramatic effect is irresistible. The tom-toms starting, in Richard Dana Skinner's apt phrase, at the rate of the human pulse beat and rising bit by bit as a fevered pulse would rise and which are of the warp and woof of the drama itself, sweep one along and up into a mighty climax and leave one without breath. Into this study of the Negro's dream of release from bondage to the whites and, upon the dream's coming true, his defeat by the very tricks of the whites which in practise have brought him release, or what he images is release, O'Neill has introduced a symbolic fancy uncommon to American dramatic writing. The succeeding *Diff'rent,* however, is of small moment, a feeble distillation of Strindberg further debilitated by its author's handling of its materials.

1921. *The First Man, The Hairy Ape.* The former, with the later *Welded,* is one of O'Neill's two worst full-length performances. Here again, in both cases, close imitation of Strindberg has brought its penalties. Aping the technic of Strindberg, as I observed at the time, O'Neill sets himself so to intensify and even hyperbolize a theme as to evoke the dramatic effect from its overtones rather than, as is the more general manner, from its undertones. His attempt is to duplicate the technic of such a drama as *The Father,* the power of which is derived not by suggestion and implication but from the sparks that fly upward from a prodigious and deafening pounding on the anvil. The attempt is a failure, for all that one gets in O'Neill's case is the prodigious and deafening pounding; the sparks simply will not come out. Now and again one discerns something that looks vaguely like a spark, but on closer inspection it turns out to be only an artificial theatrical firefly which has been cunningly concealed up the actors' sleeves. The author goes aground on the rocks of exaggeration and overemphasis. His philosophical melodrama is so full of psychological revolver shots, jumps off the Brooklyn Bridge, incendiary Chinamen, galloping horse carts, forest fires, wild locomotives, sawmills, dynamite kegs, time fuses, infernal machines, battles under the sea, mine explosions, Italian blackhanders, sinking ocean liners, fights to the death on rafts, and last-minute pardons that the effect is akin to reading a treatise on the theme of a bump-the-bumps. He rolls up his sleeves and piles on the agony with the assiduity of a coalheaver. He here misjudges, it seems to me completely, the Strindberg method. O'Neill intensifies his theme from without. He piles psychological and physical situation on situation until the structure topples over with a burlesque clatter. Strindberg magnified the psyches of his characters. O'Neill here magnifies their actions. *The Hairy Ape* is in a class apart. Partly expressionistic and written with greater restraint if with greatly increased and sounder dramatic intensity, the play dramatizes its theme of despairing humanity gazing blinded at the stars with a signal drive.

1922. *The Fountain*. A very uneven and not particularly successful fantasy dealing with the quest of Ponce de Leon. Some of the writing is eloquent, but more seems labored. The protagonist is described as "a romantic dreamer governed by the ambitious thinker in him." The protagonist's confusion is shared by the playwright.

1923. *Welded, All God's Chillun Got Wings*. As for the former, see the above comment on *The First Man*. *All God's Chillun Got Wings* is a study of miscegenation wrought with honesty, sympathetic comprehension and proficient dramaturgy. Its basic idea, the tragic difficulty in man's acceptance of reality and truth, is boiled out of the theme with a steaming emotionalism and persuasion.

1924. *Desire under the Elms*. The Strindberg influence is here again clear, but in this instance O'Neill has exercised greater caution and selection and has not allowed himself so fully to be dominated. The result is a drama of passion and incest that does not get out of hand and that by and large amounts to a satisfactory realistic treatment of some of the elements in the classic Greek drama.

1925. *Marco Millions, The Great God Brown*. *Marco Millions* is a witty satire, crossed with the poetic mood, dealing with the exploits of that prototype of the American go-getter, Marco Polo. It is everything that *The Fountain* is not. Much of the writing is delightful and the sentiment in, for example, the little Princess Kukachin's eager search for the lost suggestion of her hero's soul has real body. *The Great God Brown*, with its employment of masks, is one of O'Neill's major efforts and in many respects comes off laudably despite the difficult problems it offers to stage presentation. The psychological essences of the drama are craftily distilled and, for all the complexities projected by the frequent mask-changing on the part of the characters, the play manages much of the impression designed by its author. What confusion there is is less inherent in the theme than in the mechanical adornments visited upon it.

1926. *Lazarus Laughed*. An unsuccessful attempt at what seems to be operatic Biblical fantasy. Less a theatre play than a libretto.

1927. *Strange Interlude*. A notable contribution to the drama. On an unusually broad canvas, O'Neill has plumbed the psyche of a woman in relation to her men with a handsome understanding. His knowledge of character has never been better displayed by him. There are one or two moments when matters seem to evade him, but he thereafter recaptures his purpose and pushes ahead with entire comprehension. On the whole, a psychological drama again touched by the Strindberg philosophy which leaves its immediate subject matter convincingly exhausted.

1928. *Dynamo.* A conflict between the depths and surfaces of man resolved into a drama that is overwritten, overstuffed, and that does not come off. Isolated scenes are dramatically stimulating, but the drama in its entirety becomes lost in its own tortuous philosophical alleys and leaves one with the impression that less symbolism and more simplicity would have served the playwright's purpose infinitely better.

1931. *Mourning Becomes Electra.* A fine paraphrase of the classic Greek drama. Bringing the incestuous theme of revenge into modern recognition, O'Neill has fashioned a tragedy that stands largely on independent feet and that presents his dramaturgical gifts in full flower.

1932. *Ah, Wilderness!* Turning from tragedy to comedy, the author has here achieved the tenderest and most amusing comedy of boyhood in the American drama. It is an answer to those who believe that he is without humor, a belief held by such as have engaged some of his antecedent work with a predetermined lack of humor. (*Ah, Wilderness!* was dedicated to Nathan.)

1933. *Days without End.* Rewriting has spoiled a play that in its original conception was not without some merit. As it stands, it is an anachronistic treatment of its single-standard sex theme wedded to psychic release through religious faith. The many revisions made by the author in his several earlier drafts weakened the play's directness and have botched it. A poor performance.

1939. *The Iceman Cometh.* One of O'Neill's top achievements. A drama of the submerged tenth which, as previously noted, vaguely suggests Gorki's *The Lower Depths* but which is not only an immeasurably better play but one that explores the confused and agonized souls of mankind with rare understanding and with powerful dramatic result.

Two additional plays have been completed during the last four years and are awaiting metropolitan production: *A Moon for the Misbegotten,* already tried out in the Mid-West, and *A Touch of the Poet.* Pending a view of them, what is O'Neill's critical status to date?

That he is the foremost dramatist in the American theatre is, as has been recorded, generally granted. His eminence is predicated on the fact that no other has anything like his ability to delve into and appraise character, his depth of knowledge of his fellow man, his sweep and pulse and high resolve, his command of a theatre stage and all its manifold workings, and his mastery of the intricacies of dramaturgy. His plays at their best have in them real universality. His characters are not specific, individual, and isolated types but active symbols of mankind in general, with mankind's virtues and faults, gropings and findings, momentary triumphs and doomed defeats. He writes not for a single theatre but for all theatres of the world.

It is argued by some against him that he is no poet, and that his drama hence misses true stature. Specifically and in the conventional sense, he may not be, but he is nevertheless, as must be evident to the close student of his work, driven ever by the poetic spirit. His weakness, where and when it exists, lies in his excesses—the excesses of overlength, over-emphasis, overembroidery and overmelodramatization of the psychological aspects of his drama and of that drama itself. At his worst, these qualities edge him close to brooding travesty.

He has worked expertly in the field of tragedy, nimbly in the field of comedy, and less happily in that of fantasy. His brutality in tragedy is a handmaiden of the truth as he sees it. He cannot compromise with himself, right or wrong. Uncommonly gifted in a knowledge of the theatre, it may seem to some that he resorts occasionally to critically invalid devices to further his dramatic ends. If he does so, he does so unconsciously, never with calculation and deliberately. He would be content, I am assured, to publish his plays and forego the profits of production. He has written muddled and poor plays along with the valid, some very muddled and very poor. But the great body of his work has a size and significance not remotely approached by any other American. In a broader sense, he is certainly in no remotest degree the mind that Shaw is—his is an emotional rather than an intellectual; he is not by far the poet that O'Casey is, for in O'Casey there is the true music of great wonder and beauty. But he has plumbed depths deeper than either; he is greatly the superior of both in dramaturgy; and he remains his nation's one important contribution to the art of the drama.

Before the presentation of *The Iceman Cometh*, it was exactly twelve years and nine months since O'Neill's last previous play, *Days without End*, had seen production, and in the long intervening spell the theatre had had small news of him. Now and then came vague and contradictory reports that he was working on a cycle of eight or nine plays to be named by the general and somewhat turgid title *A Tale of Possessors Self-Dispossessed;* that he was very ill and no longer able to do any work; and that he had successively retired from the theatre to Sea Island, Georgia, and the Valley of the Moon in California, there to devote the rest of his life to nursing his health, raising Dalmatian dogs, and laughing at most of current English dramatic criticism. But from the man himself there issued not so much as a whisper. What, really, was he up to?

It happens that we have been close friends for going on thirty years now, and that I am in a position to tell. That in the period of his absence he completed *The Iceman Cometh,* along with the subsequently to be produced *A Moon for the Misbegotten* and the still later to be produced *A Touch of the Poet,* the public had been apprised. These three plays, however, were by no means all. During the twelve-odd years, he not only outlined in minute detail not eight or nine but all of eleven plays of the cycle referred to—the eleven were to be played, however, as eight with three combined into duplex units and presented, like *Strange Interlude,* on the same afternoons, evenings and nights—but further definitely completed seven of them, including the three double-length ones, and got pretty well into the eighth. In addition, he finished a separate and independent play of full length called *Long Day's Journey into Night,* production of which he will not allow, for reasons which I may not specify, for many years. Nor, yet again, was that all. Besides *Long Day's Journey into Night,* he also completed the first play of a much shorter and entirely different cycle of which no word has reached anyone. Its title, like that of the contemplated briefer series in its entirety, is *By Way of Orbit.* It runs for forty-five or so minutes and involves, very successfully I think, an imaginative technical departure from O'Neill's previous work. It contains but two characters and is laid in New York in approximately the same period as *The Iceman Cometh.* . . .

O'Neill's attitude toward criticism of his work in particular and in general has not changed. However denunciatory and stinging it may be at times, he shows no indignation and maintains at least outwardly an appearance of smiling tolerance. Unlike a number of his playwrighting contemporaries, he never makes public reply to it, though now and again to a close friend he will privately express his amusement over certain of its more capricious aspects.

An English critic recently, for example, had at O'Neill with the old, familiar contention that, though he may think of himself as a poet, he is far from one. In proof whereof, the critic delightedly quoted this speech by Marsden in *Strange Interlude:*

"We'll be married in the afternoon, decidedly. I've already picked out the church, Nina—a gray ivied chapel, full of restful shadow, symbolical of the peace we have found. The crimsons and purples in the windows will stain our faces with faded passion. It must be in the hours before sunset when the earth dreams in afterthought and mystic premonitions of life's beauty," etc.

"Didn't he realize," chuckled O'Neill, "that the attempt there certainly wasn't poetry, but poetic travesty? Marsden, as anyone must easily see, is a sentimental throwback, a kind of *Yellow Book* period reversion, and I was deliberately using that 'crimsons and purples in the windows,' 'staining our faces with faded passion' and so on stuff to indicate it."

The notion that O'Neill entertains a profound satisfaction with everything he has written and resents any opposite opinion—a notion that pops up in various treatises on his work—is nonsensical. I give you several instances out of my own personal critical experience. When his *The First Man* was produced, I wrote acidly of it, even indulging in some ridicule. Reading the criticism, O'Neill grinned. "You let it down too easy," he observed. "It's no good." When subsequently I wrote in the same vein about *Welded,* which he seemed to have faith in when he gave me the script to read, he allowed, "I know now I was 'way off; the play is all wrong; it's no good." When, on the other hand, I found certain things to my liking in *Gold,* he took me to task. "You're wrong. It's a bad play. I'm telling you." He further believes that *The Fountain* is even more defective than I found it to be, and that *Dynamo,* though granting its lapses, is considerably less so. Only in the case of *Days Without End,* which I could not critically stomach, has he vigorously opposed my opinion, and even in this case he allows that he now feels he must rewrite the play's ending for the definitive edition of his works. As originally conceived, this *Days Without End* was, as I have said before, laid back in the year 1857 or thereabout. Bringing it up to the 1930s seemed to me, among others, to render its single-standard sex idea somewhat archaic and shopworn. O'Neill, however, was not to be persuaded. What he has persuaded himself, nevertheless, is that his hero's final gesture calls for alteration, though the alteration consists simply in reverting to the dramatic scheme as he first conceived it.

He is a stickler for casting and direction. As to the latter, his constant concern is any sentimentalization of his work. "Where sentiment exists," he says, "there is sufficient of it in the characters, and any directorial emphasis would throw it out of all proportion and make it objectionable." As to casting, he is generally opposed to so-called name actors. "They distract attention from the play to themselves," he argues. "My plays are not for stars but for simply good actors. Besides, you can never count on the idiosyncrasies of stars; they may not stick to a play and may so damage its chances on the road. I'm afraid of them, as I've had some experience with them. Also, they sometimes want you to change certain things in your play. Not for me!"

To return, finally, to *The Iceman Cometh,* I have already twice remarked that it may very roughly be described as a kind of American *The Lower Depths.* Like that play of Gorki's, though it in few other ways resembles it, it treats of a group of degenerate outcasts and the advent among them of a man with a philosophy of life new and disturbing to them. Its language is realistic, at times over-violently so; its cast of alcoholic down-and-outs includes gamblers, grafting cops, circus lot sharpers, whores, pimps, anarchist riff-raff, military failures, college-educated wastrels, stool-pigeons, *et al.;* and it is written in four parts. It attests again to the fact, lost upon some of O'Neill's critics, that he is far from lacking a healthy

sense of humor. Some of the comedy writing is irresistible. It also demon-
strates again the most barbed appreciation of character known to any of
his American playwriting contemporaries. And it embraces, among many
other things, the most pitifully affecting picture of a woman—the unseen
wife of the protagonist—that I, for one, have encountered in many years of
playgoing.

Among the criticisms of the play is the argument that the characters "do
not grow." That they do not grow is O'Neill's specific dramatic theme.
Human beings sometimes change but change is not necessarily growth.
Change is frequently impermanent and retrogressive rather than advanc-
ing as O'Neill indicates. Another argument is that Hickey, the salesman of
Death, in the end "explains himself with a textbook clarity that robs him
of a truly dramatic role in the play, or a really human complexity." What of
Nina in *The Sea Gull?* And a third condescendingly observes, "As for
O'Neill's 'thesis' it would seem to be that men cannot live without illu-
sions; hardly a new or very disputable idea." Hardly new, granted; but not
very disputable? Come, come. What of the sufficient disputation on occasion of Ibsen, Strindberg, Zola, Hauptmann, Tolstoi, Wedekind, Shaw
. . . ?

Maxwell Anderson (1888–1959)

There is, at least in three cases out of five, a temptation to give a play by
Maxwell Anderson a better critical notice than it deserves. He often writes
with such a feeling for beauty that, whatever the rest of his play may be
like, a critic has a time keeping strict criticism from getting out of control,
especially in this day when a feeling for beauty is most often confined, in
the theatre, to mere settings and costumes and, in public life, to migratory
hands under night-club tables. No man writing currently for the American
theatre knows better than Anderson the great loveliness that lies in English words and the greater loveliness that may be achieved by weaving
them into delicate patterns. And no man is more happy in now and then
effectuating, with the loom of his fancy, panels of affecting poetic prose for
the adornment of his dramas. The ear is at such times so prejudiced in his
favor that the critical eye must keep itself doubly wide-awake lest it
neglect to report upon the inner deficiencies of the dramas themselves. As
with a bright Armistice parade, the swinging and exhilarating bands are in
danger of making the casual spectator overlook the many cripples in line.

Three new plays by Mr. Anderson, *The Wingless Victory, High Tor* and

From *The Morning After the First Night* (New York: Knopf, 1938), pp. 106–15. Copyright
renewed 1965 by Mrs. George Jean Nathan.

The Masque of Kings, were revealed to the theatre last season, and all three—as I have already suggested in a previous chapter—again revealed their author as a writer who is for the most part apparently determined to see poetry in everything, whether it is there or not. It has become a mania with him. Take, for example, some such thing as garbage. If a playwright like Eugene O'Neill or even Mr. Anderson's quondam collaborator, Laurence Stallings, finds himself called upon to comment dramatically upon it, in all likelihood he will satisfy himself, his play and his audience with the sufficient observation, "The garbage stinks." But not so Mr. Anderson. Instead of announcing very simply and bluntly to the point that the garbage stinks, Mr. Anderson will dreamily weave blooms in his hair and go in for some such blank verse as:

> The garbage,
> like a thousand Persian perfumes
> warring with themselves
> and stewing in the golden sun,
> flaunts the daisies that grow
> like timid, fearful and unwanted babes
> by the swill-pail's silver side.

Mr. Anderson, in short, is a glutton for poetic expression and the fact that he is an apter hand at it than any man writing for the American theatre at the present time should not make us oblivious of the second fact that his arbitrary employment of it is occasionally gratuitous and often not a little undramatic and out of key. *The Wingless Victory* here and there, as drama, suffers badly from its misrelated use. There are moments, indeed, when the Anderson muse intrudes itself into the play's movement much as might a cello into a marching brass band, and with the same droll inconsistency. The fantasy *High Tor* accepts his muse with considerably more consonance and inner grace, and it is, accordingly, infinitely the better play. Not for this reason alone, of course, but for the further reason that it enjoys a relative individuality and dramatic imagination that the other work lacks. Its fault lies in the defective orchestration of its two moods: the one fantastic, the other realistic. Mr. Anderson has tried simultaneously to direct a symphony orchestra and a swing band and the result is too often dramatically cacophonous. As for *The Masque of Kings*, it is so overly poetized that it suggests in the end nothing so much as a fire-sale of German Christmas cards.

But one point I wish to repeat. Dismissing this season's *The Star-Wagon* as a lapse perhaps resulting from his having been scared by Channing Pollock as a child, I would rather listen to the average Anderson play, whatever its dramatic defects, than look at many other American writers' plays, whatever their purely dramatic virtues in turn. As a paid critic it is my duty to indicate Anderson's shortcomings as a dramatist, but as a lay individual, it is also my duty to confess that I am a ripe sponge for the beauties inherent in the English language and that when a playwright comes along who knows how to extract and merchant them I frequently am willing comfortably to forget whether he is a great hand at drama or not.

The lay aspect of a critic, however, is uninteresting to one seeking the more sober facts of criticism, so criticism be it. In the trio of plays mentioned, Mr. Anderson again affords ample proof that if drama consisted merely of the aforesaid harmonious weavings of the English language he would be the best of present-day American dramatists. Drama, however, consists in something more than that, and it is because he has not yet mastered these vital other elements that his position remains on a very considerable and slippery rung, at least, beneath his aspiration.

Mr. Anderson's uncommon virtues and regrettable shortcomings are once more visible in the plays in point. All contain much lovely song. All— the second named in particular—disclose a mind and a point of view superior to the playwriting general. And the second combines with its other qualities a small measure of that precious after-image, a small measure of that day-after recollective warmth, which in its full is the stamp and mark of important drama. But all, the superior second as well as the inferior first and third, lack the strong, taut, purple cords to tie up and bind closely into a whole their isolatedly commendable elements and their periodic stirring notes of dramatic music. *The Wingless Victory,* accordingly, emerges simply as a poor, rickety play garnished here and there with sympathy-coddling philosophy and with some flights of ear-oiling poetry; *High Tor* is a brave attempt at fantasy much of whose language is in fine key with its plan and a number of whose separate incidents are dramatically first-rate but whose whole is defectively articulated and not a little disturbing in its failure deftly to dovetail its rapidly shifting tempers; and *The Masque of Kings* is a bastard lyric-dramatic opera sung by Thoedore Dreiser, Hervey Allen and various other such linguacious and multiloquous divas of belles-lettres.

The Wingless Victory, remotely reflecting the Medea legend and at the same time more immediately repeating the thrice-told tale of the New England sea captain who brings back to his hide-bound home a Malay woman as wife, employs the familiar materials as a funnel for a diatribe against racial, religious, and moral bigotry. What eloquence the author's well-molded phrases bring to his argument his uneloquent dramaturgy largely invalidates. One gets in the theatre the impression of a lawn full of beautifully upholstered furniture waiting to be moved into a locked house, with the movers occupying their enforced leisure in happy bouts with the booze bottle. The air is full of lush impulse and potential movement, but the door remains stubbornly closed. And gradually one grows weary with waiting. *High Tor* is an effort to combine the Rip Van Winkle legend with the creatures of today's world, an attempt to brew from a kind of modern Catskill *Midsummer Night's Dream* a contrast between the ghosts of yesterday and the flesh of today and to distil out of it the philosophy that reality suffers no escape and that the impossibility of escape is not without its compensating reward, however evanescent. The play contains episodes and passages that flick the mind and touch the heart; it sometimes, though less than the same author's *Winterset,* transforms the stage into an orchestra platform warm and vibrant with the melody of winged writing; but it remains in its entirety the dream of a drama on its way into the theatre. For such dreams, albeit unrealized, the theatre must, of course, be sentimentally grateful; it is not vouchsafed many of them in these days. Yet criticism haplessly must deplore what sentiment too often finds wholly satisfying. Mr. Anderson, applaudable as he unquestionably is, finds his rich materials in the end his master. Not his master, true, when it comes to words, but his master nonetheless when it comes to compact, coherent drama.

The publishers of the third exhibit, *The Masque of Kings,* make considerable point of the fact that they have issued the play in its full, original, uncut form. The news is somewhat disturbing. As a general rule, at least in his more recent years, Mr. Anderson is much more dramatically valuable when cut, and cut liberally. For as time goes on he seems more and more to give himself to verbosity, apparently in the belief that an eloquent nonstop talker is *ipso facto* an important and irresistible dramatist. Someone should tell him that even Shaw, the most eloquent non-stop talker in modern drama, has become something less than irresistible to audiences in late years and that his garrulous plays have sadly detracted, rather than happily added, to his importance.

It isn't that Mr. Anderson doesn't, as I have said, write and talk well. There is at the moment, as I have also said, no fellow American playwright who so often uses as rich and beautiful phrasings (or so many of them). It is, rather, that he gives one the impression of a man who, going to the bullfight that is the drama, occupies himself during its thrilling progress with lengthy poetic disquisitions on taurian zoology and with delicate comparisons of the glint of Toledo steel to the gleam in the eyes of Torquemada's best girl. I have no complaint against the disquisitions and comparisons as such. Some of them are in themselves sufficiently dulcet. But the obvious enough fact is that they get in the way of and distract people who came to see the fight. So with his plays. Just as they seem to be on the point of grasping dramatically at the attention and interest, Mr. Anderson heaves himself onto the scene with a colossal verbal squirt-gun and sprays the vital action into a theatrical extermination. He may love life, but when he enters a theatre he becomes eccentrically platonic about it. He reveals himself, in this sense, a lover who talks himself out of his beloved's favor.

In the theatre, *The Masque of Kings* was pruned and it could well have stood further pruning. Attempting to derive a philosophy, so to speak, from the familiar and now somewhat mothy record of Mayerling and the lovers[1] who met their deaths there, the playwright constitutes himself a dramatic traffic signal that flashes red every time anything starts to move. Dramatic action gets little or no password from him; he halts it constantly with speeches, nay, more often with lectures. Even before shooting himself to lie beside his Vetsera, Rudolph—with Anderson encouragingly patting him on the back—cannot resist something closely approaching an oration covering the passing of kings, the shadows cast by medieval conquerors, the rising of nations, the new leaders, the new batch of devil-faces, the despair of European youth, and the senseless killing of men on invariably blind altars.

As has been noted, much of what Anderson writes and says is of a high and lovely sound and sometimes, even, of a high and fine nobility of mind. But, as I have also noted, he writes and says so much of it that he drowns in it the struggles of his drama. And all that is left at the finish are the bubbles on the top of the flood, gurgling, gurgling, gurgling.

It has, I believe, come to be an accepted critical fact that a dramatist may distort historical facts howsoever he wishes by way of dredging up a likely play from them and by further proving whatever it is he may have in his head to prove. Mr. Anderson here takes advantage of this foolish and often offensive allowance in full measure. He brings Franz Joseph into the scene when Franz Joseph could not have been there. He introduces the Empress when fact records that she was at the time nowhere near the Hofburg. And he does various other such things to historical discomfort. It may be his acknowledged theatrical, dramatic and critical privilege, but I do not like it. I remain one of those wayward crackpots who want a historical play to be more or less accurate. At least, any historical play not written by Shakespeare, Shaw, or the Marc Connelly of *Custard's Last Stand*.

The library in all likelihood, as the library sometimes, though surely not always, does, will deceive the reader into perceiving the drama in the three plays that the stage denies them. In this, the reading eye is like the ghosts of *High Tor* as opposed to the stage's breathing, actual creatures in the same play. It represents, as faultfully as Mr. Anderson's dramaturgy, the fantastic imagination in a disjointed pilgrimage with realism. I recall once, and not so long ago, speaking to a celebrated dramatist about a play that I had recently read in manuscript—the work of a novice—one scene which had made a considerable impression upon me. "It's good, very good," he agreed. "In fact, its' damned good. The only trouble with it is that it won't play." "Why?" I asked. "The answer to that *why*," he returned, "is the difference between damned good writing and damned good playwriting."

Maxwell Anderson is a damned good writer. . . .

_____

1. Crown Prince Rudolph and the Baroness Maria Vetsera in 1889.

S. N. Behrman (1893–1973)

Since the felicitously endowed and developing Vincent Lawrence was swallowed by Hollywood, and his talent with him, Behrman has had no native competitor as a contriver of literate, intelligent and thoroughly adult comedy. There has been in him, since first be began to write, a complete and incorruptible probity and a regard only—apart from all other considerations—for himself as an artist. If he has ever thought of editorial checks or theatrical box-offices, it must have been in his sleep, and then only during the Prohibition period of bad liquor. Even his poorer work never fails of dignity. And year by year he suggests a growth visible in the instance of few of his American contemporaries. His *Rain From Heaven*, a study of present-day ethics and prejudices in fierce open clash, is a testimonial to the fellow's fine honesty, very considerable skill in drawing character in short, pithy strokes, high gift for dialogue, and steadfast avoidance of every trace and smell of facile theatrical sham. If he happens to have a theme, as he has in this case, that may best be treated with an almost complete dramatic quiescence—that is, in the Philistine critical sense—well, that is the way he treats it, and to hell with anyone, in or out of criticism or the box-office, who doesn't like it. If he feels a thing, he lets himself feel it, let audiences in turn feel whichever way about it they will, and may they go hang. It isn't that he deliberately slaps popularity in the face; it is rather that he appears never to be conscious that such a thing as popularity exists in the world, or at least in his immediate world. He is a writer, whatever he writes (which is uncritical criticism), with whom our theatre, still replete with posturers and charlatans, may be vastly satisfied.

There is one moment in *Rain From Heaven* that illustrates more nicely, I think, than any in recent dramaturgy the gulf that yawns between the new drama and the old drama of the Pineros whose influence, as Charles Morgan has lately pointed out, dominates still to no little degree the more

_____

From *The Theatre of the Moment* (New York: Knopf, 1936), pp. 270–73. Copyright renewed 1964 by Mrs. George Jean Nathan).

backward and less Anglo-American stages. That moment comes at the curtain to the second act. The scene is Lady Wyngate's house outside of London, wherein—under her hospitable roof—is gathered a party of Americans and of German and Russian refugees. Suddenly jealous of the attention his Lady is privileging the German exile Willens, the young American hero spatters at the latter the sling, "You God damned Jew!", which is immediately echoed by his elder brother. Willens, in the dead silence that follows, makes no move. Whereupon Lady Wyngate, taking his hand, in the quietest and smoothest of voices turns to the two others, still colored with bitter distaste and hate, and says, very softly, very graciously—and unexpectedly and joltingly enough in the case of the young suitor for her favor—"Remember, please, Mr. Willens is not only my lover; he is also my guest."

There never lived a Pinero, a Henry Arthur Jones, an Alfred Sutro or any other such exponent of the older drama who would not, to achieve a facile surprise second-act curtain, have turned that line hind end foremost.

Behrman's *End of Summer,* however, is a disappointment. That he remains, in spite of it, our most important writer of light comedy is still evident, but in this, his latest work, there is form so disordered and attack so periodically groping that the dramatic impression is of a usually very skilful pianist playing a composition that irritatingly keeps slipping off the rack. Some of the scenes, notably one between the predatory psycho-analyst and the attractive daughter of the woman who would have him as husband, are in the author's best vein, but a number of other scenes indicate rather clearly that he has permitted a makeshift resignation and even a certain degree of auctorial despair to fill in spaces left personally unsatisfactory through the failure of imaginative inventiveness to hearken to his pleas. Some of his lines and quotations, too, are streaked with tired cobwebs, for example, the old Bismarck animadversion on the wisdom of the Irish exchanging counties with the Dutch, the collegiate jest as to who it was who psychoanalyzed Freud himself, the character who observes that he is grateful for his deafness as it prevents him from hearing bores, etc. Behrman, to repeat, for all this exhibit, remains our first comedy writer.

Lillian Hellman (1905–1984)

Lillian Hellman's latest play, *The Little Foxes,* provides fresh evidence of its author's high position among American women writers for the stage.

From *Encyclopedia of the Theatre* (New York: Knopf, 1940), pp. 170–71. Copyright renewed 1968 by Mrs. George Jean Nathan.

Both in *The Children's Hour* and in this exhibit—even, indeed, in certain phases of her defective *Days to Come*—she indicates a dramatic mind, an eye to character, a fundamental strength, and a complete and unremitting integrity that are rare among her native playwriting gender. Her dramaturgic equipment is infinitely superior to Susan Glaspell's; her surgery of and grip on character are infinitely superior to Lula Vollmer's; and compared with her, Rachel Crothers is merely a shrewd old girl in a box-office dispensing prettily water-colored parlor tracts. Some of her other sisters enjoy pleasant little talents but there is none in the whole kit and caboodle whose work shows so courageous and unflinching an adherence to the higher and finer standards of drama. Once she has succeeded in mastering her present weaknesses—a periodic confusion of melodramatic bitterness with suggestive tragedy, intensified and unrelieved acerbity with mounting drama, and a skeletonization of episode[1] with dramatic economy—she will find herself occupying a really distinguished critical place in our theatre.

Her most recent play is a scrutiny of social and economic changes in the South at the turn of the present century. Related in terms of a middle-class family of rapacious and conniving knaves bent upon outdoing not only one another but upon sacrificing all that is proud and fine in the tradition of the old southland to the new economic slavery and the new capitalistic greed, it may flippantly be described as a Dodie Smith nightmare. It may also be less flippantly described as the very best illustration of the difference between the current cheap and squashy family drama calculatedly manufactured by English female pastry cooks and the fond intention, at least, of American women like this Hellman to bring to the stage that inner inviolable dramatic vitality and thematic meat that London critics on brief excursions to these shores have often in the past so offendedly and patriotically minimized and derogated. From first to last, *The Little Foxes* betrays not an inch of compromise, not a sliver of a sop to the comfortable acquiescence of Broadway or Piccadilly, not the slightest token that its author has had anything in her purpose but writing the truest and most honest play on her theme that is was possible for her to write.

The central characters are a woman and her two brothers who individually and apart brook no interference with their selfish determinations to get for themselves what they want out of family, community, finance, and worldly position. The woman is hard, disillusioned, and merciless to the point of contributing to the death of her invalid husband in order to perch herself on top of the heap. The brothers descend to perjury, theft, and even to veiled threat of murder-accusation to dislodge her from it. (In handling of character, the ghost of Strindberg here and there unmistakably and occasionally a bit too obviously peers over Miss Hellman's shoulder as in the treatment of theme the ghost of Ibsen—momentarily, too, the ghost of the Pinero of *The Thunderbolt*—here and there edges the spook of Strindberg to one side.) The conclusion resolves itself into a temporary triumph for the wily, slate-hearted female but with the evil of the money-hungry brothers' machinations a cloud darkening her future. And out of the parable of boiling acid there emerges the disgust and defiance of a new, young generation that throws into the face of mankind the challenge of human decency, fairness, equity, and honor.

Christopher Fry (b. 1907)

After disfranchising modern dramatic poets *in toto,* my friend the late James Agate[1] wrote to Fry: "And why must you fellows all write plays with titles like *Turn Right For The Crematorium?* Is there no other subject in the world except death? I suppose that, being youngish, you still think death is great fun. I am oldish, and don't." He further wrote to him on reading the script: "I decline to let your "A Phoenix Too Frequent" cheat me of a sigh or charm me to a tear. I get almost no pleasure from it, because it makes me work too hard. . . . And you want me to slog out to some hole in some suburban corner to listen to [among a half dozen other sarcastically listed passages]:

> *Dynamene.* What appears
> Is so unlike what is. And what is madness
> To those who only observe, is often wisdom
> To those to whom it happens.
> *Tegeus.* Are we compelled
> To go into all this?

The answer is that I am not, and won't.

To which Fry replied: "Alas, it [the play] seems to have been a very solemn affair to you and not a joke at all. . . . No, you don't win your case by quoting passages which were never meant to be poetry in order to prove that I can't write it. . . . As for the 'dreadful' line, 'And very pleasant too. Did I interrupt you?' you can't pretend to me, Jimmy, that you didn't know it was meant to be comic bathos. You know it's a trick I have all the way through following the flickers of poetry, as I prick the bubble of the love scene with 'Is your husband expecting you?' And the laughs come, and that's what I want."

To which in turn Agate: "So that's what highbrows laugh at? . . . Is *This*

From *The Theatre Book of the Year 1949–1950),* pp. 274–78.

Way To The Tomb meant to be funny too? And what started all this wild hilarity—*Murder In The Cathedral?*"

Jimmy Agate was a man of abundant humor, but it appears to have stopped suddenly short when confronted by the poetic drama, whether serious or humorous, since it was his singular conviction that "there has been no poet with any sense of drama since Shakespeare, and I don't believe there is any dramatist living today with any sense of poetry. Or any poet either."

So much for the prosecution. Now for a word from the defense . . .

Though this short play—it runs only about an hour—is admittedly and decidedly inferior in almost every respect to *The Lady's Not For Burning* . . . it nevertheless has some merit on its comparatively lesser level and has in it a number of the felicitous touches that set its author apart not only from many of the playwrights presently operating in the English language but from those who further operate in it in terms of poetry. If, as I have written before, there is at the moment another new writer for the English-speaking stage with Fry's gift of poetic imagination, humor, and wisdom—as wisdom goes these days in the theatre—I have not had the good fortune to encounter him.

The little play, announces the author, is based on a story from Jeremy Taylor, who derived it in turn from one by Petronius called "The Matron Of Ephesus." (Gotthold Ephraim Lessing, Fry may be told, also derived a one-act play from the same source and gave it the same title.) It has only three characters: a beautiful young widow, her female attendant, and a young soldier; and the scene is the tomb of Virilius, her late, tearfully mourned husband. The theme is a simple one: that love, however deep, is to be fulfilled by life alone. Or, as the widow devoted to the memory of her departed expresses it to the puzzled soldier who has at length argued a second love into her: "How little you can understand. I loved his life, not his death. And now we can give his death the power of life." The theme is related through the story of the court-martial and death that imminently threaten the young trooper set to guard the body of a hanged man which has disappeared and of the practical decision of the young widow not to allow a body that isn't there to come between them and to substitute in its place that of her beloved, deceased husband. But theme and story are of much less importance than the lilt of language and seasoning of wit with which Fry has creamed them. And, above all, the whimsical ingenuity with which he has held in check expression when in danger of becoming a bit highfalutin'.

Descriptions of poetry are usually unsatisfactory for the same reasons that descriptions of a remarkable dish of goulash are. You have to taste it to appreciate it. Descriptions of wit, furthermore, are scarcely less so, since the wit is often a matter of context and, removed from it, becomes in quotation a little suspect. The reviewer thus takes chances with his critical reader, and since I do not like to take any such gratuitous chances, I let Fry speak for himself by quoting several random samples of both.

"Life and death," he writes, "is cat and dog in this double-bed of a world." Again, "The sun itself trails an evening hand in the sultry river." Again, "It seems he has a soul as well as his other troubles." Yet again, "If I were still of the world, and not cloistered in a colorless landscape of winter thought where the approaching spring is desired oblivion." And still again, "He has a tacit misunderstanding with everybody and washes in it."

Even such direct quotation, I begin to see, loses considerable; one can't get the flavor of a juicy pineapple by nibbling the rind. Yet even the rind isn't bad after one for so long has been on a dramatic diet of peanut shells. Herewith, therefore, a few more nibbles:

Speaks the widow: "When the thoughts would die, the instincts will set sail for life. And when the thoughts are alert for life, the instincts will rage to be destroyed on the rocks. To Virilius it was not so; his brain was an ironing-board for all crumpled indecision." Again the same, savoring her cool drink, "How good it is, how it sings to the throat, purling with summer," to which the soldier adds. "It has a twin nature, winter and warmth in one, moon and meadow. Do you agree?" and the widow's, "Perfectly; a cold bell sounding in a golden month." And still again, after a fancy poetical flight: "Why should scent, why should flavor, come with such wings upon us? Parsley, for instance."

It is not that there aren't some worms in the fruit. For example, such facetiæ as "by Jove, by Jove"; such lines as the widow's "I think of you as a crisp loaf" and the soldier's "And now you'll insult me because I'm not sliceable"; such youthly philosophies, in connection with a desire to find a reason for living, as "It leads to death—that may be life's reason"; such pretty writing as "how a star ran through me, to live in the brooks of my blood forever" and as "your throat is a white branch and my lips two singing birds"; and such lingo, introduced into the poetic pattern for sudden startle effect, as the leave-taking "so long" and the colloquial "anything but." But never mind "A Phoenix Too Frequent" in the aggregate is a delectable tidbit by a man with a lot of other things in his cheek but his tongue, and by one who can make that other tongue, our English language, dance and laugh and smile and sing like no other new British or American playwright who has lately come our dusty way.

---

1. James Agate (1877–1947) English drama-critic who wrote mostly for the *London Sunday Times.*

William Saroyan (1908–1981)

In this William Saroyan, crazy or not crazy, the national theatre, I believe, has discovered its most genuinely gifted new writer. His plays singly and in combination have disclosed and further argue a talent which, as yet undisciplined, vainglorious, cockeyed and pigheaded, is nevertheless the liveliest and most bouncing that has come the way of the local stage in some equinoxes. In that talent, which still resembles a fountain contending against a strong headwind and helplessly splashing itself all over the place, we engage a whimsical imagination, a lenitive sentiment, a fertile humor and a human wonder and ache uncommon to our drama and which in sum make his plays, whatever their occasional critical subordinacies, such welcome additions to the file of American playwriting. He is a peculiar mixture, this young Saroyan, one of the most peculiar it has been my adventure to experience among writers for the lighted platform. Although his dramaturgy is sometimes as sketchy as a child's drawing of Santa Claus or a moo-moo, he not only gets the effect more usually contrived by the more precise artisan but here and there achieves it with a doubled power. And although he seems superficially to sustain his characters, orchid-like, on the thinnest of thin air, they come to us at the end rounded, whole, and completely intelligible. He writes much too hurriedly and impatiently, a symptom of his brash overconfidence. And his plays, accordingly, are not fully what care and meditation might make them. But I, for one, would rather have them in all their relative crudity than any ten dozen others sedulously polished, like old pairs of cheap shoes, into a surface acceptability.

From *The Entertainment of a Nation* (New York: Knopf, 1942), pp. 53–54. Copyright renewed 1969 by Mrs. George Jean Nathan.

Profiles of Other Writers

F. Scott Fitzgerald (1896–1940)
and Zelda Fitzgerald (1900–1947)

F. Scott Fitzgerald once told me that he planned to write a novel about me. It turned out to be *The Beautiful and Damned*.[1] Subsequently he came to me somewhat apologetically and explained that he found that he had tried, but could not lionize me in his novel. He said that he found himself unable to write a heroic character other than himself and that he had to be the hero of any novel he undertook. As I duly discovered, what he started as a heroic me resulted in a wholly minor and subsidiary character not distinguished for any perceptibly favorable attributes.

On such occasions, if he suspected he had offended a friend in any way, it was his conciliating gesture to appear at the friend's diggs the very next morning and to present him with one of his used old pocket handkerchiefs, not visibly re-laundered. That the handkerchief was embroidered with his initials did not notably impress the recipient.

Despite his personal vanity, Scott's life was wrapped up in his lovely young wife,[2] who was born Zelda Sayre in Alabama and whom he met as a young Lieutenant in an Army Training Camp in [Montgomery] Alabama. This Zelda, conscious of her beauty, was something of an exhibitionist and was given to such whimsies as disrobing herself in the Grand Central Station.

On one occasion, indeed, she went to the extreme of getting into the bathtub during a house party at the undergraduate club at Princeton to which Scott belonged and inviting the house guests en masse to come in and revel in her pulchritude, bringing about her husband's suspension from the club and causing a campus scandal of sizable proportions.

On an earlier occasion. Scott allowed that she had divested herself of her clothing and had stood in the middle of the railroad tracks in Birmingham, Alabama, and had waved a lantern and brought the startled

---

From "The Golden Boy of the Twenties," *Esquire* (October 1958), pp. 148–53.

156

passengers scurrying out of the stalled express train. Scott loved to re-count the episode in a tone of rapturous admiration.

Another incident of Zelda's exhibitionism was one that Scott used to remember with considerably less relish.

One night our friend, John Williams, the noted theatrical producer, gave a small dinner party in his apartment just off Union Square. During it the fair Zelda abruptly took off for a splash in the Union Square fountain. Followed by Williams and her husband in hot pursuit, she was encoun-tered there in her birthday clothes surrounded by at least a dozen fran-tically indignant cops.

When Scott sought to intercede with them and to explain to them that it was his wife who was doing the Godiva act, they pushed him aside and informed him that he was on the way to the hoosegow. At this point, Williams ventured to explain to them who their potential jailbird was, whereupon one of the cops, who mistook Scott for Ed Fitzgerald, the popular radio comedian of the time, deemed it his pleasure at meeting Scott and allowed that the lady in the fountain must accordingly be the comedian's wife, Pegeen. This managed to assuage the cops' wrath and to spare Scott and his wife the humiliation of arrest for disorderly conduct.

In his biography on Fitzgerald, which is full of distortions of the truth, Arthur Mizener, currently a professor at Cornell, alleges that I once tried to flirt with Zelda and so enraged Scott that he engaged me in a furious fist fight. The facts are far different.[3] While Zelda and I were accustomed to engage publicly in obviously exaggerated endearing terms which Scott appreciated and which were in the accepted vein of Dixie chivalry, our close friendship was never interrupted.

The subject of our intimate explorations was resolutely fastidious. Scott would have it no other way. It was said of him during his undergraduate days that he sent out questionnaires to prospective feminine dates as to (1) whether they had had their hair washed during the day, and (2) how many baths they had taken.

He once aroused the wrathful indignation of the colored elevator boys in the New York hotel at which he was staying by confining their tips at Christmastime to fancily wrapped bottles of a well-known deodorant. I can further testify from personal observation that it was his habit, to their consternation, to demand of any female companion in taxicabs that they open their mouths so he might determine that the insides of their teeth were free of tartar.

A one-time close friend of his mother has confided to me that, as a baby, he not only cried for Pear's soap but ate it, and with what seemed to be relish.

Once in Paris he burst into my hotel room in the early dawn, pulled me out of bed and proclaimed that he had just read the work of a new to him American writer named Hemingway who promised to be the greatest of his generation.

When in his cups it was his drollery to descend upon my working quarters in company with his friends Edmund (Bunny) Wilson, the now celebrated literary critic whom he deeply admired for his critical gifts, Donald Ogden Stewart, Ed Paramore and Edna St. Vincent Millay, all in a more or less exalted state, and to occupy his talents in applying matches to the rubber bindings on the pillows on my sofa. Their howls of glee when the rubber started to stench up the place could be heard a block away and were matched by my less gleeful own.

Scotty, as he was familiarly called, visualized himself as the banner-carrier of the youth of his generation and was such an admirer and celebrant of youth for its own sake that, although he was polite and even deferential to his elders, whom he usually addressed as "sir," it was clearly evident that he privately considered them all and sundry on the way to an old man's home or ready for the embalmer.

The only evidence of his being interested—and then strictly platonically—in any female of the species apart from his wife was an absurdly young, personable actress named Lois Moran.[4] She was a lovely kid of such tender years that it was rumored she still wore the kind of flannel nightie that bound around her ankles with ribbons and Scott never visited her save when her mother was present.

Once, while I was spending a week-end with him and Zelda in their Connecticut house, the racket made by the house party lasted so long into the night that I had to get up at dawn and, seeking quiet, went down into the cellar. Rummaging about, I came upon some notebooks marked "Zelda's Diary" and looked through them. They interested me so greatly that in my then capacity as a magazine editor I later made her an offer for them. When I informed her husband, he said that he could not permit me to publish them since he had gained a lot of inspiration from them and wanted to use parts of them in his own novels and short stories, as for example, "The Jelly Bean."

There was just one important occasion on which Fitzgerald consulted me in the matter of research on subjects which he was writing about.

It was during that fantastic era known as Prohibition, when he was beginning work on his highly regarded novel *The Great Gatsby*.[5]

Fitzgerald planned a novel about a fabulously rich Prohibition operator who lived luxuriously on Long Island, and he asked me to introduce him to such persons I happened to know who might supply him with proper patterns and the necessary atmospheric details.

When I duly made him known to one such, Nicky Bates, who except for an habitual spruce and natty shirt, closely resembled the present Yogi Berra, he protested that it was not at all what he was looking for and that he hoped I would put him in touch with a glossier specimen closer to the type upon which he sought to model his character.

On a subsequent week-end I accordingly took him to a house party on Long Island at which were gathered some of the more notorious speakeasy operators and their decorative girl friends. When we departed the scene, Fitzgerald objected that this, again, was not what he wanted and that I was guilty of playing a joke on him and introducing him to a party of Wellesley girls and their Rutgers boy friends.

Fitzgerald was spoiled by too early success. His first novel, *This Side of Paradise,* which he wrote when he flunked out of Princeton, was an immediate success and netted him more than forty thousand dollars. He afterward expected every other one of his books to be a like success and lived up to what he imagined would be his subsequent income. He could not understand why everything that followed was not as financially rosy and, though he never lost confidence in himself, one could readily detect his disappointment and even indignation.

"I am writing better than ever before," he once said to me, "and, though they seem still to like my stuff, public taste would appear to be not so good as it once was."

Fitzgerald so regarded his popular acceptance as the logical thing that when he entered a smart restaurant or even a roadside hot dog stand he was ruffled if the waiter or counterman did not greet him in terms otherwise befitting a candidate for the Presidency. He was, however, in the habit of soothing the offender's embarrassment over his delinquency by slipping him a gratuity, which paid off in terms of the embarrassed servitor's additional protestations that he had committed a dreadful *faux pas* in having failed to recognize Fitzgerald as the eminento which he was.

If any man may be said to have died of a broken heart, Scott was that one.

He himself was aware of what had befallen him since the incapacity of his dearly beloved wife and his surrender to Hollywood, and he described it without reserve in a series of utterly frank confessions which he wrote for one of the popular magazines. . . .

He himself died ultimately forsaken save for a feminine friend (now a noted Hollywood columinist)[6] who had befriended him and consoled him in his dying moments.

Yet, here was a writer who adorned his period with some lastingly lovely writing, with a very true romance in a time of so much questionable realism and, not least of all, with his own warm and friendly company.

What will be the final estimate of him I do not know, but, far from being what has been described as "someone who once kissed a Gibson Girl and told," he left his mark on a generation that will long remember him with deep and tender affection.

---

1. *The Beautiful and Damned* (1922), dedicated "To George Jean Nathan et al.," contains a caricature of Nathan in the character of Maury Noble.

2. For Nathan's relationship with the Fitzgeralds, see Nancy Milford, *Zelda* (New York: Harper & Row, 1970), pp. 97–98; see also Zelda's letter to Scott, p. 216.

3. That the flirtation was not serious is corroborated by Nancy Milford in *Zelda*, pp. 71–72.

4. Cf the 18-year-old actress Rosemary Hoyt in *Tender Is the Night*.

5. See Nathan's letter to Fitzgerald, p. 210.

6. See Sheilah Graham, *Beloved Infidel* (New York: Henry Holt, 1958).

Theodore Dreiser (1871–1945)

It was seventeen years ago that a morning's mail brought to me the brief note from Theodore Dreiser that led that same evening to what was really, save for a casual word some seven years earlier, my first meeting with him. "I urge you please to come down to my place at eight o'clock tonight. I have asked a dozen or so others as well. I want to present to you a significant and very important idea that I have in mind." My curiosity aroused by the cryptic subpoena, I appeared at the little flat on West Tenth Street in which he was then living and was ushered by him into a tiny room packed like soda crackers with a least twenty men, all of them talking at once and nine-tenths of them smoking the smelliest cigars that my nose in all its wide experience had engaged. In the group there was only one man whom I had ever seen before, George Luks, the painter. Who the rest were, I had not the faintest idea and haven't to this day, as Dreiser made no gesture toward introductions further than to announce "Nathan" upon my entrance and as the great news seemed to be completely lost in the eveloping din.

"The others will be in any minute now," he informed me. "Then we can get down to business. In the meantime, find youself a seat on the floor."

Shortly thereafter four or five more men came in. They, too, were strangers to me, as they seemed to be to one another. As Luks, whom Huneker[1] had once introduced me to, was occupied elsewhere and, as I say, I didn't know anyone else, I duly found myself a place on the floor, sat myself simultaneously on it and a small sticky piece of cake that had evidently been lying there for a couple of days, and awaited the significant and very important Dreiserian evangel. After numerous injunctions pray-

---

From *The Intimate Notebooks of George Jean Nathan* (New York: Knopf, 1932), pp. 38–53.

ing the assemblage to shut up and listen to what he had to say, Dreiser took his position in the centre of the mob, blew violently for several minutes at the thick cloud of smoke that hid the congress from his view, took out his handkerchief and, catching two ends of it with his fingers, began slowly to roll and unroll it, and proceeded:

"I've asked you all here to tell you of a plan I've thought of and to get your views on it. It's this. There are a lot of writing geniuses in America who are so poor that they can't go ahead with what they've got in them and who need help. Unless they get help, these geniuses, so far undiscovered, will never be heard of. It's my idea that what we all ought to do is to go around and try to interest rich men in these geniuses and get them to subsidize them. Let me hear your opinions."

He had hardly got the word *opinions* out of his mouth than Luks, a low fellow given, it was whispered, to an occasional indulgence in alcoholic liquor, let out such a loud and derisory hoot that poor Dreiser was a full minute in regaining his equilibrium. Fixing the offender with his characteristic cold one-eyed stare, he bade the reason for the unseemly interruption.

"Who are these neglected great geniuses?" Luks demanded, "Just you name me one!"

"That's not the point," returned Dreiser.

"Well, if that isn't the point," shouted Luks, "for God's sake what *is?* Name *one* neglected genius, old boy, and hurry up about it, as this floor is damned hard and my backside is getting sore."

"There are a lot of them," Dreiser insisted, but his confidence began perceptibly to show signs of weakening.

"All right," hammered Luks, taking a swig out of a pocket-flask that he had thoughtfully brought with him. "All right, old boy, but just you go ahead and relieve our minds by naming *one* of them!"

Dreiser continued slowly to roll and unroll the handkerchief, the meanwhile still fixing Luks with that cold left eye.

"I'm waiting, old boy," chuckled Luks, wiping off his mouth with the back of his hand. "Just you name *one!*"

We waited, but Dreiser made no move.

"Well, I guess the meeting's over," said Luks. "Let's get the hell out of here!"

And the meeting was over.

As some men's hobby is collecting postage stamps or Buxbeutels; and others, discovering out-of-the-way little restaurants or recondite cocktail mixtures, Dreiser's—like Lewis'—is discovering and collecting geniuses. Since the days of my early acquaintance with him, he has discovered and collected about him more geniuses than ever were heard of in the world before. The only trouble with Dreiser's geniuses is that, for some strange reason, no one ever considers them geniuses but himself, conceivably due to the fact, among other things, that they never seem to have done or to do anything. But though they never produce anything to suggest their dower of genius, Dreiser is in each instance sure that they are geniuses. Who they are or where they hail from, none of Dreiser's friends has ever been able to learn. What is more, their names are for the most part and remain for the most part meaningless. They do not write books or poems or plays; they do not paint or carve out marble; they do not compose music or play the piano, violin or xylophone. At least, if they do, only Dreiser seems to be privy to the news. But that they all are blessed with the divine fire to an incalculable degree, he will confidently assure anyone who will lend him an ear. I myself have met no less than two or three hundred of these great geniuses either in Dreiser's company or upon receipt of letters of introduction from him. But just what direction their genius took or what masterpieces they were responsible for I have never quite been able to make out, although I have listened patiently and politely to their voluble and enthusiastic tributes to their own talents. Looking back over all the theoretical Flauberts, Beethovens, Sardous and Raphaels of Dreiser's faith, there is only one, in point of fact, whose name appears even faintly to have ever been heard of outside of Dreiser's rooms. That one is the recently deceased Charles Fort, a writer happy in the conviction that all science is simply so much blather, and in whose enormous metaphysical and literary prowess Dreiser had fervently and steadfastly believed for all of fifteen years. What has become of his other many pets, I do not, as recorded, know.

When first I met him, Dreiser, as I have said, was living in a couple of two-by-four rooms in West Tenth Street. He was miserably hard up and was existing, he told me, on something like ten dollars a week. But he never whined, never grumbled. In all that time, indeed, I heard him complain only once and that was because whoever lived in the cellar under him—his rooms were on the first floor of a seedy and dilapidated three-story house—made so much noise at night that he couldn't work. He subsequently learned that the cellar was occupied by two foreigners engaged in the august profession of counterfeiting. The police some time afterward backed up a patrol-wagon late one night to apprehend the knaves, but the latter, while the police were gumshoeing around the front of the house, quietly departed out of the rear entrance. Thereafter, Dreiser was able to pursue belles lettres in peace.

Although his rooms looked like a brace of dry-goods boxes that had been left on a wharf during several months of severe storms, he had exercised himself to give them a tone. The aforesaid tone was accomplished by covering the two windows with red hangings which excluded all light, illuminating the *mise en scène* with candles, and maintaining a small phonograph in constant operation upon three mournful Russian musical records. There, for hours on end, he would sit in the dim candlelight, rolling and unrolling his handkerchief, and listening in rapt taciturnity and open-eyed wonder to the dolesome emanations from the wax—at intervals of every five or ten minutes opening his mouth only to ejaculate, "Beautiful, beautiful!"

Now and again in those days, Mencken and I would seek to lighten our friend's obstinate moodiness with facetiæ of one species or another, but never with the faintest degree of success. It was one of our juvenile monkeyshines to fill the mail-box outside his door with a variety of objects, including small American flags accompanied by scrawls issuing Black Hand threats, letters ostensibly written by the President urging him to come at once to the White House for a confidential talk, menus of Armenian restaurants affectionately inscribed to him by Robert W. Chambers, Elinor Glyn and Harold Bell Wright, frankfurters tied with red, white and blue ribbons, beer-bottle labels, photographs of the Czar bearing the inscription, "To Theodore, gentleman and scholar—well, anyway, scholar," and other such nonsenses. Dreiser's invariable retort was to go out, buy a ten-cent Street and Smith paper-back by Bertha M. Clay and present it to us with the sour remark that it was the only kind of literature either of us could understand. This was his single form of humorous repartee. I still have, among the works of the Mlle. Clay that he presented to us, such masterpieces as *Redeemed by Love, or Love Works Wonders, For a Woman's Honor, The Gipsy's Daughter, A Heart's Idol, Another Man's Wife, Gladys Greye* and *His Perfect Trust.*

On one occasion, knowing how badly he needed money, Mencken and I consulted an acquaintance connected with the moving pictures in an effort to get him some kind of offer that might bring him easy funds and permit him to pursue in comfort the novel[2] that he was then working on. We finally got an offer for him of two thousand dollars. All that he would have to do was to pose before the camera in his own person, seated at a desk writing. The picture dealt with a novelist and it was the idea to show a well-known novelist at work by way of an introduction. He was not to figure in the story; after the short series of shots his job would be done and the two thousand dollars would be his. Not without a feeling of satisfaction over our achievement, since it involved no invasion of Dreiser's dignity, we hurried down to tell him of it. Firmly convinced, despite our protestations, that we were up to another joke at his expense, he grew excessively indignant, cursed us out roundly, and refused us the honor of personal contact with him until further notice.

It was fully six months before I saw him again. We found ourselves seated next to each other at a small stag dinner given by T. R. Smith in a private room at the Beaux Arts restaurant. Dreiser, who had succumbed to the geniality of the wassail bowl, was in high spirits, roaring with laughter over any and everything, pulling chairs out from under the guests, offering toasts to the glory of Jehovah, and making loud Swiss music on the table glasses with his knife. "So here you are again, by God!" he bellowed, clapping me lustily on the back and mussing up my hair. "So here you are again. Well, well, well! Look who's here, fellows! It certainly is an awful sight. Yes, sir, it certainly is! Take a look, all of you. My God, what a face! So here you are again!" And so on for fully fifteen minutes, all to the accompaniment of reverberating yowls of pleasure and chuckles of self-satisfaction over his great sardonic humor. So tickled was he, indeed, over his imagined complete retaliation for the moving picture episode that we became friends again in his eyes and have so remained, without further interruption, until this day.

Only once was that friendship even mildly threatened and that was when Mencken and I, then editing *Smart Set,* after publishing a number of his manuscripts of the usual more or less despondent nature, suggested to him that he do a story for us of a somewhat different character. "What kind of story?" he wanted to know. "Why not a society story," suggested Mencken, swallowing a grin. "Something very swell and tony. Get out of the tenements and dirty undershirt atmosphere for a change. It'll do you good." Oblivioius of Mencken's jocosity, Dreiser allowed that he might try his hand at some such story and, lo and behold, about two days later the result arrived.[3] The scene was laid in Cincinnati and the occasion was a great ball given by the leader of the élite in that city. The very air quivered with *ton*. There were "no less than dozens of butlers" and the heroine, "an heiress of the *beau monde,* swept down the great staircase attired in very trig green satin." Other ladies present were also attired in "trig green satin" and the climax of the "trig affair" came when the hostess confronted the "fashionable multi-millionaire, Mr. Diamondberg" and accused him, in the middle of the ballroom, of having swindled her husband out of a street-railway franchise. When we sent the story back to him, he was surly over our failure to appreciate its elegances and held me equally responsible with Mencken for having wasted his time and energy.

As, gradually, money came to him from his writings and life became easier for him, his nature expanded in many directions. His attitude toward his work did not change; for nothing, I believe, could ever change that. If he had ten dollars in his pocket or ten hundred thousand, nothing or no one could influence him once he took pen in hand. Even in the poor days when at times he was forced by necessity to write on order, he wrote with complete honesty, the best he knew how, and—whether it was liked and accepted or not—with a sincerity that was not to be mistaken. If he has ever done hack work, he at least did not regard it as such. Even the story about the heiress of the *beau monde* attired in trig green satin was an honest job so far as he himself viewed it. But, if affluence altered his attitude toward his work no whit, it altered—and why not?—his manner of living. The first large round sum of money that came to him, the proceeds of the sale of *An American Tragedy* to the moving pictures, resulted in the installing of himself in an elaborate duplex studio apartment, with a brace of colored girls in white caps and aprons to add a note to the scene, with monthly soirées and receptions involving the activities of Hungarian violinists, Russian colatura sopranos, and an international and marvelous assortment of dubious pianistic professors; with a cut-glass punch bowl, banked with lettuce sandwiches, caviar sandwiches and *petits fours,* glistening in splendor on the dining-room table. There also followed the purchase of an estate up the Hudson, with a remodeled house large enough to hold a good part of the Authors' League of America, and with a swimming pool, a small lodge house for visiting bachelors, and a set of very dégagé after-dinner coffee cups. There appeared on the scene, as well, what is known as "a man," a colored gentleman whose profession embraced the taking of cards at the door, the pressing of trousers, the service of beverages and a close scrutiny of the behavior of any visiting poets. "Is it possible that that host of ours was Dreiser, *Theodore Dreiser?*" Fannie Hurst once demanded of me in ironic perplexity upon leaving one of the studio gatherings. "Say what you will, I won't believe it!"

Dreiser's simiplicity, however, for all the great change in his external surroundings, is still his simplicity of the days when he hadn't a cent. His friends are still the friends of those days; his cast of mind is still exactly the same; his diversions are still composed of such innocent adventures as going to the movies, having an occasional dinner in some side-street Italian or Chinese speakeasy, or taking a trip to Coney Island, Asbury Park or Atlantic City. "What I am still looking for," he has told me, "in the midst of all this success that seems to have come to me, is some little greasy one-horse publisher who wouldn't know a mahogany desk if he saw one but who has a high and very real love for literature and who, though he may be poor in money, will have time to talk sincerely with me about my work, and understand the kind of man I am, and let me talk with him through the nights of all that is in my mind and heart. I am sick of these business-men publishers with their offices that look like the *lle de France* and with their minds that look on books as if they were so many boxes of merchandise."

A socialist—"Equitist" he calls it—in philosophy, and a very indignant one to boot, with a passion for writing letters to newspapers and magazines inveighing against the rank injustices of the capitalistic systems, he is so absolutely earnest in his convictions that I honestly believe that if the issue were brought to a head he would be the first to give every cent he owned in the world into the common fund. "I really don't need or want money," he has said to me, "though under the existing order of things you may be damned sure I want and get every dollar that is coming to me. But I could still live on ten dollars a week and probably be just as happy on it." The trip to Russia[4] that he undertook several years ago made a tremendous impression upon him. Among the things other than economic, governmental and the like that moved him deeply and set him to a profound ponderation was Russian art. Immediately upon his return, he sought me out and bade my help in introducing one of the greatest phenomena of this art to America. "It's wonderful!" he proclaimed. "There's nothing in the whole world like it! It will be a revelation to this country!" I asked him what it was. "The Russian ballet," he gravely informed me. "But," I protested, "Americans already know almost as much about the Russian ballet as the Russians. It has been shown here time and again." Dreiser looked at me, disbelief all over him. "You don't say so!" he remarked. "Well, isn't that odd now." He was very much disappointed.

One always finds Dreiser surprised and amazed at what has long been familiar to most persons. When he sees something for the first time, it is discovered to the world so far as he is concerned. Once, returning from a trip through the West, he hotly demanded why no one had ever remarked on the majesty of the Grand Canyon. "It's gorgeous, beautiful, that's what it is!" he announced. "People should be told about it." Going to Europe for the first time at forty, he subsequently delivered himself of a book full of wide-eyed marvelings at various Continental cities, peoples and customs that had already been written about by hundreds of authors before him and that were subjects of long-standing knowledge to almost everybody else.

Even more greatly so than O'Neill is Dreiser fundamentally a lugubrious fellow. Despite his fitful excursions into a swollen humor, his nature is cast o'er with melancholy; and even his occasional search for diversion of one kind or another has implicit in it a tendency toward and taste for the glum, the depressing and the morbid. While I will not go so far as to say that his favorite form of melody is the requiem, it is pretty safe to say that nothing really appeals to him in the way of music save that which, in the bumpkin expression, is described as "sad." In the movies, to which he often goes, only the more drab and despairful Russian films make any impression upon him, although there is a single qualification here in the instance of the comedy films of Laurel and Hardy, which he peculiarly delights in. He cannot stand high lights and, wherever he lives, his rooms have the aspect of an undertaker's boudoir. When he goes to a restaurant, he prefers one that is so dimly illuminated that he can hardly make out whether he is eating spaghetti or chop suey. He spends many hours in drugstores examining the stocks of pills, medicaments, embrocations and tinctures, which he lays in by the wholesale, never traveling out of reach of a pharmacy without carrying with him a suit-case chock full of his grim purchases. Any man with whiskers is immediately accepted by him as a distinguished and very learned person. His taste in reading is for novels in which everyone dies a horrible death and in which the groans fill at least one hundred and fifty of the book's pages.

Of all the writers whom I know intimately, Dreiser is the only one who actually enjoys the physical business of writing. Whereas the rest of these men hate the actual business of putting their thoughts and inspirations upon paper, complain bitterly of the dreadful chore that literary composition is, and do all sorts of things to try to divert themselves from the misery that envelops them when they sit down to their desks, Dreiser would rather write than do anything else. He looks forward to the day's job as another writer looks impatiently ahead to the hour when it will be finished. "I am a writer; I like to write; and I am wretched when I don't write," he has told me. "If I don't produce three thousand words a day, I'm unhappy." He writes, writes, writes. Commonly regarded as being mainly devoted to the novel form, he has written in more various literary forms than any other American of repute. Aside from novels, he has turned out poetry, long plays, short plays, short stories, travel books, special articles on all kinds of subjects, political and economic *feuilletons,* special newspaper assignments, Sunday supplement feature stories, pamphlets, essays, personality sketches, magazine articles, newspaper editorials, dramatic criticism, fashion articles, autobiography, novelettes and magazine fillers. He has written on women violinists, interior decoration, carrier pigeons in war time—"Their Use on Warships and Capabilities in Carrying Swift Information," life stories of successful men, electricity in the household, American portrait painters, Japanese home life, the horseless age, American women playwrights, American female harp players, the Society for the Prevention of Cruelty to Animals, the food problem, the subway, the history of the horse, the rural free mail delivery, Hollywood, Ty Cobb, movie actors, antique furniture, American foreign relations, chicken ranches, baseball, railroad wrecks, street-car strikes, insects, matrimonial problems, Marshall Field, Thomas A. Edison, Philip Armour, Chauncey Depew, Mrs. Clara Shortridge Foltz "A Modern Portia," cats and dogs, babies, metal workers, photography, "Artistic and Literary People in the Picturesque Bronx," the cash register business, sweat shops, the right to kill, applied religion, the Authors' League of America, and diseases. . . .

Almost any kind of movement or cause finds in him a ready-made and excitedly eager sympathizer. Ever since he helped organize something known as the National Child Rescue Campaign back in 1907, he has either been helping to organize or serving on committees to rectify one or another national, political, economic, social or literary ill. His name has figured on more letterheads proposing crusades for or against any and everything than even Mr. Lincoln Steffens' or Mrs. Charles Sabin's. He has been on anti-censorship committees, Sacco-Vanzetti committees, Mooney committees, assistance for starving Armenians committees, baby milk committees, free library committees, committees for a better understanding of the Soviet, bread-line committees, committees for a better understanding of socialism, committees for a truer understanding of communism, committees to raise funds for monuments, tenement investigation committees, committees for better movies, committees to re-open wrongful convictions of alleged criminals, literary committees, committees to protest against the sewage conditions at Far Rockaway, anti-noise committees, committees to beautify Greenwich Village, civil liberties committees, committees to look after the welfare of poets' widows, Indiana state anthem committees, committees to erect statues to his late brother,[5] tree saving committees, sailors' aid committees, committees in protest against the deportation of alleged radicals, committees to investigate the white slave traffic, committees to investigate the condition of mine workers and mill-hands, committees protesting the lynching of Negro Lotharios, committees against child labor, committees against the high cost of living, pro-Ben Lindsey committees, pro-Jurgen committees, anti-Prohibition committees, and scores of others. If he has ever turned down anyone who asked him to serve on a committee, provided only that it did not involve him in the necessity of attending a banquet, there is no record of the fact.

As to criticism of his writings,[6] favorable or unfavorable, he has for the last twenty years displayed a sublime and complete indifference. Indignant over many things, what is said against him personally or professionally is of not the slightest concern to him. When some friend of his wrathfully brings to his notice some particularly ignorant, prejudiced and hasty critical comment on his work, he quietly rolls and unrolls his handkerchief, chuckles softly and says, "Oh, yes?" That is his invariable rejoinder, amplified only on rare occasions with an adagio ejaculation of the *mot de Cambronne*. In all the long time that I have known him, I recall only three instances when anything printed about him invaded his composure in the remotest degree. On each of these occasions what was said about his writings did not interest him in the least; it was the reflection on him personally that mildly tried his temper. The first instance was when James L. Ford asserted in the New York *Herald* that any man who wrote the kind of stuff that Dreiser wrote should be shot, and that it was impossible for any person in decent society any longer to speak to him. The second instance was when the New York *Times*, in an article on Zola's death, pointed out that Zola "had died falling in his own vomit" and that "it would be well for an American writer named Dreiser, a disciple of Zola, to take note." The third instance was when a reviewer on a Montreal paper—I believe it was the *Star*—observed that only a man who had plumbed the depths of perversion could write such a novel as *The Genius*.

One night about a year ago, on the eve of his sixtieth birthday, we sat together over the rosy waters contemplating the literary scene. I telescope a few snatches from his conversation: "Take Shaw. The old fellow makes a sad idiot of himself trying to convince himself through other people that he's still young and spry. I had lunch with him in his flat when I was last in London and guess what the bug did! After each course, he jumped up from the table, grabbed hold of two chairs, placed them some five and a half feet apart, adjusted his chin on one and his feet on the other, and then—in a horizontal position—chinned himself up and down on them for a couple of minutes. When lunch was over and I was safely out of the place, he probably had to go to bed and rest up for twelve hours from the exertion of having impressed me, as he believed, with his remarkable youthful vitality. . . . Take Wells. A notable man, but so persistently damned British in his point of view that I can no longer carry on any correspondence with him. We corresponded for quite a time, but it got so not long ago that his unyielding British prejudices made it impossible for me to get any satisfaction out of trying to exchange opinions with him . . . . Take George Moore. I had a visit with him several years ago and hope to have a long chat on literature with the old fellow. And what do you imagine he spent the whole three hours talking about? About his prostate gland! . . . The trouble with literary men is that they leave widows. When you once wrote that a widow is the financial remains of a love affair, you said a mouthful, my boy! I tried lately to get together a collection of short stories by poor So-and-So, who died some ten years ago, write an introduction to them, and so not only help perpetuate his reputation but get a little money for his widow. And what did the old girl do? She accused me of a plan to make money for myself, together with a reputation, at her dead husband's expense? A fact! All widows of literary men ought to be buried with them. They're generally all the same. I've run up against any number of them in my time and they always imagine that any friend of their late lamenteds is some kind of ghoul. . . . Andreyev is the world's greatest dramatist. His *Devil in the Mind* is a tremendous play. I know it is, because I happen to know a man who's exactly like his central character. . . . David Graham Phillips was as overestimated as hell. But Harold Frederick and Will Payne were two real geniuses of Phillips' day who were never properly appreciated. . . . Don't talk to me of current American literature. The profound amours of amateur emotions—that's what the bulk of it is . . . . I don't believe in saints, but there's one man on this earth who strikes me as being one, and he's Abraham Cahan. . . . Plagiarism? The hell with it! Take Gross, the Chicago merchant who was a friend of mine, and Rostand, who stole his play and made it into *Cyrano de Bergerac*. I thoroughly believe Rostand swiped my friend's play and I helped my friend out in his law-suit. But Rostand made it into a beautiful thing, didn't he, so what are the odds? . . . Critics are getting too rich. More of them ought to starve to death. Every time I hear of a critic who is hardly getting enough to eat I laugh until I bust my galluses. Nothing personal, however, nothing personal, mind you. Ha-ha-ha. . . ."

1. James Huneker (1860–1921), American critic and novelist; author of *Painted Veils* (New York: Random House, 1920). Nathan held him in very high esteem.

2. *An American Tragedy,* which would be published in 1925 by Boni and Liveright and emancipate him from indigence.

3. The story's working title was "The Trig Affair."

4. See *Dreiser Looks At Russia* (New York: Boni and Liveright, 1928).

5. Paul (1857–1906), who changed his name from Dreiser to Dresser; co-author, with Theodore, of the song "On the Banks of the Wabash Far Away."

6. See Richard Lingeman, *Theodore Dreiser: At the Gates of the City* (New York: Putnam, 1986), p. 279 and Lazarus's review in *Indiana Magazine of History* (December 1987), pp. 379–82.

Somerset Maugham (1874–1965)

The recent revival of W. S. Maugham's *The Circle* is at once the occasion for pleasure and regret. It is the first because after these many seasons it remains one of the brightest comedies to have come to the English-speaking stage in our time. It is the second because it once more focuses into our consciousness the sad fact of its talented author's defection from the theatre. About a year ago I asked him if he was determined never again, as was his declaration, to write plays. "I have said that I shall write no more plays," he answered. "But"—and his right eye maneuvered something resembling a wink—"I have left myself a loophole. If ever I get an idea that doesn't fit into a novel and that is essentially theatre, I may change my mind." So there is still hope.

The gift that Maugham brought to later-day British comedy was three-fold: Not only is he one of the most skillful writers of his period and not only is he an expert in the handling of character, but in almost everything he does there is discernible the force of an independent and richly fertile personality. It is the common allegation against him that he is arbitrarily cynical and bitter. Nothing could be more ridiculous. No one who has read him closely or who closely has scrutinized his plays can fail to perceive that he is cynical and bitter only when a particular theme is itself naturally

From *The Encyclopedia of the Theatre* (New York: Knopf, 1940), pp. 250–53. Copyright renewed 1968 by Mrs. George Jean Nathan.

cynical and bitter and when any other treatment of it would be false and corrupt. And even when he engages such a theme there is plenty of evidence that the unruly sentiment that may be at the bottom of even the profoundest cynic gets its free and gracious and liberal play from him.

Take, for a single example, this *The Circle*. Stamped by nine critics out of ten a cynical excursion into comedy, it actually contains quite as much sentiment as the average exhibit by the average English sugar-treat confectioner. It would not, indeed, be too much of an exaggeration to say that this widely accepted specimen of Maugham cynicism is one of the most romantic comedies of the modern British theatre. Cynical? Bitter? Bosh! It simply smiles sympathetically with love on the wing. It cries into its beer over the lost stage beauties of an earlier day—Mrs. Langtry, Ellen Terry, Mary Anderson. It devotes itself to the considerate tenderness of love grown old. It plays wistfully with old albums and it is gentle with mistakes of even those who have done us grievous wrong. It moons over the beauty of first loves and sighs for the loveliness of places where long ago one had been happy. It flatters old age in men and even momentarily extenuates it in women. It is, in a word, one long laugh at cynicism, only at rare intervals punctuated with the relieving injection of a little acid.

Further proof? Maugham, the reputed sourball, makes his young hero a business man, insists he is purely a business man, and then makes him, contrary to popular cynicism, at the same time a heroic and romantic lover. He pursues the hokum romantic point of view by causing his sagacious old Champion-Cheney, quondam member of Parliament, to be outwitted by a young woman. He goes in for such sentiments as: "When I drive about in a Callot frock and a Rolls-Royce I envy the shopgirl in a coat and skirt whom I see jumping on the tailboard of a bus." He argues with a perfectly straight face that the best way to make a woman love a man is for him to give her a black eye, surely the conviction of dyed-in-the-wool sentimentalists determined to hide their sentimentality. He evokes sentimental pictures with passages about cocoanut trees, azaleas, camellias, winding coast lines, and blue seas. His heart is in such a purple song as "The moon's shining, Elizabeth. We'll drive all through the night. We'll drive through the dawn and through the sunrise." And at the conclusion he cheers his young lovers through the gates and on the warm tropics with (I quote) their blue skies and palm trees all along the beach.

Maugham a cynic? In your hat!

Gertrude Stein (1874–1946)

It is Miss Stein's stout argument that the meaning and sense of words placed together is of no importance; that it is only their sound and rhythm

From *Passing Judgments* (New York: Knopf, 1935), pp. 171–74.

that count. This, in certain specific phases of artistic enterprise, may—for all one's initial impulse to impolite titter—be not entirely so silly as it sounds. Beautiful music often is meaningless (in the same sense of the word) and yet finds its effect and importance in sound and rhythm. Poetry, also, often finds its true reason for being in a complete lack of intelligence[1] and in the vapors of lovely sound and lulling rhythms. Painting, too, need not have "meaning," nor "sense," but may project its power alone by form (which is rhythm) and by color (which is the equivalent of sound). Even drama itself may have little meaning and sense, yet may evoke a curious meaning-without-absence-of-meaning (regards to Dreiser) none the less; for example, Strindberg's *Spook Sonata* or—to go to extremes in even absurdity—something like Mr. Lawson's *The International*.

Up to this point, there conceivably may be something in Miss Stein's literary bolshevism. But now let us see how she combines theory with practice. In demonstration and proof of her conviction that the meaning and sense of words are of infinitely less significance than their sound and rhythm she presents to us, in her *chef d'œuvre Four Saints in Three Acts* such verbal matrimony as the following (I mercifully quote but three samples):

> *One*. To know to know to love her so. Four saints prepared for saints. It makes it well fish. Four saints it makes it well fish.
> *Two*. Might have as would be as would be as within nearly as out. It is very close close and closed. Closed closed to let letting closed closed closed closed closed in justice in join injoining. This is where to be at at water at snow snow show show one one sun'nd sun snow show and no water no water unless unless why unless. Why unless why unless they were loaning it here loaning intentionally. Believe two three. Would could be sad beside beside very attentively intentionally and bright.
> *Three*. The difference between saints forget-me-nots and mountains have to have to have to at a time.

Repressing a horse-laugh and hitching up our earmuffs, let us meditate this archdelicatessen. That Miss Stein is absolutely correct in announcing that it has not either meaning or sense, I hope no one will be so discourteous as to dispute. But if Miss Stein argues that, on the other hand and to its greater virtue, it has rhythm and beautiful sound, I fear that I, for one, will have to constitute myself a cad and a bounder and inform her that she is fish and it does not make it well fish either. In point of fact, anyone with half an ear to rhythm and sound (whether in song, in reading, or in recitation) can tell her that any such arrangement of words—to pick at random—as "beside beside very attentively intentionally and bright" is not only lacking in rhythm and pleasant sound but that, in addition, it is painfully cacophonous. It is perfectly true that words shrewdly strung together may be meaningless and may still sound better than words strung together with some meaning—take Edgar Guest's poetry, for instance—

but one fears that Miss Stein has not mastered the trick which she so enthusiastically sponsors and advocates. I am no Gertrude Stein, but I venture constructively to offer her a laboratory specimen of what she is driving at and fails to achieve. The example: "Sell a cellar, door a cellar, sell a cellar cellar-door, door adore, adore a door, selling cellar, door a cellar, cellar cellar-door." There is damned little meaning and less sense in such a sentence, but there is, unless my tonal balance is askew, twice more rhythm and twice more lovely sound in it than in anything, equally idiotic that Miss Gertrude ever confected.

The contention of a number of music critics who have reviewed Miss Stein's opera is that, inasmuch as one can catch very few words in the average opera and, not being bi-lingual, would understand most of them not at all even if one did catch them, it is of no consequence that Miss Stein's lyrics are completely meaningless and absurd. If both Miss Stein and her sympathetic critics are right—that is, if sense does not figure in the matter, if the rhythm and sound are all that count, and if in opera one can, anyway, only at very rare intervals decipher the words that are being sung—may it not be suggested that Miss Stein abandon in her future operas all such hash as she writes—which unnecessarily irritates the intelligent and the judicious—and achieve a sound name and operatic position for herself by substituting for it such simple and beautifully rhythmical sequences as eenie, meenie, minie, mo, or the even more simple and effective do re, me, fa, so, la, ti, do? Miss Stein, further, is not sincere. Though she professes to be the arch-enemy of the apostles of meaning in the written word, she every now and again halts abruptly in the midst of her verbal monkeyshines and writes some such grammatically orthodox, clear and simple sentence as, "If it were possible to kill five thousand Chinamen by pressing a button, would it be done?" One begins to believe that Gertie is a very shrewd and sapient girl who deliberately plans her writing performances as absurdity and who appreciates that if you keep up absurdity long enough, and with a perfectly straight face, there will always be critics who will mistake the *tour de force* for some strange and inscrutable kind of wayward genius.

---

1. Compare Archibald McLeish's "Ars Poetica," which concludes, "A poem should not mean but be."

H. L. Mencken (1880–1956)

I first laid eyes on the cherub-faced man with the golden hair parted in the middle and slapped down like a barber's on a Sunday morning, and in a

---

From "The Happiest Days of H. L. Mencken" (*Esquire,* October 1957), 46–150.

stiff, starched Herbert Hoover collar on a morning in the early May of 1908. It was in the offices of the old *Smart Set* Magazine, where we had been called in to be offered the respective jobs of literary and dramatic critic. The stranger thrust out his hand to me and exclaimed, "I'm H. L. Mencken from Baltimore and I'm the biggest damned fool in Christendom and I don't want to hear any boastful reply that you claim the honor." Fifteen minutes later, after we had completed our business, we were seated together drinking a mutual congratulatory Florestan cocktail in the bar of the old Beaux Arts Café a block and a half away. "What's your attitude toward the world?" he asked, and continued before I had a chance to open my mouth: "I view it as a mess in which the clowns are paid more than they are worth, so I respectfully suggest that, when we get going, we get our full share."

When we subsequently got going we found ourselves in the posts of co-editors of the magazine in whose offices we had first met. "I see a magazine as something to make the idiotic and the crazy crazier," was his dictum. "So I hope you will agree with me when we propose, first, to get the proper amount of fun out of our jobs and to pray that the money, if any, will respectfully oblige us by duly coming in afterwards."

The popular belief that friendships and even acquaintances met on shipboard, save possibly in the instances of chorus girls, never last and that one subsequently runs as from the plague if one again encounters them after landing takes a twist worthy of O. Henry and even Horatio Alger at his most imaginative in the break that eventually landed Mencken and me in the post of the *Smart Set*'s co-editors and, eventually, co-owners. One day on the return trip of the *Europa* from Europe a stranger approached me on the deck and asked me where I had obtained my exact duplicate of a tweed overcoat that he was wearing. After I imparted the information he requested, he suggested that I join him for a drink in the smoking-room. "What's your name?" he bade me. When I told him, he allowed that I was the only writer he had ever met personally and that he had a proposition for me. "I have just acquired the *Smart Set* Magazine and I offer you the editorship starting as soon as we land." I inquired his name—it was Eltinge F. Warner—and told him that if my recently made friend, Mencken, would serve as co-editor with me I would accept the job. The rest is magazine history.

Mencken said that he would go with me and when, several days later, we arrived at our editorial sanctum, the first thing he did was to cock his shoes up on the handsome mahogany desk to the anguish of our publisher and to inquire of me what I had in mind as our editorial policy. Before I had a chance to answer he interrupted, "After all, that can wait. More magazines are spoiled by the announcement of an editorial policy that their editors soon find they have to abandon if their magazine is to survive

than even magazines with too much money in the bank. Much more important is that we go to work setting up a free lunch for poets. "Poets," he went on, "can no more be expected to write anything worth-while in the way of poetry on an empty stomach or the kind of garbage they have to subsist on in Greenwich Village than Shakespeare, as witness the *Sonnets*. We can't afford to pay them enough money if they are good so the least we can do for them is to content their bellies." The rest of the morning was spent in setting up a delicious lunch on a marble slab that Mencken foresightedly had shipped from Baltimore and that consisted of stacks of liverwurst, pretzels, anchovies, olives, celery and pots of cheese, not to mention ham sandwiches with mustard, Saratoga chips, and a shotgun to frighten off Harry Kemp, the Greenwich Village genius[1] who was destined to be our most assiduous customer.

"I have always maintained, along with the discoverer of that miraculous cure-all of a bygone century called 'Peruna'—which contained enough alcohol tonic to make an arthritic kangaroo jump into the air like a Mordkin coached by a Russian chiropractor—that a man without personal peculiarities was either an unimaginative clodhopper or, I say it with becoming modesty, a genius." Mencken certainly had his share of idiosyncrasies. His favorite cigar—which once as a youth he had rolled in his father's cigar factory and which bore the name of "Uncle Willie" and cost all of five cents—was the priceless gift he bestowed on his carefully chosen acquaintances. These benefactions, each encircled with a handsome cigar band voluptuously engraved with the name of some three-dollar brand, he would bestow with a flourish upon whomever he chose to honor, and always with the words, "I give you this token of my esteem which I have imported from distant parts at a prohibitive cost and with which I beseech you to honor me in return by blowing some of the fragrance in my direction." He insisted that he never felt completely at home and at ease without a cuspidor nearby, and when we set up office at our magazine he brought up from his family's old home in Hollins Street, Baltimore, three brass souvenirs that had once been the proud property of his paternal grandfather. When our fastidious partner caught sight of the ornaments and let out a howl Mencken conciliated him by conceding to drape, at his own expense, the spittoons with cretonne coverings whenever lady authors appeared on the scene. He always said that every man ought to feel rich whether he had a cent or not to his name, and to that end had a habit of distributing ten-dollar bills in out-of-the-way corners of his jackets and pants pockets. "When I accidentally come upon one of the bills," he assured me, "I always feel a satisfactory glow come over me and the

---

1. Irony; actually they regarded him as a clod.

surprise does me no end of good." Whereupon he would lead me into the nearest drink house and set them up.

One of his pet philosophies was, "Whom the gods would destroy they first make popular." But, though he was not in the least gregarious, he always got along with people, even those whom he disliked, and it is a fact that even when he encountered someone he elected to consider an enemy, he was soon in comradely arm in arm with him and so full of good will and joyous spirits that the imagined foe soon became a loving friend.

He hated New York, which he always referred to in his correspondence as Sodom and Gomorrah and was always eager to get back to his home in Baltimore. When he was in New York, which was every other week, it was our custom to walk up Fifth Avenue each morning to our offices. "There is nothing like the smell of gasoline odors to invigorate one more than the Adirondacks," he would observe. "The main trouble with this wicked city of yours is that people here judge and esteem every man according to the amount of money he has, which gives me an idea. Let's impress the booboisie with our eminence by piling up some big mazuma, which should be easy for two such remarkable geniuses as we are, not to say crooks."

He accordingly, with some eloquent assistance from me, concocted a plan to get out a pulp magazine on the side which would be such an atrocity that we would hide when any of our friends mentioned it in our presence. The magazine which we duly published, and which sold out its first issue completely in a single day and netted us and our partners a tidy small fortune, was called *The Parisienne* and catered to the French-American sentimentalists during the First World War. It was adorned with a cover picturing a saucy French minx and contained frisky tailpieces at the bottom of every page consisting of drawings in the manner of those adorning the Paris boulevard magazines. Mencken insisted it be printed on green paper which, he told the readers in an editorial, like the green grass and billard tables, was much easier on the eyes than the white paper on which other magazines were printed and which would guarantee to the readers the welfare of their eyes, otherwise risking serious strain and even occasional blindness. The paper, because of the shortage imposed upon publishers by the restrictions of war, was obtained for us by our senior partner, Eugene F. Crowe, the paper tycoon, who was of a humor on a par with Mencken's. The paper he got us was, haplessly, so rough and so full of wood pulp that Mencken allowed that if the readers found fault with it they could at least use it for toothpicks.

Although those who did not know him sometimes mistook Mencken's air of supreme self-confidence for brag, he often said privately that he considered himself a failure. He was personally a modest man about himself, though he said that even if he was not modest to the point of self-embarrassment he fully realized his potentialities and abilities. He was, indeed, so modest that he always—even after he had achieved literary fame and had published among fifty other books, his monumental *The American Language*—referred to himself as merely a newspaperman. His prankishness, however, never deserted him and among his pet diversions was affectionately autographing photographs to himself of Otto von Bismarck, the German Kaiser and various American Presidents like Calvin Coolidge, Martin Van Buren and Abraham Lincoln. His best-known hoax was the publication of an article that claimed the first bathtub ever to be used in the White House was installed during the Millard Fillmore administration. This news was solemnly reprinted in the *Congressional Record,* has been included in various encyclopdias and has been popularly accepted as gospel.

During Prohibition he imported a famous brewmaster from the celebrated Pschorrbräu brewery in Munich and installed him in the cellar of his Baltimore house. The beverage, which Mencken dispensed to his delighted cronies, was eight per cent in alcohol content and on one occasion it exploded and the brew flooded the house of the next-door neighbor.

Those were the gala days in our friend's life. He said that never thereafter did he enjoy himself so hugely. This was true. For when, subsequent to our sale of the *Smart Set,* we as co-editors founded *The American Mercury* with our good friend Alfred A. Knopf, a change overcame Mencken and, though he never lost his fondness for waggishness, a much more serious attitude infected him. His relative sobriety took the alarming form of a consuming editorial interest in politics and a dismissal of his previous interest in *belles-lettres,* which had been so great a factor in the propensity of our former periodical. The newspaperman in Mencken superseded the literary man and he favored filling the *Mercury* with pieces written by assorted jailbirds, hobos, politicians and riff-raff of all species. The magazine, however, because of the novelty of such material, nevertheless promptly caught on, and though it sold for fifty cents and was very expensive to produce (Knopf had a new type-face manufactured that was so beautiful we found no one could read it and also imported an especial celery paper from Japan on which to print the magazine), it actually made one dollar profit on its first issue. Knopf, incidentally, who is lavish in everything he undertakes, including unheard-of delicacies at his dinner table and shirts so be-hued that they caused Mencken to remark that "Alfred must think he is an Easter egg," went along with us in complete agreement with whatever course, foolish or otherwise, we chose to follow. We didn't, true, go in for such editorial whimsies as, in the case of *Smart Set,* giving over an entire single issue to a full-length novel about an undertaker and his modern methods of advertising (including reproductions of his imbecile advertisements). Nor did Mencken broadcast a request to agents that they send us any and all manuscripts that had been rejected by the loftily self-called Quality Group of magazines, namely, *The Century, Harper's, The Atlantic Monthly, Scribner's,* etc., which manuscripts gave us our most sensational success, Somerset Maugham's "Miss Thompson," subsequently dramatized into the mint known by the title *Rain.* Rather, Mencken endorsed such contributions as a graph-filled treatise on the population growth in Mississippi. But, though it seemed to some that a new and unusual gravity had been imposed upon him by his new editorial post his former ebullience could not be suppressed. As heretofore, he professed, despite his perfect health, to be always dying and he would appear in our office affecting the walk of an old Dixie family retainer suffering from an acute pain in the kidneys. In addition, he would counter everyone else's catalogue of ailments with a lengthy list of his own (This was a favorite device of his to spare himself the necessity of listening to the others' malaises.)

"As for me," he would always write to me, "I am enjoying my usual decrepitude. A new disease has developed hitherto unknown to the faculty. A dermatitis caused by the plates I wear for my arches. No one seems to know how to cure it. I shall thus go limping to the crematory. My ailments this morning come to the following:

    a. A burn on the tongue (healing)
    b. A pimple inside the jaw
    c. A sour stomach
    d. Pain in the prostate
    e. Burning in the gospel pipe (always a preliminary of the hay-fever season)
    f. A cut finger
    g. A small pimple inside the nose (going away)
    h. A razor cut, smarting
    i. Tired eyes."

He was, in short, a walking compendium of mankind's complaints of all natures. If it wasn't one thing it was another. When he appeared in the office one morning, he loudly lamented that, while he did not mind his Negro cook's filching almost everything in his icebox to take home, he objected to having to supply her with a Ford to cart it away. He allowed that he considered it something of an imposition. During Prohibition he complained that his favorite beer hall in Union City, New Jersey, had a sign pasted on its front window reading. "This place closed by the Prohibition Agents," and directly beneath it another adorned with an arrow: "Kindly use rear door," thus necessitating his walking, and in his decrepit condition, at least thirty feet away.

Another grouse was that Julius Klein, the violinist at Lüchow's Restaurant in Fourteenth Street, played his favorite Strauss waltzes altogether too quickly and that he accordingly could not keep accurate time with them with his foot.

When anyone complimented him on the sudden prosperity of the *Mercury* he would reply with his pet rejoinder: "Whom the gods would destroy they first make popular."

"We are pretty good," he would concede to me, "but let's not forget that the embalmer may be waiting just around the corner."

Reverting to his regular complaints, one letter from him had this to say: "I have been trying to start my new book, but an infection in the sinuses has got into my larynx and I am uncomfortable. *Immer traubel!* I begin to give up hope." At another time: "My sister is making a really extraordinary recovery; should she recover completely I assume that I'll be the next to be laid up. I pray, but without hope." And again: "Hay fever has me by the ear and I am making the usual rough weather of it. It seems to be rather more severe than usual. What a world!"

His credo was that we never got a good editorial idea save only over a beer table at night, but that the trouble with it was that when morning came around the idea proved to be no good.

His favorite low burlesque comedian was George Bickel and when he met Ethel Barrymore and discovered that she shared his enthusiasm for the artist, he founded a George Bickel Alumni Association on the spot, and presently gathered into the fold such of the literary elect as Theodore Dreiser, Edgar Lee Masters and Joseph Hergesheimer. Having been a dramatic critic in his young newspaper days, and having seen only the performances of a stock company in his native Baltimore, he seemed to think that the theatre in his later period was constituted in its entirety mainly and only of bad imitations of Ibsen plays and steadfastly refused to be lured into it. Reprimanded on one occasion by our friend, John D. Williams, the Harvard brains of the Charles Frohman offices, who insisted that he was a dolt for his attitude and who assured him that he would change his mind if he were to see a play by the great Italian dramatist, Dario Niccodemi, which in truth was a horrible turkey, Mencken, impressed, was inveigled not only into going to the play but, dressing himself up in evening finery, he sat stoically in a box through the performance without saying a word. But as its end he gave Williams a poke in the eye, with the words, "That was the most dreadful hogwash that ever poisoned my nose!"

He maintained that the wittiest line that the *Smart Set* ever printed was from an anonymous contributor: "When love dies, there is no funeral; the corpse remains in the house." Perhaps his own remark that pleasured him most was, "Hamlet has been played by 5,000 actors; no wonder he is crazy."

He professed to be a disciple of Nietzsche's "Be Hard!" philosophy.

But he never failed to spend hours shopping for Christmas toys for his little niece, collecting fancy cigar bands for her, obediently eating turkey on Thanksgiving Day and getting a tear in his eye whenever an orchestra played *Roses from the South.*

He always referred to himself and me as "two retired porch climbers."

He was proud of the fact that he had an uncle who still drew a pension as a Civil War veteran. He confided that the uncle had patriotically suffered his wounds when Federal draft agents entered a saloon in Baltimore and his uncle slipped on the floor suds and broke a leg in trying to evade them.

Sinclair Lewis (1885–1951)

Late one afternoon eleven years ago, our mutual friend, T. R. Smith, then managing editor of the *Century Magazine,* telephoned Mencken and myself at our office and bade us come up to his flat that evening for a drink. When we got there, we found with Smith a tall, skinny, paprika-headed stranger to whom we were introduced as one Lewis. The fellow was known to neither of us save as the author of a negligible serial that had appeared in the *Saturday Evening Post* and that had subsequently been gathered between book covers and, to me specifically, as the author of a play called *Hobohemia,* produced the year before down in Greenwich Village and exquisitely—if I may be permitted so critically indelicate a word—epizoötic.[1]

Barely had we taken off our hats and coats and before Smith had an opportunity even to fish out his *de luxe* corkscrew from behind his *de luxe* sets of the works of the more esoteric Oriental and Polack amorists, when the tall, skinny, paprika-headed stranger simultaneously coiled one long arm around Mencken's neck and the other around mine, well nigh strangling us and putting resistance out of the question, and—yelling at the top of his lungs—began: "So you guys are critics, are you? Well, let me tell you something. I'm the best writer in this here gottdamn country and if you, Georgie, and you, Hank, don't know it now, you'll know it gottdamn soon. Say, I've just finished a book that'll be published in a week or two and its the gottdamn best book of its kind that this here gottdamn country has had and don't you guys forget it! I worked a year on the gottdamn thing and it's the goods, I'm a-telling you! Listen, when it comes to writing a novel, I'm so far ahead of most of the men you two think are good that I'll be gottdamned if it doesn't make me sick to think of it! Just wait till you read the gottdamn thing. You've got a treat coming. Georgie and Hank, and don't you boys make no mistake about *that!*"

From *The Intimate Notebooks of George Jean Nathan* (New York: Knopf, 1932), pp. 8–21.

Projected from Smith's flat by the self-endorsing uproar—it kept up for fully half an hour longer—Mencken and I jumped into a taxicab, directed the driver to speed up posthaste to a tavern where we might in some peace recover our equilibrium and our ear-drums, and looked at each other. "Of all the idiots I've ever laid eyes on, that fellow is the worst?" groaned Mencken, gasping for breath. . . .

Three days later I got the following letter from Mencken, who had returned to Baltimore:

Dear George: Grab hold of the bar-rail, steady yourself, and prepare yourself for a terrible shock! I've just read the advance sheets of the book of the *Lump* we met at Schmidt's and, by God, he has done the job! It's a genuinely excellent piece of work. Get it as soon as you can and take a look. I begin to believe that perhaps there isn't a God after all. There is no justice in the world. Yours in Xt.,

M.

The book was *Main Street*.

As is sufficiently known, it not only became a best-seller overnight, but it promptly established its author as one of the most observant, penetrating and significant writers in America.

It was more than a year before I ran across our friend again. I had dropped in late one night at a beer conference of four or five literary compeers in a mughouse off Union Square, where we were then in the custom of gathering. We were in the midst of a quiet, if somewhat malty, conversazione when the door flew open and our friend entered. Who had bidden him to come or how he had learned of our meeting-place, no one knew. Jamming down his hat on one of the wall-pegs, he yelled for a Seidel, grabbed a chair and pulled it up to the table, bounced himself up and down on it for three minutes as if it were a mechanical gymnasium horse, and began loudly to sing something in pig-German, accompanying his melodic gifts with gestures that swept two glasses, three Schweitzer cheese sandwiches and one sizable order of Bismarck herring off the table. The song concluded and paying not the slightest heed to our grunts and maledictions, he next yelled for a fresh Seidel (fondly embracing the waiter, whom he addressed familiarly and endearingly as leetle Owgoost), complained bitterly of the slowness of the service, demanded of the assemblage if it did not regard him as the best gottdamn writer in this here gottdamn country, got down at one big gulp three-quarters of the contents of the delivered pipkin, pushed his chair from him, mounted to his feet, cleared his throat several times, and launched into the following declamation:

"Ladies und Chentlemens: It is gewiss a great pleasure, gottinhimmel, für me to have been envited to shpeak to you dis eefining. In rising to address mit you, mit my impromptu shpeech in mine vest pocket, I am reminded uff der shtory uff der zwei Irishers, Pat und Mike, who vas riding on der choo-choo car. Pat und Mike, I forgot me to tell you, vas sailors in der Navy. It seems Pat had der unter berth and by and by he heard such a noise von der ober berth und he called oop asking warum? Und Mike he answered, 'Shure and begorra how can Oi ivver get a night's shlape at all, at all? Oi've been tryin' to get into this damn hammock ivver since eight bells!' Now, ladies und chentlemens, shtanding up here before you great folks, I feel me a whole lot like Mike und maybe after I've sprechen along für a while, I may feel so darn shmall, I'll be able to crawl me into a choo-choo hammock mineself mit no trouble at all, at all."

At this point, he paused just long enough to shout for another Seidel and to drop what he evidently desired us to believe were rich German and Irish dialects. Then—"Gentlemen," he proceeded, aiming an imaginary hunk of chewed plug-cut at a remote corner of the wall, "it strikes me that each year at this annual occasion when friend and foe get together and lay down the battle-ax and let the waves of good-fellowship waft them up the flowery slopes of amity, it behooves us, standing together eye to eye and shoulder to shoulder as fellow-citizens of the greatest city in the world, to consider where we are both as regards ourselves and the common weal. It is true that even with our two hundred and fifty-two or practically two hundred and fifty-three thousand population, there are by the last census almost a score of larger cities in the United States. But, gentlemen, if by the next census we do not stand at least tenth, then I'll be the first to request any knocker to remove my shirt and to eat the same, with the compliments of yours truly! It may be true that New York, Chicago and Philadelphia will continue to keep ahead of us in size. But aside from these three cities, which are so overgrown that no decent white man, nobody who loves his wife and kiddies and God's great out-o'-doors and likes to shake the hand of his neighbor in greeting, would want to live in them—and let me tell you right here and now, I wouldn't trade a corner lot in this fine city of ours for the whole of any one of them—aside from these three, gentlemen, it's evident to anyone with a head for facts that this grand city of ours is the finest example of American life and prosperity to be found anywhere on God's earth! I don't mean to say we're perfect. We've got a lot to do in the way of extending the paving of motor boulevards, for, believe me, it's the fellow with four to ten thousand a year, say, and an automobile and a nice little family in a bungalow on the edge of the town, that makes the wheels of progress go round! That, gentlemen, take it from yours truly, is the type of fellow that's ruling America today; in fact, it's the ideal type to which the entire world must tend if there's to be a decent, well-balanced Christian, go-ahead future for this little old planet. Once in a while I just naturally sit back and size up this Solid American Citizen with a whale of a lot of satisfaction."

For at least twenty-five minutes more he kept on in this vein, occasionally lapsing for a few seconds into dubious German, Irish or French dialect and interrupting himself only with admonitions to leetle Owgoost. Finally exhausted, he dropped with a bang into his chair, spilling half the contents of his Seidel over himself, and waited for some sign of approval of his great comedic gift. There bloomed only a grim silence, save for a quiet remark from one end of the table that the lock on the outer door, evidently defective, had better promptly be replaced with a triple-Siegel. Not in the least disconcerted by the captious lull, our visitor pulled himself together, mopped up the hop moisture from his trousers, and—getting to his legs— lifted the remains of his Seidel above his head and clamorously proposed a toast to the novel he was then working on.

Concluding by this time that there was nothing to be done about it, the assembled literati decided to make the best of things. One got up and raised his Seidel "To our distinguished guest, Sinclair Lewisohn." Another "To Upton Sinclair, author of *Main Street.*" A third observed that it was an honor to have Alfred Henry Lewis present, while a fourth ventured to inquire if the guest could by any chance be May Sinclair.

"Well, anyway, what did you guys think of my speech?" demanded leetle Owgoost's best customer.

The answer was a volume of inelegant mouth-noises.

A few months later the speech was found to be the keynote of one of the sharpest, most bitingly satirical and best novels ever written by an American. Its name, if you haven't already identified it, was *Babbitt.*

I began to meet our friend more frequently. He would stop in at my apartment in the late afternoon for a Florestan cocktail, sometimes so moody that he didn't speak five words and at other times so excited and voluble that he would stand up and, apropos of nothing at all, make speeches at me for an hour on end. These speeches, generally couched in dialect of one species or another, were invariably on one of two subjects: himself—in terms of a facetious self-appraisal predicated upon critics who did not sufficiently appreciate him, and myself—consisting for the most part in deplorings of the unhappy facts that I didn't drink enough, that I didn't have the sense to recognize *Hobohemia* for a swell play, that Mencken and I were nice enough fellows all right but that we ought to get married, and that something ought to be done about our recognizing Stuart Sherman anyway. At other times I would call on him in whatever hotel room he was occupying that week. He never used a chair in any such room, but always favored a far end of the bed, the rest of the bed usually being taken up by a varying and various assortment of individuals who gave one the impression that he had run down into the street and herded them in indiscriminately a few minutes before. Who most of them were, I never had the faintest idea. Many of them looked like a comic-strip artist's idea of anarchists; they all talked at once about everything under the sun;

and they all drank his liquor very proficiently. He called them all by diminutives of their Christian names, always duly announced in introducing each one of them that each was a grand guy, and confidently and enthusiastically predicted to me on each and every occasion that no less than six of those present were virtuosi of one sort or another who one day would take the critics off their feet. None of them—there were at least eighty or ninety he thus eulogized in the period of my visits—has yet been heard of.

He had been living in London for several weeks with Paul De Kruif, his collaborator, working on *Arrowsmith*—originally called *Dr. Martin Arrowsmith*—before I got there on my annual spring trip. The day I arrived I went to a lunch party, where I found myself seated between John Drinkwater and Philip Guedalla, neither of whom I had previously met. I had not sat down before Guedalla said to me, "You are an American and I have a message for you. If your country doesn't recall Sinclair Lewis at once, there will be war between England and the United States!" It did not take a confidante of the oracles to imagine what had been happening. Our friend Red, as his nickname goes, had all too evidently been living up to his sobriquet, if not to its communistic implications, at least in its taurian sense. It developed that the moment he had set foot on the English shore he had begun to make speeches. These speeches—according to Guedalla—amounted up to the hour to a total of something like two or three hundred and delivered in dialect on every conceivable occasion at the rate of a dozen or so daily, or rather nightly—these had mainly to do, it appeared, with the shameful failure of the English critics, excepting only Hugh Walpole, to take a proper interest in American literature. Our friend, despite the German, French, Italian, Cockney and Way Down East dialects in which he couched his diatribes, may have minced words but certainly not meanings. While calling loudly for 'arf and 'arf or a spot of whiskey, old top, named not only names, but also dates, places and weather conditions. Every now and then, by way of prolonging international amity for a little while longer, it had been necessary for De Kruif, a veritable Sandow of a man, to grab hold of his colleague, pull him down into a chair, and sit on him.

On one occasion, I was informed, our genial friend, being entertained by a lady of title and being congratulated by those present on his literary gifts, had indicated his whole-hearted concurrence in the wisdom of the encomiums by running around the room and imprinting a very moist buss on the lips of all the female guests. On another, during a gathering of celebrated English men of letters, he had—after, as is his custom, promptly addressing everyone by contractions of their given names— wound his arms around two of the sedate valetudinarians present and insisted that he be allowed to teach them the American jazz dances. On a third, invited to a dinner in his honor by an English woman essayist and novelist, he had brought along with him two strange Germans, a Russian, three Americans whom he had picked up at the American Express Company that afternoon, and two taxicab drivers, both boiled.

With the completion of *Arrowsmith,* which further established him as one of the most important American novelists of his time, our friend returned to his native land and, finding himself in need of some ready money, applied himself to the writing of a deliberately commercial novel, *Mantrap,* that would need only a camera-man standing behind it and a peroxide blonde in front of it to make a popular moving picture. Always forthright and completely honest with himself, whatever the effect of the forthrightness and honesty may be on the delicate sensibilities of such as leetle Owgoost, Englishmen, Pulitzer prize committees and suddenly kissed dowagers, he made no bones of what he was doing, but frankly announced to anyone who would listen that he was, to use his own locution, turning out a swell piece of cheese to grab off some easy gravy.

His literary cheese duly manufactured, he disappeared from New York for a number of months, traveling the West to gather material for his next piece of work. The night that he got back, he was put to bed with a high temperature, but the next morning—the temperature having dropped to 102—he telephoned Mencken and me to come to dinner with him that night, assuring us that he was in great shape and never felt better in his life. We arrived at about quarter to seven and found that he was still in bed, now with a temperature of 103. No sooner had we entered his bedroom and hardly had we begun to denounce him for a mule for having asked us to dine with him when he was obviously a pretty sick man, than he jumped out of bed, the tails of his short white old-fashioned nightgown flapping about him, and—striking an attitude—began:

"Brothers and sisters, don't you listen for one second to these wishy-washy fellows that carry water on both shoulders, that love to straddle the fence, that are scared of the sternness of the good old-time Methodist doctrine and tell you that details don't mean anything. They do! Let me tell you, brothers and sisters, that justification means something! Baptism means something! It means something that the wicked and worldly—and here I point to some of our fellow-citizens—stand for this horrible stinking tobacco and this insane alcohol, which turns men into murderers, but we Methodists must keep ourselves pure and clean and undefiled. But tonight, on this first day of getting acquainted with you, brothers and sisters, I don't want to go into these details; I want to get right down to the fundamental thing that details merely carry out—and what is that fundamental thing? What is it? I'll tell you, brothers and sisters. It is the Lord Jehovah and his love for each and every one of us, big or small, rich or poor, drunk or sober. Love! Love! Love! How beauteous the very word!

Not carnal love, not love of the flesh, but the divine presence. Love is the rainbow that stands out in all its glorious many-colored hues, illuminating again the dark clouds of life. It is the bright morning and the evening star that, in glad refulgence, there on the awed horizon, call all our hearts—and that goes for yours, Georgie, and yours, Hank—to an uplifted rejoicing in God's marvelous firmament! Round about the cradle of the babe, sleeping so quietly while o'er him stands in almost agonized adoration his loving mother, shines the miracle of Love, and at the last sad end, comforting the fond hearts that bear its immortal permanence, round even the quiet tomb, shines Love. What is great art—and I am not speaking of ordinary pictures but of those celebrated Old Masters with their great moral lessons—what is the mother of art, the inspiration of the poet, the patriot, the philosopher and the great man of affairs, be he business man or statesman—yes, brothers and sisters and Georgie and Hank, what inspires their every effort? Love! Love! Do you not sometimes hear, stealing o'er the plains at dawn, coming as it were from some far distant secret place, a sound of melody? (Shut up, you two bums, and listen!) When our dear sister here plays the offertory, do you not seem sometimes to catch the distant rustle of the wings of cherubim? And what is music, lovely music, what is sweet melody? 'Tis the voice of Love! 'Tis the magician that makes royal kings and queens out of plain folks like us! 'Tis the perfume of the wondrous rose, 'tis the strength of the athlete, strong and mighty to endure 'mid the heat and dust of the valorous conquest. Ah, Love, Love! Without it, we are less than beasts; with it, earth is heaven and we are the gods! Yes, brothers and sisters and you two lice, that is what Love—created by the Almighty and conveyed through all generations by His church, particularly, it seems to me, by the great, broad, wholesome, democratic, liberal brotherhood of the Methodist Church—that is what Love means to us!"

His temperature having now evidently shot up again, he let out a loud whoop, informed us that we were both low infidels bent for Hell, fell back into bed and, exhausted, was sound asleep a few moments later.

At dinner in a nearby restaurant shortly afterward, Mencken contented himself with a single word of comment. It was: "Bughouse!" At dinner in the same restaurant not very much later as time goes, we were congrat-ulatingly buying our friend drinks on the elaboration of the boudoir harangue—where it figured almost word for word—into his now famous and finely ironic novel, *Elmer Gantry.*

One can always tell a new novel coming on when the oratorical mood in any one, single thematic direction assails our friend. *The Man Who Knew Coolidge* was nothing more that a series of such orations gathered to-gether, with not a word changed. They had been delivered in a variety of places and at a variety of times, including the corner of Fifth Avenue and Fifty-sixth Street at high noon, a beer-house in Hoboken at eleven o'clock at night, another beer-house in Union Hill, New Jersey, at two in the morning, the bathroom of my apartment, the men's lavatory at the Rennert Hotel in Baltimore, a publisher's tea at the Sherry-Netherland, several taxicabs, two New York theatre lobbies on opening nights, and the steps of St. Ignatius' Church. *Dodsworth,* a year later, was heralded both before and directly after our friend's European material-seeking trip by innumerable vaudeville performances in the British dialect, aided and abetted by a monocle that he had purchased for the further embellishment of his histrionic talents.

One afternoon a year or so ago, our hero called me up and somewhat mysteriously hinted that I had better be at his house in West Tenth Street at seven o'clock that evening if I didn't want to miss something good. Since he is generally about as mysterious as a traffic cop, my curiosity was aroused and at seven promptly I was on the scene. Three other male guests, as mysteriously summoned, they told me, were already there: one a writer, one a labor leader (our friend at the time was planning a labor novel), and one an intermittent producer of theatre plays. After a cocktail or two, we were bidden to sit to dinner. In the middle of the meal, our host arose and excused himself. Returning a few minutes later, he informed us that he had to have a minor operation performed and had just telephoned the surgeon to come over. We had been invited, it appeared, to stand around and be company while the operation was going on. Protest being of no avail, we had to entertain Lewis while the surgical performance was in progress. "Looking at you guys gives me such a pain," he observed, "that the other one in comparison won't seem so bad."

When some months later the news was flashed over the wires that our friend had been awarded the Nobel Prize, the immense gratification that a number of us felt was slightly modified by qualms as to how the fellow would conduct himself in the presence of Swedish royalty. It was our firm conviction, based upon years of close intimacy, that he would in all likelihood run right up to the Queen, call her by her first name and lodge an aqueous smack upon her lips, and that when he was presented to His Majesty he would promptly and affectionately whack him on the back, put his arm around him, and call him "you old son-of-a-gun." Consequently, on the night the award was announced, some of us gathered together with him and solemnly engaged to offer him sage counsel and instruction in the finer shades of the punctilio.

"For example," we asked him, "what are you going to say to the King when you meet him?"

"What am I going to say?" he roared, waving his arms in the air and knocking over two lamps. "What am I going to say? Well, just you guys listen! 'Your Gracious Majesty and Officers of the Coldstream Guards: It is a great pleasure, let me tell you, for a little feller from Sauk Centre to meet you big Swedes. I feel proud and honored, believe me, boys, and when I get back home and tell the folks of the swell reception you've given me, they're going to be not only proud of me but of you too. After all, we're all brothers in Kiwanis, whether we're Swedes, Americans or Bohunks, and our hearts are in the right place. So what do you all say to going out, King, and having a little drink?' "

Yet once again our old friend fooled us. Just as his whistle, however wet and riotous it may be when he is not in the grip of literary labor pains, is ever of an unremitting and almost Pythagorean aridity when he really sits himself down to work, so his conduct at Stockholm turned out to be so formal and proper—that his August Majesty, together with several members of his court, privy to the eccentricities of American comportment, actually inquired of our hero if he was not, at least on one of his parents' side, partly British.

---

1. That is, disease-ridden

T. S. Eliot (1888–1965)

The play [*The Cocktail Party*], though it scarcely comes under the heading of art, nevertheless betrays further evidence of its Missouri-born-converted-Englishman-converted-Anglo-Catholic author's credo and incidental confessional, expressed early in his career, that art is not a revelation but an escape from personality. His attempts to escape from personality, both inborn and acquired, have been a mark of much of his life. He has put on a show for himself and often no sooner has the curtain gone up on it than he has tried, not always successfully, to sneak out on it unobserved and preserve his *amour propre*. "We may well inquire," Llewellyn Powys wrote some years ago, "how it has come about that this poet, so adept at identifying himself with the predilections of London society, has enjoyed so universal a recognition. His popularity may be accounted for in two ways. First, from his disposition to champion orthodoxy. Secondly, because of the dramatic interest of his personal predicament. . . . Mr. Eliot is a poet who, partly through accident, has allowed himself to become entrammeled by convention and society, and the reading world has been as intent to watch his spiritual struggles as it would be intent to watch an animal in a lethal chamber. His complicated symbols of despair are the outcome of his revolt against the suffocating environment

---

From *The Theatre Book of the Year 1949–1950* (New York: Knopf, 1950), pp. 197–202.

from which he has been too weak or too disillusioned to extricate himself."

Since the review of a play is hardly the place for a psychograph of its author, an expansion of any such inquiry into Eliot's mental composition would be somewhat amiss, but it may sufficiently serve here to say that the play itself offers considerable food to anyone wishing to pursue the matter. It presents, in a way, a chart of his attempted substitution of one personality for another, his psychological vacillations, and his personal doubts and uncertainties. It is, in brief, a tussle between his individual thought and thought gained at second-hand from others, between his personal conventionality and a more worldly unconventionality, and between his realistic self and his adopted spirituality. It is orthodoxy with an incongruous feather in its brain, and with one foot on the earth and the other in the skies. But the play *per se,* for all its marked defects, is at the same time, and this is the more immediately relevant critical point, an honest dramaturgical experiment in the employment of verse in connection with contemporary people which, though not basically anything novel, since other playwrights have already assayed it, has been most satisfactorily maneuvered.

In this direction, Eliot has again subscribed to Lytton Strachey's view of poetry: "It is not the nature of poetry to be what anyone expects. . . . If we look at the facts, where do we find poetry? In the wild fantasies of Aristophanes, in the sordid lusts of Baudelaire, in the gentle trivialities of La Fontaine." Eliot has here sought it in even wholly negligible people of the day and age, and in his surface appraisal of them. In an analysis of his intentions and purposes, he has stated his position in part thus: "Poetic drama must try the most daring thing, and surrender any momentary advantage that may be got from making up with nice poetry what is lacking in dramatic quality. Specifically, I have been trying myself to get away from the chorus. . . And now I have written a play in verse with no chorus whatever. . . . My second notion is that I only want to write plays of contemporary life. For me, at least, a play set in the past, or in some fictitious place or time, would be an evasion of the immediate task. I think that if poetic drama is to establish itself again, after three hundred years, it has got to show that it can deal with what appears to be the most refractory material: a plot of contemporary people, such as the men and women we know, in the usual clothes that they wear today, in the same perplexities, conflicts and misunderstandings that we and our acquaintances get involved in, and uttering no lines that are not relevant to the situation, the mood and the dramatic action."

He continues: "But, if this is our aim, we may be asked what is to be gained by writing in verse instead of prose? Why go to all that trouble, and add to the difficulties of both actor and audience, by saying in verse what can be said as well in prose? Well, of course, the answer is that we also have to show that it can not be said so well in prose. The purpose of the verse should be to operate upon the auditor unconsciously, so that he shall think and feel in the rhythms imposed by the poet, without being aware of what these rhythms are doing. All the time, these rhythms should be preparing the ear of the audience for the moments of intensity, when the emotion of the character in the play may be supposed to lift him from his ordinary discourse, until the audience feels, not that actors are speaking verse, but that the characters in the play have been lifted up into poetry. For the effect of first-rate verse drama should be to make us believe that there are moments in life when poetry is the natural form of expression of ordinary men and women. In fact, I should say that poetry should be the norm for dramatic expression; and that it is more possible for poetry to adapt itself to the uses of prose than for prose to perform the functions of poetry. We have to show that, if poetic drama is restricted in its scope, prose drama is still more restricted; and that without poetic drama we are cut off from the expression on the stage of some of the most intense and subtle kinds of feeling."

In other words, as Eliot's friend, associate and present stage director, Mr. Browne, interprets it: "If the characters' speech is confined to the ordinary, to the prosaic dialogue people normally use, they must grope helplessly for expression at the moments of deepest emotion, and they must largely fail to explain their deepest thoughts. The range of expression is widened when the poet takes charge." That there is some sense in all this is fairly clear, though prose has scarcely handicapped dramatists of genuine talent, as some of Shaw's plays, for example, have amply and very handsomely proved. But Eliot has done nicely by his theory and has come off well. His auditor, as he has hoped, does think and feel in the rhythms imposed upon him, at least in the theatrical sense; and the verse is unobtrusive; and the effect, it is to be admitted, is one of naturalness. So far, so good.

But we come now to the matter of the play itself, that is, the play as a play. I trust that I may not be charged with an undue levity when I remark that it might have profited Eliot if he had heard the Joe E. Lewis song, "Sam, You Made The Pants Too Long," for his exhibit needs considerable shortening to make it dramatically tolerable. As it stands, it is so excessively windy that only by bracing one's self with that hope which ever springs eternal in the reviewer's breast can one drag one's self, after a first act that is more endlessly talkative than an encouraged parrot, to return for the second. The allusion to a parrot is apt, since Eliot's observations on human relationships in that initial, interminable act are one long string of cuckooed platitudes and, in view of the fact that they deal mostly with the idiosyncrasies of married and unmarried love, would impel one, if one were not above such things, to describe him as a Porto-nouveau-Riche.[1]

The aforesaid hope in the reviewer's breast this time, however, stands him in fair stead, for the second act, though also calling for Sam's attention, takes a turn for the better and, while not entirely escaping platitude and while still clouded by Eliot's commercial mysticism, is not only comparatively fresh and lively but brings to its materials, particularly in the scenes between the psychiatrist and the characters bedevilled by their amorous problems, both some theatrical ingenuity and humor, if little practical sense. Eliot's religious philosophy, insofar as one can penetrate its opium smoke, here suggests that of a sophomore Methodist boning up for examinations in Catholicism; and his sexual philosophy is no less that of a man whose dalliance with women seems to have been confined to hand-holding in an ivory tower. As an example, consider his treatment of what is really his principal distaff character. He gives us a young and obviously inexperienced, beautiful young woman who has been having a passionate affair with a married man which, she hopes, will ultimately lead, after his conjectural divorce, to marriage. When he informs her that he can not and will not marry her and that their affair must end, she hurries distraught to an all-wise psychiatrist, vaguely identified as the Deity. To him she woefully confides that something has gone out of her that never again, she feels, can she give love or receive it; that, in short, the love impulse has died within her. The all-wise one thereupon advises her that there is but one means for her salvation, and that is in self-sacrifice. He dispatches her, accordingly, to a savage, plague-ridden land in the East where she selflessly serves the mortally ill and is rewarded for her pains by being crucified by the natives.

Passing over the largely irrelevant Saviour analogy, what have we here? We have, plainly, both sprinkled with mystic cologne. The young woman's conviction that her disappointment and grief have permanently made her immune to love has been the conviction of thousands of sensitive young women who have experienced the same doubts since almost the world began. What she needed was not a psychiatrist with its rigmarole of self-sacrifice but rather a period, more or less indefinite, of waiting until memory became less acute and bitter and until another man came along and made her forget and reawakened love in her. But that is too simple for Eliot, and too unintelligible. He must needs climb stairs backwards and on his knees, with a punk stick in his hand. . . .

To revert briefly to Eliot's dramaturgy, it will be argued by some that one of its most conspicuous shortcomings is his too frequent employment of the door bell and telephone bell to interrupt the long speeches of his characters. I can not agree. The bells to my mind are not employed frequently enough.

---

1. The *nouveau-riche* pun, here, alludes to Georges de Porto-Riche (1849–1930), a French playwright who wrote psychological dramas of marital triangles—e.g., *Amoreuse* (1891).

Profiles of Directors and Producers

Florenz Ziegfeld (1869–1932)

The difference between Florenz Ziegfeld and his imitators is illuminatingly revealed in a comparison of one of the Ziegfeld roof revues with such a show as John Murray Anderson's *What's in a Name?* This differnce is not a matter of costumes—Anderson's are as beautiful as Ziegfeld's; it is not a matter of lighting—Anderson's lighting is, if anything, better than Ziegfeld's; it is not a matter of wit or humor or music—there is little if any wit or humor or music in the exhibitions of either the one or the other; it is not a matter of scenery—Anderson's is often as attractive as Ziegfeld's. It is, rather, that the touch of Ziegfeld is the touch of an artist, whereas the touch of such a man as Anderson is the touch of a showman. It is this touch of Ziegfeld's that takes a bag of canvas, costumes, lights and girls and converts the whole, with an unerring instinct for form, into something of fluid light, fluid color, and fluid beauty. It is this lack of touch that, in the instance of the Andersons, brings from the same bag a sometimes beautiful but always chaotic, and never fluid, vaudeville show.

It is only recently that Ziegfeld has been recognized for the man he is. In a theatre that holds David Belasco, Augustus Thomas and Nance O'Neil to be in their several ways great artists, it is not unnatural that a genuine theatrical artist, an artist of penetrating taste, fine feeling and delicate perception, should be overlooked. And not merely overlooked, but shouldered aside, at the mere thought of him, with breezy derision. And so it came about that this Ziegfeld, save for the clear vision of the few who observed in him the temperament and execution of the real craftsman of the theatre, was slow to be recognized for the fine skill that is his. It is, of course, as difficult for the average American theatregoer, who habitually confuses the Swiss cheese with the mustard, to persuade himself that an artist and a music show may in any way be related as it is for him to recognize the artist in a man who, like George Ade,[1] writes in slang or in one who, like Montague Glass, writes mere magazine stories about the low-comedy creatures of the cloak-and-suit trade.

From *The Theatre, the Drama, the Girls* (New York: Knopf, 1921), pp. 145–48.

There is no producer in the world today who, in his field, in any degree approaches to this Ziegfeld. I have sat under them all. Out of the vulgar leg-show, Ziegfeld has fashioned a thing of grace and beauty, of loveliness and charm. He knows colors as a painter knows colors; he knows form; he knows quality and mood. He has lifted, with sensitive skill, a thing that was mere food for smirking baldheads and downy college boys out of its low estate and into a thing of symmetry and bloom. To appreciate what he has done, it is only necessary to have surveyed the efforts of such of his competitors as Butt and de Courville in England, Meinhard in Germany and Volterra in France. A man of manner in its nicest sense (rather than in its indiscriminate sense of tribute to any actor who doesn't pull up his trousers when he sits down), the fellow is. And those who see in his *Follies* and *Frolics* merely a number of young women running around the stage half-naked are the same yokels who believe that Brieus, the amiable satirist of *Les Hannetons,* is an inferior artist to Brieux, the indignant literalist of *La Robe Rogue.*

As to the claims of the others who, opposed to this Ziegfeld, are regarded as truer artists of the native theatre, Schopenhauer did away with such as Belasco when he observed that "It is essential to a work of art that it should give the form alone without the matter. . . . This is really the reason why wax figures produce no æsthetic impression and, therefore, are not, in the æsthetic sense, works of art at all; although if they were well made they produce an illusion a hundred times greater than the best picture or statue could effect; so that if deceptive imitation of reality were the object of art, they would have to take the first place." As for Thomas, recall Derely's "In an age when the struggle for life has become more exclusive than ever, it is not an empty anachronism to represent on the stage only the struggle for women?" And of such as O'Neill, her celebrated fellow-mime's, "The actor may mark with his imprint the parts that he interprets; but his imprint must be so well confounded with the reality of the personage as not to be realized by the spectator without reflection and comparison. . . ." It took the American theatre ten years to realize that George M. Cohan had other talents than catarrh and hair that bobbed up and down. It has taken the American theatre quite as long to realize that Ziegfeld has other talents than Martha Mansfield and Lillian Lorraine.

---

1. See A. L. Lazarus, ed., *The Best of George Ade* (Bloomington: Indiana University Press, 1985).

Max Reinhardt (1873–1943)

Preceded by that species of irrelevant and trumpery press-agency which, somewhat disconcertingly, he would seem fond of allowing to make him appear rather like German silver, Max Reinhardt, the foremost active producer in the world theatre, has lately come again across the Atlantic to display his wares. That this virtuoso of dramatic production should permit himself publicity devices that Peaches Browning and even Otto Kahn might balk at is gagging to those of his critics who peculiarly believe that art and dignity should have something in common and who have difficulty in determining just what connection there can be between some of the very finest dramatic presentations of the modern stage and a lot of free lunches at Salzburg, to say nothing of widely disseminated photographs showing the impresario and Miss Julia Hoyt posed against the façade of Schloss Leopoldskron eating sizeable hunks of *Wiener Lungenbäuscherl.* For while such stuff may be all right on the part of self-advertising vaudeville actors and pentecostal clergymen it is hardly an admirable business for a man of Reinhardt's attainments. He may thus impress a senate of doodles, but in the minds of others he lowers himself considerably.

That Reinhardt is the most talented director and producer operating in the theatre in these years is certainly not news, except perhaps to a few Russians. With Craig, the greatest genius of them all, in forced retirement in Genoa, with Stanislavsky, a skillful fellow, calmly relying for eminence upon a few already ancient achievements, with Danchenko, very little better than a second-rater, idiotically frittering away his time out in Hollywood and with Pitoëff going in simply for a series of exaggerated imitations and caricatures in France, Reinhardt has the field pretty well to himself. He is an extraordinarily fertile and alive figure, indefatigable, imaginative and resourceful; he works like a Trojan; he has, unlike these other producers, a sense of internationalism—all drama, whatever the land of its origin, is of interest to him; he has a mind that adapts itself to a diversity of drama and a fancy that filters it with a various force and beauty onto a fluid and galvanic stage. It is Reinhardt's outstanding characteristic indeed, and the quality that has raised him to leadership among the active producing talents of the day, that he is, in a sense, a different man in the instance of each separate production that he makes. Where the majority of producers have a very definite and unmistakable personal label that sticks betrayingly to each of their presentations, however essentially different the dramas themselves may be, Reinhardt changes his directing person-

From *Art of the Night* (New York: Knopf, 1928), pp. 292–96. copyright renewed 1955 by George Jean Nathan.

ality according to the drama he happens to be dealing with. There is not one director Reinhardt—there are a dozen director Reinhardts. But there is only one Stanislavsky, one Gemièr, one Granville-Barker, one Copeau or one Sierra, be the play farce or comedy, tragedy or allegory, spectacle or what not. The signature is genuine, but the contents of the bottle are often spurious. For these directors and others like them are bent upon impressing their own idiosyncratic personalities on a variety of drama where Reinhardt is concerned chiefly with so adjusting the many facets of his directorial personality that the one of them that most patly suits the particular drama in hand shall not obscure the latter to his own vainglory and to its own infinite damage.

Going into the theatre of any outstanding director and producer save Reinhardt, one can discern the director's arbitrary method and technique, be the exhibit Shakespeare or Racine, Lenormand or Oscar Wilde. The label is there as flamboyantly—and as dubiously—as on a bottle of bootleg Scotch. Everything is sacrificed to make a Roman holiday for the producer himself, and for his personal *kudos*. The dramatist is simply a tool wherewith he seeks to fashion his own monument. Among directors both big and little the world over one finds this vain adherence to and exposition of an inflexible technique or style, as set in each of its several ways as the writing tricks of the more celebrated popular fictioneers or the steps of the more celebrated colored hoofers. Thus, one need not refer to the playbill to know a Stanislavsky production, whether of Chekhov or Maeterlinck: the Stanislavsky idiosyncrasies periodically thrust themselves forward willynilly, and the devil take the dramatist. . . .

In Reinhardt's theatre, as I have noted, technique of production is no such more or less exactly pigeonholed business. For each separate drama a new technique is devised. For one, we have the Craig concepts visualized by the Reinhardt imagnation; for another, the principles of the *commedia dell'arte* elaborated and edited; for still another, music and the spoken word deftly orchestrated; for still another, the Sixteenth Century moralities beautified by a Twentieth Century looking imaginatively backward; for yet another, modernism plus modernism; and for yet another still, impressionism and expressionism enjoying a picnic of acutely critical production. In this lies the estimable and protean Max's directorial expertness and felicity: that all manner of drama is grist for his mill and that, more important, that mill revolves not by a single wind, as with the other producers, but to whatever wind the drama in point may blow. There are times, it may be, when Reinhardt plainly strains himself for effect, when a trace of illegitimacy insinuates itself into his work and causes one transiently to suspect the mountebank, when those snapshots of Max kneeling piously before a ten-foot crucifix in Schloss Leopoldskron with Fanny Brice, Morris Gest and other such devout fellow Christians[1] come to mind, but in the general run of things the honest artist is clearly to be felt and seen beneath and beyond the momentary posturer. Reinhardt, with Papa Craig peeping over his shoulder, has brought more actual life to the modern stage than any other practising director and producer of his time. His influence has spread over all lands and seas. He has been Gordon Craig's Paul.

---

1. Christians . . . Nathan's intended irony may be lost here. Actually, Reinhardt (born Max Goldmann), Fanny Brice, and Morris Guest were Jewish.

Winthrop Ames (1871–1937)

Mr. Henry Miller once said that the trouble with the business he was in was that it was too theatrical. One sometimes feels that the trouble with the business Mr. Winthrop Ames is in is that it isn't theatrical enough. There is a something to the efforts of the latter—a slight aloofness, an undue reticence, mayhap—that one feels handicaps on a measure the theatre he cicerones. A talented, educated fellow and one pleasant to behold in play-world people, as is the present day play world, so largely by ex-sidewalk-solicitors for the Newsboys' Home, Ames brings to his work a sense of discrimination, a sense of beauty and ideals and at once charming and timeful. And as for the contention one hears now and again from serious clowns that he is impracticable, it may be dismissed with the statement that the difficulty with the theatre at the present time is that there are already altogether too many practical producers in it. As a writer for a better theatre, give me any day a so-called impracticable man like Ames above a hundred practical Moroscos. But what one wishes Mr. Ames had more of is that direct bluntness, that saucy fire, which injects into even the best of acted plays a better and warmer glow.

When I sit in Mr. Ames' Little Theatre, I am, by the very feel in the air, charmed as I am charmed in the home of a congenial host—and when I am not pleased with what Mr. Ames presents me I feel somehow the same distaste for finding fault, however deserved, that I feel upon arising from a friend's dinner table (though in such cases no one has ever accused my manners getting the better of my feelings)—yet I often in that lovely little playhouse feel like whistling or giving my nose a lusty blow or doing something disgraceful by way of injecting into the surroundings an air of greater excitement and camaraderie. I am quite certain, knowing Mr.

From *Mr. George Jean Nathan Presents* (New York: Knopf, 1917), pp. 278–81. Copyright renewed 1944 by George Jean Nathan.

Ames as I do, that he would be the last man in the world to object to my doing such a thing—he would, indeed, probably like me to do it—but I am equally certain, knowing the gentleman as I do, that he would be the last man in the world to ask me to do such a thing. Yet I wish he would. It would, I feel sure, help the both of us.

Aside from the merits of the play *Hush* by Miss Violet Pearn, with which Mr. Ames reopened his theatre for a recent season (personally I was not at all beguiled by it for it seemed to me to lack the satiric wit absolutely essential to the telling of a tale of a young pseudo-radical who seeks vainly to shock people), one could not help believing that a more bourgeois showmanship would have better projected into the auditorium the materials in the manuscript. Mr. Ames staged the play carefully and attractively and, in the main, cast it efficiently, but one missed in its exhibition and maneuvering the nearness and warmth that one must feel in the playhouse. The Little Theatre stage was probably not more than twenty-five feet from my seat on the aisle in J, but it seemed a full quarter of a mile away. I could see plainly; I could hear clearly; but I couldn't feel at all. In the great spaces of the late New Theatre Mr. Ames once made two manuscripts glow—*The Piper* of Josephine Preston Peabody and the *Strife* of John Galsworthy—two of the very finest instances of staging the modern theatre has known. The paradox of the very vastly less great spaces of the Little Theatre and the corresponding diminution of the sense of warm propinquity, I leave for explanation to some critic more penetrating than I.

The notion, incidentally, that the New Theatre failed because its auditorium was too big is the merest gabble. The auditoriums of the famous theatres of thirty years and more ago—the particular theatres, that is, from which have come down to us the best traditions of our stage—were in several cases as hulky as the auditorium of the New Theatre. The notion that the New Theatre failed,[1] further, because the plays presented there were poor plays is equally sorry. Look over the list of productions made in that theatre and compare them, in any way you choose, with the list of productions made in a corresponding period of time in any other theatre in America. Ames probably did as well with the New Theatre as any man one can summon to mind could have done with it. The New Theatre failed, very simply and very uncritically, for the same reason that the Ritz hotels have succeeded. It was too democratic and not sufficiently exclusive. It made a good start and then slipped. For, after its first month and with high prosperity staring it in the face, it began with diligent gusto to inform the yokelry that it did not have to put on evening dress to get in. And the yokelry, thus persuaded that any mere hooligan might attend, remained sniffishly away. Had the New Theatre let it be felt that no person unadorned with a boiled shirt could enter, it would have been quite as impossible to get a seat at its box-office as it was to get a table in the Savoy supper room in London during the American traveling season.

---

1. After the failure of his New Theatre Repertory Company, Mr. Ames erected, and directed successful plays in, The Little Theatre and the Booth Theatre.

George Abbott (b. 1887)

George Abbott does not drink or smoke, thus preserving his unimpaired energy for rumba dancing, which he engages in nightly for six or seven unflinching hours, and for the kind of direction that converts his stages into a cross between the Preakness and an intercollegiate hockey match. His success is chiefly with musical shows and farce-comedy, at which he is a foxy hand. When he tries that hand at the more elevated species of drama, it loses its cunning. Give him something in which three men rush madly about a hotel room tearing frantically at their neckties, the while the pants fall off one of them, and worrying how they can raise five dollars either to pay their bill, bet on a horse, back a play, waggle a movie deal or get control of a gold-mine, the while in turn they ejaculate "Nuts," "It stinks" or "How about calling up Jock Whitney?", and the next morning you are certain to read my colleagues' tributes to his remarkable genius, along with the news that the line of art-lovers at the box-office is a quarter of a mile long. But give him a play in which human emotions impel their possessors to sit down quietly once in a while and to speak their thoughts without once resorting to such facetiæ as "Sez you" or "I wonder what Lee Shubert is writing on the table cloth at the Astor," and he gives the impression of being lost.

In the way of what is often too restrictedly called popular entertainment (for after all, such a play as *Tobacco Road* has run much longer than Abbott's most successful runner, *Three Men On A Horse,* such a one as *The Children's Hour* longer than *Boy Meets Girl,* and such as *Rain, The Green Pastures* and *Street Scene* longer than *Brother Rat*)—in the way of this so-called popular entertainment Abbott at present has few rivals. But if someone like O'Neill or O'Casey were perchance to send him a script, he would be so puzzled and confused that you would probably find him that night doing the minuet under the impression that it was the conga.

From *The Entertainment of a Nation* (New York: Knopf, 1942), pp. 118–19. Copyright renewed 1969 by Mrs. George Jean Nathan.

Selected Letters

From Gordon Craig

January 9, 1916.

DEAR MR. NATHAN:

A copy of your book on the Theatre[1] has come here—I have read it through and enjoyed and marked much of it. I like so much the amazing Americanisms—

I had a note on "applause" (under the name of Adolphe Furst) in *Mask. Volume I. Page 247.* Not unlike yours on the same subject. After having read your book I sent for your portrait and was surprised to find you so young a man. I wish you the best of success.

I suppose you know *The Mask.*[2] Are there any publications you would like me to send you from here that you have not got? There are one or two of interest—not periodicals but things to do with the new movement are here. That same *'new movement'* is now playing the ass. I am not disheartened by its behaviour but it seems a little silly. The big men in it are practically all united. I hear from most of them regularly and if we looked at it from our own point of view we should have no regrets. But the hundreds and even thousands of new-comers all of whom seem bent on copying some 10-year-old scrap which one of us gave out at the time are rather unsatisfactory . . .

"They say" I am coming over to America—how they know, *you know*. I was invited and I sent my conditions—They wanted the biggest thing ever done—that's just what I want them to want—but I have not yet heard from them—I hear that a lot of little European affairs are being exhibited just now. And a donkey wrote to me saying it had heard that SIR Beerbohm Tree was going to ask me to "stage" *The Tempest* for him in New York. I wonder what the devil use I could be to a man who can't stage the play for himself—It is all so pitifully *small*—quality the Theatres of all lands delight to develope. What? I want a manager—*an impressario!* and *one rich man* and I'll make their fortunes if they'll do as I want—that is catch my step and "fling along Sambo"—Your book has hit me and to that you must attribute this letter—

I see today that Liebler is without means. Would he be a man for me? I haven't one idea—I have 30 ripe ones—and 60 or 70 coming on excellently, thank you. It takes 3 weeks for a letter to get over to the States—I thought I'd say, what I might have kept, straight away.

With all good wishes for another eye-opening book from you

Yours sincerely,

GORDON CRAIG

---

1. *Another Book on the Theatre* (New York, Knopf, 1915).
2. Craig's magazine.

From Eugene O'Neill

WEST POINT PLEASANT, N.J.[1]
May 1st 1919.

MY DEAR MR. NATHAN:

I am sending under separate cover, for Mr. Mencken and yourself, two volumes of my book[2] which has just appeared. I hope you will accept them as small remembrances that I remember how much of my gratitude I owe both of you for your encouragement and constructive criticism. I feel that in a great measure the book is already yours since you published three of the plays and had the very first peep at one of the others.

Your name, it appears, does not adorn the jacket in spite of the fact that, when I suggested to Boni and Liveright that they use what recognized critics had said about my work for the cover instead of any self-appointed boost, I carefully placed some words of yours regarding "The Moon Of The Caribbees" at the head of the list. All this matter is puerile, of course; but as I value your commendation more than that of all the others put together, it rather makes me peevish.

One of my two long plays—*Chris Christopherson* is typed and now in the hands of the agent. (Yes, Williams' dilatory tactics drove me to an agent—The American Play Company.) Williams probably has it by this time since my contract with him gives him first choice on future plays. I intended sending you a copy at once but I find my two carbons need doctoring and so will wait until my next trip to New York—about the middle of the month—when I shall bring it around to the office personally in the hope of finally meeting you.

With sincerest regards to Mr. Mencken and yourself,

Very sincerely yours,

EUGENE G. O'NEILL

---

1. Former home of Agnes Boulton, O'Neill's second wife.
2. *Moon of the Caribbees and Six Other Plays of the Sea* (New York: Boni & Liveright, 1919).

From Eugene O'Neill

PROVINCETOWN, MASS.[1]
Nov. 4, 1919.

MY DEAR MR. NATHAN:

Your letter and the script arrived by the same mail. That you found genuine merit in *The Straw* is the most encouraging boost to my spirits I have received since the play was written. Your stamp of approval gives me renewed confidence in my own valuation.

The Theatre Guild[2] have seen the play and rejected it. They said it was most excellent but not the kind of play for their public. Since *John Ferguson* inoculated them with the virus of popular success—quite contrary to their expectations—I'm afraid they've become woefully worried about the supposed tastes of "their public." I speak not only from my own experience. Before *Ferguson* set them on horseback they had decided to do Susan Glaspell's "Bernice" this season. But now they have discovered "their public" would never— And the latest I hear is that James K. Hackett is to star for them in *Silas Lapham*. My God! The trouble seems to be that you can't eliminate the weakness of the old Washington Square Players by merely changing the name. . . .

Boni and Liveright are to publish both *Chris* and *Beyond the Horizon* this winter. Perhaps they might do *The Straw* later.

I don't expect to be in New York before the middle of next month, but will surely drop in when I do come.

My sincerest gratitude for your words of encouragement.[3] They certainly mean a lot to me!

Cordially,

EUGENE O'NEILL

---

1. Remodeled former Coast Guard Station on Peaked Hill Bar, Cape Cod.

2. The Theatre Guild was organized in 1919 by Lawrence Langner and other members of the old Washington Square Players.

3. To Boni & Liveright, Nathan had written "Here one detects the first springs of a talent that, rapidly coming to flower . . . is at present surely the finest in the American theatre."

From The George Jean Nathan Collection, Olin Library, Cornell University.

From Nathan to Fitzgerald

[New York City, New York
circa November 14, 1919]

F. Scott Fitzgerald, esq.
599 Summit Avenue,
St. Paul, Minn.

Dear Mr. Fitzgerald:

Both your short story[1] and your one-act play[2] please us—the play particularly. We are accepting both manuscripts. The office sends you its cheques on Thursday morning.

I wish, in my office of dramatic critic, personally to congratulate you on the play. You have a decidedly uncommon gift for light dialogue. Keep at the dramatic form. You will do things. I believe that your talent is superior to Clare Kummer's.

Our best thanks to you for the credos.[3] Three of them are excellent. We shall use them.

With best wishes,

George Jean Nathan

---

1. "Dalrymple Goes Wrong."
2. "Porcelain and Pink"; both the short story and the play were published in *Smart Set* (January 1920).
3. Fitzgerald had submitted twelve pieces for the "American Credo" department of *Smart Set* and claimed that all twelve had been printed in the book, *The American Credo* (1920) edited by Nathan and Mencken.

From the Fitzgerald Scrapbook, I-18. Published with permission of Princeton University Library and the Fitzgerald Estate.

From Eugene O'Neill

PROVINCETOWN, MASS.
March 12, 1920.

MY DEAR MR. NATHAN:

This is a late day for me to be writing to thank you for your note of congratulation, but I really have a valid excuse. I have been up to my ears in troubles ever since the opening date of "Beyond."[1] First my mother acquired the flu with a touch of pneumonia; then I caught it from her and was laid up in the hotel for four weeks; then my father had a stroke and has been dangerously ill ever since; then, just as I was tottering up to my first "Chris" rehearsals, I received a wire from her calling me to return to a very sick wife! Can you beat it? If this be the payment demanded of me for the big splash made by "Beyond," then I am tempted to remark with Jurgen[2] that "it does not seem quite fair."

Thank you again for your note. I am sure glad *Beyond the Horizon* pleased its godfather.

My sincerest gratitude for your words of encouragement. They certainly mean a lot to me!

Sincerely,

EUGENE O'NEILL

1. *Beyond the Horizon* (London: Jonathan Cape, 1920).
2. Protagonist of the novel of the same name by James Branch Cabell (q.v.).

From the George Jean Nathan Collection, Olin Library, Cornell University.

From Eugene O'Neill

PROVINCETOWN, MASS.
June 19, 1920.

DEAR MR. NATHAN:

Many thanks for your note. It is darned encouraging to learn that you think *Gold* is a progressive step beyond *Beyond*. Your verdict is the more welcome because I was beginning to have doubts about it myself. I gave Williams all my scripts of the play right after finishing it, have not had a chance to look at it since, and so, lacking all proof to the contrary, was commencing to wonder what it was all about, and whether I had at all accomplished what I set out to do.

I suppose I shall be credited on all sides with having made "Where the Cross Is Made" into a long play—yet the reverse is the real truth. The idea of *Gold* was a long play, one from its inception. I merely took the last act situation and jammed it into the one-act form because I wanted to be represented on the Provincetown Player opening bill two seasons ago and had nothing else in mind for them at the time. I mention this only because I know how impossible it is to expand a natural short play into a long one, and would hardly make such a futile mistake. *Gold* was always full length to me.

I wrote John Williams to be properly persuasive on my behalf in urging you to join him in a visit up here. I hope he has been so, and that you will find time to come. Putting aside the very natural pleasure I shall feel in having you here, there is for me a very special inducement also. I have wanted for a long time to talk over with you something which has been growing in the back of my head for the past year. It is an idea for future work—a scheme quite on a grand scale, and as far as my knowledge goes, an original plan in play writing. I do not mean by this that there is any heavy blank verse, soggy symbolism or bizarre innovations connected with it; but it is an idea which is so large in outline that, even having the temerity to grant one's ability for it, it will take some years of intensive and difficult labor to fill in. The question in my mind still is, is this thing as big as I think; is it worth the labor involved, and from a purely practicable standpoint, can it be done? So, standing on this threshold, I would sure like to have your opinion. At least, whether you find it worth the while or not, I am sure you will be interested.

So regard this letter as a S.O.S.—and do come!

Sincerely,

EUGENE O'NEILL

---

1. John Williams, New York theatrical producer

From The George Jean Nathan Collection, Olin Library, Cornell University

From Eugene O'Neill

PROVINCETOWN, MASS.
Feb. 1, 1921.

MY DEAR MR. NATHAN:

Your criticism certainly probes the vital spot. The devil of it is, I don't see my way out. From the middle of that third act I feel the play[1] ought to be dominated by the woman's psychology. And I have a conviction that with dumb people of her sort, unable to voice strong, strange feelings, the emotions can find outlet only through the language and gestures of the heroics in the novels and movies they are familiar with—that is, that in moments of great stress life copies melodrama. Anna forced herself on me, middle of third act, at her most theatric. In real life I felt she would unconsciously be compelled, through sheer inarticulateness, to the usual "big scene," and wait hopefully for her happy ending. And as she is the only one of the three who knows exactly what she wants, she would get it.

And the sea outside—life—waits. The happy ending is merely the comma at the end of a gaudy introductory clause, with the body of the sentence still unwritten. (In fact, I once thought of calling the play *Comma.*)

Of course, this sincerity of life pent up in the trappings of theatre is impossible to project clearly, I guess. The two things cancel and negate each other, resulting, as you have said, in a seeming H. A. Jones[2] compromise. Yet it is queerly fascinating to me because I believe it's a new, true angle.

One thing that I realize, on a rereading of the last act, is that I haven't done enough to make my "comma" clear. My ending seems to have a false definiteness about it that is misleading—a happy-ever-after which I did not intend. I relied on the father's last speech of superstitious uncertainty to let my theme show through—and on. It does not do this rightly. I now have it in my mind to have the stoker not entirely convinced by the oath of a non-Catholic although he is forced by his great want to accept her in spite of this. In short, that all of them at the end have a vague foreboding that although they have had their moment, the decision still rests with the sea, which has achieved the conquest of Anna.

Do you think this would help—in the way of holding up the theme at the end? I sure pine to talk over this play with you, but just how soon I will be able to get to town again is uncertain.

My sincerest thanks for your letter!

EUGENE O'NEILL

---

1. *Anna Christie*, produced in 1921 and published in 1922
2. Henry Arthur Jones (1857–1929), q.v. in glossary.

From Eugene O''Neill

Provincetown, Mass.
Jan. 2, 1922

My dear Mr. Nathan:

. . . I believe you are going to be very much interested in this play[1] whatever your verdict may be on the complete result. It is a very experimental departure from the form of all my previous work. Perhaps it follows the method of "Jones"[2] closer than any other. But it does not fit into any of the "isms" although there is a bit of all of them in it. I feel confident I have succeeded in what I set out to do, but in doing so I have not hesitated to use everything I could find in the theatre or life that could heighten and drive home the underlying idea . . .

[As for *The Fountain*][3] so many folk have objected to the blank verse rhythm . . . on the grounds, seemingly, that it is not beautiful verse. Whereas I used it to gain a naturalistic effect of the quality of the people and speech of those times, to place them, with little care for original poetic beauty save in the few instances where it is called for. I wanted to make ordinary speech of ordinary thoughts stilted, bigoted, narrow, sentimental and romantic, pretentiously ornate . . .

I'd like to hear what you feel is wrong and if you detect any false spots.

All best to you,
Eugene O'Neill

---

1. *The Hairy Ape* (1922), an expressionist play in which Yank, the protagonist, is a zoo-like creature who has lost his harmony with nature. O'Neill's "experimental departure" foreshadows *Strange Interlude,* which was to emerge in 1928.
2. *The Emperor Jones* (1921)
3. *The Fountain* was not to be produced before 1925.

From The George Jean Nathan Collection, Olin Library, Cornell University

From Eugene O'Neill

BROOK FARM[1]
RIDGEFIELD, CONNECTICUT

May 7, 1923.

Dear Nathan:

Nevertheless, I am convinced *Welded*[2] is the best yet. I'm glad to get Mencken's letter but I must confess the greater part of his comment seems irrelevant as criticisms of my play. To point out its weakness as realism (in the usual sense of that word) is to confuse what is obviously part of my deliberate intention.

Damn that word, "realism"! When I first spoke to you of the play as a "last word in realism," I meant something "really real," in the sense of being spiritually true, not meticulously life-like,—an interpretation of actuality by a distillation, an elimination of most realistic trappings, and intensification of human lives into clear symbols of truth.

Here's an example: Mencken says: "The man haranguing the street-walker is surely not a man who ever actually lived." Well, he surely is to me, and what is more to my point, he is also much more than that. He is Man dimly aware of recurring experience,[3] groping for the truth behind the realistic appearances of himself, and of love and life. For the moment his agony gives him vision of the true behind the real.

I can't agree that the speeches in this scene are "banal" or the ideas "rubber stamp." In fact, I'm positive it's the deepest and truest, as well as the best written scene I've ever done. Perhaps it isn't "plausible"—but the play is about love as a life-force, not as an intellectual conception, and the plausibilities of reason don't apply. Reason has no business in the theatre anyway, any more than it has in a church. They are both either below—or above it.

But I won't rave on. I'll grant this much for your criticism—that parts of the dialogue are still, I find, "speechy" and artificial but that will all be gone over and fixed. It's the slopping-over of too much eagerness to say it all.

Thank Mencken for me for reading it. I'm sorry it didn't "knock him dead" to repay him for his trouble.

Well, just wait until you see it played! If it's done right, I'm hoping that may make you recant.

My best to you both.

Sincerely,
Eugene O'Neill.

---

1. O'Neill bought this as a winter home, late in 1922. In the summers, he still used Peaked Hill Bar, Cape Cod.

2. Produced by the Selwyns. q.v. in March 1924 at the 39th Street Theatre in New York. *Welded* was published the next month by Boni & Liveright in a volume that also contained *All God's Chillun Got Wings*.

3. "Recurring Experience" echoes Nietzsche's *Also Spake Zarathustra*, q.v. in glossary.

From Eugene O'Neill

BROOK FARM
RIDGEFIELD, CONNECTICUT

Sunday. [December 1923]

Dear Nathan:

Here's the proofs.[1] I won't guarantee that I've been much help on them where spelling, etc., are concerned, but I've done my best.

What do you think of our new group.[2] I think we're going to do some really original stuff in the way of production. My ideas are playing an active part here—not like the old P. P.[3] where I simply handed in plays but kept out otherwise. I think we've worked out an amusing scheme for *The Spook Sonata*.[4] Be sure & see it. I'll bet we do it more interestingly than it's ever been done abroad!

I'm desperate for a production! I no longer believe in Hopkins. When it comes right down to bedrock, he's just another member of the P. M. A.,[5] a bit brainier & more courageous than most, perhaps—but also a lot lazier and less efficient. There's no hope for me with him. He hasn't given me a square deal either. So, as there is no one else I'll have to help create a new outlet—or remain gagged.

I'll be in town very soon. Shall hope to see you there for a few minutes if you're not too darn busy.

Here's to your first number.[6]

Eugene O'Neill

---

1. *All God's Chillun Got Wings* was published in the *American Mercury* (February 1924), pp. 129–48; later in a book by Boni & Liveright (1926).

2. In the autumn of 1923, when Susan Glaspell (q.v.) and her husband, George Cram Cook, left Provincetown for the Continent, a new Provincetown Players Company was organized by Kenneth Macgowan, Robert Edmond Jones, and Eugene O'Neill. The playhouse then reopened. In January 1924.

3. The Provincetown Players

4. By August Strindberg (q.v.) on O'Neill's suggestion

5. The Producing Managers' Association

6. *The American Mercury,* succesor to *Smart Set*

From F. Scott Fitzgerald

To Bernard Vaughan[1]
December 1923

Great Neck, L.I.

Dear Bernard: You ask me for the news from literary New York. Outside of the fact that Rebecca West and Frank Swinnerton are in town, there isn't any. Tom Boyd, after being feted on all sides by admirers of his books, got off for France and is sending back short stories for Scribner's Magazine by every boat . . .

But the real event of the year will, of course, be the appearance in January of *The American Mercury.* The *Smart Set* without Mencken and Nathan is already on the stands, and a dreary sight it is. In their nine years' association with it those two men had a more stupendous and far-reaching influence on the whole course of American writing. Their influence was not so much on the very first-rate writers, though even there it was considerable, in many cases, as on the cultural background. Their new venture is even more interesting. We shall see what we shall see.

You ask for news of me. There is little and that bad. My play *(The Vegetable)* opened in Atlantic City and foundered on the opening night. It did better in subsequent performances, but at present is laid up for repairs.

—Scott Fitzgerald

---

1. A St. Paul, Minnesota, journalist. See glossary.

From Matthew Bruccoli et al., eds., *Correspondence of F. Scott Fitzgerald.* New York: Random House, 1980. Pp. 137-8. On p. 137 the source is noted as "unlocated."

Dear Menck—

Pending your return to New York, I suggest that you leave the Dunsany and Max Beerbohm matters in my hands. While I am in full accord with you regarding the Dunsany piece, I consider you an utter ass when it comes to Beerbohm. The essay is mere flafla—Max trying to grab some easy money in the gullible American magazine market. Let him sell it to Tom Smith for the *Century*. Tom admires Beerbohm because Beerbohm's brother, Beerbohm Tree, was a celebrated actor-manager and wore silk spats. Moreover, the readers of the *Century* will like the thing . . . I doubt that it would interest our customers. They are, in the main, too sinful to be intrigued by literary sinfulness. The mere name of Beerbohm will not land them. They are hep to all the old magazine dodges, and we can never fool them with gaudy names as Hearst does. As you know, I esteem Beerbohm highly, but it seems to me that he hasn't turned out a decent piece of work for five years. . . .

Let us stick to our agreement to print nothing that we are not both sure of—that is, if we can get enough stuff of that sort. We surely get very little out of the magazine save the fun that is in our jobs, so why bother ourselves with questions of "advisability" and the like? More magazines have been wrecked by this search for advisability than by anything else I can think of, save it be too much money. What are the two greatest magazine successes of recent years in America? Obviously, the *Saturday Evening Post* and the *Atlantic Monthly,* two corpses revived into tremendous vigor. Well, neither Lorimer of the *Post* nor Sedgwick of the *Atlantic* bothers specifically about what is advisable to print, nor even about what the public wants. Each simply prints what he likes himself. Both have made fortunes for themselves and the entrepreneurs behind them as assuming that what *they* like will also be liked by thousands of other right-thinking men. Our opportunity is just as clear. Let us assume that there are thousands of other Americans who have just as little virtue in them as I have, and just as little taste as you.

I am against printing any more so-called poetry by K——[1] even if it happens to be good, which is not likely. This K—— has cheapened himself by becoming a public character down in Greenwich Village. An amiable fellow personally, and with enough talent, perhaps, to save him from the public hangman, yet he has converted himself into something that surely doesn't belong in the magazine—something that seems silly to you and me, and hence must seem silly to most of our readers. If you think he ought to be aided, then pay him a pension out of your privy purse.

I have invented a new cocktail—very fetching: one third Gordon gin, one third sloe gin, and one third tangerine juice well iced. Two fill the heart with confidence in God. Three make even such piffle as the Beerbohm essay seem good. I shall limit you to two.

Don't forget to send me the address of R——.[2] My *Popular Theatre*[3] will greatly mellow and enrich her mind. . . .

G

---

1. Probably Harry Kemp (1883–1960) "the vagabond poet"
2. Lizette Woodworth Reese (1856–1935), for many years a Baltimore high-school teacher and according to Carl Bode, Mencken's favorite American poet. See Bode, *Mencken* (Carbondale: Southern Illinois University Press, 1969), p. 64.
3. George Jean Nathan, *The Popular Theatre* (New York: Knopf, 1918)

From *The Intimate Notebooks of George Jean Nathan* (New York: Knopf; 1932).

To F. Scott Fitzgerald

Spring, 1925

Dear Scott:

A thousand congratulations! *The Great Gatsby* is an excellent job! It is leagues in advance of anything you have ever done.

As ever,
George Jean Nathan

From the Fitzgerald Scrapbook, used by permission of the Princeton University Library.

From Eugene O'Neill

BROOK FARM
RIDGEFIELD, CONNECTICUT

October 31, 1925

Mr. George Jean Nathan,
The American Mercury
730 Fifth Avenue,
New York City.

Dear Nathan:

I am at present working hard on a new play[1] but expect to be in town a week from Monday to start rehearsals. I will call you up as soon as I get in. All best.

Eugene O'Neill.

P.S. By the way, you ask where am I going to stop. I don't know yet. My problem is this: I'll be in New York some four or five days a week steadily for two months as *The Great God Brown* immediately follows *The Foun-tain*. What I want to do is to find a place where I can work with some degree of quiet until noon, and where my acquaintances can't get at me. Can you recommend The Royalton?[2] I know nothing about it or how expensive it is, but I'd be glad to hear a word from you about it.

---

1. *Lazarus Laughed*, q.v. in Glossary.
2. Nathan's residence for many years. Is O'Neill fishing for an invitation?

From Eugene O'Neill to Isaac Goldberg

Bermuda
June 14, 1926

My dear Mr. Goldberg:

[In response to your query] . . . I can't for the life of me recall much about my first meeting with Nathan. It was with John D. Williams at some restaurant, I believe, and I was three-fourths 'blotto.' I remember thinking how much he looked like an old friend of mine who wrote animal stories at that era for Street and Smith. The second meeting was, if memory serves—mine is damned bad on such matters, let me add!—at the Royal-ton in his apartment, and I still have a letter written by Nathan a few days later in which he speaks of being gratified at discovering that I was as proficient at drinking cocktails as at concocting dramas.[1] So you see. Suffice it that I found him warm and friendly and human where I half-expected an aloof and caustic intelligence completely enveloping and hiding the living being. *Half*-expected,—for his letters to me had given me an inkling. And a point to make is that we have corresponded—at rare intervals, it is true—for some years before we met, and I had sent him all my scripts for criticism as soon as the plays were written . . .

---

1. O'Neill later became a teetotaler.

Isaac Goldberg, *The Theatre of George Jean Nathan* (New York: Simon & Schuster, 1926), p. 77.

From Eugene O'Neill

Hamilton, Bermuda.
June 16th. '27

Dear Nathan:

Many thanks for your note. I will look forward to reading the article on *Strange Interlude*.[1] It is hard for me to say how deeply gratified I have been ever since you read the play to know your high opinion of it. I am not, except for rare monomaniacal moments, one of those to-be-envied ones who seem so happily certain that everything they write is "a darb." My days of doubt can do with a lot of reassurance and your appreciation is, as always, capable beyond all others' of reviving my groggy self-esteem.

Have you sent the script to Madden? I ask merely because, in that case, I must write him what to do with it.

Do you think Hopkins would be a good producer for *Interlude?* As I told you, the Guild is not definitely committed, and I am entitled to submit it elsewhere, provided I let the subcommittee know the circumstances of the option which expires Oct. 15th. There is a twofold advantage to be gained here: I might find a producer ready to take it up immediately: [if] the Guild let go—and if the Guild knew someone else wanted it, it would help them to decide to do it! But, at that, I think they will do it anyway.

All best to you,
Eugene O'Neill.

---

1. George Jean Nathan, "The Theatre: O'Neill's Finest Play," *American Mercury* (11 August 1927): 499–506.

From Eugene O'Neill

Bermuda
August 26, 1928

[Excerpt]

It [*Dynamo*] is really the first play of a trilogy[1] that will dig at the roots of the sickness of today as I feel it—the death of the old God and the failure of Science and Materialism to give any satisfying new One for the surviving primitive religious instinct to find a meaning for life in, and to comfort the fears of death with. It seems to me anyone trying to do big work nowadays must have this big subject behind all the little subjects of his plays or novels, or he is simply scribbling around on the surface of things and has no more real status than a parlor entertainer.

---

1. *Mourning Becomes Electra,* the trilogy that was to emerge in 1931. Later, returning to the conviction expressed in this letter, O'Neill sent to George Jean Nathan an article that Nathan published in *The American Spectator* (January 1933, p. 2). In this article, O'Neill wrote "[We need] a theatre returned to its highest and sole significant function as a Temple where the religion of poetical interpretation and symbolical celebration of life is communicated in human beings starved in spirit by their soul-stifling daily struggle to exist as masks among the masks of living!" Cf. "Struggles to Exist" with Nietzsche's *Also Sprach Zarsthutra,* glossary.

From The George Jean Nathan Collection, Olin Library, Cornell University

From Eugene O'Neill

> Villa Les Mimosas,
> Cap d'Ail, A.M., France
> March 29*th* '29

Dear Nathan:

Just a line to retract about thirty percent of my defense of *Dynamo* in my last! After laboring for ten days on the proofs, I have to admit that the play as it reached you in script sure had its slovenly fuzzy defects! The last act was particularly messed up and incoherent. I say "was." I hope I've cleared the whole play up by the drastic treatment I've given it and that it is now thirty percent better.

I let it out of my hands too soon, before I had any perspective on it. And I did too much writing in the medium of sets throughout. This last cannot be remedied at this late date. It's inherent in my idea of the play. But it's boring and confusing for a reader. As far as sets are concerned I'm going in for absolute simplicity in future—a dome and a few suggestive details— plenty of lighting—complete freedom of movement. At least that's how I've felt about it for the past four months—perhaps a reaction I got from the Chinese theatre.

But more of this when I see you.

I still claim *Dynamo,* as will be in the book, is a sound piece of work, in spite of some questionable techniques, and really represents me on a good level.

This is all confidential, of course. I don't want to appear to be defending this play, or to admit, as a lamentable post-mortem that the Guild might justly resent, that I sent it to them too soon—or to give out any detail of my future plans at present. Mum and then again mum is the proper course for me now.

Carlotta joins in all best to you. We are counting on your visit.

> As ever,
> Eugene O'Neill

From Eugene O'Neill

LE PLESSIS
SAINT-ANTOINE DU ROCHER
INDRE-ET-LOIRE

> August 31*st* '29

Dear Nathan:

I was damn glad to get your letter. We both were—for Carlotta was delighted with it. I have been intending to write to you or Lillian about the

Interlude suit,[1] but there isn't any news except the discouraging fact that the case is on the calendar and may not come up for trial until a year and a half! This business of the law irritates me to the exploding point! Here is a case manifestly absurd and cooked-up on the face of it and yet our legal lights of the Guild, Liveright[2] & O'Neill can't seem to do anything to get it dismissed. We have to go through with it at endless trouble and much expense. . . . I told Harry Weinberger[3] to get in touch with you . . .

No need to say how grateful I will be for your help in this affair. What is needed most are examples of the use of the hereditary insanity and the eugenic baby motive in modern literature . . .[4]

I'm still stewing around on the preliminary mulling over of the work[5] I outlined to you—and there is still a lot to get thought out clearly before I start actual dialogue. It is going to be difficult, this! It would be so easy to do *well*. The story would see to that—and that's the danger I want to avoid. It has got to have an exceptional quality to lift it above its easy possibilities and make it worthy in some sense of its classic antecedents—or it will be a rank flop in my eyes no matter what others may think of it. So I'm going to do a lot more of tentative feeling out and testing before I start.

Also I'm waiting until I see many uninterrupted months straightaway before me. There have been visitors, necessary trips to Paris, etc. breaking in. And the latter part of Sept. I've got to go through a long painful session with the dentist (extractions & new bridges). So I won't be on my way until October. But I grow more and more enthused by this idea for the next work. It keeps growing richer and I don't grudge the delay because I know it's moving.

My nineteen-year [old] son, six foot-two, 180 lbs., Eugene Jr.[6] has been visiting us after a tour of Germany I staked him to. He seems to have got a lot of valid stuff for himself out of Europe. He isn't the usual college youth from Yale; and yet he has enough of that about him to be no intellectual young prig. A fine youth, truly! I am proud of him—and I think he is of me—and our relationship is naturally brotherish with none of the forced "pal-father-son" bunk to it. When I survey his merits and think of the rotten mess of a life I was at his age, I have no fatherly superiority assumptions, believe me! He fits in very well with us. Carlotta likes him and he likes her, and I'm sure he feels more at home with us than he ever did when with me in the past. So all's well.

You don't say anything about the English plan?[7] Are you going to take them up?

It was grand to have you here, and it was grand to get to know Lillian.[8] She is simple and charming, and I sure admire her! Carlotta aussi! Put it down in the old date book that you're coming to us next year—and really stay for a while!

And think upon this: There are lots of chateaux for sale in this neighborhood. You had better look them over when you visit us.

All our affectionate best to you both!

As ever,
Eugene O'Neill.
August 31st, '29

---

1. Claiming that *Strange Interlude* had stolen much from her novel *The Temple of Palace Athene* (1924), Georges Lewys filed a plagiarism suit against O'Neill (May 27, 1929). In March 1930, the case was dismissed as being without merit. Nathan was a key witness in O'Neill's defense.

2. Horace Liveright (1886–1933) had founded the Boni & Liveright publishing firm.

3. O'Neill's lawyer; also the lawyer for the Provincetown Playhouse

4. O'Neill asked Nathan to identify other literary treatments of these themes.

5. *Mourning Becomes Electra*

6. Eugene Jr. was born on May 5, 1910, during O'Neill's first marriage (to Kathleen Jenkins).

7. Refers to the *London Daily Express*'s invitation to GJN to become a contributing critic. (He later accepted.)

8. During the summer of 1929 Nathan and Lillian Gish visited Le Plessis. The couple had previously denied that they were engaged—"only good friends." (*New York Times*, June 23, 1927).

From Eugene O'Neill

Le Plessis, November 12th, '29

Dear Nathan:

Your letter arrived a few days ago and we were both damn glad to hear from you. We had just returned from Paris where we spent three weeks—I with a daily visit to the dentist all that time! Now my teeth are fixed for the present and I can concentrate on work. Which I have been doing since our return, and I now feel I am at least off on the right foot. It should come with a rush from now on. All elaborate schemes have been cast aside and the aim now is to do this big job[1] with the utmost simplicity and naturalness. . . . Then I'll set it aside for six months—take a trip somewheres and then write the first draft of another idea that has grown ripe . . .[2]

One thing that has made the preliminary work on this new trilogy extremely arduous has been the tremendous difficulty of seeing every character through all the situations in different plays. With *Interlude* that was simple. They followed fairly straight lines of development in that work. But this is another story. . . .

And in Paris I saw my first "Talkie"—*The Broadway Melody*—and, think what you will of me, I was most enthusiastic! Not especially at the exhibit itself, naturally, but at a vision I had of what the "Talky" could be in time when it is perfected. Looked at from the personal angle, I saw how its technique could set me free in so many ways [that] I feel still bound down—free to realize a real Elizabethan treatment and get the whole meat out of a theme. Not that the "Talky" folk are ever liable to let me realize any of these dreams but I think the day may come when there will develop a sort of Theatre Guild "talky" organization that will be able to rely only on the big cities for its audiences. As for the objection to the "talkies" that they do away with the charm of the living, breathing actor, that leaves me completely cold. "The play's the thing," and I think in time plays will get across for what their authors intended much better in this medium than in the old. Also I believe a play written for the "Talkies" can have just as much literary value in printed form as any done for the regular stage. And again I am certain plays can be written that could be played as written on either the regular stage or as a "talky"—with a little help in the way of elasticity in the contrivings of our stage scenic designers. At any rate, my inspirations on this subject have had one practical result that I see the next play after the trilogy (an idea I set aside because I couldn't see how to do it) as a stage play combined with a screen talky background to make alive visually and vocally the memories, etc. in the minds of the characters. Keep this notion of mine a secret, of course.

I am most eager to talk to Lillian[3] about all this—after she has made *The Swan*[4]—hear all about the inside of this new technique. Perhaps we can eventually get together on something worth doing for both of us. Be sure to bring her here next summer!

Carlotta joins in all good wishes to Lillian & you. We are looking forward to your coming here next year. Don't let anything stop you!

As ever,

Eugene O'Neill

---

1. *Mourning Becomes Electra*
2. *Days Without End*
3. Lillian Gish
4. a project that fell through

From Zelda Fitzgerald to her husband, out of town

Late summer/early fall 1930

Dear Scott:

I have just written to Newman[1] to come here to me. You say that you have been thinking of the past. The weeks since, I haven't slept more than three or four hours, swathed in bandages sick and unable to read.

There was:

The strangeness and excitement of New York, of reporters and furry

smothered hotel lobbies, the brightness of the sun on the window panes
and the prickly dust of late spring: the impressiveness of the Fowlers[2] and
much tea-dancing and my eccentric behavior at Princeton. . . .

There was George's apartment [The Royalton] and his absinth cocktails . . .

We swam in the depth of the night with George before we quarrelled
with him and went to John Williams'[3] parties where there were actresses
who spoke French when they were drunk. George played "Cuddle up a
Little Closer" on the piano . . .

1. Newman Smith, husband of Zelda's sister Rosalind.
2. Ludlow Fowler and his wife Elsie. Ludlow had been one of Fitzgerald's classmates at
Princeton. He became the model for "Anson Hunter," protagonist of Fitzgerald's story "The
Rich Boy," *Redbook Magazine* (February 1926).
3. John Williams was a New York producer.

From the Fitzgerald Collection, Box 41, Folder 62, published with permission of Princeton
University Library and the Fitzgerald Estate.

From Carlotta O'Neill

February 21, 1931
[Handwritten note by Carlotta]

Dearest George Jean,

In looking over some clippings today I found one in which you stated
that "Eugene O'Neill was happy in his new marriage!" I thank you.—
We're both for matrimony—you'd better try it!!

Carlotta

From Theodore Dreiser

(Early in 1932 Theodore Dreiser was invited, along with Eugene
O'Neill, James Branch Cabell, Sherwood Anderson, and Ernest Boyd, to
share both the profits and the editorial responsibilities of the new *American Spectator,* which Nathan and Mencken were about to establish.
Dreiser was at first not aware that Nathan wished to devote the *Spectator*
to literature, theatre, and the other arts, whereas Mencken preferred to
stress politics, the economy, and other public affairs. Before Dreiser, who
leaned toward a combination of the two visions, learned of the founders'
disagreement, he delivered to their office on August 7, 1932 "My Idea of a
balanced issue.")

My idea of a balanced issue would be:

1. A poem—lyric, free verse, or prose.
2. Scientific presentation of something—preferably an examination of an important scientific fact or an interesting speculation.
3. Philosophic discussion of an abstraction after the manner of Santayana, Spencer, James, or whomsoever (not over 1000 words)
4. Critical or picturesque study of a literary or artistic personality (painter, novelist, poet, actor, dancer, singer, musician or composer)
5. Brief but colorful picture of the special state of a community, tribe, sect, cast, anywhere on the face of the earth.
6. A bit of adventure (important) by one who has done the adventuring—Byrd, Lindbergh, Post and Gatty, Amelia Earhart, Stefanson, or whomsoever.
7. A defense of someone or something either by the accused or a partisan of the thing attacked.
8. A picture of the difficulties, pleasure, profits, amusement, annoyances, reward, etc. of some profession by one in it—priest, lawyer, doctor, engineer, scientist, educator, administrator, banker, industrialist, or what you will.
9. A presentation of something by a technician.
10. A skit or playlet ridiculing some phase of something in the State or Nation or world—religious, political, artistic, athletic, dramatic, social, intellectual, etc.
11. A worth-while protest against some definite ill—savage and uncompromising.
12. A short story.
13. A discussion of a single important play.
14. Ditto a really important book (just one)
15. One or more genre commentaries by world celebrities anywhere— such as Hauptmann, Mussolini, the Pope, Stalin, Greta Garbo, Shaw, or one of the reigning Chinese Generals

From Robert Elias, ed., *Letters of Theodore Dreiser, a Selection* (Philadelphia: University of Pennsylvania Press, 1959), pp. 598–9.

From Theodore Dreiser

Old Bedford Road
R.F.D. 3
Mt. Kisco, New York
September 19, 1932

Dear George:

I want to tell you how valuable I feel the meaning of Friday evening to be.

In every worth-while enterprise, to say nothing of a distinguished one, there must always be, as you know, unintentional disagreements of action, thought, and, consequently, results. Unfortunately, maybe, you will always find me aggressive and insistent, probably irritatingly so, but the target and the goal is that evanescent thing, perfection.

One thing I want to say, and it springs not only out of that evening, but all else that has gone before in this instance, is this: There is that about your courageous, diplomatic, optimistic approach and efforts in connection with this really big thing which gratifies me enormously, and evokes my sincere respect. I think you are due a banquet and this is it.

In the case of Ernest,[1] I feel constantly an often wordless but really priceless aesthetic value there which can and will do as much with this venture as anything else that will be done by anybody to give charm and strength to this paper. To me his aesthetic approach is like a flag in the wind indicative of an important and so necessary ideal. Some good came of this thing, I know.

More important and most important, if it can possibly be arranged and that quickly, is to bring to New York, for conference, both Cabell and O'Neill. Regardless of the merit of their names, you know and I know that mere names at a masthead, unless joined with active co-operation, mean nothing. I cannot sufficiently emphasize how meaningful I hold this to be. If I could persuade it into immediate being, I would do so. If I could brutally command it, the order would go forth now.

As it is, with five equal temperaments trying to harmonize themselves, the best I can do is to urge you to use your personal persuasiveness and force to bring it about. Will you do this? You know me.

                                                        T.D.

---

1. Ernest Boyd, a member of the *American Spectator* Editorial board

---

From Robert Elias, ed., *Letters of Theodore Dreiser, a Selection* (Philadelphia: University of Pennsylvania Press, 1959) pp. 598–9.

From Eugene O'Neill to Saxe Commins, an editor at Random House

                                                [ca. October 12, 1932]
Dear Saxe:

This in haste to supplement my wire. I object to Nathan in this instance because when a volume including as many plays as this is put out it will stand in everyone's mind as representing the whole significant trend of my work—and, between us, I don't like leaving such a choice to Nathan. In spite of my friendship for him and my respect for his judgment along many lines, I by no means believe, or have ever believed, that he is any infallible critic of my work or has a comprehensive understanding of its inner spiritual, as opposed to its material outer dramaturgical, trends. He has too many (frankly confessed by him) blind spots. He is too Latin-rationalistic-sceptic-sentimental in the influences that have moulded his critical viewpoint. He is antipathetic to all plays with a religious feeling (he liked *Brown*[1] for its other aspects), all plays involving any tinge of social revolution. He liked *The Fountain, Gold!*[3]—he despised *Lazarus*, totally misunderstood what I was driving at in *Dynamo*,[5] thought *Hairy Ape*[6] was radical propaganda and disliked it for that, considered *Desire*[7] imitation Strindberg. I will say nothing about the many Nathan conceptions of life he has read into my plays and praised to my irritated amusement.

Don't misunderstand this as any panning of Nathan or any lack of gratitude for all the fights he has made for me. I'm only saying things about his criticism that I've often said in my arguments with him.

And on practical grounds I think in a case of this kind it's always a mistake to do the obvious thing that everyone accepts without interest as predetermined. Nathan is the obvious thing here. It's poor business, it has no imagination, no drama to it. The only comments on his choice and his foreword will be: "Of course. Old stuff." And I think it's bad policy from Liveright's as well as my end to always have Nathan as sponsor. If he were the only prominent critic who appreciated my works—but there are plenty of others—Krutch, Young, Atkinson, Gabriel, W. P. Eaton, etc., etc., etc.

My suggestion is to let *me* select *ten* plays. In a couple of sentences of foreword—no more—I would say my selection was based on my own good judgment and what the best criticism all over the world had said about either productions or the printed play. Then I would suggest that the Book Month ask one prominent American critic to do a *short* appreciation of a single play—ten critics for the ten plays—such appreciations to include a dire panning of the rest of my work by comparison, if the critic felt that way about it. I append a list of my selections of plays and possible critics for each play. This, of course, is tentative. By looking up your press records & old jackets you could probably add greatly to this list of alternatives of critics for each play. Let every critic appreciate his pet play as *the* best, that's the idea. Broun, for example, and Woollcott would probably say kind words about *Jones* or *Glencairn* if they were allowed to add that all my work since then has been trash! You get the idea? Difference of opinion, clash, argument ensuing, fresh interest and angles from the public and press standpoint—with my choice of ten plays as the background. . . .

If this thing is worth doing, it's worth doing well. Trouble is with any organization like the Book M. too lazy to take trouble—do the obvious—and lose out.

Or if B. of M. won't do this then I suggest choice of plays to be made from consensus opinion of one poet (Robinson or Jeffers, say) one novelist (Dreiser or Lewis) one historian (Beard or Adams) one dramatic critic (Krutch or Atkinson or Young or—endless list of possibilities) & one psychologist (White or Jeliffe or—another endless list) & one publisher (?). And Nathan to do foreword.

The above second suggestion is just dashed-off suggestion—may have nothing to it. What I'm after in this suggestion is to get away as far as possible in the choice matter from arbitrary choice by one dramatic critic whose opinion is already well known followed by foreword by same critic. Sabe? The list of plays to be submitted to parties to have all long plays on it except ones I barred. Of course, its doubtful if you could find one person in each class who had read or seen the plays! But some other scheme along these lines might be thought out. The good points about such a consensus scheme is that noone but the boobs would regard such a selection as having any real artistic authority! Whereas it would be interesting & comment-provoking. . . .

As ever,
Gene

---

1. *The Great God Brown* (New York, 1926)
2. *The Fountain* (New York, 1926)
3. *Gold* (produced in Provincetown in 1921)
4. *Lazarus Laughed* (New York, 1928)
5. Dynamo (New York, 1929)
6. *The Hairy Ape* (New York, 1922)
7. *Desire Under the Elms* (New York, 1924)

From Eugene O'Neill

Sea Island Beach
Georgia
Nov. 3rd 1932

Dear George:

Grand news, that of your card of the 28*th!* About the 4*th* printing,[1] I mean. Damned if I would ever have believed such was possible in this depressed era! It trends on the miraculous! But it's grand stuff, eh? You must feel very gratified after all the time and thought you have put in on it . . . .

Hmmm. That stock certificate. You wouldn't care to give me some more in exchange for some St. Louis & San Francisco Pfd., would you? No? Why, that's strange! Well then, make a suggestion: What can one do with Frisco Pfd.? Even the receivers don't seem to want it. I hope you appreciate these remarks are richly humorous—born of a twenty thousand dollar & more experience in R.R. financing by a playwright.

Working hard but bogged down in a bad spot.

C. joins in love to Lillian & you. We have seen no reports of *Camille*[2] but hope it was a grand smash. As ever,

Gene.

---

1. *The American Credo,* originally published by Knopf in 1920.
2. *Camille,* in which Lillian Gish starred, was a "smash."

From Eugne O'Neill

Sea Island Beach,
Ga.

Nov. 28, 1932

Dear George:

Well, how is the *Spectator*[1] coming along on its second number? If it's out, none have come this way yet. I have tried to think up something to send in but nothing whatever has come to me. This damned play has a strangle hold on the old bean. And, I'm sorry to say, without any satisfying results. I just finished what amounts to a second draft and am already starting to rewrite from top to bottom. Read what I'd done and it seemed to me a horrid mess—not even worth getting typed. At this rate, there won't be any play ready for production next season, either. Which, from what I hear of prevalent conditions in the N.Y. theatre—and due to get worse instead of better—may be just as well. *Electra* on the road is doing miserably. I expect any day to get the bad news that it has been called in.

Carlotta and I were planning to take a trip to N.Y. sometime around New Year's but we've had to call that off. Simply can't afford it, the way things are shaping up. Is there any chance of you and Lillian getting down here? We hope so but are afraid you are too tied up with the *Spectator* to make it. It's too damned bad we are so far off and it's such a jump to get here. But it's worth it, in weather and health, once you're here!

I have no news of any kind. Got a few English clipping[s] about *Spectator* which were very superior and snotty. You will have seen them, of course. All I see now are International clippings—and that only to track down productions over there. I cut out the American clips before I left New York. Expensive, and not one in a hundred that was worth a nickel to look at.

We're both "in the pink" in spite of various worries. Here's hoping you and Lillian are!

What do you hear now about the financial outlook for us [in the] U.S.? Love from us to you both!

As ever,
Gene

---

1. *The American Spectator*

From Eugene O'Neill

CASA GENOTTA
SEA ISLAND
GEORGIA

Dec. 29*th* 1932

Dear George:

My deepest sympathy,[1] I know what you have been going through and what it must have done to you. I also realize how futile it is for me to say anything that can mean anything—but again, my deep sympathy.

Don't you think that possibly if you got away down here now for a few days, it would be a good relief for you after such a prolonged period of mental and nervous strain? You know, just wire you're coming any time you care to.

As ever,
Gene.

---

1. Nathan's mother died on December 23, 1932.

From Theodore Dreiser

[*The American Spectator*
12 East 41st Street
New York, N.Y.]
April 17, 1933

Dear Nathan:

I have read "Sex Life in Hollywood" by Kearney,[1] and like it. Actually I see little wrong with it except where he gives the impression that he is apart from and above all this. Why declare himself either way? Just leave it out.

A thing that is entirely uninformed is his opening statement that the legends of wild orgies, dope parties, current about ten years ago have no foundation in fact. This is pure ignorance. Kearney was not there. I happened to be there at the time and know details and can give details aplenty, but one is sufficient: The party in the St. Francis Hotel thrown by Fatty Arbuckle which caused the death of the young actress whose name I forget, but the orgy phases of which are a part of the criminal records of San Francisco.[2]

These things were as common as pig tracks, beginning at the end of any day on which a director or producer decided to throw one. All the attractive girls that could be commandeered were called off the lot, brought into the party; and work ceased insofar as they were concerned until the party was over and they were in shape to go to work again. To ignore this truth is just nonsense. Either leave it out or state the facts.

Otherwise, I think the article, edited, would be valuable, and I cannot see, since it is so, how it happens to fall below our editorial dignity, particularly after "The Barbary Coast" and some others.[3]

T.D.

---

1. Patrick Kearney's article was submitted but not published.
2. Arbuckle's trial for manslaughter ended in acquittal (1922).
3. "Pretty Waiter Girls" and "A Forgotten American Christian" by Herbert Asbury, *The American Spectator* (January 1933, p. 3) and (April 1933, pp. 1–2).

From Robert Elias, ed., *Letters of Theodore Dreiser, A Selection* (Philadelphia: University of Pennsylvania Press, 1988, p. 628).

From F. Scott Fitzgerald

La Paix, Rodgers' Forge
Towson, Maryland,
July 27, 1933.

Dear George:

My interest in finding the *Spectator* in six pages this issue reminded me that you asked me to contribute. My phantom novel which is now really in its last stages absorbes every second of time that I don't have to devote to making a living so that for months even all correspondence has gone by the boards. As a matter of fact I have several pieces which I would like to work up for you but that eventuality seems some months off.

Please give my affectionate souvenirs to Ernest[1] whose letter I also omitted to answer. We often think of you and read everything you write but we seem to see each other only at intervals of three years.

With cordial best wishes always,

F Scott Fitzgerald

---

1. Ernest Boyd, one of Nathan's associate editors on *The American Spectator*.

From The George Jean Nathan Collection, Olin Library, Cornell University.

From Theodor Dreiser

> *The American Spectator*
> 12 East 41st Street
> New York, [N.Y.]
> December 13, 1933[1]

Nathan:

With regard to Lina Goldschmidt, I think the suggestion she made "About What Do People Laugh in Moscow" is a good one. The Slav sense of humor is very different from the Western European or American sense of humor, and if it were analysed it would be a good thing for the paper.

I like the fourth one, too: "Is There Romanticism on the Russian Stage?" I certainly think that should be analysed in the light of the very realistic communist program. Ideologically and philosophically, I think the government belittles it, but the Russian temperament is at once mournful and romantic, and how this point works out in connection with their program, if she could indicate that, would be valuable to us.

> T. D.

---

1. Although in a letter of October 7, 1933, Dreiser wished to be "disassociated" with the *American Spectator,* he did not formally resign until January 1, 1934. The *Spectator* folded in 1935.

From Robert Elias, ed., *Letters of Theodore Dreiser, a Selection* (Philadelphia: University of Pennsylvania Press, 1959), p. 655.

[On an *American Spectator* Letterhead]

> January 11, 1934

Dear Sean O'Casey:

My hope, now, for an American production of *Within the Gates*[1] lies with Sidney Phillips. I have had several long talks with him and the only remaining problem is a financial one on his part. He has fifteen thousand dollars to give to the production but agrees with me that the investment should be double that amount in order to keep the play going if business at the outset is not sufficiently prosperous. It is possible, he tells me, that he will be able to raise the extra amount from one of his friends. We shall see. I should have a report from him within the week.

Our other more eminent producers to whom I have submitted the play are either ignorant cowards or with full schedules for the remaining part of the season. It is amazing what stupidity I have encountered in that direction. Madden has been of great help to me in ferreting out the financial competence of the men I have approached. He is a valuable aid.

I am determined to get a production for you here and shall leave no stone unturned. I have even got into touch with one of our best young actresses[2] who would be ideal for the role of Jannice and she is so excited about doing it that she volunteers herself to contribute to the necessary treasury.

O'Neill's new play, *Days Without End,* is a failure. And deservedly. It is one of the poorest pieces of work that he has thus far contrived. He is pretty sad about it, but I cannot, on this occasion, sympathize with him. He has in recent years isolated himself so greatly from life that this play smells violently of grease-paint.

My every good wish to you,

As ever,
George Jean

---

1. Produced in Dublin, 1933; in New York, 1934.
2. Probably Lillian Gish, now in her thirties. "George and Lillian are still pretty thick," wrote Ring Lardner to F. Scott Fitzgerald about this time. See Matthew Bruccoli et al., eds., *Correspondence of F. Scott Fitzgerald* (New York: Random House, 1980), p. 177.

From Eugene O'Neill

CASA GENOTTA
SEA ISLAND
GEORGIA

Dear George,

I've just finished reading the script.[1] It certainly works out most amusingly! The jump from Romeo and Juliet seemed to me to come off remarkably well although I felt a little at sea on the Othello ending. The gap to the Shrew was harder to leap. I think you may find that additional small cuts in the first part of this third act, which would tone down the too-essentially Shrewish quality of the dialogue in the beginning, might help your cause. You see what I mean. If you could possibly insinuate an audience into the Shrew without their being too aware of it until they had accepted it, it would work all to the benefit of the rest of the act, and also be more amusing, I think. I may be all wrong. It's just the feeling that hit me that I could believe in Romeo-Othello and Juliet-Desdemona changing into Petruchio and Katherine if their too-Shrewish dialogue was toned down a bit when I first met them so the jolt of changed character wouldn't be so abrupt.

Thank you for sending the script. I had a lot of fun reading it. It's a grand stunt and the reactions to a production I am grinning at in advance. But, for God's sake, my dear Elizabethan confrere, do everything to keep your end of it dark until after the official unveiling!

Carlotta joins in love,
Gene

July 14th 1935
P.S.
The script is being returned to you under separate cover.

---

1. Nathan's play, *The Avon Flows*, a humorous pastiche of *Othello, Romeo and Juliet*, and *The Taming of the Shrew*, was published by Random House in 1937.

From Eugene O'Neill

4701 West Ruffuer St.
Seattle, Wash.[1]
[November 1936]

Dear George:

The past few days have been damned hectic, as you may imagine, what with ducking interviews of all sorts, radio & newsreel men, etc. But things appear now to have calmed down a bit. I'm still in a daze and don't know what to make of it all. The Nobel[2] caught me with my pants down, so to speak. I had absolutely no thought of it this year and did not believe the rumors—had it all doped out a Frenchman was due, Gide or Valéry.

A million thanks for your congrats—and let me take this opportunity to again thank you for all your friendship and encouragement has meant to me and my work. But I guess you know how I feel about that!

Still feeling all shot physically—no chance to rest yet and all this excitement is hell on the nerves. No definite plans, except that I can't possibly get to Sweden in time for the festival (don't feel physically up to it, anyway)—and am waiting now for a letter from the Swedish Academy with whatever suggestions they have to make.

Again, all gratitude, Friend!

Gene

---

1. The O'Neills had bought a home overlooking Puget Sound.
2. O'Neill was awarded the Novel Prize for Literature in 1936.

From Eugene O'Neill

TAO HOUSE
DANVILLE
CONTRA COSTA COUNTY
CALIFORNIA

Dear George,

Well, we are almost settled in the new home. I say almost because we've been living amidst carpenters, painters, electricians, ever since I last wrote you and it seems too good to be true that we are at last to have a little peace. But all discomforts will be justified in the final result. Carlotta has done a wonderful job in the interior—better than Casa Genotta—as you will agree when you visit.

I've just finished [reading] *The Morning After The First Night*. I like it better, I think, than any book of yours in years. Or, if that is because I see this one clearer, having just read it, than I remember the others, then I like it as well, and that means liking it a hell of a lot! The amazing thing, looking back over all your critical books, is that you never let yourself let down; each book has the same vital integrity, wit, clear vision, zest and love of the theatre. When I consider the twenty or more boring evenings in the Showshop Racket you have to pay for one interesting one in the theatre—season after season for so many years—well, my hat is off to you! It seems miraculous that just the wear and tear of the job doesn't weary your spirit into a let-down year now and then. I don't mean in the integrity of your criticism, of course. You couldn't do that. I mean in the vitality of your writing, in general quality—that that never becomes overstrained or stale. I guess we better begin to call you Iron Man!

What's new with you? We haven't heard from you in ages.

We had a letter from O'Casey a few weeks ago. He seemed as pleased about the *Electra* London lauds as if it were his own play. A grand guy, Sean, if there ever was one! As you probably know, *Electra* has moved to the West End after packing them in at the Westminster. The joker in this record Westminster business is that capacity gross there is a little above [that of] the old Provincetown Playhouse. Even at the West End theatre it has moved to, three hundred pounds a performance is S.R.O. So I'm not liable to grow rich on royalties—British Income Tax taking 25% and agents' cut further reducing them. The last report I had, business was steadily building at the new theatre but by no means capacity yet . . .

Love from us,
Gene

Feb. 7th '38

To Sean O'Casey

The Royalton Hotel, 44 W. 44th Street, New York
May 14, 1939

My very dear Sean:

Because of the European jitters [Hitler, etc.] I shall probably abandon my English visit this summer . . . maybe go to California and swim around with Gene [O'Neill]. . . . I hope autumn may bring you to America. For it is lovely here—impudently peaceful—the thrill of life with a smile in the air.

The Critics' Circle party this year was the best thus far; nobody got home before 9:00 a.m. . . . Dick Watts, Joe [Joseph Wood] Krutch and I sang trios to an accompaniment of a hurdy-gurdy played by a couple of New York cops . . . also we picked up two beautiful girls.

All the best,
George

From the George Jean Nathan Collection, Olin Library, Cornell University

From Eugene O'Neill

TAO HOUSE
DANVILLE
CONTRA COSTA COUNTY
CALIFORNIA

Dear George:

Much gratitude for the birthday note! It did a lot toward making me feel reconciled. And it arrived right on the dot, the morning of the 16th. Wartime mail service being what it is, that was surely luck.

There is nothing much of news to report. Carlotta is again suffering from her bad back, but keeps on with the job in spite of it. I'm feeling a bit better and hope to start work again soon. If and when, I'll let you know what I'm at.

Again, my gratitude, George—and our love to you and Julie.[1]

As ever,
Gene

October the 20th 1943.

1. Julie Haydon, who became Mrs. George Jean Nathan in 1955.

(From Nathan, the Royalton, New York, 1 December 1948, to August Mencken, Baltimore)[1]
Dear August: If there is anything at all I can do for Henry, please let me know. I am ready to come down to Baltimore at any time, though his secretary informs me that he must rest and be alone for a spell.

Yours,

George Jean Nathan

(From the Royalton, 22 December 1948, to H. L. Mencken, 1524 Hollins Street, Baltimore)
Dear Menck: August has conveyed to you my joy over your recovery and my hope that it will not be long now before I may again set an eye on you. I have saved up all the tasty gossip and the catalogue of my own ills and shall pour them into your ear in due course.

Best—

George

(From The Royalton, 28 January 1950, to 1534 Hollins Street, Baltimore)
Dear August: As I asked Blanche Knopf to report to you, I have been laid up with a relapse of virus flu, which has brought back my old torturing neuralgia and made me miserable . . . I hope HL is in pretty good shape. What wrecks we two once robust men are! But may God again be kind to us!

Ever—

George

(From The Royalton, 17 August 1950, to Hollins Street, Baltimore)
Dear August: . . . As soon as the weather clears, I'll come down for a visit. I miss seeing the old boy. Tell him that [Lawrence] Spivak has sold the *Mercury* to Clendenin Ryan for a fancy figure. Also that Harold Ross [of the New Yorker] asks about him regularly.

Ever—

George

---

1. Mencken, a widower since 1935, had suffered another stroke. In a long convalescence, he was cared for by his younger brother August.

These letters to August Mencken are in the Mencken Room of the Enoch Pratt Library, Baltimore, and are used by permission of the trustees of the Henry Mencken estate.

(From The Royalton, 28 November 1950, to Hollins Street, Baltimore)
Dear August: I think you are most wise to keep HL in the hospital until all danger is past. . . . When you next visit with him, read him my stuff about him in the current *New American Mercury* [November, 1950], probably the worst magazine ever published. I wrote the piece three months ago as

notes toward an ultimate autobiography. But now that damned heart attack has me . . . If I should get really worse, tell Henry I'll come down to the Hopkins [Johns Hopkins University Hospital] and crawl into the bed next to him.

Ever—

George

(From The Royalton, 26 May 1951, to Hollins Street, Baltimore)
Dear August: . . . I do hope the warm weather (it is 78° here today) will help Henry. I continue to believe that he would get a lot of distracting amusement out of a pet dog. My own certainly has passed the time for me. . . .

May the day come when I'll be able to see you and H again.

Ever—

George

(From the Royalton, 5 September 1951, to Hollins Street, Baltimore)
Dear August— . . . Knopf is off on [another] Western mountain pack trip. . . . He has purchased equipment at an outlay of 740 dollars, very handsome, including a purple rosette for the donkey's behind.[1] I lunched with him before he left and gave him a St. Christopher's charm to safeguard him.[2] Pat [Knopf's daughter] and I are growing marijuana on his country place during his absence. We obtained the seeds in Harlem and should get rich. My best to both of you—

George

---

1. Nathan writes in another letter (1 October 1951) "Alfred tells me his behind is normal save for a deep saddle mark on the left cheek." In still another letter (about 1956): "Alfred is spearing sharks off the coast of Santa Domingo. There has been no man like him since the late Frank Buck."
2. Knopf was Jewish, and Nathan would not be converted to Catholicism until his marriage to Julie Haydon in 1955.

(From The Royalton, 1 July 1953, to Hollins Street, Baltimore)
Dear August: Is all well with you both? The weather is so infernal here that I am planning to get away from it for a couple of weeks on July 17. I have booked a cruise on the *Santa Rosa* of the Grace Line and will be back in New York on the 29th.[1]

The Indiana trip was a happy and gratifying one, and you may now address me as Herr Doktor. They [Indiana University] conferred the Litt D. degree on me at the same time that they gave Harold Urey, who won the Nobel Prize, the D.Sc. You should see my robe! Lillian Russell would have died of envy. . . .

Best—

George

(From The Royalton, 12 August 1953, to Hollins Street, Baltimore)

Dear August: Is all well with you and H? I am back in town from the trip to South America, which I enjoyed a lot, and am attempting to return to my desk chores. I discoverd a spot in Venezuela not far from Porto Cabello that comes close to being paradise. A lovely small club-hotel in a forest of palms and on a silent beach where for little more than $100 a week one can have a small suite with two walls opening to the sea and all meals with excellent service. When the years crowd too heavily upon me, I shall retire there, perhaps with a young native girl and make faces at Willie Maugham.

Best—

George

---

1. It was on the *Santa Rosa* in 1955 that Nathan married Julie Haydon.

Photo Gallery

George Jean Nathan (Courtesy of the Cornell University Library)

Nathan and Mencken (Courtesy of Thomas Yoseloff)

Lillian Gish (Courtesy of Lillian Gish and James Frasher)

Nathan and Julie Haydon (Courtesy of Thomas Yoseloff)

Sean O'Casey (Courtesy of Thomas Yoseloff)

Eugene O'Neill (Courtesy of Thomas Yoseloff)

Zelda and Scott Filtzgerald (Courtesy of Princeton University and the Fitzgerald Estate)

Sinclair Lewis (Courtesy of Viking)

Theodore Dreiser (Courtesy of Pennsylvania University)

Gordon Craig (Courtesy of Simon & Schuster)

Glossary

Abbreviations

aka	also known as
ca.	(circa) about
cf.	compare
d.	died
ed.	editor
eds.	editors
et al.	and others
fl.	flourished
p.	page
pp.	pages
(q.v.)	which see or whom see
tr.	translated

ABBEY THEATRE, DUBLIN

Opened in 1904 on Abbey Street, on the site of the former Mechanics' Institute. The first director/managers were W. B. Yeats (q.v.) and Lady Augusta Gregory (q.v.). Succeeding them as manager was Lennox Robinson (1886–1958). From its beginnings, the Abbey was devoted to the revival of interest in Irish folklore and legends, and Irish cultural and national issues, which militants in the audience took very seriously, so that that audience became noted for its disorderly conduct. The opening presentations were Yeats's *On Baile's Strand* and Lady Gregory's *Spreading the News*. In 1907 the Abbey produced *Playboy of the Western World*, a controversial play by John Synge (q.v.), which caused a virtual riot. In 1924 the Abbey received a large grant from the Government of Eire, thus becoming the first government subsidized theatre in the entire English-speaking world. The Abbey burned down in 1951 and was not rebuilt until 1966.

See Lady Gregory, *Our Irish Theatre* (NY: Oxford Press, 1913); Lina Ellis-Fermor, *The Irish Dramatic Movement* (London: Methuen, 1939); and Robert Hogan, *After the Irish Renaissance* (Minneapolis: University of Minnesota Press, 1967).

ABBOTT, GEORGE (b. 1887)

American playwright and director. He specialized in comedies and was the author, with Ann Bridges, of *Coquette* (1928); with John Held, *Three Men on a Horse* (1935); and *The Boys from Syracuse* (1938). Abbott also directed many Broadway hits, including *Boy Meets Girl* (1935), *Room Service* (1938), *Damn Yankee* (1955), and *Fiorello* (1959), See Nathan's profile of Abbott in *The Entertainment of a Nation* (New York: Knopf, 1942), pp. 118–19.

245

ABIE'S IRISH ROSE (1922)

A play by the American playwright Anne Nichols (1891–1966). Based on the love of an Irish girl for a Jewish boy, this play ran on Broadway for 2,327 performances (1922–27).

ACADÉMIE FRANÇAISE

In France a distinguished cultural and learned society. It was founded in the early 1600s to discuss critical and linguistic standards, which it disclaimed it was "setting." After the first forty members, ("the immortal forty"), a new member was admitted only to replace one deceased. Over the years, the Academy's members have included such celebrities as Moliere (q.v.), Rousseau (q.v.), Balzac (q.v.), Flaubert (q.v.), Stendhal (q.v.), and Zola (q.v.). The Academy issued a dictionary as early as 1694. In modern times, in association with the Minister of Public Instruction, the Academy's activities have included the preparation of revised dictionaries (1932–) and grammars (1932–), and in general the awarding of literary grants and prizes.

ACT

1. Except in one-act plays (for example, Susan Glaspell's "Trifles," 1920) a section or division of a play indicated by the raising and lowering of the stage curtain. Ideally the end of each act except the last conveys a sense of suspense so that the audience is eager to see what happens next.

Most modern plays consist of three acts (beginning, middle, and end). Ancient Greek and Roman plays were not formally divided into acts. Shakespeare's plays now appear in five acts, although it was not before 1709 when Nicholas Rowe (q.v.) sorted out Shakespeare's plays into acts and scenes. Nineteenth-century English and Continental plays characteristically used four acts. An exception was Rostand's *L'Aiglon* (1899), which used six. An unusual nine-act play is O'Neill's *Strange Interlude* (1927), which requires the audience to return for a second seating.

Critics who have negative reactions to a play are known to walk out after the second act.

2. to act—to create an illusion of reality preferably by underemoting as opposed to "hamming it up." See Stanislavsky.

ACTION

See Plot.

"THE ACTRESS"

A one-act play by Molnar (q.v.)

ADAMS, JAMES TRUSLOW (1878–1949)

American historian whose distinguished books include *The Epic of America* (1931).

ADAMS, MAUDE (1872–1953)

American actress, born Maude Kiskadden. She was best known as the leading lady opposite John Drew (q.v.). Under the management of the Frohman Syndicate (q.v.), she starred for the most part in plays by James M. Barrie (q.v.): in 1897, *The Little Minister;* in 1901 *Quality Street;* in 1905, *Peter Pan,* her most memorable role; in 1908, *What Every Woman, Knows.* See Phyllis Robbins, *Maude Adams, an Intimate Portrait* (New York: G. P. Putnam's Sons, 1956). See Nathan's profile p. 95.

ADDISON, JOSEPH (1672–1719)
English essayist. *See* Richard Steele.

ADE, GEORGE (1866–1944)
American humorist and playwright. A native Hoosier, he attended Purdue University, where his classmates included Booth Tarkington (q.v.) and the Mc-Cutcheon brothers John and George Barr (q.v.). In his humorous columns and stories, Ade captured the slangy vernacular of his Chicago environment. His columns in the *Chicago Record* were collected in *Stories of the Streets and of the Town* (1893) He was also the author of *Artie* (1896), *Pink Marsh* (1897), *Doc Horne* (1899), *Fables in Slang* (1900), *The Girl Proposition* (1902), *Breaking into Society* (1903), and other humorous books. In 1903, three of his satirical plays ran simultaneously on Broadway: *The Sultan of Sulu,* a burlesque on gunboat diplomacy; *The County Chairman,* reflecting his hobnobbing with politicians whom he hosted at Hazelden, his Indiana country estate; and *The College Widow,* which was said to mirror college life at Wabash College, Crawfordsville, Indiana. *The College Widow* became a popular movie. It also was made into the musical comedy *Leave It To Jane* with music by Jerome Kern (q.v.) See A. L. Lazarus, ed., *The Best of George Ade.* (Bloomington: Indiana University Press, 1985.)

AESCHYLUS (525–456 B.C.)
Greek playwright of tragedy, first of the great trio (Aeschylus, Sophocles, Euripides). He fought at Marathon and Salamis (476 B.C.) Of the 90 odd plays he wrote, only seven survive, including *The Suppliants* (date unknown) about the marriages of the daughters of Danaüs; *The Persians* (ca. 472 B.C.) celebrating the Athenian victory at Salamis; *The Seven against Thebes* (467 B.C.), about the heroes who avenged, on the Theban usurper Eteocles, his banishment of Oedipus; *Prometheus Bound* (date unknown), which protests the cruelty of the gods against mankind; and the prize-winning *Oresteia* trilogy, a history of the house of Atreus—*Agamemnon, Choephoroe (The Libation Bearers),* and *The Eumenides.* Except for the *Oresteia,* which uses three actors, most of Aeschylus's other plays use only one actor apiece besides the chorus. Aeschylus's choruses sing poetic and philosophical comments on the actors' actions. In 1841 *Prometheus Bound* was translated by Robert Browning; also, *Agamemnon* in 1877.

AGATE, JAMES E. (1877–1947)
English drama critic for the *Manchester Guardian* and the English *Saturday Review.* See Nathan's profile of Christopher Fry, p. 152.

AGE OF INNOCENCE (1928)
The dramatization by Margaret A. Barnes of the novel (1920) by Edith Wharton (q.v.). See Nathan's profile of Katharine Cornell, p. 101.

AH, WILDERNESS! (1932)
A play by Eugene O'Neill (q.v.) It was "fondly" dedicated to Nathan.

AKINS, ZOË (1886–1958)
American playwright and screen writer who dramatized Edith Wharton's *The Old Maid* (1935).

ALBUMAZAR (805–885)
Arabian astronomer.

ALDOBRANDINI, IPPOLITO (1536–1605)
Italian artist and art patron who became Pope Clement VIII.

ALEXANDER, SIR GEORGE (1858–1918)
English actor.

ALGER, HORATIO (1832–1899)
Writer of hundreds of popular books for boys. He was the son of a Unitarian minister. See Nathan's profile of Theodore Dreiser, p. 160.

ALGONQUIN HOTEL
59 West 44th Street, New York, across from Nathan's apartment at the Royalton. The Algonquin's Round Table Room has long been the rendezvous for celebrated literati and editors.

ALIEN CORN (1933)
A play by Sidney Howard (q.v.).

ALLEN, HERVEY (1889–1949)
American novelist and biographer best known for his picaresque novel *Anthony Adverse* (1933), a historical figure. See Nathan's profile of Maxwell Anderson.

ALL GOD'S CHILLUN GOT WINGS (1923)
A play by Eugene O'Neill (q.v.).

ALL MEN ARE ALIKE (1941)
A play by Vernon Sylvaine (1897–1957).

ALL MY SONS (1947)
A play by Arthur Miller (q.v.).

ALSO SPRACH ZARATHUSTRA (IN 4 PARTS, 1883–92)
Nietzsche's treatise that defines his vision of the highest type of human character. He rejects Christian "original sin" as obstructing all that is courageous in mankind. His doctrines of "will to power" (derived from Schopenhauer) and "eternal return" (to power) are emblazoned on the banner of every heroic person who fights against all that is tragic in life. This new heroic man ("superman") is foreshadowed in Zarathustra (Zoroaster) the Persian religious leader. "Eternal return" is consciously more aggressive than "eternal recurrence."

AMERICAN CREDO, THE (1920)
Essays by Nathan in collaboration with H. L. Mencken; revised as *The New American Credo* (New York: Knopf, 1927).

AMERICAN LANGUAGE, THE (1919; 1936)
A philological lexicographical study by H. L. Mencken (q.v.). The first edition was published in 1919 by Alfred Knopf, New York.

AMERICAN MUSIC HALL
Erected originally as a church in 1852 at 139–141 East 55th Street, it was converted into a theatre on 14 March 1934 with the presentation of the melodrama *The Drunkard* by William Henry Smith (1806–1872). This melodrama, which had played on tour hundreds of times during the late 1800s, now played for hundreds more times at the American Music Hall. Here, at each performance, ironically, beer was served.

AMERICAN SPECTATOR, THE
A short-lived (1932–1935) magazine founded and edited by Nathan in collaboration with Ernest Boyd, Theodore Dreiser, Sherwood Anderson, James Branch Cabell, and Eugene O'Neill. See the footnote to O'Neill's letter of 26 August 1928 to Nathan.

AMES, WINTHROP (1871–1937)
American theatrical producer who managed theatres in Boston and New York. In 1909 he produced *Strife* by John Galsworthy (q.v.). Ames also wrote and produced *Snow White* (1913). From 1926 to 1929 he revived the operettas of Gilbert and Sullivan (q.v.).

AMORGOPULA
One of the Greek islands. See Nathan's essay "Intelligence and the Drama."

ANDERSON, DAME JUDITH (b. 1898)
Australian-born actress, famous for her performances in classical Greek and Shakespearian tragedies. She also triumphed in modern roles on stage and screen, notably in *Rebecca* (1940) and *Cat on a Hot Tin Roof* (1958). Nathan regarded her as one of the most accomplished actresses in America. See Nathan's essay "Helen Hayes and Her Rivals," p. 104.

ANDERSON, JOHN MURRAY (1886–1954)
American theatrical producer. See Nathan's profile of Ziegfeld, p. 192.

ANDERSON, MARY (1859–1940)
American actress.

ANDERSON, MAXWELL (1888–1959)
American playwright; he started his career with teaching at Stanford University and at Whittier College. He then turned to journalism, working on the *New York World,* where he met Lawrence Stallings (q.v.), with whom he collaborated on several plays, including *What Price Glory?* (1924). This was later made into a successful motion picture. Plays by Anderson himself include *Saturday's Children* (1927); *Elizabeth the Queen* (1930), in blank verse; *Both Your Houses* (1933), a Pulitzer Prize winner; *Mary of Scotland* (1933), which starred Helen Hayes (q.v.); *Valley Forge* (1934); *Winterset* (1935), a verse tragedy concerned with the Sacco-Vanzetti case; *Masque of Kings* (1936); *The Wingless Victory* (1936); *High Tor* (1937); *Joan of Lorraine* (1946); *Anne of the Thousand Days* (1948); and *Barefoot in Athens* (1951), about the Greek philosopher Socrates.
See Nathan's profile of Maxwell Anderson. See also Laurence Avery, ed., *Letters of Maxwell Anderson* (Chapel Hill: University of North Carolina Press, 1977).

ANDERSON, SHERWOOD (1876–1941)
American fiction writer and playwright. In 1932 Anderson joined Nathan, Mencken, and others in founding *The American Spectator* (q.v.). Several of Anderson's plays—especially from his group *Winesburg, Ohio, and Other Plays* (1937)—were produced in New York by the Provincetown Players (q.v.). But Sherwood Anderson is best remembered as the author of a collection of short stories entitled *Winesburg, Ohio* and especially—in that collection—for the story "Hands," which has been frequently anthologized.

ANDREYEV, LEONID (1871–1919)
Russian playwright; author of *He Who Gets Slapped* (1914). See Nathan's profile of Theodore Dreiser, p. 160.

ANGELIN, MARGARET (1876–1958)
Canadian actress who starred in the Hudson Theatre production of *Camille* (1904).

ANNA CHRISTIE (1920)
The play that won for O'Neill his second Pulitzer Prize.

ANNIE LAURIE (1927)
An MGM film directed by D. W. Griffith (q.v.) and starring Lillian Gish (q.v.).

ANOTHER BOOK ON THE THEATRE (1915)
A book by Nathan. New York: Knopf.

ANOTHER PART OF THE FOREST (1946)
A play by Lillian Hellman (q.v.).

ANOUILH, JEAN (1910–1987)
French playwright, author of more than 40 dramas, most of which center in the protagonists' heroic attempts to maintain integrity in the face of corruption. His best known plays include *The Ermine* (1931), *Jezebel* (1932), *The Savage* (1934), *Traveler Without Luggage* (1937), *Eurydice* (1942), *Antigone* (1942), *Medea* (1946), *Cry of the Peacock* (1950), Thieves' Carnival (1952), *The Lark* (1953), *Tiger at the Gates* (1955), *The Restless Heart* (1957), *Becket* (1959), *Rendezvous at Senlis* (1961), *The Rehearsal* (1961), and *The Honor of God* (1962). See Nathan's profile of Anouilh in *The Theatre Book of the Year 1949–1950* (New York: Knopf, 1950), pp. 262–65.

ANTA (AMERICAN NATIONAL THEATRE & ACADEMY)
A professional organization chartered by Congress in 1935 to encourage outstanding drama and theatre in the United States.

ANTA THEATRE
245 West 52nd Street between Broadway and 8th Avenue, New York City; it opened in December, 1954 with a dramatization of *Portrait of a Lady* by Henry James (q.v.). The Anta Theatre was originally the Guild Theatre, which had opened in April 1925 with a production of *Caesar and Cleopatra* by George Bernard Shaw (q.v.).

ANTHEIL, GEORGE (1900–1959)
American pianist and composer. Author of "Jazz Symphony" (1927) and *Bad Boy of Music* (1945), he was a member, along with Hemingway, Fitzgerald, and Malcolm Cowley, of what Gertrude Stein called "the Lost Generation." With those and other "expatriates," he sojourned in France during the 1920s. He typified the jazz pianists that Fitzgerald portrayed in Jay Gatsby's East Egg, Long Island, wild parties. Even more specifically, Antheil was the model of the musician Abe North in the French Riviera beach gatherings in Fitzgerald's novel *Tender is the Night* (1934). Cf. Zelda Fitzgerald's account of a party "fling" in New York, p. 217.

ANTHONY, KATHARINE (1877–1965)
American biographer; she was the author of *Catherine the Great* (1925), *Louisa May Alcott* (1938), and other books that were borrowed from for dramatizations.

ANTI-MASQUE
See Masque.

ARCHER, WILLIAM (1856–1924)
Scottish-American drama critic and scholar; noted for his translations of Ibsen's plays.

ARISTOPHANES (448 B.C.–388 B.C.)
Celebrated Greek playwright of comedies who used the chorus (q.v.) extensively and hilariously. He almost surely wrote more than eleven plays, but those that survive include *The Athenians* (425 B.C.), an attack on the Peloponnesian wars; *The Clouds* (423 B.C.), which satirizes Sophists like Socrates; *Lysistrata* (411 B.C.), a hilarious exposé of war, in which the women band together to withhold sex from their husbands to force them to give up going to war; and *The Frogs* (405 B.C.), lampooning the seriousness of Aeschylus (q.v.) and Euripides (q.v.). From *The Frogs* a group of Yale University students borrowed the cheer "Breke ko-ex, ko-ex, ko-ex!"

ARLEN, MICHAEL (1895–1956)
English novelist and playwright (born Dikran Kouyoumdjian). He is best known as the author of *The Green Hat* (1924). He also wrote *The London Venture* (1920), *These Charming People* (1923), *Men Dislike Women* (1931), *Hell! Said the Duchess* (1934), and *The Flying Duchman* (1939). *The Green Hat* was made into a play and was produced in 1925 at the Broadhust Theatre in New York. It was also made into a movie starring Greta Garbo, who played the role of Iris March.

ARLISS, GEORGE (1868–1946)
English actor on stage and screen. He performed with Mrs. Patrick Campbell (q.v.) in *The Second Mrs. Tanqueray* by Pinero (q.v.); also in *Disraeli* (1911). His role as Disraeli is among his best remembered, especially in the 1930 screen version, for which he won an Academy Award. His other screen performances include *The Green Goddess* (1920), *Old English* (1930), *Alexander Hamilton* (1931), *The House of Rothschild* (1934), and *Cardinal Richelieu* (1935). His autobiography, *Up the Years from Bloomsbury,* appeared in 1927. It was published in London by John Murray.

ARMOUR, PHILIP (1832–1901)
American industrialist.

ARSENIC AND OLD LACE (1944)
A popular play by Joseph Kesselring (b. 1902).

ARTAUD, ANTONIN (1896–1948)
French surrealist playwright and actor. See Surrealism.

ASBURY, HERBERT (1891–1963)
American journalist; author of *Life of Carry Nation* (1929) and *The Barbary Coast* (1933).

ASCAP
American Society of Composers, Authors, and Publishers. *See* Victor Herbert.

ASIDE
A character's parenthetical remark stage-whispered to the audience as opposed to another character or characters, who are not supposed to hear the remark. The aside was used in many plays of the eighteenth and nineteenth centuries and also in the early 1900s. It was a favorite device of Oscar Wilde (q.v.). Cf Soliloquy.

ASTOR THEATRE
1537 Broadway, New York; it opened 21 September 1906, with a production of Shakespeare's *A Midsummer Night's Dream*.

ATKINSON, BROOKS (1894–1983)
Celebrated drama reviewer and critic who wrote for the *New York Times*, among other periodicals. See his estimate of Nathan, p. 11.

AURELIUS, MARCUS ANTONINUS (121–180)
Roman emperor and Stoic philosopher originally named Marcus Ennis Verus. He remains best known for his *Meditations*. See Stoicism.

AUSTIN, MARY (1868–1934)
American poet, novelist, and playwright. She was a feminist and champion of native American Indians and Hispanic Americans. She was the author of *The Land of Little Rain* and *The American Rhythm* (1923). Her most popular play was *The Arrow Maker* (1910). *See* Karen Langlois, "Mary Austin and the New Theatre . . . ," *Theatre History Studies*, vol. 8, 1988.

AUTOBIOGRAPHY OF AN ATTITUDE
A book by Nathan. New York: Knopf, 1925.

AWARD, THE GEORGE JEAN NATHAN
In accordance with the provisions in the will of Nathan, the George Jean Nathan Award was established "to encourage and assist in developing the art of drama criticism and the stimulation of intelligent theatre going." The selection committee, consisting of the English department chairmen of Cornell, Yale and Princeton universities, meets annually to cite "the best piece of drama criticism published during the previous year." The award carries a stipend of $4,000.

BACH JOHANN SEBASTIAN (1685–1750)
German organist and composer.

BACK TO METHUSELAH (1922)
A play by George Bernard Shaw (q.v.).

BAGNOLD, ENID (1889–1981)
English novelist; author of *National Velvet* (1935), which was later dramatized into a movie starring Elizabeth Taylor.

BAHR, HERMANN (1863–1934)
Austrian playwright, critic, and theatre manager; author of *The Master* (1916).

BAKER, GEORGE PIERCE (1866–1935)
Professor of playwriting at Harvard and of play production at Yale. At Harvard in 1906 Baker founded his experimental "Workshop 47," in which many later-to-be celebrated plays were drafted, criticized, revised, and tried out on the stage of Agassiz House. The students of Workshop 47 included Edward Sheldon, Eugene O'Neill, Philip Barry, S. N. Behrmann, John Dos Passos, Sidney Howard, John Mason Brown, and Thomas Wolfe. Here, Edward Sheldon wrote his melodrama *Salvation Nell* (1908), later popularized by Minnie Maddern Fiske (q.v.). Thomas Wolfe's novel *Of Time and the River* (1935) contains a portrait of Baker in the character Professor Hatcher. The success of Workshop 47 prompted several emulators. For example, at the University of Michigan, in the late 1920s, Professor Kenneth Rowe established the playwriting workshop that was to develop many a Hopwood Award (q.v.) winner. It was in Rowe's workshop that Arthur Miller developed a first draft (1935) of a play that would be called *All My Sons* (1947).

In 1925 Professor Baker, disheartened by "lack of appreciation" by colleagues in the Harvard English Department, transferred to Yale, where the Harkness Theater was built for him. About four years after his death, John Mason Brown edited a collection of memorial tributes to him (1939). Baker's own books include *Dramatic Technique* (1919) and *The Development of Shakespeare as a Dramatist* (1907). See W. P. Kinne, *George Pierce Baker and the American Theater* (Cambridge: Harvard University Press, 1954).

BALDERSTON, JOHN L. (1889–1954)
English playwright.

BALDWIN, JAMES (1924–1987)
American novelist, essayist and playwright. His play *Blues for Mr. Charlie* (1964) was not as well received as were his other works, including *Go Tell It on a Mountain* (1953), *Notes of a Native Son* (1955), *Nobody Knows My Name* (1961), *Another Country* (1962), and The *Fire Next Time* (1963).

BALZAC, HONORÉ DE (1799–1850)
French novelist, best known for his series of realistic novels, *La Comédie Humaine* including *Eugene Grandet* (1833) and *Le Pere Goriot* (1834).

BARA, THEDA (1885–1955)
Née Theodosia Goodman, American actress of silent films, including *Cleopatra* (1917), *Dubarry* (1917), and *Salome* (1918). In her time she created the image of the siren or vamp.

BARBER, JAMES NELSON (1784–1858)
American playwright best known for his dramatization of Sir Walter Scott's *Marmion* (1812), which played off and on for thirty years. Barber's other plays included *The Indian Princess* (1808), *The Court of Love; or How to Try a Lover* (1817), and *The Madras House,* which was produced posthumously in 1921. See Nathan's essay "Literature and the Drama," p. 66.

BARLOW, REGINALD (1867–1943)
Anglo-American actor.

BARNUM, PHINEAS T. (1810–1891)
American circus showman. See Irving Wallace, *The Fabulous Showman* (New York Knopf, 1959).

BARRETTS OF WIMPOLE STREET, THE (1930)
Rudolph Besier's play about Elizabeth Barrett and her family and Robert Browning (q.v.).

BARRIE, JAMES M. (1860–1937)
Scottish playwright. He was the author of *Quality Street* (1901): *The Admirable Crichton* (1902); *Peter Pan* (1904), which in America starred Maude Adams (q.v.); *What Every Woman Knows* (1908); and *The Twelve Pound Look* (1910). See Nathan's profile, p. 121.

BARRY, PHILIP (1896–1949)
Amrican playwright, a graduate of the Harvard Workshop 47 under George Pierce Baker (q.v.). Barry was the author of *Holiday* (1929); *Hotel Universe* (1930); *The Animal Kingdom* (1932); *Here Come the Clowns* (1935); and *The Philadelphia Story* (1939), starring Katharine Hepburn.

BARRYMORE, ETHEL (1879–1959)
American stage and screen actress. She was the sister of John Barrymore (q.v.) and Lionel Barrymore. She starred in numerous productions, among them *A Doll's House* (1905) and *The Constant Wife* (1926). Nathan lists her among the few rivals of Helen Hayes. See "Helen Hayes and Her Rivals," p. 104.

BARRYMORE, JOHN (1882–1942)
American actor and screen idol. His stage performances included leading roles in *Beau Brummel* (1916), *Don Juan* (1921), *Hamlet* (1922 and 1924–25), and *The Royal Family* (1927). He starred in many screen roles, the best known perhaps in *Grand Hotel* (1930) in which he played opposite Greta Garbo. After his death there appeared the biography *Good Night, Sweet Prince* (1943) by Gene Fowler; also Lionel Barrymore's *We Barrymores* (1951).

BARRYMORE, MAURICE (1847–1905) AND FAMILY
Maurice Barrymore was born Herbert Blythe in India. He was married to Georgianne Drew, the daughter of the actor John Drew (1827–1862). Maurice and Georgianne became the parents of Lionel (1878–1954), Ethel (1879–1959), and John (1882–1942). In *The Royal Family* (1927), Edna Ferber and George S. Kaufman poke fun at this theatrical family.

BARTON, BRUCE (1886–1967)
American journalist and advertising executive.

BATAILLE, FELIX HENRY (1872–1922)
French poet and playwright. He was obsessed with visions of nymphomaniacs, especially in his plays *La Femme Nue* (tr. *The Nude Woman,* 1908) and *Le Scandale* (1909).

BATHOS
Literally "depth"; effects of a plunge from loftiness to unintended humor. Example: "Advance the fringed curtain of thy eyes / And tell who comes yonder." See "Christopher Fry."

BATTLE(S) OF BULL RUN (1861 AND 1862)
in the American Civil War.

BAUDELAIRE, CHARLES (1821–1867)
French poet and critic, best known as the author of *Flowers of Evil* (1857), a collection of symbolist poems. See Nathan's profile of T. S. Eliot, p. 188.

BEACH, REX (1877–1949)
American critic and novelist.

BEACH, SYLVIA (1877–1962)
Expatriate American bookseller and publisher who presided over the Shakespeare & Company bookshop in Paris (1919–1941). She published James Joyce's *Ulysses* (1922). *See James Joyce's Letters to Sylvia Beach,* eds. Melissa Banta and Oscar Silverman (Bloomington: Indiana University Press, 1988).

BEARD, CHARLES A. (1874–1948)
American historian and essayist best known for *The Rise of American Civilization* (1927), which he wrote in collaboration with his wife, Mary Ritter Beard (1876–1958).

BEAUMARCHAIS, PIERRE-AUGUSTE (1732–1799)
French playwright and critic, best known for his plays *The Barber of Seville* (1775) and *The Marriage of Figaro* (1784), which inspired operas, respectively, by Rossini and Mozart.

BEAUTIFUL PEOPLE, THE (1941)
A play by William Saroyan (q.v.).

BEAUX ARTS CAFÉ
In 1919 near 34th Street and 8th Avenue, New York; frequented by Nathan and H. L. Mencken.

BECKETT, SAMUEL (b. 1906)
Anglo-French playwright, author of *Waiting for Godot* (1953), *Endgame* (1957), and *Krapp's Last Tape* (1959).

BECQUE, HENRY FRANCOIS (1837–1899)
French playwright. He was the author of *La Parisienne* (1885) and *La Ronde* (tr.

The Merry-go-Round, 1913), both of which strongly influenced French literary naturalism (q.v.).

BEERBOHM, HERBERT TREE (1853–1917)
English actor and theatre manager, half-brother of Max Beerbohm (q.v.). In 1914 "H. T." founded what was to become the Royal Academy of Dramatic Art. See Hesketh Pearson, *Beerbohm Tree* (London: Methuen, 1956). See Nathan's letter of 1924 to Mencken, p. 209.

BEERBOHM, MAX (1872–1956)
English essayist, caricaturist, and drama critic. As the drama critic for the English *Saturday Review,* he succeeded George Bernard Shaw (q.v.). Beerbohm was the author of *A Book of Caricatures* (1907) and *A Christmas Garland* (1912), which contains caricatures and parodies of such authors as G. K. Chesterton (q.v.); Joseph Conrad (q.v.), and H. G. Wells (q.v.). One of Beerbohm's best known novels remains *Zuleika Dobson* (1913). See Nathan's letter of 1924 to Mencken, p. 209.

BEGGAR ON HORSEBACK (1924)
This comedy, by George S. Kaufman (q.v.) and Marc Connelly (q.v.), with music by Deems Taylor, was based on a satirical German play, *Hans Sonnenstösser's Hoellerfahrt (Trip to Hell)* by Paul Apel (fl. late 1800s).

BEHOLD THE BRIDEGROOM (1927)
A play by J. E. Kelley (1915–1964).

BEHRMAN, S. N. (1893–1973)
American humorist, playwright, and screenwriter. He had been a member of the Harvard Workshop 47 under George Pierce Baker (q.v.). Behrman was the author of *The Second Man* (1927), *End of Summer* (1936), *Amphitryon '38* (1937), and *No Time for Comedy* (1939). See Nathan's profile of Behrman, p. 149.

BEINECKE LIBRARY OF AMERICANA
Yale University. Curator is Donald Gallup.

BELASCO, DAVID (1853–1931)
American actor, playwright, and producer. Belasco was brought up in a family of theatre people in San Francisco, where at the age of 19 he was made stage manager of the Baldwin Theatre. His real apprenticeship, however, occurred in Virginia City, Nevada, under the tutelage of showman Dion Boucicault (q.v.). In 1880 Belasco toured the country with a series of melodramas that attracted the attention of the Frohman Syndicate (q.v.). Two years later, in New York, the Frohmans made him stage manager of the Lyceum Theatre. Because he demonstrated inventiveness in stage sets and, especially, in lighting, the Frohmans were sorry to lose him, when in 1895 he left them to become an independent producer. He was so successful that in 1910 he bought the old Stuyvesant Theatre (West 44th Street) and renamed it The Belasco.

An eccentric personality, Belasco affected the role of an Episcopalian priest, wore a clerical collar, and became known as "The Bishop of Broadway." In accordance with his policy of the "star system," he helped develop the talents of such stars as Minnie Maddern Fiske, David Warfield, Lenore Ulric, Ina Claire, Fannie Brice, and the controversial divorcée Mrs. Leslie Carter. Of over 400 plays that he produced, he wrote several and revised most. His own plays include *Du Barry* (1901) and *Girl of the Golden West* (1905). The latter inspired *La Fanciulla del West* (1908), the opera by the Italian composer Giacomo Puccini (1858–1925), the first opera on an American theme. See Craig Timberlake, *The Life and Work of David Belaso, the Bishop of Broadway* (New York: Library Publishers, 1954). See also Nathan's profile of Belasco, *Mr. George Jean Nathan Presents* (New York: Knopf, 1917), pp. 66–79.

BELASCO THEATRE
West 44th Street between Broadway and Avenue of the Americas (6th Avenue); originally the old Stuyvesant Theatre, which David Belasco (q.v.) had purchased.

BELCH, SIR TOBY
In Shakespeare's *Twelfth Night,* Olivia's uncle; caricature of a roistering knight.

BELDEW, COSMO KYRLE (1886–1948)
American actor; star of *Raffles* (1910).

BELLEVILLE, FREDERIC DE (b. 1911?)
Anglo-French actor.

BELLEW, HAROLD KYRLE (1855–1911)
English actor.

BELLINI, GIOVANNI (1430–1536)
Italian who painted *Madonna, Child, and Six Saints,* among other masterpieces.

BELLINI, VINCENZO (1801–1835)
Italian who composed the opera *Norma* (1831) among others.

BELLOW, SAUL (b. 1915)
American novelist; Nobel Laureate of 1976.

BELLOWS, GEORGE (1882–1925)
American painter and lithographer. He specialized in such landscapes and sporting scenes as *Up the Hudson* and *Stag at Sharkey's.* See Nathan's profile of O'Neill, p. 135.

BEN-AMI, JACOB (1890–1976)
Yiddish actor who, because of his inappropriate accent, was dismissed from O'Neill's play *The Fountain.*

BENELLI, SEM (1877–1949)
Italian playwright. See Nathan's profile of John Barrymore, p. 98.

BENÉT, STEPHEN VINCENT (1898–1943)
American poet, short-story writer, and playwright. He was the author of *John Brown's Body* (1928), an epic poem with a memorable invocation. The poem was dramatized by Charles Laughton and produced in New York in 1953, ten years after Benet's death. Benet's best known story was "The Devil and Daniel Webster," which was made into an opera (1943) by Douglas Moore and later into a successful movie.

BENÉT, WILLIAM ROSE (1886–1950)
    American poet, playwright, and *Saturday Review* editor. He was the brother of
Stephen Vincent Benet (q.v.). William Rose Benet's second wife was the poet
Elinor Wylie (q.v.). His poetry collections include *Merchant from Cathay* (1913);
his plays include *Day's End* (1939), which is addressed to children.

BEN HUR (1880)
    A popular novel by Lew Wallace (q.v.). It has been dramatized for stage and
screen; screen versions, over the years, have starred several matinée idols including Ivor Novello and Charlton Heston. The 1958 screen version was written by
Christopher Fry (q.v.).

BENNETT, ARNOLD (1867–1931)
    English novelist; author of *The Old Wives' Tale* (1908).

BENNETT, JAMES GORDON JR. (1841–1918)
    American editor; founder of the Paris edition of the *Herald Tribune*. In 1869 it
was he who sent journalist Henry Morton Stanley to Africa to find missionary and
explorer David Livingstone.

BENNETT, RICHARD (1872–1944)
    American actor and producer. Among other plays, he produced O'Neill's *Be-
yond the Horizon (1920)*. Richard Bennett was the father of the movie actresses
Constance and Joan Bennett.

BENSON, SALLY (1900?–1972)
    American novelist and playwright; author of *Junior Miss* (1941) and *Meet Me in
St. Louis* (1942).

BENTHAM, JOSEPHINE (b. 1925?)
    American novelist and playwright; co-author with Herschel Williams (b. 1909)
of the play *Janie* (1944), based on her novel of the same name.

BENTLEY, ERIC (b. 1916)
    Anglo-American critic of drama. His books include *The Playwright as Thinker*
(1946). He is quoted in Nathan's profile of O'Neill.

BENTLEY, HAROLD W. (b. 1899)
    American actor.

BERGMAN, INGMAR (b. 1918)
    Influential Swedish screen writer and director. His films include *The Seventh
Seal* (1956) and *Wild Strawberries* (1957).

BERGNER, ELIZABETH (b. 1900)
    Austrian-American actress; she began her career in playing Shakespearian
roles; later she gravitated toward Ibsen and Shaw. She also starred in such films as
Catherine of Russia (1934) and *Escape Me Never* (1947).

BERKELEY SQUARE (1926)
    A play by J. R. Balderston (1889–1954) and J. C. Squire (1884–1958).

BERLIN, IRVING (1888–1989)

American songwriter. Born Irving Baline in Russia, he came as a child to the United States. During World War I, he served in the Army, an experience that inspired many songs (he has written more than 800), along with the musical comedy *Yip Yip Yaplank,* which he later rewrote as *This Is the Army* (1942). He also wrote songs for the *Ziegfeld Follies,* for *As Thousands Cheer* (1933), *Annie Get Your Gun* (1946), *Miss Liberty* (1949), *Call Me Madam* (1950), and *Mr. President* (1962).

In 1926 Berlin married Ellin MacKay, daughter of John W. MacKay, president of the internationally prestigious Commercial Cable Company.

Berlin's best known songs include "Alexander's Ragtime Band," "Easter Parade," "White Christmas," "God Bless America," and "There's No Business Like Show Business."

BERNARD, SAM (1889–1950)

American actor.

BERNHARDT, SARAH (1844–1923)

Celebrated French actress who first used the name of Rosine Bernard. She made her debut in 1862 at the Comèdie Française (q.v.). From 1866 to 1872 she performed at the Odéon (q.v.). She starred in Coppé's *Le Passant* (1869), in Racine's *Phaedre* (1874) and in Hugo's *Hernani* (1877). Her most celebrated roles were in Dumas' *Le Dame aux Camelias* (1852) and in Rostand's *L'Aiglon* (1900). In the latter she played the role of Napoleon's young son (the "eaglet"). In 1915, because of an accident, her left leg was amputated; but with characteristic courage and élan she carried out her acting commitments, especially at the war front. She later toured Europe and America. In Cleveland she was a guest of Nathan's Uncle Nixon, where she put a ring on the finger of young Nathan. She was a close friend of the playwright Victorien Sardou (q.v.), in whose many melodramas (notably *Fedora*) she starred. Oscar Wilde called her "divine Sarah." See Iris Noble, *Great Lady of the Theatre, Sarah Bernhardt* (New York: Messner, 1960).

BERRA, YOGI (b. 1925)

American baseball player, born Lawrence Peter Berra. See Nathan's profile of F. Scott Fitzgerald.

BESIER, RUDOLF (1878–1942)

English playwright; author of *The Barretts of Wimpole Street* (q.v.).

THE BETROTHAL (1910)

A play by Maurice Maeterlinck (q.v.); a sequel to his better-known play *The Bluebird* (1909). Maeterlinck's play *The Betrothal* is to be distinguished from the better known Italian novel of the similar name *The Betrothed* (*I Promessi Sposi,* 1825) by Alessandro Manzoni (1785–1873).

BEYOND THE HORIZON (1918)

First full-length produced play by Eugene O'Neill (q.v.).

BICKEL, GEORGE (1863–1941)

American burlesque comedian and author of numerous monologues.

BICKERSTAFFE, ISAAC (1735–1812)
Irish playwright and librettist, author of *Love in a Village* (1762) and several other comedies; also of *The Hypocrite* (1769) adapted from *Tarfuffe* by Moliere (q.v.). This Bickerstaffe is to be distinguished from the fictional person of the similar name in Joofnathan Swift's *The Tatler* periodicals of 1709.

BIGGERS, EARL (1884–1933)
American playwright and fiction writer. His mystery novel *Seven Keys to Bald-pate* (1913) was made into a play by George M. Cohan (q.v.) and later into a movie. Biggers' best known series of mysteries both in print and on the screen are built around the scrutable Chinese detective Charlie Chan.

BIJOU THEATRE
209 West 45th Street between Broadway and 8th Avenue, New York. It had opened on 1 April 1917 but was re-opened and named the D. W. Griffith Theatre in October 1962. Since the early 1900s many an American theatre (both legitimate and movie) has been named The Bijou, from the French for gem.

BILL OF DIVORCEMENT, A (1921)
A play by the celebrated actress Eleonora Duse (q.v.). Both in its stage and in its screen version it has provided roles for famous actresses, including Ethel Barrymore, Katharine Cornell, and Helen Hayes. See Nathan's profile of Katharine Cornell, p. 101.

BILLY BUDD (1951)
A play by Louis Coxe and Robert Chapman based on the short novel of the same name by Herman Melville (1819–1891). Faithful to Melville, the authors retain the Christian symbolism—for example, the yardarm from which Billy is hanged represents the crucifixion, and the splinters represent relics from the cross.

BILLY ROSE THEATRE
208 West 41 Street, between 7th and 8th Avenues; it opened in October 1959 with a production of Shaw's *Heartbreak House*. This theatre was originally named The National; as such it had opened in September 1921.

BIOGRAPH FILMS
The silent movies developed by D. W. Griffith (q.v.) in the early 1900s.

BISMARCK, OTTO VON (1815–1898)
German "Iron" chancellor. See Nathan's profile of S. N. Behrman, p. 149.

BJÖRNSON, BJÖRNSTJERNE (1832–1910)
Norwegian poet, playwright and fiction writer; Nobel Laureate of 1903. From 1857 to 1859 he served as director/manager of the Ole Bull Theatre of Bergen, which had been immortalized by Ibsen (q.v.). From 1865 to 1867 Björnson served as director/manager of the Norwegian National Theatre at Christiana (Christiana is now Oslo). He was the author of 20 plays, including *Halta-Hulda* (1858), *Kong Sverre* (1861), *Sigurd Slembe* (1862), *The Bankrupt* (1914), and *The Editor* (1914). His fiction includes some memorable short stories, mainly about Norwegian peasants: "Thond" (1857), "Trust and Trial" (1858), "Arne" (1859), and "The Father" (1860).

One of the defenders of Alfred Dreyfus and oppressed minorities in general, Björnson was active as an essayist and pamphleteer in the social and political life of his times. After reading Charles Darwin, Ernest Renan, and Hippolyte Taine, he underwent a religious crisis, culminating in his rejection of Christian dogma. See the biography by Harold Larson, *Björnson, a Study in Norwegian Nationalism* (New York: King's Crown Press, 1944).

BLACK HAND, THE
At the turn of the century a secret terrorist society associated with the Italian Mafia.

BLAVATSKY, HELENA (1831–1891)
Russian theosophist and occultist.

BLUE ANGEL, THE (1928)
A novel by Heinrich Mann (q.v.), which was adapted to the screen by Carl Zuckmayer (q.v.) in a film (1930) directed by Josef von Sternberg (q.v.), starring Marlene Dietrich (b. 1900).

BLUE BIRD, THE (1909)
A play by Maurice Maeterlinck (q.v.).

"BOARDING HOUSE, THE"
A short story by James Joyce (q.v.); first published by Nathan in *Smart Set*, it was later reprinted in Joyce's collection *Dubliners* (1914).

BOAS, FRANZ (1858–1942)
American anthropologist whose books include *The Mind of Primitive Man* (1911) and *Race, Language, and Culture* (1940).

BOHÈME, SCENES DE LA VIEDE (1848)
A romance of Parisian student life by Henry Murger (1822–1861), it was the basis of Puccini's opera *La Bohème*. The MGM film of the same name appeared in 1926, directed by D. W. Griffith (q.v.) and starring Lillian Gish (q.v.).

BOOBOISIE, THE
The non-intelligentsia, a term coined by H. L. Mencken (q.v.).

BOOK WITHOUT A TITLE, A (1920)
A book by Nathan.

BOOTH, EDWIN (1833–1893)
American actor who excelled in Shakespearian roles, notably that of Richard III. In 1864 at the Winter Garden Theatre his Hamlet ran for 100 performances. In 1869 he built the Booth Theatre in New York. In 1889 he performed in several plays with Helene Modjeska (q.v.). He was the founder and first president of the Players Club, New York. He was the brother of Abraham Lincoln's assassin.

BOOTH, JOHN WILKES (1839–1865)
American actor who made his stage debut at age 17 and thereafter starred in numerous Shakespearian roles. Unlike his brother Edwin (q.v.), John was an

ardent Confederate and political activist. Shortly after 10 p.m. on 14 April 1865, John Wilkes Booth assassinated President Lincoln in his box at the Ford Theatre, Washington D.C., and was captured and killed in the same year.

BOOTH THEATRE
222 West 45th Street between Broadway and 8th Avenue, New York. It was built originally by Edwin Booth (q.v.) after its predecessor, The Winter Garden Theatre, burnt down. In 1913 the Booth Theatre was acquired by the Shubert Theatre Corporation and Winthrop Ames (q.v.). See Nathan's profile of Winthrop Ames.

BOOTHE, CLAIRE (1903–1987)
American journalist and playwright who wrote the play *Kiss the Boys Goodbye* (1938). She married Henry Luce, U.S. Editor and publisher; founder of *Life* magazine.

BOSWELL, JAMES (1740–1795)
Biographer of Samuel Johnson (q.v.).

BOTTOMS UP
A melodrama by Nathan. (New York: Philip Goodman, 1917).

BOUCICAULT, DION (1820–1890)
Irish-American playwright and producer born Dionysus Lardner Boursiquot. He came to the United States in 1853. A precocious and prolific writer (he was only 19 when his first play *London Assurance* was produced); he was the author of *The Octoroon* (1859), which he took on tour throughout the United States along with several other melodramas, missing no opportunity to produce in provincial towns if they were railroad stops. For example, the Lafayette, Indiana, Opera House playbills of the late 1800s (preserved in the Tippecanoe County Historical Society's archives) reveal that the Opera House hosted his plays on a regular basis. Before going on tour, Boucicault, perhaps attracted by the same excitements that attracted Mark Twain, made his base of operations in Virginia City, Nevada. Here, too Boucicault's path crossed with that of the precocious David Belasco (q.v.). Boucicault took on Belasco as a protegé. In 1865 Boucicault collaborated with Joseph Jefferson (q.v.) in adapting, for the stage, a version of Washington Irving's story "Rip Van Winkle," See Nathan's profile of Jefferson.

BOUFFES PARISIENS
Comic operas, follies, and other Bohemian attractions.

BOULTON, AGNES (b. 1905?)
American fiction writer; Eugene O'Neill's second wife. She was the author of many short stories and of the autobiographical *Part of a Long Story* (London: Peter Davies, 1958).

"BOUND EAST FOR CARDIFF" (1914)
A one-act play by Eugene O'Neill (q.v.).

BOURGET, PAUL (1852–1935)
French poet, novelist, and critic. Several of his poems were set to music by Debussy.

BOURNEUF, PHILIP (b. 1918?)
American actor. He has performed in many plays, among them *Children of Darkness* (1930) and *Winged Victory* (1943). See Nathan's profile of Jefferson.

BOWDLER, THOMAS (1754–1825)
English physician and editor of *The Family Shakespeare* (1818), which omitted or changed passages that "could not with propriety be read aloud in a family." Hence to "bowdlerize" is to expurgate, to remove from a literary work any word or expression considered obscene or indelicate. See Noel Perrin, *Dr. Bowdler's Legacy* (NY: Atheneum, 1969); also Bertrand Russell, "Dr. Bowdler's Nightmare," *Nightmares of Eminent Persons* (London: The Bodley Head, 1954).

BOYD, ERNEST (1887–1946)
One of the co-editors, with Nathan, of *The American Spectator*. Boyd was originally an Irish critic, writing for several publications in Dublin. After coming to the United States, he published, among other books, a biography of H. L. Mencken (1925). See F. Scott Fitzgerald's letter of 27 July 1933, to Nathan, p. 224. See also Dreiser's letter of September 19, 1932, to Nathan, p. 218.

BOYD, THOMAS (1898–1935)
American writer, author of *Mad Anthony Wayne* (1929). See F. Scott Fitzgerald's letter of December 1923, to Bernard Vaughan, p. 208.

BOYER, CHARLES (b. 1899)
French-American actor.

BRADY, "DIAMOND JIM" (1856–1917)
American financier and philanthropist, born James Buchanan Brady. He became wealthy by collecting precious stones. A connoisseur of New York City night life, he was attracted to several celebrated women, among them Lillian Russell (q.v.). Brady also had several celebrated male friends—among them, Colonel William F. Cody ("Buffalo Bill") and the boxer John L. Sullivan. See Parker Morrell, *Lillian Russell, the Era of Plush* (New York: Random House, 1946).

BRALEY, BURTON (1882–1966)
American journalist and versifier.

BRECHT, BERTOLT (1898–1956)
German playwright and composer who was a devotee of expressionism (q.v.) and naturalism (q.v.); he was also a confirmed Marxist. He wrote lyrics for several of his musical plays. One of his internationally popular lyrics is "Mack the Knife," from his play *Die Dreigroschen Opera* (1928), which was based on John Gay's *Beggar's Opera* (1728). Brecht was also the author of *Mother Courage and Her Children* (1941), *The Good Woman of Setzuan* (1943), and *The Caucasian Chalk Circle* (1955). In 1961 there appeared *Seven Plays by Bertolt Brecht* translated by the eminent drama critic Eric Bentley. (New York: Grove Press). See Nathan's profile of Brecht in *The Theatre Book of the Year 1945–1946* (New York: Knopf, 1946), pp. 27–28.

BRICE, FANNY (1891–1951)
American comedienne, born Fanny Borach. From 1910 on, she starred in the

Ziegfeld Follies (q.v.). See Norman Katkor, *The Fabulous Fanny* (New York: Knopf, 1953). See also Nathan's profile of Max Reinhardt.

BRIEUX, EUGENE (1858–1932)

French playwright, a favorite of George Bernard Shaw (q.v.) and his wife. Shaw's wife, Charlotte Payne Townshend, translated three of Brieux's plays, a circumstance that prompted Nathan to call Brieux "Shaw's dramatic gigolo" in the essay "Intelligence and the Drama," p. 77. An ardent feminist, Brieux was the author of forty plays, including *The Three Daughters of M. Dupont* (1897), *The Red Robe* (1900), *Damaged Goods* (1901), *The Sweetheart* (1902), *Maternity* (1907), *Woman on Her Own* (1916), and *False Gods* (1929).

BROADHURST, GEORGE H. (1866–1952)

English journalist and playwright, he was the author of The *Man of the Hour* (1907) and *Bought and Paid For* (1913), which later became a popular movie. He also adapted the play *Hallo* by the Hungarian playwright Imre Földes (1903–   ), giving it the title *Over the Phone* (1917).

BROOKS ATKINSON THEATRE

256 West 47th Street between Broadway and 8th Avenue, New York; it opened on September 12, 1960. Originally it had been the Mansfield Theatre, which had opened in February 1926.

BROTHER RAT (1936)

A farce by John Monks (b. 1910) and Fred Finklehoffe (b. 1910).

BROTHERS KARAMAZOV, THE (1879)

A novel by Fyodor Dostoyevski (1821–1881). It was dramatized in 1928 by Jacques Copeau (1878–1949), and in 1931 by Alec Guinness (b. 1914). See Nathan's profile of Helen Hayes.

BROUN, HEYWOOD (1886–1939)

New York drama critic who helped found the Newspaper Guild.

BROWN, HARRY (1917?–1972)

American director and producer.

BROWN, JOHN MASON (1900–1968)

American drama critic. At the University of Montana he taught a course in the history of drama. He contributed reviews and criticism to the *Theatre Arts Monthly,* the *New York Post,* and the *Saturday Review.* He was the author of several books, including *The Modern Theatre in Revolt* (1929) and *Seeing Things* (1946). For his evaluation of Nathan as critic, see p. 9.

BROWNE, MAURICE (1881–1955)

English theatrical producer. See Nathan's profile of T. S. Eliot.

BROWNING, ROBERT (1812–1889)

English poet whose poetic plays *Strafford* (produced 1837 in Covent Garden) and *Sordello* (1840) are now regarded as "closet dramas" (q.v.). He is best remembered for *Pippa Passes* (1841); for his long narrative poems, especially *The*

Ring and the Book (1868–1869); and for his translations including Aeschylus's *Agamemnon* (1877). In 1846 he married the English poet Elizabeth Barrett (author of *Sonnets from the Portuguese*). Their relationship was plagued by her invalidism and by her parents' hostility. This circumstance provided the substance of the play *The Barretts of Wimpole Street* (1931) by Rudolf Besier (1878–1942).

BRUNETIÈRE, FERDINAND (1849–1906)
French literary critic. Like T. S. Eliot, Brunetière believed that literary works should treat moral issues responsibly. He was opposed to naturalism (q.v.). His best known work remains his *History of French Literature* (1897). In 1894 Brunetière tried to identify the one indispensable element of drama that distinguishes that genre from all others. His theory, known as "Brunetière's Law" can be compressed into one phrase: a will striving toward a goal. Cf. Plot.

BRUNHILDE
The beloved of Siegfried in the *Ring of the Nibelung* operas (1848) by Richard Wagner (q.v.).

BRYAN, WILLIAM JENNINGS (1860–1925)
American statesman; editor of the *Omaha World Herald*. Thrice he was nominated for President of the United States but thrice was defeated. Advocated "free silver" coinage; author of the "Cross of Gold" speech in Chicago in 1896. As a fundamentalist and anti-evolutionist, he was ridiculed by Clarence Darrow during the Scopes trial of 1925.

BUCHMANISM (OR MORAL RE-ARMAMENT)
An international movement established by Frank Buchman (1878–1961), an American Southern evangelist. Much of the opposition to Buchman arose because of his open admiration for Adolf Hitler. See Nathan's profile of the Lunts.

BUCK, FRANK (1884–1950)
American explorer and movie producer. He was the author of *Bring 'Em Back Alive* (1930) in collaboration with Edward Anthony. See Nathan's letter of 5 September 1951 to August Mencken, p. 231.

BUCK, PEARL (1892–1973)
American novelist (born Pearl Sydenstricker) best known for her Pulitzer Prize-winning novel *The Good Earth* (1931), which is set in China and which has been dramatized for stage and screen. In 1938 she won the Nobel Prize for Literature.

BUCKINGHAM, GEORGE VILLIERS
Second Duke of, (1628–1687). See *The Rehearsal*.

BULWER-LYTTON, E. G. (1803–1873)
English novelist and playwright. He is best known for his novel *The Last Days of Pompeii* (1834). His plays include *The Lady of Lyons* (1838), *Richelieu* (1939), and *Money* (1840). See Nathan's profile of August Strindberg.

BURKE, BILLIE (1884–1970)
American stage and screen actress. In 1914 she married Florenz Ziegfeld (q.v.). She appeared in several of the Ziegfeld Follies; also, on stage, she appeared in *The*

Vinegar Tree (1931). Her screen roles included those in *Dinner at Eight* (RKO, 1932), *Becky Sharp* (RKO, 1935), *Topper* (MGM, 1937), and *Wizard of Oz* (MGM, 1939).

BURLESQUE
1. In literature and the literary threatre, a farce or satirical takeoff. For example, the operettas of Gilbert and Sullivan (q.v.) burlesque certain 19th century empire-builders, along with ridiculously formal rites and ceremonies of Japanese courts. See Simon Trussler, ed., *Burlesque Plays . . . 18th Century* (New York: Oxford University Press, 1969).
2. During the 1920s and 1930s in big-city music halls, a clothing takeoff or strip-tease popularized by the Minsky brothers (q.v.).

BURROWS, ABE (b. 1910)
American playwright and director who wrote the book for *Guys and Dolls* (1950) and for *Can-Can* (1953) for which Cole Porter (q.v.) wrote such songs as "I Love Paris," and "C'est Magnifique."

BUSINESS
See Stage Business.

BUSKIN (OR COTHURNUS)
Stylized elevated boot worn by actors in early Greek tragedies.

BUXBEUTELS
Coin purses. See Nathan's profile of Theodore Dreiser, p. 161.

CABELL, JAMES BRANCH (1879–1958)
American novelist, editor, and historian. When asked about the proper pronunciation of his name, he said, "It rhymes with rabble." In 1932 he joined Nathan, Mencken, and others in founding *The American Spectator*. He remains best known, however, for his novel *Jurgen* (1919), in which the character of Helen was said (by biographer Albert Bigelow Paine) to have been inspired by Nathan's friend Lillian Gish. Cabell's epic fiction series *Poictesme* (written between 1917 and 1930) is set in the fictitious French medieval province of the same name. In that series of novels, the best known is *The Cream of the Jest* (1917), a moral allegory. Because of alleged obscenities, Cabell's novels met with suppression by watch-and-ward societies. His non-fiction includes *Beyond Life* (1919) and *Here Let Me Lie* (1947). See Hugh Walpole, *James Branch Cabell*. (Port Washington and London: Kennikat Press, 1967; reprint of an earlier, out-of-print edition).

CAHAN, ABRAHAM (1860–1951)
Russian-American-Yiddish editor and author; he was admired by Dreiser and by Nobel Laureate Isaac Bashevis Singer. See Nathan's profile of Theodore Dreiser.

CAIN, JAMES M. (1892–1977)
American journalist, novelist, and playwright. He is best known as the author of the novel *The Postman Always Rings Twice* (1934), which was made into a play (1936) and into a melodramatic movie (1946).

CALDERON DE LA BARCA, PEDRO (1600–1681)
Celebrated Spanish playwright. He was the author of more than 100 plays, 70 of

which were one-acts. His earliest include *La donna duende (The Lady Fairy)*. His best known plays include *El magico prodigioso (The Wonderful Magician)* and *La vida es sueño (Life is a Dream)*.

CAMILLE (1860)

English translation of *La Dame aux camelias* (1852) by Alexandre Dumas fils. In the cross-country tour of 1932, the star role of Marguerite was played by Lillian Gish (q.v.). See Nathan's profile of Lillian Gish.

CAMP, WALTER (1859–1925)

American football coach who devised the "daily dozen" calisthenics.

CAMPBELL, MRS. PATRICK (1867–1940)

English actress, born Beatrice Tanner. She was celebrated for several Shakespearian roles, including those of Ophelia and Lady Macbeth. She also starred in Ibsen's *Hedda Gabler*, Shaw's *Pygmalion*, and Pinero's *The Second Mrs. Tanqueray*. After an absence of 14 years from Broadway, she starred in a play entitled *The Adventurous Age*, in which she had to negotiate a ladder-climb to a second-story window. The audience applauded this feat, but Nathan considered this applause either prurient or patronizing or both. He faulted them for this in his essay on Mrs. Campbell in *Art of the Night* (New York: Knopf, 1928), pp. 61–63.

CAMUS, ALBERT (1913–1960)

Algerian-French novelist and playwright, Nobel Laureate in Literature (1957). While still a student at the University of Algiers, he initiated a theatre group in which he acted and directed. During World War II he joined the Parisian Resistance and edited the underground paper *Combat*. Often associated with existentialism (q.v.), he preferred to be regarded as a humanist, as expressed in his essay *The Myth of Sisyphus* (1953). His best known novels include *L'Étranger (The Stranger*, 1942), *La Peste (The Plague*, 1947), and *La Chute (The Fall*, 1956). His short stories were collected in 1957. His best known plays include *Le Malentendu* (1944), *Caligula* (1945), and *State of Siege* (1948). See Albert Camus, *American Journals* (New York: Paragon House, 1987).

CANDIDA (1893)

A play by George Bernard Shaw (q.v.), which was adapted as a musical comedy by the poet Richard Wilbur and the playwright Lillian Hellman (q.v.). See Nathan's profile of Hellman.

CANDIDE (1759)

A satirical romance by Voltaire (q.v.) that pokes fun at the optimism of Rousseau (q.v.) and the philosopher Gottfried Wilhem von Leibniz (1646–1716) for maintaining that this is the best of all possible worlds.

CANTOR, EDDIE (1892–1964)

Vaudevillian singer and entertainer.

ČAPEK, KAREL (1890–1938)

Czechoslovakian playwright best known for his play *R.U.R.* (1921). The initials stand for Rossum's Universal Robots, which introduced the word *robot* into the dictionaries of the world. This play is a good example of German expressionism (q.v.) in drama.

CAPTAIN BRASSBOUND'S CONVERSION (1900)
A play by Shaw (q.v.).

CAPTAIN OF KOEPENICK (1931)
A satirical comedy by Carl Zuckmayer (q.v.), which pokes fun at Prussianism and Nazism.

CAPUS, ALFRED (1858–1922)
French novelist. See Nathan's essay "Literature and Drama," p. 66.

CAREW, JAMES (1875–1938)
American actor.

CARNEGIE HALL
154 West 57th Street on the southeast corner of 7th Avenue. This concert hall was built in 1847, remodeled in 1881, and again in 1987. It was the gift of Andrew Carnegie (1835–1919), Scotch-American steel magnate and philanthropist.

"CARTEL OF FOUR"
Influential French drama critics and arbiters.
Georges Pitoëff (1886–1939) (q.v.), Gaston Baty (1885–1952), Charles Dullin (1865–1949), and Louis Juvet (1887–1951).

CASANOVA, GIOVANNI (1725–1798)
Italian libertine; author of *History of My Life* (tr. 1860). This was the basis of the play *Casanova* (1923) by Louis de Azertis.

CASTLE, IRENE (1893–1969) AND VERNON (1887–1918)
Choreographers and popularizers of several ballroom dances in England and America.

CATASTROPHE
Falling action of a tragedy. Cf. dénouement.

CATEGORICAL (ALSO MORAL) IMPERATIVE
See Kant.

CATHARSIS
The spectators' emotional purging as they identify with the feelings and experiences of the characters, especially in tragedies; Aristotle identified the two chief tragic emotions as "pity and terror."

CATHER, WILLA (1876–1947)
American journalist and fiction writer. She worked on *McClean's* Magazine, among other periodicals. Her best known novels include *O Pioneers* (1913), *My Antonia* (1918), *The Professor's House* (1925), and *Death Comes for the Archbishop* (1927). One of her best known short stories, "Neighbor Rosicky" (1930) is reprinted in Robert Freier et al., eds. *Adventures in Modern Literature,* 5th Ed. (New York: Harcourt Brace Jovanovich, 1962). See Sharon O'Brien, *Willa Cather: the Emerging Voice* (New York: Oxford University Press, 1986).

CATTULUS, GAIUS (CA. 84 B.C.–54 B.C.)
Roman lyric poet.

CENACOLO (*THE LAST SUPPER,* 1498)
A painting by Leonardo da Vinci (1452–1519).

CENTLIVRE, SUSANNAH (1841–1891)
English actress.

CHAMBERS, ROBERT W. (1865–1933)
American writer and illustrator.

CHAPLIN, CHARLES (1889–1977)
English comedian actor, writer, and producer. His best known films include *The Kid* (1920), *The Gold Rush* (1924), *City Lights* (1931), *Modern Times* (1936), and *The Great Dictator* (1940). In 1943 Chaplin married Eugene O'Neill's 18 year old daughter Oona. See Parker Tyler, *Last of the Clowns* (New York: Vanguard Press 1947; reprinted 1972).

CHAPMAN, GEORGE (CA. 1559–1634)
English poet and playwright; one of the translators of Homer, he inspired John Keats' sonnet "On First Looking Into Chapman's Homer." Chapman's plays include the comedies *All Fools* (1605) and *Eastward Ho!* (1605), which he wrote in collaboration with Ben Jonson (q.v.) and John Marston (1576–1634). See Nathan's profile of George Bernard Shaw.

CHARLEY'S AUNT (1892)
A farce by Brandon Thomas (1849–1914).

CHEKHOV, ANTON (1860–1904)
Celebrated Russian playwright and short-story writer. The son of serfs, he worked hard for his education, becoming independent at the age of 16. In 1886 he became a physician but practiced little, preferring to earn his living through publication.

His major plays include *The Sea Gull* (1896), *Uncle Vanya* (1899), *The Three Sisters* (1901), and *The Cherry Orchard* (1904). The anguished brooding of his characters, along with their hesitation to take decisive steps, has caused his plays to be called "dramas of inaction."

His numerous short stories, which tend toward lighter, often humorous, themes include "Grisha" (1886), "Pripadok" (Brothel, 1888), "The Boors" (1897), "The Betrothed" (1903), "Gooseberries" (1913), and "The Chorus Girl" (1915). See S.S. Koteliansky and Philip Tomlinson, eds., *The Life and Letters of Anton Chekhov* (New York: Doran, 1925). See Nathan's profile of Max Reinhardt.

CHERRY, CHARLES (1872–1931)
English actor.

CHERRY ORCHARD, THE (1904)
A play by Anton Chekhov (q.v.).

CHESTERTON, GILBERT KEITH (1874–1936)
English essayist, poet, novelist. As demonstrated in *Tremendous Trifles* (1904),

one of his collections of essays, he was a master of paradox. His novel *The Man Who Was Thursday* (1908), along with its sequels, features the popular detective Father Brown. Chesterton's best remembered poem is "The Battle of Lepanto." His essays in literary criticism include those on Browning, Dickens, Shaw, Blake, and Stevenson. Chesterton's plays include *Magic* (1913) and *Judgment of Dr. Johnson* (1927). See Nathan's comments on *Magic* in the profile of Jean Giraudoux, p. 132.

CHIAROSCURO
1. In paintings, the effects of light vs. shade, especially in impressionism (q.v.).
2. In several art forms, including literature and the theatre, the effects of contrast (for example, loud/soft, explicit/suggested, happy/sad).

CHICAGO (1927)
A satirical comedy by Maurine Watkins (fl. 1900s).

CHILDREN'S HOUR, THE (1934)
A play by Lillian Hellman (q.v.); to be distinguished from "The Children's Hour," a poem by Henry Wadsworth Longfellow (1807–1882).

CHODOROV, JEROME (b. 1911)
American playwright, director, and screen writer; co-author of *Junior Miss* (1941) and *The Ponder Heart* (1956), adapted from the novel by Eudora Welty (b. 1909).

CHOPIN, FREDERIC (1810–1849)
Polish composer and pianist. Close friend of George Sand (1804–1876).

CHORUS
1. From the Greek *chorein,* to sing; in Greek tragedies, especially those of Aeschylus (q.v.), a poetic/philosphic commentary on the actions of the main character(s);
2. In popular songs, the repreated verse or refrain; usually the more memorable lines.
3. In modern theatre a group of singers and dancers, as in *Chorus Line*.

CHRIS (1914)
An early version of *Anna Christie* by Eugene O'Neill (q.v.).

CHRISTIANS, MADY (1900–1951)
Austrian-American actress.

CIBBER, COLLEY (1671–1757)
English actor, theatre manager, playwright, and poet laureate. He was the author of *Love's Last Shift* (1696). He was also the butt of Alexander Pope's satirical poem *The Dunciad* (1743).

CLAIRE, INA (b. 1892)
American actress, née Fagan. (She performed both in London and in New York music halls. She appeared in several Ziegfeld Follies and in *The Confidential Clerk* (1954) by T. S. Eliot (q.v.) In 1939 she played in the film *Ninotchka*. Nathan comments on her in his profile of Helen Hayes, p. 107.

CLAY, BERTHA (1836–1884)
Pen-name of Charlotte Braeme, an English novelist. This pen-name was un-scrupulously appropriated by the American publishers of some paperback dime novels. See Nathan's profile of Theodore Dreiser.

CLIMAX
In a plot, the crisis or turning point; highest point in the suspensive rising action or highest point of emotional excitation; from the Greek word for "ladder."

CLOSET DRAMA
Whether intentionally or not, a play that proves more successful in the reading than in the production on stage. Some examples: Milton's *Samson Agonistes* (1671), Shelley's *The Cenci* (1819), Browning's *Pippa Passes* (1841), and F. Scott Fitzgerald's *The Vegetable* (1923).

CLURMAN, HAROLD (1901–1980)
American drama critic and theatre director, he directed over 50 plays. With Lee Strasberg (q.v.), he founded the Group Theatre, New York, where he helped to develop the talents of Clifford Odets, William Saroyan, and others. Clurman contributed many drama reviews and critiques to several New York periodicals. His collections of essays in drama criticism include *Lies Like Truth* (New York: Macmillan, 1958). In 1959 he was the first winner of a George Jean Nathan Award (q.v.).

COBB, TY (1886–1961)
American baseball player and manager.

COCKTAIL PARTY, THE (1949)
A play by T. S. Eliot (q.v.).

COHAN, GEORGE M. (1878–1942)
American actor, song-writer, playwright, and producer. He is well remembered as the "Yankee Doodle boy" from his production of *Little Johnny Jones* (1904). He dramatized Earl Biggers' novel *Seven Keys to Baldpate* (1913). His numerous songs include "Over There," "Give My Regards to Broadway," "Grand Old Flag," "I'm a Yankee Doodle Dandy," and others. Nathan comments on him in the profile of Ziegfeld, p. 192 See Ward Morehouse, *Prince of the American Theatre* (Philadelphia: Lippincott, 1943).

COLERIDGE, SAMUEL TAYLOR (1772–1834)
English romantic poet and critic. A friend of William and Dorothy Wordsworth, Coleridge collaborated with Wordsworth on *Lyrical Ballads*. (1798) He agreed with Wordsworth, in the famous preface to that collection of their poems, that the language of poetry should be close to the language of everyday speech. Also, in that collection, he contributed his famous poems "Rime of the Ancient Mariner," "Kubla Khan," and "Christabel." Unlike Shakespeare, who used similes and metaphors, Coleridge preferred to create his resonances through striking singular images (seasnakes, for example, and caverns of ice). Despite an addiction to opium, Coleridge managed to write some astounding poems and, in *Biographia Literaria* (1817), some astute literary criticism.

COLLINS, DR. JOSEPH (b. 1896)
See Nathan's profile of Luigi Pirandello.

COMEDIANS ALL
A book by Nathan. (New York: Knopf, 1919).

COMÉDIE FRANÇAISE
1. One of the earliest French comedy movements. It was led by Moliere (q.v.) and his associates
2. A theatre in Paris.

COMEDY OF HUMOURS
English medieval and renaissance writers assumed that people's dispositions were governed by four body fluids—blood, choler, bile, and phlegm. These "humours" were thought to be in balance only in a healthy person. Any person experiencing an "ascendancy" of blood was thought to be too sanguine or overly cheerful; of choler, too grumpy or crotchety; of bile, too melancholy or lovesick; of phlegm, too phlegmatic or stolid. Thus, in *As You Like It,* Jacques was suffering from melancholy; in *Twelfth Night,* Malvolio was afflicted with sanguine, bumptious conceitedness.

Aside from the stock humours, above, certain more specialized psychosomatic traits informed one's behavior: possessiveness, for example, affectation, misogyny, self-righteousness, and the like. Classic examples occur in *Every Man in His Humour* (1598) by Ben Jonson (q.v.). Hence a comedy of humours is a comedy in which the chief character exhibits one or another of the psychosomatic traits described above.

COMEDY OF MANNERS
A label loosely given to English Restoration comedies (1660–1688). These comedies, as a backlash against the Puritan closing of the theatres (1642), celebrated libertine manners and morals, including the loose morals and sexual inuendo of the upper social classes. Nevertheless, such comedies as George Etherege's *Man of Mode* (1674), William Wycherly's *The Country Wife* (1675), and William Congreve's *Way of the World* (1700) sparkle with urbane wit and repartee.

Comedies of manners retained their popularity well into the eighteenth century, especially with such frequently produced plays as Oliver Goldsmith's *She Stoops to Conquer* (1773) and Richard Brinsley Sheridan's *School for Scandal* (1777). The most representative collection remains Howard Mumford Jones, ed., *Plays of the Restoration and 18th Century.* (New York: Henry Holt, 1931).

COMEDY THEATRE
108–112 West 41st Street between Broadway and Avenue of the Americas (6th Avenue); opened 6 September 1909. Owned by Sam and Lee Shubert (q.v.); it was reopened in November 1910 as William Collier's Comedy Theatre. In November 1937 it was reopened as the Mercury Theatre. It was demolished in 1939.

COME OF AGE (1934)
A play by Stanley Kauffman (fl. 1900s). See Nathan's profile of Helen Hayes.

COMMEDIA DELL'ARTE
Literally "comedy of the profession," a kind of theatrical entertainment performed by traveling troupes of professional actors and mimes. It was popular in Italy from the sixteenth through the eighteenth centuries. It was characterized by pantomime, stock situations, and such stock characters as Harlequin, the romantic hero; Columbine, his sweetheart; and Pantaloon, the clown. Some of the

conventions of this art form originated in Attelan Comedy as reflected in the *Fabulae Attelanae* of early Rome; such conventions, for example, as the stock plots, the *concetti* (stock responses for given emotions), and the *lazzi* (stock stage business). Harlequin usually wore a black mask and a costume spangled with diamond-shaped patches of red, blue, and green; he also carried a wooden sword (forerunner of the slap-stick). His sweetheart, Columbine, wore no mask; nor did any of the other female characters or any of the male characters who had speaking—as opposed to pantomime—roles. Another character, Pedrolino, forerunner of the clown Paliaccio and of the French Pierrot, acted the part of a dreamer with a sad, whitened face. Later there was added the character Pulcinello, a villain and forerunner of the English Punch in the English Punch and Judy shows.

Aside from the influence that the commedia dell'arte exerted on later mimes, it proved to be the source of certain characters in the comedies of humours (q.v.). With a few modifications the commedia is still kept alive in several European cities, notably in Copenhagen's outdoor theatre in the Tivoli Gardens; cf. Grand Guignol. See Mel Gordon, *Lazzi: Comic Routines of the Commedia dell'Arte.* (New York: Performing Arts Publications, 1987).

COMIC RELIEF
In serious plays a humorous scene, an incident, or speech injected to relieve the intensity; best known example is the Porter's scene in *Hamlet.*

COMMINS, SAXE (1892–1958)
American editor who worked chiefly at Random House. Regarding a proposed collection of Eugene O'Neill's plays, see O'Neill's letter of 12 October 1932 to Saxe Commins, p. 219.

COMPLICATION
In any plot, usually within the rising suspensive action, an unexpected twist dealt by a character or by fate that necessitates a change in the main character's originally intended route toward the goal. Cf. Peripety.

CONGREVE, WILLIAM (1670–1729).
See Comedy of Manners.

CONNELLY, MARC (1890–1980)
American playwright who helped develop the North Carolina Folk Theatre. He was the author of *Beggar on Horseback* (1924) and *The Green Pastures* (1929), among other plays. He was one of several playwrights who collaborated with George S. Kaufman (q.v.). See Nathan's profile of Maxwell Anderson.

CONRAD III (1093–1152)
A German king.

CONRAD, JOSEPH (1857–1924)
Polish novelist, born Teodor Josef Korzienowski. In 1878, while working as a seaman on an English merchant ship, he began to master the English language, in which he was to write his novels. He later became a British subject. His short story "The Heart of Darkness" (1902) is often cited (along with Henry James's "The Beast in the Jungle") as among the most masterful in English. Conrad's best known novels include *Almayer's Folly* (1895), *The Nigger of the Narcissus* (1898), *Lord*

Jim (1900), and *The Secret Agent* (1907). Conrad's autobiography, *A Personal Record*, was first published in Boston in 1912 by Garland Press.

COQUELIN, BENOIT-CONSTANT (1841–1909)
French actor associated with the Comédie Française (q.v.). His best known role was Cyrano in Rostand's *Cyrano de Bergerac*. See Nathan's profile of Rostand.

CORELLI, MARIE (1855–1924)
Pseudonym for Mary MacKay, English novelist and playwright.

CORN IS GREEN, THE (1940)
A play by Emlyn Williams (q.v.).

CORNEILLE, PIERRE (1606–1684)
Celebrated French playwright devoted to classical tragedy. His best known plays include *Medea* (1635), *Le Cid* (1637, and *Polyeucte* (1643). See F.P.G. Guizot, *Corneille and His Times* (New York: Harper, 1852).

CORNELL, KATHARINE (1898–1974)
American actress, wife of the director/producer Guthrie McClintic (q.v.). In 1917 she made her stage debut with the Washington Square Players (q.v.). Her best remembered roles include those in *A Bill of Divorcement, The Green Hat, The Age of Innocence, The Barretts of Wimpole Street, Alien Corn, Saint Joan,* and *The Constant Wife*. See Nathan's profile of Katharine Cornell, p. 101. Nathan lists Katharine Cornell among the few rivals of Helen Hayes. See his essay "Helen Hayes and Her Rivals," p. 104.

CORNELL UNIVERSITY LIBRARY
To Cornell University, his alma mater, Nathan bequeathed his personal library and his letters. Curator of the Nathan Collection is Donald Eddy. The collection includes 129 letters to Nathan from Eugene O'Neill and 23 letters to Nathan from Carlotta Monterey O'Neill. Most of Nathan's letters to O'Neill have not as yet been found. For a collection of O'Neill's letters to Nathan, see Nancy L. Roberts and Arthur W. Roberts, *As Ever, Gene*. (Rutherford, N.J.: Fairleigh Dickinson University Press, 1987).

COUNTRY FAIR, THE (1916)
A play by Charles Barnard and Neill Burgess (both fl. late 1800s).

COUPEAU, JACQUES (1879–1949)
French theatrical director. See Nathan's profile of Max Reinhardt.

COURTENAY, WILLIAM (1875–1933)
American actor.

COUSINS, NORMAN (b. 1912)
American editor and essayist. From 1940 to 1971 he was the editor of *Saturday Review* and the champion of many liberal causes. His many books include *Modern Man is Obsolete* (1945) and *In God We Trust* (1958). Having overcome a serious health problem, he has shared his conviction that a proper mental attitude can be therapeutic. As a visiting professor he has lectured at UCLA.

COVENT GARDEN THEATRE
Covent Garden, London, originally a produce and flower market, added a theatre in 1712. This burned down in 1808 as did its replacement in 1856. The present Covent Garden Theatre, built in 1858, is devoted primarily to Italian Opera. In the Covent Garden mall, the Theatre Museum traces the history of London performing arts to modern times from the times of Shakespeare and his contemporaries. See Ronald Bergan, *The Great Theatres of London*. (San Francisco and London: Chronicle Books, 1988).

COWARD, NOËL (1899–1973)
English actor, playwright, and composer. His most popular works include *Hay Fever* (1925), *Bitter Sweet* (1929), *Private Lives* (1930), *Cavalcade* (1931), *Words and Music* (1932), and *Blithe Spirit* (1941). He was also the author of several screen plays. His best known songs include "I'll See You Again," "Someday I'll Find You," "Mad About the Boy," and "Mad Dogs and Englishmen." See Nathan's profile of Beatrice Lillie, p. 103.

COWL, JANE (1883–1950)
American actress and playwright. She was a native of Boston, where she tried out most of her six plays. Her own most celebrated acting role was that of Juliet in Shakespeare's *Romeo and Juliet*. Her best known play was *Payment on Demand* (1950).

Nathan gave her mixed reviews, and in his essay "Episode in the Career of a Critic," (*Comedians All,* [New York: Knopf, 1919], pp. 169–74) he derogates her rather harshly. But he does acknowledge her excellence as Juliet. See Nathan's essay "Helen Hayes and Her Rivals."

COWLEY, HANNAH (1793–1809)
English playwright.

COWLEY, MALCOLM (1898–1989)
American critic and essayist; member of the 1920s expatriate group in France. He relates this episode in *Exile's Return* (1929). For many years he was book-review editor for the *New Republic*. In 1951 he co-edited with F. Scott Fitzgerald a revised edition of *Tender Is the Night*.

CRAFT CYCLES.
See Morality Plays.

CRAIG, EDWARD GORDON (1872–1966)
English actor, designer, critic, editor, and a fan of Nathan's. (See his letter of 9 January 1916 to Nathan, p. 199.) Craig, the son of Ellen Terry (q.v.), edited *Mask* Magazine from 1908 to 1929. In 1911, in Florence, Italy, he founded the Craig School for the Art of the Theatre. His books include *On the Art of the Theatre* (1911) and *Scene* (1923). In his honor the Craig Theatre, 152 West 54th Street between 7th Avenue and Avenue of the Americas, was opened on 24 December 1927, with a production of *Potiphar's Wife*. The honor was short-lived, however, for in 1934 that theatre reopened as The Adelphi and again, in 1958, as the Fifty-fourth Street Theatre.

CRITIC AND THE DRAMA, THE (1922)
A book by Nathan.

CRONYN, HUME (b. 1911)
Canadian/American actor, playwright, director, and screenwriter. While a student at McGill University, he performed in several productions of the Montreal Repertory Theatre. His first appearance on Broadway was as a janitor in *Hipper's Holiday* (1934). Thereafter he rose to more substantive roles, including that of the Stage Manager in *Our Town* (1938). During the 1940s and 1950s he starred in and/or directed scores of plays. In 1942 he married the actress Jessica Tandy (q.v.). He and his wife have received numerous awards. During the 1960s he appeared in a number of plays at the Guthrie Theatre, Minneapolis. The films he starred in include *The Seventh Cross* (MGM, 1944), *The Postman Always Rings Twice* (MGM, 1946), *Sunrise at Campobello* (WB, 1960), and *Cleopatra* (1963). His numerous appearances on television with this wife include his own production of the Appalachian *Foxfire* (1987) under the auspices of the Hallmark Hall of Fame.

CROTHERS, RACHEL (1878–1958)
American feminist playwright and director. She was devoted to writing comedies concerned with women's problems. Her plays include *The Three of Us* (1906), *A Man's World* (1909), *He and She* (1911), and *Susan and God* (1937). See Nathan's profile of the Lunts, p. 99.

CROUSE, RUSSEL (1893–1966)
American journalist, playwright, and producer; best remembered for his nostalgic history *Mr. Currier and Mr. Ives* (1930). In 1931 he wrote the libretto for *The Gang's All Here*. In 1934 he collaborated with Howard Lindsay on *Anything Goes;* and in 1939, with Clarence Day (q.v.) on *Life with Father*. In 1940 Crouse produced *Arsenic and Old Lace,* and in 1960 he wrote the book for *The Sound of Music*.

CROWE, EUGENE (FL. EARLY 1900S)
At one time the financial partner of *Smart Set* magazine.

CRY OF THE PEACOCK (1950)
A play by Jean Anouilh (q.v.).

CURTAIN RAISER
A skit or short play designed to warm up the audience before the main presentation or a device to introduce the main play. Cf. INDUCTION. To be distinguished from play-within-a-play q.v.

CURTIS, MARGARET (b. 1897)
English novelist and playwright who was the author of *Highland Fling* (1943) and *Planter's Punch* (1962).

CUSTARD'S LAST STAND (1943)
A farce by William D. Fisher (fl. 1900s).

CYRANO DE BERGERAC (1897)
A play by Edmond Rostand (q.v.).

DADAISM
A European aesthetic movement characterized by anti-rational, nonsensical, often outrageous improvisations in literature, theatre, music, and other arts.

Dadaists used props and artifacts designed to shock (for example, bedpans, urinals, and exploding balloons) in protest of war and other inhumane acts. The movement was started in Zurich in 1916 by the Romanian expatriate Tristan Tzara and the Alsatian Hans Arp. A few years later Tzara took it to Paris, where it captivated young poets, artists, and playwrights. The movement spread to Berlin and several other cities of Europe. Dadaists published handbills, manifestoes, and little magazines—among them the journal *Dada,* its title connoting nonsense or nothingness. Chief contributors, besides Tzara, included André Breton, Louis Aragon (inventor of the "glass syringe"), and Phillipe Soupault (inventor of the "musical urinal"). They gave concerts, lectures, and dramatic skits that elicited the ridicule of establishment critics. As reflected in the play *Pandora's Box* (1918) the German expressionist playwright Frank Wedekind (1869–1918) (q.v.) was a kindred spirit not only of expressionism (q.v.) but also of dadaism. During the 1920s, with the ascendancy of André Breton (1896–1966), who had published his own *Manifesto* (1924), the movement merged with surrealism (q.v.). Cf. Expressionism and Immediate Theatre.

DADDY LONG LEGS (1912)
A novel by Jean Webster (1876–1916), which was later made into a movie. See Nathan's profile of Molnar, p. 126.

"DALRYMPLE GOES WRONG" (1919)
A short story by F. Scott Fitzgerald (q.v.). See Nathan's letter of 14 November 1919 to Fitzgerald, p. 202.

DALY, ARNOLD (1875–1927)
American actor.

DALY, AUGUSTIN (1838–1899)
American playwright and theatrical producer. After 1859 he served as drama critic on several New York newspapers. From 1867 on, he adapted and produced several foreign plays, mostly German and French. He was the author of one of the most popular melodramas, *Under the Gaslight* (1867). In 1869 he opened his own theatre, The Fifth Avenue, and a few years later the famous Daly's Theatre on Broadway. He developed a regular company of players that included John Drew (q.v.) and Ada Rehan (q.v.). See Marvin Felheim, *The Theatre of Augustin Daly* (Cambridge: Harvard University Press, 1956).

DAMROSCH, WALTER (1862–1950)
American composer and conductor.

DANA, RICHARD HENRY (1815–1882)
American author best remembered for his *Two Years Before the Mast* (1840).

DANCHENKO, VLADIMIR (1859–1943)
Russian director and producer; cofounder with Stanislavsky (q.v.) of the Moscow Art Theatre (q.v.).

DANE, CLEMENCE (1888–1965)
English actress and playwright, born Winifred Ashton. See Nathan's profile of Katharine Cornell, p. 101.

D'ANNUNZIO, GABRIELE (1863–1938)
Italian poet and novelist whose novels include *The Flame of Life* (1900), which is believed to have been based on his relationship with the celebrated Eleonora Duse.

DANTES, EDMOND
Protagonist in the *Count of Monte Cristo* (1845) by Alexandre Dumas père.

DARRIEUX, DANIELLÉ (b. 1917)
French actress.

DARWIN, CHARLES (1809–1882)
English naturalist celebrated for his theories of evolution. His works include *Voyage of the Beagle* (1839, to the Galapagos Islands), *Origin of Species* (1859) and *The Descent of Man* (1871).

DAUMIER, HONORÉ (1808–1879)
French painter, sculptor, illustrator, and caricaturist. His caricatures were published first in the weekly periodical *Caricature,* later in *Charivari.* See Nathan's profile of O'Neill.

DAVENPORT, HARRY (1866–1949)
American actor.

DAVIS, ELMER (1890–1958)
American journalist and essayist. His books include *But We Were Born Free* (1954).

DAVIS, OWEN (1874–1956)
American journalist and adapter. For the stage, he adapted Fitzgerald's *The Great Gatsby,* Pearl Buck's *The Good Earth,* and Edith Wharton's *Ethan Frome.* See Nathan's essay "On Adaptation," p. 74.

DAVIS, RICHARD HARDING (1864–1916)
American journalist and essayist associated with the *New York Sun* and with *Harper's Weekly.*

DAY, CLARENCE (1874–1935)
American humorist best known for his book *Life With Father* (1935), which was made into a play and a movie.

DAYS WITHOUT END (1933)
A play by Eugene O'Neill (q.v.).

DEATH AND THE FOOL (1893)
A verse play by Hugo von Hofmannsthal (1874–1929), who is better known as the author of the light opera *Der Rosenkavalier* (1912). See Nathan's profile of Jean Giraudoux, p. 131.

DEATH OF A SALESMAN (1949)
A play by Arthur Miller (q.v.).

DEATH TAKES A HOLIDAY (1929)
A play by Walter Perris (fl. 1900s).

"DEBUTANTE, THE"
A one-act play by F. Scott Fitzgerald. It was first published by Nathan in *Smart Set* (November 1919), pp. 85–96.

DEEPING, WARWICK (1877–1950)
English novelist whose books include *Sorrell and Son* (1925). See Nathan's profile of Luigi Pirandello, p. 124.

DEKOVEN, REGINALD (1859–1920)
American musician and composer. His works include the opera *The Canterbury Pilgrims* (1917) and the well-known song "Oh Promise Me."

DE KRUIF, PAUL (1890–1971)
American bacteriologist who collaborated with Sinclair Lewis on *Arrowsmith* (1925) and with Sidney Howard (q.v.) on *Yellowjack* (1934).

DE MILLE, AGNES (b. 1909)
American dancer and choreographer. See her autobiography, *Dance to the Piper* (Boston: Little, Brown, 1952).

DE MILLE, CECIL B. (1881–1959)
Major American film producer. His best known films include *The Ten Commandments* (1923), *The Plainsman* (1937), *Samson and Delilah* (1949), and *The Greatest Show on Earth* (1952).

DE MILLE, HENRY CHURCHILL (1853–1893)
American playwright who collaborated with David Belasco (q.v.) in producing, among other plays, *The Charity Ball* (1889) and *Men and Women* (1890).

DE MILLE, WILLIAM CHURCHILL (1878–1955)
American playwright who collaborated with his brother Cecil (q.v.) in writing *The Genius* (1904) and *The Royal Mounted* (1908). See Anne Edwards, *The DeMilles* (New York: Abrams, 1988).

DÉNOUEMENT
Literally, "unraveling"; the resolution of a plot or of one of the final complications of a plot in a play or novel. Thus, by the end of Act V of Shakespeare's *The Tempest,* the conspirators against Prospero are exposed; the lovers of Ferdinand and Miranda are engaged to be married; and the problems of even such minor characters as Stephano, Trinculo, Caliban, and Ariel are resolved.

DEPEW, CHAUNCY (1834–1928)
American lawyer and railroad magnate.

DESIRE UNDER THE ELMS (1924)
A play by Eugene O'Neill (q.v.).

DEUS EX MACHINA
Literally "god out of a machine," a derogatory phrase for a contrived rescue or a

solution to a major problem, as opposed to a solution achieved through the wits and efforts of the protagonist. For example, in Euripides' *Orestes,* the god Apollo is let down on pulleys above the palace and commands Orestes to marry Hermione instead of killing her. This kind of sham was derogated as early as Sophocles (ca. 496 B.C.–406 B.C.), who denounced it. Yet intermittently, through the years, stage contraptions and rescue-devices have persisted. For a description of some of these, see Lily Bess Champbell, *Scenes and Machines on the English Stage.* (Berkeley: Univ. of California Press, 1923). See also C. Thomas Ault, "Baroque Stage Machines." *Journal of Theatre History,* xxviii-2 (November, 1987), pp. 101–2.

DEVIL, THE (1908)
A play by Molnar (q.v.) which starred George Arliss (q.v.).

DIALOGUE
The words or lines spoken by the characters in drama and fiction; the chief communication medium of drama. Cf. Repartee and Stichomythy.

DICKENS, CHARLES (1812–1870)
English novelist and elocutionist. From 1856 to 1867 he managed amateur theatricals. On tour in England and America, he also gave popular readings from his novels and sketches. He was the author of *Sketches by Boz* (1836–37), *The Pickwick Papers* (1836), *Oliver Twist* (1837), *Nicholas Nickleby* (1838–39), *The Old Curiosity Shop* (1843), *A Christmas Carol* (1843), *David Copperfield* (1849–50), *Bleak House* (1852), and *A Tale of Two Cities* (1859). Most of his novels appeared first in monthly installments in such magazines as *Household Words* and *All the Year Round.*

During the 1980s the Old Vic Theatre Society produced a triumphant dramatization of *Nicholas Nickleby* in England and in the United States. See Edgar Johnson, *Charles Dickens, His Tragedy and Triumph* (New York: Viking/Penguin, 1986).

DIEUDONNÉ, MAURICE (1831–1922)
French actor and playwright. See Nathan's essay "Literature and Drama."

"DIFF'RENT" (1920)
A one-act play by Eugene O'Neill (q.v.); to be distinguished from "Different," a one-act play by Sherwood Anderson (q.v.).

DILLINGHAM, CHARLES (1868–1934)
Broadway producer.

DISRAELI, BENJAMIN (1804–1881)
English statesman and writer. A favorite of Queen Victoria, he was twice a prime minister—in 1868 and from 1874 to 1880. He was the author of a number of novels, including *Vivian Gray* (1826), *Coningsby* (1844), *Sybil* (1845), *Tancre* (1847), *Lothair* (1870), and *Endymion* (1880). One of the best known biographies remains *Disraeli* by Andre Maurois (New York: Modern Library, 1955).

DITRICHSTEIN, LEO (1865–1928)
American actor.

DIXEY, HENRY (1859–1953)
American actor and stage manager.

DIXON, THOMAS (1864–1946)
American racist minister and novelist. He was the author of *The Clansman* (1905) and *The Birth of a Nation* (1914), which encouraged the revival of the Ku Klux Klan. But the motion picture version of *Birth of a Nation* by D. W. Griffith (q.v.) exposed the Klan's evils. See Nathan's essay "Negroes in the American Theatre," p. 76.

DOCTOR'S DILEMMA, THE (1906)
A play by George Bernard Shaw (q.v.).

DODSWORTH (1929)
A novel by Sinclair Lewis (q.v.).

DON GIOVANNI (1787)
An opera by Wolfgang Amadeus Mozart (q.v.). See Nathan's essay "Intelligence and the Drama," p. 77.

DOS PASSOS, JOHN (1896–1970)
American novelist, playwright, and screenwriter. He was the author of *Three Soldiers* (1921) and the "USA" trilogy—*The 42nd Parallel* (1930), *Nineteen Nineteen* (1932), and *The Big Money* (1936).

DOUGLAS, KENNETH (CA. 1875–1923)
English actor.

DOVE, THE (1925)
A play by Willard Mack (1878–1934). The play was based on a story by George Beaumont (fl. late 1800s). See Nathan's profile of Helen Hayes.

DOWLING, EDDIE (1894–1975)
Born Joseph Nelson Goucher, Dowling became an actor, director, and producer in England and the United States. In London he sang in the Boys' Choir of St. Paul's Cathedral. In the United States he acted in vaudeville (q.v.) and in several of Ziegfeld's Follies (q.v.). In 1939 he participated as an actor and assistant director in a touring company of Thornton Wilder's celebrated play *Our Town*. Later the same year, in association with the Theatre Guild (q.v.) he produced William Saroyan's (q.v.) *The Time of Your Life*. In 1945, in Chicago, in association with Margo Jones (q.v.) he produced Tennessee Williams' *The Glass Menagerie,* starring Julie Haydon. In 1948 he directed O'Neill's *The Iceman Cometh*. During World War II he organized, and was the first president of, the USO shows. In 1961 he founded the Eddie Dowling University Theatre Foundation.

DRAMATIC IRONY
A dramatic effect in which the audience is aware of a circumstance that a given character is unaware of; for example, when Oedipus vows revenge on the murderer of his father, the audience is shocked because it knows, as Oedipus does not, that he himself is the murderer. See Bert States, *Irony and Drama: A Poetics* (Ithaca: Cornell University Press, 1971).

DRAMATIS PERSONAE
Cast of characters; originally in Greek and Latin a *persona* was a mask, an artifact worn over the face to indicate whether the play was a comedy or tragedy.

(In the New Testament, Paul's observation "God is no respecter of persons" uses "persons" as a transliteration—that is, God is no respecter of masks.) With respect to masks, modern playwrights have not, of course, followed primitive Greek conventions except for Eugene O'Neill in *The Great God Brown* (1921) and Bertolt Brecht in *The Good Woman of Setzuan* (1938). Cf. the Japanese Kabuki and Nō plays.

DREISER, THEODORE (1871–1945)
American novelist and playwright. Born into an impoverished family in Terre Haute, Indiana, he worked at odd jobs, then moved to Chicago, where he worked on various newspapers. In 1894 he moved to New York, where he continued working on newspapers and as a freelance writer. He soon became noticed by Nathan and by H. L. Mencken. In 1932, when Mencken and Nathan launched *The American Spectator,* they invited Dreiser to join them as an editor and partner. See Dreiser's letter to Nathan, p. 218.

Dreiser's best known books include *Sister Carrie* (1900), a novel which soon after publication was withdrawn from distribution because of its frank treatment of sex; *Jennie Gerhardt* (1911); *The Financier* (1912); *The Titan* (1914); *The Genius* (1915); and *An American Tragedy* (1925). His short-story collection *Free and Other Stories* (1918) contains "The Lost Phoebe," which Robert Penn Warren and F. O. Mathiessen regarded as his masterpiece. After a visit to Russia, Dreiser published *Dreiser Looks at Russia* (NY: Boni and Liveright, 1928). A collection of his short plays, *Plays Natural and Supernatural* (London: John Lane) appeared in 1916. One of his best known autobiographical books remains *Newspaper Days* (NY: Liveright, 1931). "The Lost Phoebe" has been reprinted in *The Indiana Experience* (Bloomington: Indiana University Press 1971.) See Nathan's profile of Dreiser.

DRESSER, LOUISE (1882–1965)
American actress and singer, born Louise Kerlin. She was a friend of, but she was not related to, Theodore and Paul Dreiser. Paul persuaded her to change her name to Dresser, as he had done with his own name. When she was a vaudeville headliner, she introduced Paul's song "My Gal Sal." She later became a movie actress.

DRESSER, PAUL (1857–1906)
American song writer, brother of Theodore Dreiser, with whom he collaborated on the song "On the Banks of the Wabash, Far Away." On is own, Dresser composed a number of popular songs, including "My Gal Sal."

DRESSLER, MARIE (1869–1934)
Canadian actress, born Leila Koerber. In 1904 she joined the New York Company of Weber and Fields (q.v.) as leading comedienne. In 1914 she moved to Hollywood, where she starred with Charles Chaplin in the Mack Sennett movie *Tillie's Punctured Romance.* Her performance in *Min and Bill* (1931) won her an Academy Award. Her other screen performances included those in *Tugboat Annie* (1933) and *Dinner at Eight* (1933).

DREW, JOHN JR. (1853–1927)
American actor and matinée idol. In 1875 he joined the company of Augustin Daly (q.v.), playing several Shakespearian roles, starring especially as Petruchio in *The Taming of the Shrew.* He later joined the Frohman Syndicate (q.v.) in several

modern plays with Maude Adams (q.v.). He died on tour while playing in Pinero's *Trelawney of the Wells.*

DREW, JOHN SR. (1827–1862)
Irish actor and producer, father of John Drew Jr.

DRINKWATER, JOHN (1882–1937)
English poet and playwright. He founded and managed the Pilgrim Players Company in 1907, which later became the Birmingham Repertory Theatre. He was the author of *Collected Poems* (1923). His plays include *Richelieu* (1914), *Abraham Lincoln* (1918), *Oliver Cromwell* (1921), *Robert E. Lee* (1923), *Robert Burns* (1925), and *A Man's House* (1934). Nathan's profile of Drinkwater in *Materia Critica* (New York: Knopf, 1924) is uncomplimentary.

DRURY LANE THEATRE
Drury Lane, London; built in 1663 by Thomas Killigrew under a charter granted by King Charles II. Also known as the Theatre Royal, it burned down in 1672. In 1674 it was rebuilt from plans devised by the celebrated architect Christopher Wren. Another fire occurred there in 1809, destroying the Wren structure. In 1812 the architect Benjamin Wyatt designed and supervised the building of the present structure. It remains the oldest London theatre still in use. Many plays, operas, and even circuses have been produced here. See Ronald Bergan, *The Great Theatres of London*. (San Francisco and London: Chronicle Books, 1988.)

DRYDEN, JOHN (1631–1700)
English poet, playwright, and critic. He was appointed Poet Laureate in 1668. His plays include *The Conquest of Granada* (1670–71); *All for Love* (1677), a play in blank verse which is regarded as his masterpiece; and *Marriage a la Mode* (1672). In 1681–82 there appeared his celebrated political satire in verse, *Absalom and Achitophel*. His best known work in literary criticism remains his *Essay of Dramatic Poesy* (1668). See James Winn, *John Dryden & His World* (New Haven: Yale University Press, 1980).

DU BARRY, MADAME MARIE (1746–1793)
The beautiful provincial woman who was the mistress of King Louis XV of France and a victim of the guillotine.

DUBLIN, LOUIS I. (b. 1892)
Former president of the Metropolitan Life Insurance Company.

DUBLINERS (1914)
A collection of short stories by James Joyce (q.v.).

DUMAS, ALEXANDRE FILS (1824–1895)
French novelist and playwright. He was the author of *La dame aux camélias* (1852), which portrays the love affair of a courtesan and was the basis for Verdi's opera *La Traviata*. Dumas is one of the personalities in André Maurois's collective biography *The Titans* (1957; reprinted in New York: Modern Library, 1971).

DUMAS, ALEXANDRE PÈRE (1802–1870)
French novelist and playwright. He was the author of *The Three Musketeers*

(1844) and *The Count of Monte Cristo* (1845). A dramatization of the latter was made famous by the actor James O'Neill (q.v.). This Dumas is also one of the subjects of André Maurois's biography *The Titans* (cited above).

DU MAURIER, GEORGE (1834–1896)
English artist and novelist on the staff of *Punch* for many years. He was the author of *Trilby* (1894) and *Peter Ibbetson* (1892), which was dramatized in 1915 and was later made into an opera by Deems Taylor (1885–1966).

DUNNE, FINLEY PETER (1867–1936)
American journalist and humorist, a Chicago contemporary of George Ade (q.v.), Eugene Field, and the McCutcheon brothers. Dunne was the creator of "Mr. Dooley" for his column in the *Chicago Post* and later became editor of *Collier's Magazine*. For a profile of Dunne, see James De Muth, *Small Town Chicago* (Port Washington and London: Kennikat Press, 1980).

DUNSANY, LORD EDWARD (1878–1957)
English playwright. Born Edward Moreton Drax Plunkett, 18th Baron, he became a soldier and a sportsman. For a brief period he was also associated with the Abbey Theatre (q.v.). He is best remembered as the author of the one-act play "A Night at an Inn" (1916). Nathan gave him high marks.

DURBIN, DEANNE (b. 1922)
Canadian-American singer and actress born Edna Mae Durbin.

DÜRER, ALBRECHT (1471–1528)
German painter and engraver who specialized in mythological and Biblical subjects.

DUSE, ELEONORA (1859–1924)
Italian actress descended from a theatrical family. In 1873, at age 14, she played Juliet in Shakespeare's *Romeo and Juliet*. In 1893, under the auspices of the Frohman Syndicate (q.v.), in New York and London she starred in Dumas' *La dame aux camélias*. Acclaimed as the only rival of Sarah Bernhardt (q.v.), Duse was romantically linked with the poet Gabrielle D'Annunzio (q.v.).

DUTCH TREAT CLUB
A New York City Tuesday luncheon club of writers, artists, editors, and publishers, whose invited after-luncheon speakers included celebrities like Minnie Maddern Fiske (q.v.), H. L. Mencken, and George Jean Nathan. Long-term members included the playwrights George S. Kaufman, Booth Tarkington, and Julian Street; bibliophile Christopher Morley, who would be producing melodramas in Hoboken; the illustrator Montgomery Flagg; the publishers Charles Scribner, George Putnam, and Edward Dodd; magazine editors Charles Hanson Towne, and Frank Crowninshield; the novelist George Barr McCutcheon, and others. See A. L. Lazarus and Victor H. Jones, *Beyond Graustark* (Port Washington and London: Kennikat Press, 1981), p. 129.

DYNAMO (1923)
A play by Eugene O'Neill (q.v.).

EAST IS WEST (1918)
A play by S. Shipman (1883–1937) and J. B. Hymer (b. 1917?).

EAST LYNNE (1861)
The English novelist Ellen Wood, aka Mrs. Henry Wood (1814–1887) wrote a tear-jerker, which in 1861 was dramatized as *East Lynne* by Clifton Tayleure (dates unknown). After a successful tour in England, this melodrama achieved a phenomenally long tour in the United States, playing in every town and hamlet that could be reached by train or overland stage-coach. In 1878 it played at the Lafayette (Indiana) Opera House, for example, starring Anne Pixley and later Minnie Maddern before she became Mrs. Fiske. In 1926 *East Lynne* was revived in New York at the Greenwich Village Theatre, where it did not succeed. But when it moved in 1932 to the John Golden Theatre, it played for 900 performances.

EASTMAN, MAX (1883–1969)
American journalist and essayist. His many books include *Enjoyment of Laughter* (1936), which describes humor as "the pleasant disappointment of an expectation." He began his career as a teacher at Columbia University and as a devotee of aesthetics. After World War I he embraced Marxism. He had helped found two periodicals, *The Masses* (1911) and *The Liberator* (1917).

EATON, WALTER PRICHARD (1878–1957)
American educator, essayist, and critic. He taught at several Ivy League colleges and served as drama critic for the *New York Herald Tribune*.

ELIOT, T. S. (1888–1965)
American-born poet, playwright, and critic; in 1927 he became a British subject. In 1948 he won the Nobel Prize for Literature. His best known poetry includes *Prufrock and Other Observations* (1918), *The Waste Land* (1922), *Ash Wednesday* (1930), and *Four Quartets* (1935). He was also the author of the humorous *Old Possum's Book of Practical Cats* (1939), featuring "McCavity," which inspired the musical revue *Cats* (1981). His plays include *Murder in the Cathedral* (1935), which was made into a movie; *The Family Reunion* (1939); *The Cocktail Party* (1950); *The Confidential Clerk* (1954); and *The Elder Statesman* (1959). His best works of literary criticism include *The Sacred Wood* (1920), *The Use of Poetry and the Use of Criticism* (1933), *Elizabethan Essays* (1938), and *Notes Toward a Definition of Culture* (1945). Among the best biographies is *Great Tom* by Thomas S. Matthews (London: Thomas Stanley, 1974). Among the best critical studies are those by Linda Wagner, *T. S. Eliot: A Collection of Criticism* (New York: McGraw-Hill, 1974); and A. W. Litz and L. Lipking, *Modern Literary Criticism 1900–1970* (New York: Atheneum, 1972).

ELMER GANTRY (1927)
A novel by Sinclair Lewis (q.v.).

EMPEROR JONES, THE (1920)
A play by Eugene O'Neill (q.v.).

EMPIRE THEATRE
Opened 25 January 1893, at the southeast corner of Broadway and 40th Street with a production by Belasco of Franklyn Fyles's *The Girl I Left Behind Me*. This theatre building also housed the main New York offices of the Frohman Syndicate

(q.v.). When the building was demolished in 1953, cheering onlookers included thespians who had been slighted by the Frohmans.

ECHEGARAY, JOSÉ (1832–1916)
Spanish playwright who earned the soubriquet of "Renaissance man" because of his erudition. In 1904 he shared the Nobel Prize for Literature with Frederic Mistral (1830–1914). See Nathan's profile of O'Neill.

EDEL, LEON (b. 1907)
American biographer and Henry James scholar.

EDISON, THOMAS (1847–1931)
American inventor. See Nathan's profile of Dreiser.

EDWARD, MY SON (1947)
A play by Noel Langley and Robert Morley (q.v.). It was produced in 1948 at the Martin Beck Theatre, New York. See Nathan's essay "Myself," p. 33.

ENCHANTED COTTAGE, THE (1922)
A play by Sir Arthur Wing Pinero (q.v.)

ENCYCLOPEDIA OF THE THEATRE (1940)
A book by Nathan. Cf. Martin Esslin, *The Field of Drama* (New York: Methuen, 1987).

END OF SUMMER (1936)
A play by S. N. Behrman (q.v.).

ENEMY, THE (1928)
An MGM movie directed by D. W. Griffith (q.v.), which starred Lillian Gish (q.v.)

EPIGRAM
A brief witty saying, often in verse. For example, "I do not like thee, Dr. Fell; the reason why I cannot tell . . ." Epigrams are to be distinguished from epigraphs. (An epigraph is a brief quotation or motto prefaced to a written work and used to suggest its theme. For example, at the beginning of *For Whom the Bell Tolls,* Hemingway uses a quotation from John Donne "No man is an island." Cf. *epilogue* and *epitaph* (along with their derivations from Greek roots.) See, on p. 119, Nathan's profile of Oscar Wilde, whose plays abound in epigrams and other witty remarks.

EPISODE
A scene that follows another without any cause-effect chain, without any rising suspensive action or conflict; hence, in drama criticism, a derogatory epithet.

EQUITISM
Theodore Dreiser's synonym for Socialism (q.v.).

ERLANGER, ABRAHAM (1860–1930)
A theatre manager employed by the Frohman Syndicate (q.v.).

"ETERNAL MYSTERY, THE" (1912)
A one-act play by Nathan. It was produced at the Princess Theatre, New York, but did not survive its first performance because it was considered sacrilegious.

ETHEREGE, GEORGE (1635–1692)
English playwright, author of *The Man of Mode* (1676).

EURIPIDES (CA. 489 B.C.–406 B.C.)
Greek tragedian. Unlike the more successfully produced Aeschylus (q.v.) and Sophocles (q.v.) Euripides won only four first prizes in the annual Festivals of Dionysus at Athens. Of Euripides' surviving plays, the best known remain *Alcestis* (438 B.C.), *Medea* (431 B.C.), *Hippolytus* (428 B.C.), *Andromache* (426 B.C.), *Hecuba* (425 B.C.), *The Suppliants* (420 B.C.), *The Trojan Women* (415 B.C.), *Electra* (413 B.C.), *Helena* (412 B.C.), *Iphigenia in Taurus* (date unknown), *The Phoenician Women* (409 B.C.), and *The Bacchae* (405 B.C.). *The Phoenician Women* is built around the legend of the "seven against Thebes." Euripides was lampooned by Aristophanes (q.v.).

EUROPE AFTER 8:15 (1914)
A book by Nathan in collaboration with H. L. Mencken and W. H. Wright (q.v.).

EVANS, MAURICE (b. 1901)
Anglo-American actor. See Nathan's profile, p. 108.

EXISTENTIALISM
A philosophic movement (as opposed to a system) in revolt against traditional philosophies. Several so-called existentialist writers resisted the label among them, Karl Jaspers (1883–1969); Martin Heidigger (1889–1976); and—especially— Jean Paul Sartre (1905–1980), author of *Being and Nothingness* (1943). Perhaps the one emphasis they share is a fierce individualism, echoing Hamlet's "To be or not to be?" (that is, to exist or not to exist). Extended, the question becomes "to submit or not submit to the forces of depersonalization?" This is the theme in *Either/Or* (1842) by Soren Kierkegaard (1813–1855) and in Isaac Bashevis Singer's *Love and Exile* (1984). Existentialists also stress the need for *(a)* the individual's self-actualization through self expression; *(b)* finding ways toward morality that have their foundation in the human condition rather than in theological dogmas; and *(c)* becoming involved in whatever benefits society. In *Fear and Trembling* (1843) Kierkegaard argued that each individual needs to find God within himself; because all too many religious organizations tend to depersonalize.

Well known religious existentialists include Martin Buber (1878–1965), Jewish; Jacques Maritain (1882–1973), Catholic; and Paul Tillich (1886–1965), Protestant. See Walter Kaufman, ed., *Existentialism from Dostoevsky to Sartre.* (New York: Meridian Books, 1956) and Bert States, *On the Phenomenology of Theatre* (Berkeley: University of California Press, 1985).

"EXORCISM"
A one-act play by Eugene O'Neill (q.v.).

EXPOSITION
Factual elements such as time, place, and circumstances (especially circum-stances antecedent to the main action). These are usually established during the second chapter of a novel or the first part of a play. Ideally, however, in both fiction

and drama, exposition is revealed through the characters' emotions and dialogue, which will at the same time move the action forward. Cf. *flashback* which is a more formal re-creation.

EXPRESSIONISM

An artistic movement of the 1920s in which poets, novelists, playwrights, and painters went further than had the impressionists (q.v.) in expressing their most subjective (often all too private) impressions of experience. Thus Franz Kafka (1883–1924), for example, in his story "The Metamorphosis," instead of only suggesting that his protagonist feels like a detested cockroach, has him awake one morning to find himself turned into an actual cockroach. The expressionists, reflecting the influence of Karl Marx (1818–1883), also revolted against the mechanization of labor and life. Thus in *The Adding Machine* (1923), a play by Elmer Rice (q.v.), the protagonist, Mr. Zero, a bookkeeper, is replaced by an adding machine, which motivates him to kill his employer. Reflecting the influence of Sigmund Freud (1856–1939) and Carl Jung (1875–1961), the black protagonist in Eugene O'Neill's play *The Emperor Jones* (1921) relives the history of his oppressed race. Most of the psychological and cultural influences on the expressionists unite in the novel *Finnegan's Wake* (1939) by James Joyce (q.v.). In the theatre the expressionist movement was especially popular in Europe thanks to the works of the German playwright Frank Wedekind (q.v.) and his followers. See Eric Bentley *The Playwright as Thinker* (New York: Harcourt Brace 1967) and B. S. Meyers, *The German Expressionists* (New York: McGraw-Hill, 1963). See also Nathan's essay on expressionism, p. 71.

FALSTAFF

See Fastolfe, Sir John.

FAMILY REUNION, THE (1939)

A play by T. S. Eliot (q.v.). See Nathan's profile of Eugene O'Neill.

FANTASTIKS, THE (1900)

A play by Edmond Rostand (q.v.).

FARCE

A nonsensical comedy based on contrived situations and characterizations. Among well known examples is *Charley's Aunt* (1892) by Brandon Thomas (1849–1914), in which the male protagonist in woman's clothing tries to pass as a woman. See J. H. Huberman, *Late Victorian Farce* (Ann Arbor: UMI Research Press, 1986).

FASTOLFE, SIR JOHN (1378–1459)

English soldier in the French wars of Henry V. Independently wealthy, Fastolfe contributed to Cambridge University and to Magdalen College, Oxford. Hence it is unlikely that he inspired Shakespeare's egregious character Sir John Falstaff. See Nathan's profile of Maurice Evans, p. 108.

FATHER, THE (1887)

A play by August Strindberg (q.v.). See Nathan's profile of Strindberg.

FAVERSHAM, WILLIAM (1868–1940)

English actor.

FERBER, EDNA (1887–1968)
American novelist and playwright. She was the author of several novels, among them *So Big* (1924) and *Show Boat* (1926), which was later made into a stage play and a movie. With George S. Kaufman (q.v.) she collaborated on such plays as *The Royal Family* (1927), *Dinner at Eight* (1932), and *Stage Door* (1936). See her autobiography, *A Peculiar Treasure* (New York: Doubleday, 1936).

FESTSCHRIFT
A collection of testimonial letters and essays written by colleagues, students, and friends of a retired or deceased person. For example, see Ray Browne and Donald Pizer, eds., *Themes and Directions in American Literature, Essays in Honor of Leon Howard* (Lafayette, Ind.: Purdue University Press, 1969).

FIELD, MARSHALL (1834–1906)
American merchant (Chicago). See Nathan's profile of Dreiser.

FIELDS, LEWIS OR "LEW" (1867–1941)
Partner of Joe Weber (q.v.). At the turn of the century Weber and Fields flourished as the most popular team of vaudeville performers and burlesque-house owners.

FILLMORE, MILLARD (1800–1874)
Thirteenth President of the United States.

FIREBIRD, THE (1932)
A play by Lajos Zilahy (fl. early 1900s). See Nathan's profile of Helen Hayes. This play is to be distinguished from the ballet *The Firebird* (1910) by Igor Stravinsky (1882–1971).

FIRST MAN, THE (1921)
A play by Eugene O'Neill (q.v.), which was at first tentatively entitled "The Oldest Man." *The First Man* was first produced at the Neighborhood Playhouse, Greenwich Village, New York.

FISKE, MINNIE MADDERN (1865–1932)
American actress and singer. She was born into a New Orleans family of actors. She made her stage debut at the age of 3 as the child Duke of York in Shakespeare's *Richard III*. She later played several other boys' roles, among them the Gamin in *Under the Gaslight* (1869), Little Frantz in *Our German Cousin* (1870), Paul in *The Octoroon* (1874), and Rackstraw in *H. M. S. Pinafore* (1880). During the late 1800s she also sang (as herself) in many a musical. By 1889 she had starred in enough Shakespearian plays to have attracted the attention of the *New York Dramatic Mirror* editor, Harrison Grey Fiske, whom she married in 1890.

This event almost broke the heart of George Barr McCutcheon (q.v.) the Lafayette, Indiana, newspaper editor, aspiring playwright, and an admirer from afar. He had seen her perform at the Lafayette Opera House on several of her tours, which had been arranged by the Frohman Syndicate (q.v.). See A. L. Lazarus and Victor Jones, *Beyond Graustark* (Port Washington and London: Kennikat, 1981), pp.20–22.

In New York, Mrs. Fiske starred as Nora in Ibsen's *A Doll's House* (1894) and in 1901 she opened the new Manhattan Theatre with roles adapted from Hardy's Tess and Thackeray's Becky Sharp. Meanwhile she and her husband, outraged by the monopolistic practices of the Frohmans, excoriated them in an open letter in the *New York Dramatic Mirror*. This elicited a libel suit, which the Fiskes won.

In her interpretation of Shakespeare and Ibsen, especially the latter, Mrs. Fiske developed a reputation as an intellectual. Nathan, however, in one of his reviews of her work, expressed the opinion that this reputation was not earned. See Archie Binns, *Mrs. Fiske and the American Theatre* (New York: Crown, 1955). See also *Mr. George Jean Nathan Presents* (New York: Knopf, 1917), pp.182–203.

FITCH, CLYDE (1865–1909)
American playwright who was the author of *Beau Brummel* (1890), *Barbara Frietchie* (1984), *Nathan Hale* (1899), *Captain Jinks of the Horse Marines* (1901), and *The Girl with the Green Eyes* (1902). Nathan derogated his plays as "superficial."

FITZGERALD, BARRY (1888–1961)
Irish actor at first associated with the Abbey Theatre (q.v.); later, in America, an actor in the movies.

FITZGERALD, F. SCOTT (1896–1940)
American novelist, short-story writer, and playwright. He was a descendent of Francis Scott Key, author of "The Star Spangled Banner." Fitzgerald was as a beginner encouraged and published by Nathan. Fitzgerald and his wife, Zelda (q.v.), were members of what Gertrude Stein called "the Lost Generation" and prototypes of the Jazz Age.

Fitzgerald's best known novels include *This Side of Paradise* (1920). *The Beautiful and Damned* (1921), *The Great Gatsby* (1925), and *Tender Is the Night* (1934). His autobiographical *The Crackup and Journals* (1936) was edited by his Princeton friend Edmund ("Bunny") Wilson (q.v.). See Nathan's profile of Fitzgerald.

FITZGERALD, ZELDA (1900–1947)
Ballet dancer, painter, and fiction writer. She was talented in her dancing and painting, and brilliant in her writing, as evidenced in her letters and short stories. As a teenager in Montgomery, Ala., during World War I, she met F. Scott Fitzgerald, who was stationed in a nearby Army camp. (He had left Princeton University in 1917 to join the Army and probably also to escape suspension because of his disorderly conduct and his failure to master spelling.) After a hectic courtship, she married him in 1920, the year his first novel, *This Side of Paradise,* became a bestseller, enabling the couple to move to New York and indulge in a madcap lifestyle.

In 1921 their daughter Frances ("Scottie") was born, but this event failed to inhibit Zelda from her exhibitionist behavior—for example, disrobing in outdoor public fountains. Such behavior probably foreshadowed her subsequent mental breakdown. Her flirtation with Nathan was not, however, serious, as Nancy Milford reports in *Zelda, a Biography* (New York: Harper & Row, 1970). By 1930 Zelda's health had deteriorated to the extent that she had to be confined to sanitariums, including one in Zurich, Switzerland. Still, she remained lucid enough to write the novel *Save Me the Waltz* (1932). In 1947 she was killed in a fire. See Nathan's profile of Scott and Zelda, p. 156. See also Zelda's letter of 1930, p. 216.

FLASHBACK
In fiction and drama the technique of deliberately re-creating a scene or incident that occurred before the main action. Cf. Exposition.

FLAUBERT, GUSTAVE (1821–1880)
French novelist, best known for his novel *Madame Bovary* (1856). He was a leader in realistic fiction, especially in his mastery of close rendering of details. See Nathan's profile of Theodore Dreiser.

FLOWERS OF EVIL (1857)
A collection of symbolist poems by Charles Baudelaire (1821–1967).

FLOWERS OF THE FOREST (1924)
A play by John Van Druten (q.v.).

FOIL OR CHARACTER FOIL
In fiction and drama, along with other genres, a character whose traits contrast markedly with those of another character; for example, in Shakespeare's *Henry IV, Part I,* young Hal and Falstaff; in George Eliot's *Silas Marner,* Godfrey and Dunstan; in Joseph Conrad's "The Secret Sharer," Mr. Leggatt and the Captain; in Herman Hesse's *Demian,* Demian and Emil; and in John Knowles' *A Separate Peace,* Gene and Phineas. Cf. *Doppelgänger* or "double."

FÖLDES, IMRE JOLAN (b. 1903)
Hungarian playwright, author of *Hallo* (1916), which in 1917 was adapted as *Over the Phone* by George Broadhurst (1866–1952).

FOLIES BERGÈRE
A place of entertainment which opened as a restaurant-with-floor-show April 11, 1917, at 210 W. 46th Street. The original owners were Jesse Lasky and Henry Harris. On October 11, 1917 it re-opened as the Fulton Theatre. On November 21, 1955, it re-opened as the Helen Hayes Theatre.

FONTANNE, LYNN
See The Lunts.

FOOTE, SAMUEL (1720–1777)
English mimic, actor, and playwright who was indicted for libel for his caricature of Lady Kingston. In 1767 he built and later managed the new Haymarket Theatre. His plays included *An Englishman in Paris* (1753), *The Devil on Two Sticks* (1768), and *The Lame Lover* (1770).

FORBES-ROBERTSON, SIR JOHNSTON (1853–1937)
English actor and theatre manager. He was noted for his Shakespearian roles, especially that of Hamlet. Nathan called him "a master," giving him high marks and also using him as a stick with which to beat John Barrymore. See Nathan's profile of John Barrymore.

FORESHADOWING OR "PLANTING"
An image, phrase, or scene that more or less prepares the audience for another scene, usually an ultimate outcome; for example, in *Macbeth* Shakespeare uses one of the witch scenes to predict Macbeth's doom: "Thou shalt get kings though thou be none." Some foreshadowings are more subtle.

FOREVER AMBER (1944)
A risqué novel by Kathleen Winsor (b. 1919). It was described by *Life* magazine

as a story "about a beauty who went from mattress to mattress across Restoration London." See Nathan's profile of August Strindberg.

FORT, CHARLES (1873–1932)
American journalist who was a collector of anecdotes and accounts of phenomena that could not be explained scientifically. In 1931, a group of his admirers, including Theodore Dreiser and Booth Tarkington, founded the Fortean Society, "dedicated to the frustration of the sciences." They published a periodical entitled *Doubt*. See Nathan's profile of Dresier.

FORT WAYNE, INDIANA
Birthplace of George Jean Nathan, whose maternal grandfather, Frederick Nördlinger, had been a founding father and community pillar.

FOULLÉE, ALFRED (1833–1912)
French philosopher and sociologist.

FOUNTAIN, THE (1926)
A play by Eugene O'Neill (q.v.) that deals with Ponce de Leon (1460–1521), the Spanish explorer who sailed to Florida in search of the legendary Fountain of Youth. See O'Neill's letter of 2 January 1922 to Nathan, p. 205.

FOWLERS, LUDLOW AND ELSIE
Ludlow Fowler, along with John Peale Bishop and Edmund Wilson (q.v.), was one of F. Scott Fitzgerald's close friends at Princeton. Fowler was the model for the character Anson Hunter in Fitzgerald's story "The Rich Boy," *American Mercury* (February 1926). See Zelda Fitzgerald's letter of 1930, p. 216.

FOX, RICHARD K. (1846–1922)
Editor of the *National Police Gazette*. See Nathan's essay "The Old Police Gazette," p. 45.

FRANK, WALDO (1889–1967)
American journalist and non-fiction writer who was the author of *Virgin Spain* (1926), *Down in Russia* (1932), and *The Drama of Israel* (1957). Somewhat unsuccessfully he also tried his hand at fiction: *Holiday* (1928) and *The Bridegroom Cometh* (1938). He was derogated by Nathan.

FRANZ JOSEPH (1830–1916)
Emperor of Austria (1848–1916) and King of Hungary (1867–1916). See Nathan's profile of Maxwell Anderson.

FREDERIC, HAROLD (1856–1898)
American novelist.

FREGOLI, LEOPOLD (1867–1936)
European actor and impersonator.

FRENSSEN, GUSTAV (1863–1945)
Danish-German novelist and playwright who was the author of the novel *Three Comrades* (1907) and—according to Nathan—the play *Sönke Erichsen*.

FRENCH, SAMUEL (1821?–1898)
American publisher of plays.

FREUD, SIGMUND (1856–1939)
Viennese psychologist, psychiatrist, and psychoanalyst; co-founder with Jung (q.v.) of psychoanalysis. Freud was the author of *The Interpretation of Dreams* (1900), *The Psychopathology of Everyday Life* (1904), *Three Contributions to the Sexual Theory* (1905), and *Moses and Monotheism* (1939). The definitive biography is by Ernest Jones (New York: Basic Books, 1953).See Nathan's profile of Behrman.

FRIML, RUDOLF (1879–1972)
Czechoslovakian-American composer. He came to the United States from Prague in 1906 and became naturalized in 1925. He remains best known for his light operas, among them *The Firefly* (1912); *High Jinks* (1913); *Rose Marie* (1924, with its popular song "Indian Love Call"); and *The Vagabond King* (1925). He also composed the music for several movies, including "The Donkey Seranade" for the film version of *The Firefly* (1937).

FROHMAN, CHARLES (1860–1915) AND THE SYNDICATE
American theatrical producer and head of the Frohman Syndicate; Charles, his brother Daniel, and the law firm of Klaw & Erlanger managed New York's and the world's most powerful and monopolistic theatre syndicate of their times. From their main offices in the aptly named Empire Theatre building, they controlled many American, British, and Continental theatres, road-show bookings, and even some of the players' contracts. Daniel stayed in the office, while Charles traveled extensively across the country and overseas to court and hire "outsiders" resented by certain less accomplished New Yorkers. Among the out-of-town directors Frohman brought into his stable was David Belasco (q.v.) from San Francisco; among the European players, Sarah Bernhardt (q.v.) and Eleonora Duse (q.v.). Although Frohman went to great lengths to import George Bernard Shaw (see Nathan's profile, p. 116), the Syndicate's ultra-conservative stockholders balked at Shaw's iconoclasm and also voted against the plays of Henrik Ibsen (q.v.) until some strenuous lobbying by Frohman, who did know quality when he saw it.

The Syndicate's initial suppression of certain plays (for example, Ibsen's *A Doll's House*) and Charles Frohman's strangle-hold on actors antagonized Ibsen devotee Minnie Maddern Fiske (q.v.) and her husband, Harrison Grey Fiske, Editor of the *New York Dramatic Mirror*. In 1897, in an open letter in *The Mirror,* the Fiskes excoriated Frohman and were sued by Klaw & Erlanger for libel. The Fiskes won the case. (A copy of the court's decision may be viewed at the Humanities Research Center, Austin, Texas.)

To his credit, Frohman, before going down with the *Lusitania* in 1915, won the Syndicate over to Ibsen. No doubt, the Syndicate had been needled by Nathan and other critics. Nathan disapproved of monopolies, of course, but he applauded Frohman's imports of first-rate actors and playwrights. For a detailed profile of Frohman see A. L. Lazarus and Victor H. Jones, *Beyond Graustark* (Port Washington and London: Kennikat Press, 1981)

FRY, CHRISTOPHER (b. 1907)
English poet, playwright, and translator, born C. F. Harris. He was director of the Oxford Repertory Players in 1940 and from 1944 to 1946. Among his plays: *The*

Boy with a Cart (1937), *The Tower* (1939), *The Circle of Chalk* (1945), "A Phoenix Too Frequent" (1946), *The Lady's Not for Burning* (1948), and *Venus Observed* (1950). Fry also wrote several movie and television scripts. Among his translations: *The Lark* (1955) by Jean Anouilh (q.v.) and *Tiger at the Gates* (1955) by Jean Giraudoux (q.v.). Nathan gave Fry very high marks; See his profile of Fry, p. 154. See also Peter Brook, *The Shifting Point: Theatre, Film, Opera.* (New York: Harper & Row, 1987)

FUCHS, GEORG (1868?–1939)
German critic who wrote about the development of drama, especially of Munich. His book *Revolution in the Theatre* (1909) is the title as translated and edited by Constance Kahn (Ithaca: Cornell University Press, 1959).

FULTON OF OAK FALLS (1937)
A play by Parker Fennelley (fl early 1900s).

FUTURISM
A European aesthetic movement (ca. 1909–1918). In their manifestoes, the futurists espoused the benefits of the machine age, speed, violence, and war. In Russia the spokesman was Vladimir Mayakovski (1894–1930) and in Italy, F. T. Marinetti (1876–1944), an admirer of Mussolini. The futurists experimented with technological devices, anticipating the multi-media presentations of stage and screen. Cf. Dadism.

See further A. L. Lazarus and H. Wendell Smith, the *NCTE Glossary of Literature & Composition,* (Urbana: National Council of Teachers of English, 1973). pp. 128–29. For a biography of Mayakovski, see Ann and Samuel Charters, *I Love* (New York: Farrar, Straus, 1979.)

GABLE, CLARK (1901–1960)
American actor, primarily in films.

GABRIEL, GILBERT (1890–1952)
drama critic for the *New York American*.

GAIETY THEATRE
1547 Broadway, west side, between 45th and 46th Streets. It was owned by Klaw & Erlanger, the attorneys for Charles Frohman (q.v.). It opened on 31 August 1908 with a production of *The Yankee Prince*. Later reorganized, this theatre reopened in September 1943 as The Victoria.

GALLARATI-SCOTTI, TOMMASO (1878–1966)
Italian playwright; author of *Cosi sia* (1924).

GALSWORTHY, JOHN (1867–1933)
English novelist and playwright best known for his *Forsyte Saga* series of novels (1906–1921). He was the author of the plays *Strife* (1909), which is about an industrial dispute; *Justice* (1910), which criticizes prison systems; and *The Skin Game* (1920), which criticizes caste systems and class distinctions. Galsworthy considered himself a better playwright than a novelist, as he once mentioned to Nathan.

GARLAND, HAMLIN (1860–1940)
American editor, essayist, and fiction writer. Born in the midwest, he moved about frequently—from West Salem, Wisconsin; to Iowa; to the Dakota Territory; to South Dakota; to Boston; to Chicago, where he became a prominent member of the Little Room Society (q.v.). He also founded a group that he called The Cliff Dwellers before he finally settled in New York as an editor at several magazines. He developed a literary theory that he called *veritism,* similar to realism in fiction. He was the author of *Main Traveled Roads* (1891) and *Rose of Dutcher's Coolly* (1895). His best known autobiographical work remains *A Son of the Middle Border* (1921).

GARRICK, DAVID (1717–1779)
English actor (perhaps England's greatest), playwright, and producer; a pupil of Dr. Samuel Johnson (q.v.) Garrick starred in many a play of Shakespeare's, most of which he rewrote. From 1747 to 1776 he was co-manager of the Drury Lane Theatre (q.v.). Garrick wrote more than 20 plays, including *The Enchanter* (1760) and, with George Coleman Sr., *The Clandestine Marriage* (1766). See Sheila Stowell, "Actors and Dramatic Personae," *Theatre History Studies,* vol. 8 1988 (Grand Forks, N.D.: University of North Dakota Theater Arts Dept.)

GARRISON, WILLIAM LLOYD (1805–1879)
American journalist and reformer.

GATES, ELEANOR (1875–1951)
American actress and playwright; author of *The Poor Little Rich Girl* (1913), a play dramatized from her novel of the same name.

GEMIER, FIRMIN (1865–1933)
French theatrical producer.

GENERAL JOHN REGAN (1912)
A play by George Birmingham (1865–1950).

GEORGE, GRACE (1879–1961)
American actress.

GEORGE, LLOYD (1863–1945)
English statesman; active in World War I.

GEORGE M. COHAN THEATRE
1482 Broadway; it opened in February 1911. It was demolished in 1938.

GERSHWIN, GEORGE (1898–1937)
American composer; author of "Rhapsody in Blue" (1923), "Concerto in F" (1925), and "An American in Paris" (1928). He also wrote the music for *Lady, Be Good* (1924), *Girl Crazy* (1930), *Of Thee I Sing* (1931), and *Porgy and Bess* (1925). The lyrics for these were written by his brother Ira (1896–1983). For a biography, see Edward Jablonski, *Gershwin* (New York: Doubleday, 1987).

GERSHWIN, IRA (1896–1983)
Brother of George Gershwin; a popular lyricist.

GEST, MORRIS (1881–1942)
American theatrical producer. He is best known as the producer of Dr. S. I. Hsiung's *Lady Precious Stream* (1936), although Gest produced many other plays. Nathan discusses Gest's contributions in the profile of Max Reinhardt, p. 194. Nathan also discusses Gest in *The Theatre of the Moment* (New York: Knopf, 1936), pp. 131–34.

GIBSON GIRL, THE
During the early 1900s an American beauty created by the illustrator Charles Dana Gibson (1867–1944), who illustrated many books, including those by Anthony Hope and George Barr McCutcheon (q.v.). See Nathan's profile of F. Scott Fitzgerald, p. 156.

GIELGUD, JOHN (b. 1904)
Distinguished Anglo-American actor, director, and producer. See Nathan's profile of Gielgud, p. 110. See also Samuel Leiter, ". . . Sir John Gielgud, Directs," *Theatre History Studies,* vol. 8 1988 (Grand Forks, N.D.: University of North Dakota Theater Arts Dept).

GILBERT AND SULLIVAN OPERETTAS
See Gilbert, Sir William and Sullivan, Sir Arthur.

GILBERT, SIR WILLIAM SCHWENCK (1836–1911)
English playwright celebrated for his collaboration with Sir Arthur Sullivan (q.v.) in creating such light operas as *H. M. S. Pinafore* (1878), *Pirates of Penzance* (1879), *The Mikado* (1885), and *The Gondoliers* (1889). These pieces abound in satirical wit and clever rhymes.

GILLETTE, WILLIAM (1855–1937)
American actor and playwright who performed in numerous melodramas that were the staples of the late 1800s. He was the author of *The Dream Maker* (1921). See Nathan's profile of Gillette.

GILPIN, CHARLES (1878–1930)
The American actor who starred in Eugene O'Neill's *The Emperor Jones* (1920). See Nathan's essay "Negroes in the American Drama," p. 76.

GINGOLD, DAME HERMIONE (1897–1989)
English actress celebrated for her roles in such Shakespeare plays as *The Merchant of Venice, The Merry Wives of Windsor,* and *Troilus and Cressida*

GIRAUDOUX, JEAN (1882–1944)
French playwright and diplomat. His best known plays include *Amphitryon 38* (1938), which featured the Lunts; *The Mad Woman of Chaillot* (1946), whose English version was written by Maurice Valency (b. 1903); *Intermezzo* (1950); and *Tiger at the Gate* (1955). See Nathan's profile of Giraudoux.

GISH, LILLIAN (b. 1899)
American actress and author, maternal granddaughter of President Zachary Taylor. In 1904, at the age of five, she performed in Ohio in *In Convict Stripes,* a melodrama. She made her New York debut in 1913 as Marianne in *A Good Little Devil.* Her first major role was that of Helena in Chekhov's *Uncle Vanya* at the

Cort Theatre in 1930. In 1932 she starred as Marguerite in Dumas' *Camille,* a performance that elicited a rave review from Nathan (see his profile of Gish, p. 101.). By 1934 she was beginning to feel stereotyped as too virginal, and she won the role of the whore in Sean O'Casey's *Within the Gates,* which Nathan was instrumental in bringing to New York (see his letter to O'Casey, p. 225). Ever progressing from melodramas to more serious vehicles, in 1936 she starred as Ophelia in John Gielgud's production of *Hamlet.*

Before and even during her stage performances, Miss Gish starred in several movies, at first as a protegée of D. W. Griffith (1878). She starred, for example, in *The Birth of a Nation* (1915), *Intolerance* (1916), *The Battle of the Sexes* (1916), *Broken Blossoms* (1918), *Orphans of the Storm* (1922), *The Scarlet Letter* (1925), *La Bohème* (1926), *Annie Laurie* (1927), and *Portrait of Jenny* (1948). Her television appearances include that of *The Birth of the Movies* (1959). For several years she was a close friend of, and was in fact considered engaged to, George Jean Nathan, but she preferred to stay married only to her profession. Her books include *The Movies, Mr. Griffith, and Me* (1969) and *Dorothy and Lillian Gish* (1973), both published by Prentice-Hall, Englewood Cliffs, N.J.

GLASPELL, SUSAN (1882–1948)
American playwright; in 1915, along with her husband, George Cram Cook, she was one of the founders of the Provincetown Players (q.v.), which opposed the commercialism and stereotypes of Broadway. She encouraged several young playwrights, including Eugene O'Neill (q.v.).

Glaspell wrote several novels but remains better known for her plays. These include *The People* (1917), *Bernice* (1919), *The Inheritors* (1921), and *Alison's House* (1930), a Pulitzer Prize winner based on the life of Emily Dickinson. Glaspell's best known play, the one-act "Trifles" (1920), frequently performed still by amateur groups, was reprinted in Robert Freier et al., eds., *Adventures in Modern Literature, 5th Edition* (New York Harcourt Brace Jovanovich, 1962). See Nathan's profile of Lillian Hellman. See also Eugene O'Neill's letter of 4 November 1919 to Nathan, p. 201.

GLASS MENAGERIE, THE (1944)
A play by Tennessee Williams (q.v.) which starred, among others, Julie Haydon (q.v.), who in 1955 would become Mrs. George Jean Nathan. For this play, Nathan contributed, and Tennessee Williams reluctantly accepted, the drunkard scene at the beginning of scene 4. See Tennessee Williams, *Memoirs* New York: Doubleday, 1975, pp. 81–82.

GLASS, MONTAGUE (1877–1934)
English humorist. See Nathan's profile of Florenz Ziegfeld.

"GLENCAIRN, S. S."
A one-act play by Eugene O'Neill produced at the City Center Theatre, New York in May, 1948; also the collective title of four one-act plays written before 1919 and published in the 1919 edition of *Moon of the Caribbees* . . . Nathan observed, "These plays foreshadow a greatness to come."

GLYN, ELINOR (1864–1943)
British novelist, born Elinor Sutherland; she was the author of *Three Weeks* (1901). See Nathan's profile of Theodore Dreiser.

GOETHE, JOHANN WOLFGANG VON (1749–1832)
Germany's greatest poet, playwright, and critic. With his play *Götz von Berlichingen* (1773) he initiated the movement known as Sturm und Drang (q.v.). He was the author of the *Sorrows of Werther* (1774), a *Bildungsroman* or novel depicting the education and spiritual growth of the young protagonist; the play *Iphigenia in Tauris* (1787); the plays *Egmont* (1788) and *Torquato Tasso* (1790); *Wilhelm Meister's Lehrjahre* (1796) and *Wilhelm Meister's Wanderjahre* (1821) two more *Bildungsroman* types; the romance *Hermann und Dorothea* (1798); and the distinguished work of literary criticism, *Dichtung und Wahrheit* (Literature and Truth, 1811).
Goethe's masterpiece remains his closet drama (q.v.) *Faust* (part 1, 1808; part 2, 1832). This is the poetic and philosophic drama of the atheistic scholar who seduces the innocent young Gretchen, for whom he has sold his soul to the devil (Mephistopheles). Faust is redeemed in the end, chiefly by *tün* (constructive activity). The poetry and drama are lofty throughout, but part 2 is laced with obscure symbolism and ambitious business involving Helen of Troy, Lord Byron, and the wedding of classicism and romanticism. Goethe had almost surely read Christopher Marlowe's play *Doctor Faustus* (1604), but Marlowe's play centers in the legendary fifteenth century wandering conjuror and is much less complicated and symbolic than Goethe's.

GOGOL, NIKOLAI VASILYEVICH (1809–1852)
Russian novelist, short-story writer, and playwright who was the author of *Taras Bulba* (1825); the comedy *The Inspector General* (1836), which enjoyed a long run on stage and—on screen—outlived its author; a frequently anthologized short story "The Overcoat" (1842); and his masterpiece, the novel *Dead Souls* (1842).

GOLD (1920)
A play by Eugene O'Neill (q.v.) which was produced in Provincetown in 1921.

GOLD, HERBERT (b. 1924)
American fiction writer, essayist, and editor. He edited *Fiction of the Fifties* (1957) and is the author of *Birth of a Hero* (1951), *The Man Who Was Not With It* (1956), and *Therefore Be Bold* (1960).

GOLD, MICHAEL (1894–1967)
American editor, essayist, and playwright, born Irwin Granich. He was an editor of *The Masses* and *New Masses* magazines. He was also the author of the well-known essay "Toward Proletarian Literature," frequently anthologized, which originally appeared in the *Liberator* (February 1921). His plays include *Fiesta* (1925) and *Battle Hymn* (1936), the latter about the martyr John Brown.

GOLDSMITH, CLIFFORD (1899–1971)
American playwright and screenwriter best known for his radio serials *The Aldrich Family* (1943–1944). He was also the author of the play *What a Life!* (1938).

GOLDSMITH, OLIVER (1730–1774)
Anglo-Irish poet, novelist and playwright. He was the author of the long poem *The Deserted Village* (1770), the novel *The Vicar of Wakefield* (1766), and the popular play *She Stoops to Conquer* (1773).

GOODRICH, EDNA (1888–1987)
American actress; Mrs. Nat Goodwin (q.v.).

GOODWIN, NAT (1857–1920)
American actor, one of the most popular comedians of his time. In his attempts at serious Shakespearian roles, however, he failed.

GORKI (ALSO GORKY), MAKSIM (1868–1936)
Russian novelist and playwright. His best known play, *The Lower Depths* (1902), is generally believed to have inspired Eugene O'Neill's play *The Iceman Cometh* (1929), although no plagiarism was involved. See Nathan's profile of O'Neill.

GOTHAM BOOK MART
41 West 47th Street, New York. A celebrated book store presided over by Frances Steloff (1889–1989) who was a kind of angel to writers and bibliophiles that met here for readings and fraternizings. Nathan and Mencken sometimes met *Smart Set* contributors here. The Gotham has been compared to Shakespeare & Co., which expatriate Sylvia Beach (q.v.) maintained in Paris during the early 1900s. For more on Steloff, see *Publishers Weekly* (22 January 1988), p. 16; "Talk of the Town," *The New Yorker* (25 January 1988) pp. 25–26; and William G. Rogers, *Wise Men Fish Here: the Story of Frances Steloff* (New York: Harcourt Brace Jovanovich, 1965).

GRAND GUIGNOL, THE
1. A small theatre in the Montmartre district of Paris. During the late 1800s it specialized in macabre horror skits and plays.
2. A puppet or puppet show after the one that had originally opened in Lyons, France, in 1795.

GRANT, ULYSSES S. (1822–1885)
Eighteenth President of the United States. His *Personal Memoirs* (1885), suggested and published by Mark Twain (q.v.), proved a commercial failure and put the publisher in deep debt.

GRANVILLE-BARKER, HARLEY (1877–1946)
English actor, playwright, and critic. Nathan discusses him in the essay "Adaptations" (p. 74) and in the profile of Max Reinhardt (p. 194). See Dennis Kennedy, ed., *Plays by Harley Granville-Barker* (New York and London: Cambridge University Press, 1987).

GRAUSTARK (1900)
First of a number of romances by George Barr McCutcheon (q.v.) which were dramatized on Broadway and also in the movies. The movie sequels starred such celebrities as John Gilbert, Marion Davies, and Norma Talmadge. See A. L. Lazarus and Victor H. Jones, *Beyond Graustark* (Port Washington and London: Kennikat Press, 1981).

GREAT GATSBY, THE (1925)
A novel by F. Scott Fitzgerald (q.v.). See Nathan's letter of spring 1925 to Fitzgerald. p. 210.

GREAT GOD BROWN, THE (1925)
A play by Eugene O'Neill (q.v.).

GREELEY, HORACE (1811–1872)
American journalist, founder of the *New York Tribune*. He championed women's rights, profit-sharing for employees, and the abolition of slavery. In 1872, in his bid for the presidency of the United States, he was defeated by Ulysses S. Grant. Greeley's books include his autobiographical *Recollections of a Busy Life* (1868). One of Greeley's associates is credited with originating the slogan "Go West, young man!"

GREEN GROW THE LILACS (1931)
The folk play by Lynn Riggs (1899–1954), that was the basis for the musical comedy *Oklahoma* (1943) by Rodgers and Hammerstein.

GREEN HAT, THE (1924)
A novel and play by Michael Arlen (q.v.).

GREEN PASTURES, THE (1920)
An important Pulitzer Prize play by Marc Connelly (q.v.), that was developed at the University of North Carolina folkplays workshop.

GREENWICH VILLAGE THEATRE
220 West 4th Street at 2nd Avenue; one of the first off Broadway theatres. It opened in November 1917. In December 1929 it re-opened as the Irish Theatre with a production of *Playboy of the Western World* by John Synge (q.v.). In 1930 this theatre was demolished.

GREGORY, LADY AUGUSTA (1852?–1932)
Irish playwright; co-founder, with William Butler Yeats (q.v.), of the Abbey Theatre in Dublin. She was the author of *Spreading the News* (1904), *The Gaol Gate* (1906), *The Rising of the Moon* (1907), and *The Workhouse Ward* (1908). In 1973 her works were collected and edited by Hazard Adams: (Lewisburg, Pa.: Bucknell University Press).

GRIBBLE, HARRY (b. 1896)
English actor, playwright, producer, and screen writer. He was stage manager for Mrs. Patrick Campbell's production of Shaw's *Pygmalion* (1914). He was also the author of the comedy *March Hares* (1921) and the screen version of Eleonora Duse's play *Bill of Divorcement* (1932).

GRIFFITH, D. W. (1875–1948)
First major Americn film director and producer; he founded the United Artists Association. He also discovered and developed the cinematic talents of Lillian Gish (q.v.). He introduced such cinematic techniques as fade-in, fade-out, long shot, close-up, flashback, and montage. His best known films include the *Birth of a Nation* (1915). See Lillian Gish, *The Movies, Mr. Griffith, and Me,* (Englewood Cliffs, N.J.: Prentice-Hall, 1969).

GROUP THEATRE, NEW YORK
See Strasberg, Lee.

GRUNDY, SIDNEY (1848–1914)
English playwright.

GUEDALLA, PHILIP (1889–1944)
English writer. See Nathan's profile of Sinclair Lewis.

GUEST, EDGAR (1881–1959)
American versifier and columnist.

GUIMERA, ANGEL (CA. 1845–1924)
Catalan/Spanish poet and playwright; author of *Maria Rosa* (1894) and *Terra Baixa* (1896). He also translated *Marta of the Lowlands* (1914).

GUINNESS, SIR ALEC (b. 1914)
English actor and director. In 1936, after performing and directing in several London theatres, he joined the Old Vic Company, under whose aegis he performed in several Shakespearian roles.

His movie roles include those in *Great Expectations* (1947), *Kind Hearts and Coronets* (1950), *Oliver Twist* (1951), *The Lavender Hill Mob* (1951), and *The Bridge on the River Kwai* (1957), for which he won an Academy Award. See Kenneth Tynan, *Alec Guinness* (London: Rockwell, 1953).

GUITRY, LUCIEN (1860–1925)
French actor and producer.

GUITRY, SACHA (1885–1957)
French actor and playwright, the author of *Mozart* (1925). At one time he was a neighbor of the O'Neills (Eugene and Carlotta) when they lived in Le Plessis, Saint-Antoine de Rocher, Indre-et-Loire, France.

GWYN, NELL (1650–1687)
English comedienne who was the mistress of King Charles II. See Sheila Stowell, "Actors as Dramatic Personae . . .," *Theatre History Studies,* vol. 8. (Grand Forks, N.D.: University of North Dakota Theater Arts Dept. 1988).

HACKETT, JAMES K. (1869–1926)
Canadian actor and matinée idol who starred in a dramatization of Anthony Hope's *The Prisoner of Zenda* (1894). See Eugene O'Neill's 4 November 1919 letter to Nathan, p. 201.

HADLEY, HENRY (1871–1937)
American composer and conductor. At the turn of the century he conducted the San Francisco Symphony Orchestra. His best known composition remains "The Four Seasons."

HAMARTIA
Aristotle's term (in his *Poetics,* 335 B.C.). for a tragic character's key mistake that affects—in fact, predetermines—his actions. Cf. Tragic Flaw.

HAMBURGISCHE DRAMATURGIE (1967)
Milestone theatre criticism by Gotthold Lessing (q.v.).

HAMILTON, CLAYTON (1881–1946)
American playwright, critic, and teacher. At Columbia University, he was a student of Brander Matthews (q.v.). In collaboration with Augustus Thomas (q.v.), Hamilton wrote the play *The Better Understanding* (1917). Hamilton was also the author of the essay *Theory of the Theatre* (1939).

HAMILTON, PATRICK (1904–1962)
English playwright best known as the author of the melodrama *Gaslight* (1938). He was also the author of *Rope* (1929) and *The Governess* (1945).

HAMMERSTEIN, OSCAR II (1895–1960)
American lyricist who collaborated with Richard Rodgers (q.v.).

HAMPDEN, WALTER (1879–1955)
American actor and director. By 1937 he had appeared more than 1,000 times as Cyrano in Brian Hooker's translation of Rostand's *Cyrano de Bergerac* (1923). See Nathan's profile of Hampden.

HAMSUN, KNUT (1859–1952)
Norwegian/American novelist who won the Novel Prize for Literature in 1920. He is best remembered as the author of the novel *Growth of the Soil* 1920).

HANS SONNENSTÖSSER'S TRIP TO HELL
See *Beggar on Horseback*.

HAPPY TIME, THE (1949)
A play by Sam Taylor (q.v.).

HARDWICKE, SIR CEDRIC (1893–1964)
English actor and director who starred at the Old Vic (q.v.) in several Shakespearian roles, notably that of Sir Toby Belch (q.v.). In plays by George Bernard Shaw (q.v.) he starred in *Heartbreak House, Caesar and Cleopatra, Back to Methuselah,* and *Pygmalion.*

HARDY, THOMAS (1840–1928)
English poet and novelist, author of the Wessex series of novels, which include *Return of the Native* (1878), *The Mayor of Casterbridge* (1886), *Tess of the D'Urbervilles* (1891), and *Jude the Obscure* (1896). Nathan observed that Hardy's attempt to make a play out of *Tess of the D'urbervilles* proved abortive. See Nathan's essay "Literature and Drama," p. 66.

HARKNESS THEATRE, YALE UNIVERSITY
See Baker, George Pierce.

HARRIGAN, EDWARD (1843–1911)
American actor, playwright, and producer.

HARRIS, CHARLES K. (1865–1930)
American songwriter; author of "After the Ball Is Over" (1891), "Hello, Central" (1901), and several other popular hits.

HARRIS, FRANK (1856–1931)
English editor and biographer; author of *Oscar Wilde* (1918).

HARRIS, JED (1900–1979)
American director and producer. Among many other plays, he directed *The Crucible* (1953) by Arthur Miller (q.v.).

HARRIS, MARK (b. 1922)
American novelist and screen writer. His novels include *The Southpaw* (1953) and *Wake Up, Stupid!* (1959). His screenplays include *Bang the Drum Slowly* (1956). See Norman Lavers, *Mark Harris* (New York, 1978)

HART, LORENZ (1895–1943)
American lyricist. Among many other songs, he wrote "Sentimental Me," "Thou Swell," and "Blue Moon." See Richard Rodgers.

HART, MOSS (1904–1961)
American playwright who collaborated with George S. Kaufman (q.v.), with Irving Berlin (q.v.), and Cole Porter (q.v.). See Hart's autobiography, *Act One* (New York: Random House, 1959).

HARTE, BRET (1836–1902)
American short-story writer; author of *Luck of Roaring Camp and Other Sketches* (1870). Several of his short stories were dramatized for the stage, among them "M'Liss," in which Minnie Maddern starred before she became Mrs. Fiske.

HARTLEBEN, OTTO ERICH (1855–1905)
German-American playwright; author of *Rose Monday*.

HATTON, FANNY (1870–1939), FREDERICK (1879–1946), AND JOSEPH (1839–1907)
American actors and playwrights.

HAUPTMANN, GERHART (1862–1946)
German playwright best known for *Die Weber* (tr. *The Weavers,* 1892), a sociological play. See Nathan's profile of Eugene O'Neill.

HAYDON, JULIE (b. 1910)
American actress, born Donella Lightfoot Donaldson. In 1955 she became Mrs. George Jean Nathan. She began her career at an early age. In 1931 she played Ophelia in a production of *Hamlet* at the Hollywood Playhouse; also Titania in a production of *A Midsummer Night's Dream* (1944). Her many stage roles included those in *Family Affair* (1937) at the Cape Playhouse and *What Every Woman Knows* (1939). In Chicago, in 1944, she performed in the world premiere production of *The Glass Menagerie.* In 1951 she played Celia in the touring company of *The Cocktail Party.* Shortly thereafter she starred as Masha in Chekhov's *Uncle Vanya.* Other plays in which she starred include *Major Barbara, Man and Superman, The Barretts of Wimpole Street,* and *A Streetcar Named Desire.* She has also appeared in several MGM and RKO movies. She has toured universities, giving readings from Nathan's works.

HAYES, HELEN (b. 1900)
American actress, born Helen Hayes Brown. She made her stage debut in New York when she was eight years old. Her subsequent triumphant roles: as Constance Neville in *She Stoops to Conquer* (1924); Maggie Wylie in *What Every Woman Knows* (1926); Mary Stuart in *Mary of Scotland* (1933); Queen Victoria in *Victoria Regina* (1935); Portia in *The Merchant of Venice* (1938); Viola in *Twelfth Night* (1940); Harriet Beecher Stowe in *Harriet* (1943); Amanda in *The Glass Menagerie* (1948); and Nora Malody in *A Touch of the Poet* (1958). She also starred in several movie and TV productions, including *Dear Brutus* (1956) and *The Cherry Orchard* (1960). In 1928 she married the playwright Charles MacArthur (q.v.). Her awards and honors have been legion. See Nathan's profile.

HAYMARKET THEATRE, THE, LONDON
aka Her Majesty's Theatre. Built in 1705, it was remodeled in 1821 with a Corinthian portico. At the Haymarket, the satires and farces of Henry Fielding (1707–1754), especially *Pasquin* (1736), prompted the authorities to censor him and other "offenders" by passing the Licensing Act of 1737. As a result, Fielding became disenchanted with writing for the stage and turned to writing novels, including his masterpiece, *Tom Jones, a Foundling* (1749). See Ronald Bergan, *The Great Theatres of London*. (San Francisco and London: Chronicle Books, 1988).

HELEN HAYES THEATRE
210–214 West 46th Street between Broadway and 8th Avenue; it opened 1955 November 21 with a production of *Tiger at the Gates*. This theatre was originally the Follies Bergère, owned by Jesse Lasky and Henry Harris.

HAYS, WILL H. (1879–1954)
American attorney and cinema official. From 1922 to 1945 he was head of the Hays Office, the movie industry's organ for self-censorship.

HAZLITT, WILLIAM (1778–1830)
English essayist and drama critic. He was the author of *A View of the English Stage* (1818), *Characters of Shakespeare's Plays* (1818), "On the Comic Writers of the Last Century" (1819), *Dramatic Literature of the Age of Elizabeth* (1820), and *Table Talk* (1821).

HEARST, WILLIAM RANDOLPH (1863–1951)
American newspaper and periodicals publisher.

HEART OF MARYLAND, THE (1895)
A play by David Belasco (q.v.).

HECHT, BEN (1893–1964)
American novelist, playwright, and screen writer; his first fiction was published by Nathan in *Smart Set*. Hecht's plays include *The Front Page* (1928) and *Twentieth Century* (1933), both in collaboration with Charles MacArthur (q.v.). With MacArthur, too, Hecht wrote the screen dramatization (1939) of Emily Brönte's *Wuthering Heights* (1847).

HEGEL, GEORG W. F. (1770–1831)
German philosopher and teacher (Heidelberg, 1816–18; Berlin 1818–31). An idealist, he espoused *dialectical logic* which influenced Karl Marx (q.v.). This

Hegelian dialectic theory consists of three parts: thesis, antithesis, and synthesis. A thesis is a tentative or trial position that is opposed by an antithesis or contrary view. A compromise is the resultant synthesis, containing the best aspects of the first and second positions. Hegel's publications include *Phenomenology of the Mind* (1807) and *Encyclopedia of the Philosophic Sciences* (1817). Nathan felt that most kinds of logic have no place in drama.

HEGELIAN DIALECTIC
See Hegel.

HEIDELBERG UNIVERSITY
This German University was founded in 1386 on the Neckar River. Aside from being associated with the sport of fencing, which influenced Nathan, who attended here during the 1897–98 academic term, this university was the domain of some of the world's most distinguished philosophers.

HEIJERMANS, HERMANN (1864–1924)
Dutch playwright, author of *The Good Hope* (1928).

HEINE, HEINRICH (1797–1856)
German poet and essayist best known as the author of "Die Lorelei." Many of his poems were set to music by Mendelssohn, Schubert, Schumann, and others. Heine traveled through much of Europe and wrote such travel books as *Harz Journey* (1826) and *Travel Pictures* (1827). He was also the author of the play *Almanzor* (1844).

HELD, ANNA (1873–1918)
French-American comedienne and vaudeville singer. She popularized the song "Won't You Come Out and Play With Me?" In 1897 she married Florenz Ziegfeld (q.v.) before he took up with Billie Burke (q.v.).

HELIOGABULUS (1920)
A play by Nathan in collaboration with H. L. Mencken (q.v.).

HELLINGER, MARK (1903–1947)
American columnist and drama reviewer. A New York theatre was named for him.

HELLMAN, LILLIAN (1905–1984)
American playwright. She was the author of several distinguished, award-winning plays and screen scenarios—among them, *The Children's Hour* (1934), *The Little Foxes* (1939), *Watch on the Rhine* (1941), and *Another Part of the Forest* (1946). She was married to Dashiell Hammett (1894–1961). With the American poet Richard Wilbur she wrote the libretto for a musical version of Voltaire's *Candide* (1955). See her autobiography, *Pentimento,* (Boston: Little, Brown, 1973). See also Nathan's profile.

HEMINGWAY, ERNEST (1899–1961)
American fiction writer; Nobel Laureate of 1954. His death was a suicide. He was the author of many short stories and of such novels as *The Sun Also Rises* (1926), *A Farewell to Arms* (1929), *To Have and Have Not* (1937), *For Whom the Bell Tolls* (1940), *The Old Man and the Sea* (1952), and *Islands in the Stream*

(published posthumously in 1970). His non-fiction works include *In Our Time* (1925), *Men Without Women* (1927), *Death In the Afternoon* (1932), *The Green Hills of Africa* (1935) and the autobiographical *A Moveable Feast* (New York: Scribner's, 1964).

HENLEY, W. E. (1849–1903)
English editor and poet best known as the author of the poem "Invictus" (1875).

HENRY MILLER'S THEATRE
124–130 West 43rd Street between Broadway and Avenue of the Americas (6th Avenue). It opened in April 1918.

HENSON, LESLIE (1891–1957)
English director and producer. See Nathan's profile of Maurice Evans.

HEPBURN, KATHARINE (b. 1909)
American stage and screen actress. Her performances include roles in *Jane Eyre* (1937), *The Philadelphia Story* (1939), and *As You Like It* (1950), and several Shakespearian roles in the American Shakespeare Festival (Stratford, Connecticut). Her screen performances include those of *A Bill of Divorcement* (1932), *Alice Adams* (1935), *Mary of Scotland* (1936), *Quality Street* (1937), *Adam's Rib* (1949), *The African Queen* (1951), and *Long Day's Journey Into Night* (1962). She has won four Academy Awards. In 1928 she married Ludlow Smith, whom she divorced in 1934. For many years she was linked romantically with the actor Spencer Tracy. See Garson Kanin, *Tracy and Hepburn* (New York: Viking Press, 1971). Nathan profiled Hepburn in his *Encyclopedia of the Theatre* (New York: Knopf, 1940), pp. 172–73.

HERALD TRIBUNE, THE
Well known New York newspaper; the Paris edition, founded in 1887 by James Gordon Bennett Jr. (q.v.), was addressed to Americans abroad. The Paris-based international edition is also available in New York.

HERBERT, F. HUGH (1898–1958)
American comedian and playwright. During the 1930s and 1940s he played numerous comic roles in the movies. He was the author of the comedy *Kiss and Tell* (1943).

HERBERT, VICTOR (1859–1924)
American composer and a friend of Nathan's. Herbert was the author of several successful musical comedies, among them *Babes in Toyland* (1903) and *Naughty Marietta* (1910). In 1913, in collaboration with "Stars and Stripes" composer John Philip Sousa, Herbert founded ASCAP (American Society of Composers, Authors, and Publishers).

HERGESHEIMER, JOSEPH (1880–1954)
American novelist; author of several successful books, among them *Java Head* (1919). He was also a good friend of Nathan's and H. L. Mencken's. See Nathan's profile of Mencken.

HERVE, JAMES A. (1839–1901)
American actor, playwright, and producer.

HIGHLAND FLING, A (1943)
A comedy by Margaret Curtis. It was produced in 1944 at the Plymouth Theatre by George Abbott (q.v.). See Nathan's essay "Myself," p. 33.

HILLIARD, BOB (b. 1918)
American songwriter who wrote the score for the Disney movie *Alice in Wonderland* (1951).

HILLIARD, ROBERT (1857–1927)
American actor.

HIPPODROME, THE
A New York theatre built in 1905 on the site of a former horse arena (the name derives from the Greek *hippos,* horse, and *drome,* race course) on the Avenue of the Americas between 43rd and 44th Streets. Before it was demolished in 1939 it had hosted, among other attractions, in 1905, *A Yankee Circus on Mars* and *The Andersonville Raiders.*

HITCHCOCK, ALFRED (1899–1980)
Anglo-American movie director who directed and/or produced many successful films, among them *The Skin Game* (1932), *The 39 Steps* (1935), *Rebecca* (1940), *Dial M for Murder* (1954), *North By Northwest* (1959), *Psycho* (1960), *The Birds* (1963), and *Topaz* (1969). He also served as host on a television series of mystery stories. See Nathan's profile of Eugene O'Neill.

HOBOHEMIA (1919)
A play by Sinclair Lewis (q.v.).

HOFMANNSTHAL, HUGO VON (1874–1929)
Austrian poet, playwright, and librettist best remembered as the author of *Der Rosenkavalier* (1911). Early on, he was one of O'Neill's admirers, as reported by the Robertses in *As Ever, Gene.* (Rutherford: Fairleigh Dickinson, 1987) p. 28.

HOLLYWOOD
  1. a suburb of Los Angeles, California; main seat of the film industry.
  2. By extension, a term pertaining to cinema as distinguished from stage plays; also by implication, often derogatory, a term pertaining to "make-believe," "tinsel," or "formula plotting" (for example, "Hollywood ending"—always happy) as distinguished from the more realistic drama of the legitimate theatre.

HOMME À LA ROSE (1920)
A play by F. H. Battaille (1872–1922).

HOOKER, BRIAN (1880–1946)
American novelist, translator, song-writer, and librettist. In 1923 he translated *Cyrano de Bergerac* by Rostand (q.v.). Hooker wrote the popular song "Only a Rose" and collaborated on the writing of the libretto for *The Vagabond King* (1925) by Rudolf Friml (q.v.). See Nathan's profile of Walter Hampden.

HOPKINS, ARTHUR (1878–1950)
Broadway director and producer. Among other plays, he produced O'Neill's *Diff'rent* in 1938.

HOPWOOD, AVERY (1883–1928)
American playwright best remembered for his mystery melodrama *The Bat* (1920), which he wrote in collaboration with Mary Roberts Rinehart (1876–1958). Named for him are the annual Hopwood Literary Awards at the University of Michigan.

HORNUNG, E. W. (1866–1921)
English writer, the brother-in-law of Arthur Conan Doyle. Hornung was the author of *Raffles* (1930), which became a popular movie.

HORSECOUGH AND HAMILTON AND TOWSE
See Nathan's profile of Walter Hampden.

HOUSE OF SATAN (1926)
A book by Nathan.

HOUSSAY, BERNARDO (1887–1971)
A precocious Argentine physiologist.

HOWARD, BRONSON (1842–1908)
American playwright. He was the author of *Saratoga* (1870), a popular comedy; *Young Mrs. Winthrop* (1882), a drama of social criticism; *The Henrietta* (1887), a satire on certain business practices; and *Shenandoah* (1888), a drama about the Civil War. See Nathan's profile of O'Neill.

HOWARD, SIDNEY (1891–1939)
American playwright. At Harvard he was a member of George Pierce Baker's Workshop 47. Howard was the author of the plays *They Knew What They Wanted* (1924), which won a Pulitzer Prize; *The Silver Cord* (1926); *The Late Christopher Bean* (1932); and *Yellow Jack* (with Paul de Kruif, 1934). (De Kruif, a microbes specialist, had collaborated with Sinclair Lewis on *Arrowsmith*, 1925).

In 1939, after Sidney Howard's death, the Playwrights' Company established the Sidney Howard Memorial Award of $1500 given annually to an up-and-coming young playwright. *See also* Award, George Jean Nathan.

HOWARD, WILLIE (1886–1949)
German-American comedian, born Wilhelm Levkowitz. See Nathan's profile of Strindberg.

HOWE, P. P. (FL. 1900S)
English critic. See Nathan's profile of Oscar Wilde.

HOWELLS, WILLIAM DEAN (1837–1920)
American editor, critic, novelist, and playwright. Although he was an abortive playwright, he served with distinction on the editorial boards of *The Atlantic* (1871–81); and of *Harper's* (1886–91), where he conducted a regular column, "The Easy Chair." His best known novels include *The Rise of Silas Lapham* (1885), *A Modern Instance* (1887), *A Hazard of New Fortunes* (1890), and *A Traveler from Altruria* (1894). He championed realism in literature and was a mentor of Mark Twain, Hamlin Garland and others.

HOYT, JULIA (1897–1955)
American actress referred to in Nathan's profile of Max Reinhardt.

HUBBELL, RAYMOND (1879–1954)
American composer.

HUBRIS
A Greek term meaning overweening pride which precedes a fall; one of the tragic flaws (q.v.).

HUDSON THEATRE
129-141 West 44th Street between Broadway and Avenue of the Americas (6th Avenue); opened 19 October 1903; to be distinguished from the Hudson Playhouse, which became the Theatre de Lys.

HUGHES, HATCHER (1881–1945)
American playwright; author of the Pulitzer Prize play *Hell-Bent for Heaven* (1922).

HUGO, VICTOR (1802–1885)
Major French novelist and playwright who in 1851 was banished from France by Napoleon III and lived in the Isle of Guernsey until 1870. His novels include *Notre Dame de Paris* (1836), which was adapted as *The Hunchback of Notre Dame* (q.v.); and *Les Miserables* (1862), which has been dramatized for stage, screen, and television. His plays include *Cromwell* (1827), whose preface eloquently defends romanticism; *Hernani* (1830); and *Torquemada* (1882).

HUMOURS
See Comedy Of Humours.

HUNCHBACK OF NOTRE DAME, THE (1923)
A play by P. O. Shean and E. T. Louis Jr., which they adapted from the novel *Notre Dame de Paris* by Victor Hugo (q.v.). The movie starred Lon Chaney (1883–1930).

HUNEKER, JAMES (1860–1921)
American critic and novelist; author of *Painted Veils* (1920), which described artists among his contemporaries. Nathan admired Huneker—called him "Lord Jim."

HURST, FANNIE (1889–1968)
American novelist, several of whose books—among them, *Back Street* (1931)—were adapted to movies. See Nathan's profile of Dreiser, p. 165. See her autobiography, *Anatomy of Me* (New York: Doubleday, 1958).

HUSH! (1916)
A play by Violet Pearn, referred to in Nathan's profile of Winthrop Ames.

HUXLEY, ALDOUS (1894–1963)
English novelist; best known as the author of *Brave New World* (1932).

HUXLEY, THOMAS HENRY (1825–1895)
English biologist, he was a defender of the evolution theories espoused by Charles Darwin (q.v.). Huxley was nicknamed "Darwin's Bulldog." Thomas Huxley was the grandfather of Aldous and Julian Huxley.

HYMER, J. B. (1876–1953)
American playwright; author of *East is West* (1918).

IBSEN, HENRIK (1828–1906)
Norwegian playwright; one of the world's major playwrights. Early on, he abandoned a career in pharmacy and medicine to become an editor, playwright, and stage manager. From 1851 to 1857 he served as director of the Ole Bull National Theatre, Bergen; and from 1857 to 1862, director of the Norwegian National Theatre, Oslo. Among his best known plays: *Peer Gynt* (1866), which combines folklore and poetry and which inspired the musical composition of the same name by his compatriot Edvard Grieg; *Pillars of Society* (1877), social criticism; *A Doll's House* (1879), which in part is a defense of women; *Ghosts* (1881); *The Wild Duck* (1884); and *Hedda Gabler* (1890), one of his most melodramatic. In New York his plays were at first resisted as too iconoclastic but were ultimately produced largely through the persuasive influence of Nathan and the Fiskes (Harrison, editor of the *New York Dramatic Mirror;* and Minnie Maddern, who won acclaim for her interpretations of several Ibsen roles in which she starred). Here is a representative bibliography. Michael Meyer, *Ibsen* (Garden City, NY: Doubleday 1971); Rolf Fjelds, tr, *Ibsen: the Complete Major Prose Plays* (New York: NAL, 1978); Eva Le Gallienne, tr, *Eight Plays by Henrik Ibsen* (New York: Random House, 1981); Robert Brustein, *The Theatre of Revolt* (Boston: Little, Brown, 1962); Brian Johnston, *Text and Supertext in Ibsen'z Drama* (University Park, Pennsylvania: Penn State University Press, 1989); Joan Templeton, "The *Doll House* Backlash," PMLA (Jan 1989) pp. 28–40.

ICEMAN COMETH, THE (1939)
A play by Eugene O'Neill (q.v.).

IFFLAND, AUGUST (1759–1814)
German playwright and producer.

"ILE"
A one-act play by O'Neill first produced in November 1917 in Provincetown.

IMMEDIATE THEATRE
A mode of play production featuring improvisation as in dadaism (q.v.) with the addition of audience participation. Immediate theatre has given a home to the most experimental kinds of plays, experimentalism far beyond that of O'Neill's *Strange Interlude,* for example. Immediate theatre plays are performed with a minimum of scripts. Nor are the improvisations limited to minor stage business (as is allowed the insane inmates, for example, in Peter Weiss's *Marat/Sade,* 1964) but extend to the audience, as in Jack Gelber's *The Connection* (1959). The rationale for audience participation is that play-acting is or should be role-playing, that the role of the audience has all too long remained passive; that the roles of actors and spectators sometimes need to be switched as in therapeutic psychodrama. See Peter Brook, "The Immediate Theater," *Atlantic* (November 1968), pp. 82–94.

IMPRESSIONISM

An aesthetic movement that developed among artists in France at the end of the 1800s and flourished in the early 1900s. Impressionist painters strove to emphasize light reflected from objects more than objects themselves. Their paintings, however imprecise in object-outlines, remain light and airy and full of ethereal colors, which seem to differ at different times of the day. Impressionist writers, especially Flaubert (q.v.)), strove to render details as they appeared immediately to the senses. See Robert Herbert, *Impressionism* (New Haven: Yale University Press, 1988).

IMPRIMATUR

Official approval (for example, by Catholic censors) for publication of a literary work or for the production of a play; also, by extension, approval in general.

INDIANA UNIVERSITY

The state university at Bloomington, Indiana, which conferred on Nathan the degree Litt. D.; see Nathan's letter of 1 July 1953 to August Mencken.

INDUCTION.

See Curtain-Raiser and Play-Within-a-Play. Logic: from specific to general.

INFLUENCE

Traces of one author's theme or style in the work of another author. Nathan cites Nietzsche's influence on O'Neill, for example, and Strindberg's on Wilde. For a detailed account see A. L. Lazarus and H. Wendell Smith, *The NCTE Glossary of Literature & Composition* (Urbana, Ill.: National Council of Teachers of English, 1983) and Harold Bloom, *The Anxiety of Influence* (New York: Oxford University Press, 1973).

INGE, WILLIAM (b. 1913)

American playwright and teacher. In 1943 he became a drama critic for the *St. Louis Star-Times*. He was the author of *Come Back, Little Sheba* (1950), which won a Nathan Award; and *Picnic* (1953), later a movie, which won a Pulitzer Prize.

INGENUE

In comedies and melodramas the innocent young woman who plays opposite one of the more dominant males.

IN MEDIAS RES

Literally "into the midst of things"; in fiction and drama, (also epic poetry), the writer's technique of plunging right into the main action, letting preliminaries wait for flashbacks or for expository revelation.

INTERLUDE

1. in general any time frame, often with a clandestine connotation; an assignation, as in O'Neill's *Strange Interlude* (q.v.)

2. More specifically, in the history of drama, a medieval and early Renaissance (a) comic skit characterized by slapstick (q.v.), coarse language, and simplicity of plot, and addressed to vulgar, uneducated audiences; representative is John Heywood's *The Four P's* (ca. 1520), in which a pedlar, a pardoner, a palmer, and a 'pothecary vie with one another in a contest of tasteless slander against women;

(b) court interlude, addressed to a more sophisticated audience, a short comedy presented at royal courts, schools, universities, and at the homes of nobles. Court interludes approached the language and tone of the masque (q.v.). For example, Henry Medwall's *Fulgens and Lucrece* (1497), one of the earliest of these interludes was presented at Lambeth Palace. Other interludes included Nicholas Udall's *Ralph Roister Doister* (ca. 1553), addressed to students at Eton; and John Still's *Gammer Gurton's Needle* (ca. 1556), which was written for students at Christ's College, Cambridge. See Joseph Quincy Adams, ed., *Pre-Shakespearian Drama* (Boston: Houghton Mifflin, 1924).

INTERNATIONAL, THE (1928)
A play by John Howard Lawson (b. 1895). See Nathan's profile of G. Stein.

"IN THE ZONE"
A one-act play by Eugene O'Neill

IONESCO, EUGÈNE (b. 1912)
Romanian-French essayist, fiction writer, and playwright who remains best known for his dadaistic play *Rhinoceros* (1959). See Theatre of the Absurd.

I REMEMBER MAMA (1944)
A play by John Van Druten (1901–1957) based on sketches by Kathryn Forbes (fl. early 1900s).

IRISH RENAISSANCE
See Abbey Theatre.

IRVING, SIR HENRY (1838–1905)
English actor and manager, born Henry Brodribb. From 1878 to 1902, he managed the Lyceum Theatre, London. He performed in several Shakespearian roles in which the leading lady was Ellen Terry (q.v.). With Miss Terry he also performed in tours of the United States. See the biography of Terry by Gordon Craig (q.v.): *Ellen Terry and Her Secret Life*. (London: Marston, 1931).

ISHERWOOD, CHRISTOPHER (b. 1904)
English playwright and screenwriter. He was also a devotee of Vedanta and the author of *Approach to Vedanta* (1903). His stage show *Cabaret* (1966) was based on his collections of stories entitled *Goodbye to Berlin* (1935). His play *Adventures of the Black Girl in Her Search for God* (1969) was an adaptation of a novel of the same name by George Bernard Shaw (q.v.).

JAMES, HENRY (1843–1916)
One of the greatest novelists in the English-speaking world, even if a failed playwright. He was the brother of William James, the Harvard psychologist, and the son of Henry James Sr., a theologian turned free thinker. In 1876 Henry James expatriated to England, becoming a British subject in 1915. Several of James's short stories appeared in *The Atlantic* and in other prestigious periodicals. But his reputation rests mainly on his novels, especially *Daisy Miller* (1879), *Washington Square* (1880), *Portrait of a Lady* (1881), *The Bostonians* (1886), *The Tragic Muse* (1880), and *The Turn of the Screw* (1898). His most distinguished novels remain *The Wings of the Dove* (1902), *The Ambassadors* (1903), and *The Golden Bowl* (1904). Several of his novels and novelettes, especially *The Turn of the Screw,* have been

made into movies and television adaptations. *Washington Square* was adapted to stage and screen as *The Heiress* (1947) by Ruth and Augustus Goetz. From 1889 to 1895, James's attempts at playwriting proved abortive. His play *Guy Domville* (1895) elicited hoots from the audience, and James's attempts to dramatize *Daisy Miller* also failed. Still, Henry James's fiction remains among the world's greatest for psychological introspection and characters' experimental viewpoints.

The definitive biography, by Leon Edel, comes in three volumes; *Henry James: the Untried Years* (1953); *Henry James: the Middle Years* (1962); *Henry James: the Treacherous Years*. These were published in Philadelphia by Lippincott. Edel has also edited the *Diary of Alice James* (New York: Dodd, Mead, 1964).

JAMES, JESSE (1847–1882)
American outlaw.

JANIE (1941)
A play by Josephine Bentham and Herschel Williams (b. 1909). It was produced in 1942 at Henry Miller's Theatre.

JAPANESE THEATRE
See Kabuki and Noh plays

JEFFERSON, JOSEPH (1829–1905)
American actor and playwright who remains best known for his role as Rip Van Winkle in the dramatization (1865) of Washington Irving's story by Dion Boucicault (q.v.). Before bringing the production to New York, Jefferson performed the role in London 120 times. See Gladys Malvern, *Good Troupers All* (Philadelphia: Macrae Smith, 1945). See Nathan's profile of Jefferson.

JELIFFE, DR. S. E. (1866–1945)
Co-founder of the *Psychoanalytic Review* and managing editor of the *Journal of Nervous and Mental Disorders*

JOAN OF LORRAINE (1946)
A play by Maxwell Anderson (q.v.). See Nathan's profile of Anderson.

JOHN FERGUSON (CA. 1918)
A play by Eugene O'Neill (q.v.). See O'Neill's letter of 4 November 1919 to Nathan, p. 201.

JOHN THE BAPTIST (D. 30 A.D.)
The Jewish prophet who baptized Jesus.

JOHN LOVES MARY (1946)
A play by Norman Krasna (b. 1909). It was produced in 1947 at the Booth Theatre. See Nathan's essay "Myself," p. 33.

JOHNS HOPKINS UNIVERSITY HOSPITAL.
See Nathan's letter of 28 November 1950 to August Mencken, p. 230, in which Nathan writes "that damn heart attack has me . . . If I should get worse, tell Henry I'll come down to the Hopkins and crawl into bed next to him."

JOHNSON, JAMES WELDON (1871–1938)
American lawyer, poet, and teacher. He was one of the leaders, along with Langston Hughes and Countee Cullen, of the Harlem Renaissance. Johnson's books include *God's Trombones* (1927), *Black Manhattan* (1930), and *Selected Poems* (1935).

JOHNSON, PAMELA (1912–1981)
English author and critic.

JOHNSON, ROBERT UNDERWOOD (1853–1937)
American editor and poet. From 1873 to 1913, he was editor of the *Century Magazine*. His books include *Poems of War and Peace* (1916) and *Aftermath* ((1933).

JOHNSON, SAMUEL (1709–1784)
Celebrated English critic and lexicographer. He was the subject of a well known biography by the Scottish writer James Boswell (1740–1795). Johnson's books include his edition of Shakespeare (ca. 1770), *Lives of the Poets* (1779), and his monumental *Dictionary of the English Language* (1755).

JOHNSTON, DENNIS (b. 1901)
Irish playwright.

JONES, HENRY ARTHUR (1851–1929)
A Welsh playwright, he wrote over 60 plays, all mainly concerned with social and moral issues and almost all resolved by quiet rational compromise rather than by violence. The "H. A. Jones Compromise" that Eugene O'Neill cites in his letter of 1 February 1921 to Nathan refers to just that characteristic of Jones's plays. Jones enjoyed acting in some of his own plays, especially his early one-acts. His full-length plays include *Saints and Sinners* (1884), *The Middleman* (1889), *Michael and His Lost Angel* (1896), and *The Liars* (1897), considered by some his masterpiece, although Jones himself regarded his masterpiece to be *Mrs. Dane's Defense* (1900). Jones's non-violent, compromise plays may be compared with the dramas of inaction by Chekov (q.v.), except that the desperation in Jones's characters is much shallower. A *Life of* by his daughter appeared in 1930. The definitive study remains Richard Cordell's *Henry Arthur Jones and the Modern Drama* (Port Washington and London: Kennikat Press, 1968).

JONES, INIGO (1573–1652)
English architect and stage designer best remembered for the sets he created for the plays and court masques (q.v.) by Ben Jonson (q.v.). Among Jones's innovations that he contributed to the developing theatre are the proscenium arch and movable scenery. Aside from his theatre work, Jones designed the classical facade of St. Paul's Cathedral, the layout of the Covent Garden plaza, and the floor plans for Lincoln's Inn Fields (the law school). A handsomely illustrated reference is Stephen Orgel and Roy Strong, eds., *Britannia Triumphant, Inigo Jones* (London: Thames and Hudson Publishers, 1973).

JONES, MARGO (1913–1955)
American play producer. *See* Dowling, Eddie.

JONES, ROBERT EDMOND (1887–1954)
American producer and designer associated with the Provincetown Players (q.v.) He was admired by Nathan. See Nathan's profile of O'Neill.

JONES, VICTOR H. (b. 1931)
American biographer and teacher; co-author with A. L. Lazarus of *Beyond Graustark: George Barr McCutcheon, Playwright Discovered* (Port Washington and London: Kennikat Press, 1981).

JONSON, BEN (1572–1637)
English poet and playwright; author of the well-known song "To Celia" (1616), which begins "Drink to me only with thine eyes." From 1605 on, he was continually composing masques (q.v.)—among them *Pleasure Reconciled to Vertue* (1616), which is regarded as having given John Milton (q.v.) the idea for the masque *Comus* (1634). In the production of the masque *Chlorinda,* Jonson quarrelled with Inigo Jones (q.v.) and lost court patronage. Nevertheless, as one of the University Wits (q.v.) Jonson continued to write successful plays. His best known plays remain *Every Man in His Humour* (1598), with William Shakespeare in the cast; *Every Man Out of His Humour* (1599); *Volpone* (1606); *Epicene, or the Silent Woman* (1609); *The Alchemist* (1611); and *Bartholomew Fair* (1614). See Marchette Chute's brilliant biography *Ben Jonson of Westminster* (New York: Dutton, 1953). *See* Comedy of Humours.

JOURNEY'S END (1928)
A World War I play by R. C. Sheriff (1896–1975). It has been reprinted in Robert Freier et al. eds., *Adventures in Modern Literature* (New York: Harcourt Brace Jovanovich 1953).

JOYCE, JAMES (1882–1941)
Irish fiction writer; one of the giants of the century. He was the author of *Dubliners* (1914), a collection short stories, including two originally published by Nathan in *Smart Set;* also "The Dead," generally regarded as his masterpiece or one of his masterpieces. (See Pauline Kael's review of the film version made by John Huston, *The New Yorker* 14 December 1987, pp. 144–49.) In *A Portrait of the Artist as a Young Man* (1916), largely autobiographical, Joyce reveals his disenchantment with his Catholic upbringing. Joyce's controversial novel *Ulysses* first appeared in parts between 1914 and 1921 and was published as a book (1922) by Sylvia Beach, the expatriate American owner of the Paris bookstore Shakespeare & Co. As reflected in *Finnegans Wake* (1934) Joyce was a virtuoso with languages, allusions, and clever plays upon words. For example, the impotent Earwicker fears that his "craft is ebbing" an allusion to the German sexologist Krafft-Ebing (1840–1902).

JUNG, CARL GUSTAV (1875–1961)
Swiss psychologist and psychiatrist. From 1902 on he was on the staff of the Berghölzi Asylum, Zurich, where one of the patients was Zelda Fitzgerald (q.v.) Early on, he developed the theory of complexes and, with Freud (q.v.) founded the practice of analytic psychology. Although initially Jung shared with Freud several basic theories and tenets, in 1912 Jung broke with Freud on the appearance of the latter's *The Psychology of the Unconscious.* Jung accorded to the sex drive certain basics of behavior but disagreed with Freud on its autocracy. Jung believed, rather, that if there is one paramount life force, it is the will to live. Jung developed a

classification system that divides humans into extroverts and introverts. He also developed the theory of archetypes and the collective unconscious. His chief works include *On the Psychology of Dementia Praecox* (1907), *Psychological Types* (1921), *Modern Man in Search of a Soul* (1933), *Psychology and Religion* (1939), and his autobiographical *Memories and Dreams* (1961) with posthumous editions edited by colleagues.

JUNIOR MISS (1941)
A play by Jerome Chodorov (q.v.) and Joseph Fields (b. 1895). See Nathan's essay "Myself," p. 33.

JUNO AND THE PAYCOCK (1924)
A play by Sean O'Casey (q.v.). See Nathan's profile of O'Casey.

KABUKI
The classical drama of Japan that originated during the early 1600s. It involves the actors as singers, dancers, acrobats, and sometimes swordsmen. See Earle Ernst, *The Kabuki Theatre* (New York: Oxford University Press, 1956).

KAFKA, FRANZ (1883–1924)
Major Austrian fiction-writer. An existenialist (q.v.) and expressionist (q.v.), he greatly influenced novelists and playwrights devoted to expressionism. In *The Metamorphosis* (1912), for example, Gregor, the protagonist, wakes up one morning to find himself transformed into a gigantic cockroach. Kafka's other works include *Amerika* (1912), *The Trial* (1914), *In the Penal Colony* (1914), *Letter to the Father* (1919), *The Castle* (1922), and *Investigations of a Dog* (1922). See Max Brod's biography of Kafka (Frankfurt: Fischer Verlag, 1954): also Wilhelm Emrich, *Franz Kakfa: A Critical Study of His Works* (New York: Ungar, 1968).

KAHN, OTTO (1894–1962)
American financier and patron of theatre arts. See Nathan's profile of Max Reinhardt.

KAISER, GEORG (1878–1945)
German expressionist playwright. See Expressionism.

KALLMAN, CHESTER (1921–1975)
American playwright, composer, and lyricist who collaborated with W. H. Auden (q.v.) on *The Rake's Progress* (1951) and on *Elegy for Young Lovers* (1961). Also with W. H. Auden, Kallman translated and wrote librettos for Mozart's *The Magic Flute* and *Don Giovanni*.

KALMAN, EMERICH (1882–1953)
Hungarian composer

KALMAR, UNION OF
From 1397 to 1814, an alliance of Denmark, Norway, and Sweden under the aegis of Sweden's queen.

KANT, IMMANUEL (1724–1804)
German idealist philosopher; he argued that *noumena*—things beyond experience—are unknowable while only *phenomena*—tangible experiences—are

knowable. Also, contrary to what one would expect of an idealist, he argued that the three problems of metaphysics—God, immortality, and freedom—are un-knowable by conventional means. But in his ethics he was the true idealist and is in fact best remembered for his categorical or moral imperative—namely, that as a rule for motives and behavior, a person should act as if setting an example for everyone else in the world. Kant's works, include *Critique of Pure Reason* (1781) and *Critique of Practical Reason* (1790). For a biography, see Lucien Goldmann, *Immanuel Kant* (London: Duckworth, 1971).

KÄRNTNER RING (1800S)
A set of romantic operettas set in the Carinthia hills of Austria. In 1276 Carinthia fell to Rudolf of Hapsburg, to be distinguished from the Austrian Archduke Rudolf (1858–1889), who, with his mistress the Baroness Maria Vetsera, perished myste-riously at Mayerling, near Vienna. See Mayerling.

KAUFMAN, GEORGE S. (1889–1961)
American playwright and critic; he collaborated on more than 40 plays, among them: with Marc Connelly (q.v.) on *Merton of the Movies* (1922) and *Beggar on Horseback* (1924); with Ring Lardner (q.v.), on *June Moon* (1929); with Edna Ferber (q.v.), on *The Royal Family* (1927), *Dinner at Eight* (1932), and *Stage Door* (1936); with Morrie Ryskind on the Pulitzer prize play *Of Thee I Sing* (1931), which boasted music by George Gershwin (q.v.); with Moss Hart (q.v.), on *You Can't Take It With You* (1936) and *The Man Who Came to Dinner* (1939). Kaufman was a popular member of the Dutch Treat Club (q.v.).

KEAN, CHARLES (1811–1868)
English actor.

KEAN, EDMUND (1787–1833)
English actor. Aside from his romantic roles, he remains best remembered for his role as Shylock in *The Merchant of Venice,* in which he played at the Drury Lane Theatre (q.v.) starting in 1814.

KEATON, BUSTER (1895–1966)
American comedian of stage and screen. He began his career as a child actor with his parents in vaudeville. Regarded, along with Charles Chaplin, as one of the greatest comedians in cinema history, Keaton was stereotyped as a deadpan who overcame incredible odds. His roles in the movies include those in *The Navigator* (1924), *The General* (1926), and *Steamboat Bill* (1927). After semi-retirement, he returned to the screen with supporting roles in *Sunset Boulevard* (1929), *Limelight* (1952), and *A Funny Thing Happened on the Way to the Forum* (1966). See Buster Keaton, *My Wonderful World of Slapstick* (Garden City: Doubleday, 1960).

KEIGHTLY, CYRIL (1875–1929)
Australian actor.

KELLY, GRACE (1929–1982)
American stage and screen actress. In 1956 she married Prince Ranier III of Monaco, becoming Princess Grace. She was killed in an automobile accident in Monaco in 1982.
On stage she had performed in *The Father* (1949), *The Cocktail Party* (1951), and *The Moon Is Blue* (1953). Her movie roles included those in *High Noon* (1952),

Dial M for Murder (1954), *The Bridges to Toko Ri* (1954), *To Catch a Thief* (1955), *The Swan* (1956), and *High Society* (1956). She won an Academy Award for her performance as Georgie in *The Country Girl* (1954). She also won high marks for her 1961 television performance in J. R. Balderston's *Berkeley Square*.

KEMBLE FAMILY, THE
English actors. Roger (1721–1802) formed their touring company; his children were Sarah Siddons (q.v.), John Philip (1752–1823), George Stephen (1758–1822), Elizabeth (1761–1836), and Charles (1775–1854).

KEMBLE, FANNY (1809–1893)
English actress, granddaughter of Roger Kemble (q.v.). She was born Frances Anne. She specialized in Shakespearian roles—among them, those of Juliet, Portia, Beatrice, and Lady Macbeth.

KEMP, HARRY (1883–1960)
American poet derogated by Nathan. See Nathan's letter of 1924 to H. L. Mencken, p. 209.

KENNEDY, CHARLES RANN (1871–1950)
Anglo-American playwright and moralist. See Nathan's profile of Maurice Maeterlinck in *Comedians All* (New York: Knopf, 1919), pp. 40–52.

KERN, JEROME (1885–1945)
American composer of scores for light operas and musical comedies. He remains best known for his work on *Show Boat* (1926), with its famous song "Ol' Man River."

KEYNES, JOHN MAYNARD (1883–1946)
English economist.

KIKI (1921)
A play by Andre Picaré (1874–1926) adapted by David Belasco (q.v.). See Nathan's uncomplimentary assessment of Belasco in *Mr. George Jean Nathan Presents* (New York: Knopf, 1917), pp. 66–79.

KIND LADY (1935)
A melodrama by Edward Chodorov (b. 1914) based on a novel of the same name by Hugh Walpole (1884–1941). Referred to in Nathan profile of Helen Hayes.

KINGSLEY, SIDNEY (b. 1906)
American playwright, director, and producer; not one of Nathan's favorites. Kingsley was the author of *Men in White* (1933); *Dead End* (1935), which generated the phrase "dead end kids" and *Darkness at Noon* (1951), based on the 1944 anti-Nazi and anti-Stalinist book of the same name by Arthur Koestler (b. 1905). Kingsley adapted all his major stage plays to the screen.

KINSEY, ALFRED (1894–1956)
American biologist who was the author of *Sexual Behavior of the Human Male* (1948) and *Sexual Behavior of the Human Female* (1953). Nathan uses Kinsey as a stick with which to beat Tennessee Williams (1914–1953); see Nathan's assess-

ment of Williams in *Theatre Book of the Year 1950–1951* (New York: Knopf, 1951), pp. 209–212.

KIPLING, RUDYARD (1865–1936)

English writer, born in India, who in his later years lived in the United States. He was the first English Nobel Laureate in Literature (1907). He was the author of *Departmental Ditties* (1886) and *Barrack Room Ballads* (1888); such poems as "Mandalay," "Gunga Din," "Recessional," and "If"; also *Plain Tales from the Hills* (1888); *The Light That Failed* (1890); *The Jungle Book* (1894); *Captains Courageous* (1897); and *Kim* (1901), which was praised by T. S. Eliot. In 1892, he married Caroline Balestier, an American, in London and went with her to Vermont.

KISMET

A play by Edward Knoblaugh (1874–1945) first produced in 1911, it starred Otis Skinner (q.v.).

KISS AND TELL (1943)

A comedy by F. Hugh Herbert (q.v.).

KISS FOR CINDERELLA (1916)

A play by James M. Barrie (q.v.).

KISS THE BOYS GOODBYE (1938)

A play by Claire Boothe (1902–1987).

KLEIN, CHARLES (1867–1915)

English actor and playwright associated with David Belasco (q.v.) and David Warfield (q.v.). See Nathan's profile of O'Neill.

KNOPF, ALFRED (1892–1989)

American publisher who, with his wife, Blanche, founded the Alfred A. Knopf Company in 1915. See Nathan's profile of H. L. Mencken, p. 173; also his letter of 5 September 1951 to August Mencken, p. 231.

KOTZEBUE, AUGUST VON (1761–1819)

German playwright; author of more than 200 plays, several of which became the bases for librettos by Beethoven and Schubert. Many of the Kotzebue's melodramas were very popular in so-called opera houses of the frontier and even on flatboat theatres that plied the Mississippi between Cincinnati and New Orleans. One of his most popular plays was *Father and Son* (1801).

KRAPP'S LAST TAPE (1959)

A play by Samuel Beckett (b. 1906), Anglo-French playwright and novelist.

KRASNA, NORMAN (b. 1909)

American playwright and producer; he has written and/or adapted several plays for the screen. He is the author of *Small Miracles* (1934), *Dear Ruth* (1944), and *John Loves Mary* (1947).

KRUTCH, JOSEPH WOOD (1893–1970)

American critic and essayist. From 1924 to 1952 he served as the drama critic of

The Nation. His books include *Comedy and Conscience after the Restoration* (1924), *The American Drama Since 1918* (1939), and *The Measure of Man* (1954). He was one of Nathan's close friends.

KUMMER, CLAIRE (1873–1958)
American playwright, born Claire Rodman Bacher. She was the author of several light comedies. See Nathan's letter of 14 November 1919, p. 202.

LADIES AND GENTLEMEN (1939)
A play by Ben Hecht (q.v.) and Charles MacArthur (q.v.).

LADY OF LYONS, THE (1838)
A play by E. Bulwer-Lytton (q.v.).

LADY WINDERMERE'S FAN (1892)
A play by Oscar Wilde (q.v.) that was said to be inspired by Lily Langtry (q.v.). See Nathan's profile of Wilde.

LA FOI (1912)
A play *(False Gods)* by Eugene Brieux (q.v.). See Nathan's profile of Oscar Wilde.

LA FONTAINE, JEAN DE (1621–1695)
French poet best known as the author of *Fables* (1668.) See Nathan's profile of T. S. Eliot.

L'AIGLON (1900)
A six-act play *(The Eaglet)* by Edmond Rostand (q.v.). It is based on the life of Napoleon's son. The role was popularized by Sarah Bernhardt (q.v.). See Nathan's profile of Rostand.

LAKE, THE (1933)
A play by Dorothy Massingham (1899–1933); referred to by Nathan in his profile of Katharine Hepburn in *Encyclopedia of the Theatre* (New York: Knopf, 1940), pp. 172–173.

LAMARR, HEDY (b. 1915)
German-American movie actress and ecdysiast.

LAMB, CHARLES (1775–1834)
English essayist and critic who used the pen-name Elia. He gave up an intended marriage to care for his sister, Mary Ann, who in a fit of insanity killed their invalid mother. He is best known for his *Essays of Elia* (1823). With his sister, he wrote, for children, *Tales from Shakespeare* (1807). During the early 1800s he contributed drama reviews to English periodicals.

LAMSON, GERTRUDE (1874–1974)
American actress (aka Nance O'Neill).

LANDOR, WALTER SAVAGE (1775–1864)
English essayist, poet, and playwright. At one time, in Venice, he was financially assisted by Robert Browning (q.v.). Landor remains best known for his essays in

Imaginary Conversations (1824) He also wrote the plays *Don Julian* (1812) and *Antony and Octavia* (1856).

LANGLEY, NOËL (b. 1911)
American playwright, director, and screenwriter. He wrote the screen script of *The Wizard of Oz* (MGM, 1939). He also collaborated with Robert Morley (q.v.) on the play *Edward, My Son* (1947), which was successfully produced in 1948 at the Martin Beck Theatre.

LANGNER, LAWRENCE (1890–1962)
A Welsh playwright, Langner came to New York in 1911. In 1914 he organized the Washington Square Players (q.v.), and in 1919 he founded and managed the Theatre Guild (q.v.). He also founded the American Shakespeare Theatre and Academy at Stratford, Connecticut, and he produced several of Eugene O'Neill's plays.

LANGSIDE, BATTLE OF
Scotland, 1568. This was the last battle of the war between Mary, Queen of Scots, and Archibald Campbell, fifth Earl of Argyle. As a result of her defeat here, Mary fled to England, where as a threat to Elizabeth I, she was executed. In the play *Mary of Scotland* (1933) Helen Hayes achieved one of her triumphant roles.

LANGTRY, LILY (1852–1929)
Born Emilie Charlotte Le Breton, on the Isle of Jersey, England, she became a glamorous although not an accomplished actress. Her striking beauty, however, attracted several well-known men, including King Edward VII. She is said to have inspired Oscar Wilde's *Lady Windermere's Fan* (1892). For an account of her marital and extra-marital relations, see Pierre Sichel, *The Jersey Lily* (Englewood Cliffs, N.J.: Prentice-Hall, 1958).

LARDNER, RING (1885–1933)
American humorist; best known as the author of *You Know Me Al* (1916), which successfully reproduces the early 1900s Chicago vernacular much in the manner of George Ade (q.v.). With George M. Cohan (q.v.) Lardner collaborated on the play *Elmer the Great* (1928); and with George S. Kaufman (q.v.), on the play *Blue Moon* (1929). See James De Muth, *Small Town Chicago: the Comic Perspective of Finley Peter Dunne, George Ade, and Ring Lardner* (Port Washington and London: Kennikat Press, 1980); and A. L. Lazarus, ed., *The Best of George Ade* (Bloomington: Indiana University Press, 1985).

LA SCALA
Internationally renowned house of opera in, Milan, Italy.

LAUREL AND HARDY MOVIES
See Nathan's profile of Dreiser.

LAWRENCE, VINCENT (1890–1946)
American playwright discussed by Nathan in his assessment of Elmer Rice, *Passing Judgments* (New York: Knopf, 1935), pp. 163–65.

LAWSON, JOHN HOWARD (1894–1977)
American journalist and expressionist playwright.

LAZARUS LAUGHED (1927)
A play by Eugene O'Neill. According to the New Testament (John 11:1–44) Lazarus was raised from the dead. O'Neill endows his Lazarus with first-hand knowledge that there is life after death. Freed of man's inveterate fear of death, Lazarus laughs and rejoices. The first act of this play was published in *The American Caravan* (September 1927) by Van Wyck Brooks et al. In November 1927, Boni & Liverwright published the whole play. On 9 April 1928, the play was produced at the Pasadena (Calif.) Community Playhouse. See Nathan's profile of O'Neill.

LEFT BANK, THE (1931)
A play by Elmer Rice (q.v.).

LEFT BANK, PARIS, FRANCE
Left bank of the Seine River; a section also known as the Latin Quarter.

LE GALLIENNE, EVA (b. 1899)
Anglo-American actress and director who starred in plays by Shakespeare, Ibsen, and Chekhov. In 1926 she founded the Civic Repertory Theatre. In 1941 she produced O'Neill's *Ah Wilderness!* In 1946 with Margaret Webster (q.v.) she founded the American Repertory Theatre. See her autobiography *With a Quiet Heart* (New York: Viking Press, 1953).

LEGITIMATE THEATRE
Spoken drama performed by live actors as distinguished from scripts taped or recorded or reproduced on radio, television, or cinema.

LEIBER, FRITZ (1883–1949)
American Shakespearian actor. See Nathan's profile of John Barrymore.

LEIPZIG ILLUSTRIERTE ZEITUNG
A German illustrated periodical that regularly publishes reviews of plays.

LEIPZIG, NATE (1873–1939)
Swedish magician and vaudeville performer.

LENORMAND, HENRI-RENÉ (1882–1951)
French playwright and devotee of Freud (q.v.). See Nathan's profile of Max Reinhardt.

LESSING, GOTTHOLD (1729–1781)
German playwright and one of the most influential critics in eighteenth century Enlightenment Europe. He was the author of the plays *Minna von Barnhelm* (1763) and *Nathan the Wise* (1779), which reflected his deistic convictions. His well-known essays in criticism include *Laokoön* (1766) and the *Hamburgische Dramaturgie* (1767), which faulted the French classical theatre for rejecting the truly classical, or Aristotelian, unities (q.v.). Although that side of his criticism is now negligible, what endures is his remarkably astute constructive advice to players and playwrights. The *Hamburgische Dramaturgie* was one of the books Nathan had read at Heidelberg University (q.v.). He and Lessing were kindred spirits not only in religious convictions but also in major issues of dramaturgy.

LETTER, THE (1927)
A play by W. Somerset Maugham (q.v.). See Nathan's profile of Maugham.

LEWIS, SINCLAIR (1885–1951)
American novelist, the first American Nobel Laureate in Literature (1930). He was a close friend of Nathan, H. L. Mencken, and Theodore Dreiser (q.v.). Lewis was the author of *Main Street* (1920), *Babbitt* (1922), *Arrowsmith* (with Paul de Kruif, 1925), *Elmer Gantry* (1927), *Dodsworth* (1929), and *It Can't Happen Here* (1935). The last was dramatized by Lewis and by John Moffitt and was produced in 1936 by the Federal Theatre Project. See Nathan's profile of Sinclair Lewis.

LEWISOHN, LUDWIG (1882–1955)
German-English author and artist. His books include *The Modern Drama* (1915), and the autobiographical *Upstream* (1922).

LIBBEY, LAURA JEAN (1862–1924)
American sentimental novelist.

LIBRETTO
The text or "book" consisting of dialogue and lyrics.

LILLIE, BEATRICE (b. 1898?)
Canadian-American actress, singer, and movie star. She devoted most of her career to performing in London music halls and in American vaudeville. Her best known film remains *Thoroughly Modern Millie* (1967). See Nathan's profile of Beatrice Lillie.

LISTON, VICTOR (1838–1913)
English actor.

"LITTLE CLOUD, A"
A short story by James Joyce (q.v.) in his collection *Dubliners* (1914).

LITTLE FOXES, THE (1939)
A play by Lillian Hellman (q.v.).

LITTLE ROOM [SOCIETY], THE
A Chicago club of artists, writers, and publishers that flourished in the late 1800s and early 1900s. It met on Friday evenings in the Fine Arts Building in the studio of the artist Ralph Clarkson. The name of the group ostensibly suggested the physically limited space of the meeting room, but in reality it came to connote the exclusivity of the membership, which, like that of the comparable Bloomsbury Group of London, was by invitation only, even if a little nepotism occasionally crept in. The members included Chicago's foremost architect, Louis Sullivan; the avant-garde artist Lorado Taft; the author and editor Hamlin Garland (q.v.) along with his new bride, Zulime (née Taft); Harriet Monroe, founder and editor of the celebrated *Poetry* magazine; the novelist Henry Fuller; Herbert Stone, the publisher of *Graustark; Graustark*'s author, fiction writer and would-be playwright George Barr McCutcheon (q.v.); George's brother John T. McCutcheon, who would become a Pulitzer Prize winning cartoonist; and John's roommate, George Ade (q.v.). See A. L. Lazarus and Victor H. Jones, *Beyond Graustark: George*

Barr McCutcheon, Playwright Discovered (Port Washington and London: Kennikat Press, 1981).

LITTLE THEATRE MOVEMENT

The term is generic; it refers to a small, local, off-broadway, non-commercial group of actors and producers. Characteristically the group is an on-going assembly of amateurs, often with an on-going repertoire, who perform in small, often improvised facilities, even in barns. British and American little theatres are known to have started as early as the 1500s. In modern times one thinks of the Provincetown Players (q.v.), who were the first to produce plays by the young, upcoming Eugene O'Neill (q.v.). On the opposite coast, a well-known little-theatre group developed at the Pasadena (Calif.) Community Playhouse in the early 1920s. During the 1960s thousands of little theatre groups operated all over the country, if one includes groups associated with churches, YMCAs, YMHAs and the like. See Arthur Hobson Quinn, *A History of the American Drama* (New York: Harper and Row, 1923; revised 1943).

LOGAN, JOSHUA (1909–1988)

Stage and screen director and producer. He may best be remembered for his productions of *South Pacific* and *Annie, Get Your Gun*.

LOLLARDS.

See Oldcastle, Sir John.

LOMBARD, CAROLE (1909–1942)

American movie actress. Wife of the actor Clark Gable, she was killed in a plane crash.

LONDON, JACK (1876–1916)

American fiction writer. Born the illegitimate son of W. H. Chaney and Flora Wellman, Jack was adopted by John London, his step-father. For the most part, Jack was self-educated, his books supplied by Jim Coolbirth, a librarian friend. Most influential among the books were those by Darwin (q.v.), Marx (q.v.), and Nietzsche (q.v.). To support himself, Jack worked at odd jobs, including, for example, janitor at the University of California, Berkeley; newspaper vendor; pin boy in bowling alleys; cannery worker, longshoreman; able-bodied seaman; and gold prospector. Although he committed suicide at age 40, his experiences at sea and in the gold mines had inspired a large oeuvre of fiction. He was the author of many short stories, several of which were first published in the *Overland Monthly*. One of his best known stories remains "To Build a Fire." His best known novels include *The Call of the Wild* (1903), *White Fang* (1906), *Martin Eden* (1909), and *Cruise of the Snark* (1911). For a fictionalized biography, see Irving Stone, *Sailor on Horseback* (New York: Doubleday, 1938).

LONG DAY'S JOURNEY INTO NIGHT (1956)

A posthumously published play by Eugene O'Neill (q.v.).

"LONG VOYAGE HOME" (1925)

A one-act play by Eugene O'Neill (q.v.).

LORRAINE, LILLIAN (1892–1955)

American actress, born Mary Ann Brennan. See Nathan's profile of Ziegfeld.

LOUIS, JOE (1914–1981)
American boxer nicknamed "The Brown Bomber."

LOUIS VII (CA. 1120–1180)
French king, "Le Juen (the young)" who participated in the Second Crusade (1147–1149).

LOVE, PHYLLIS (b. 1925)
American actress who has performed in plays by Tennessee Williams (q.v.).

LOWER DEPTHS, THE (1902)
A play by Maxim Gorki (q.v.). See Nathan's profile of Strindberg.

LÜCHOW'S RESTAURANT
Originally on East 144th Street; See Nathan's profile of H. L. Mencken.

LUKS, GEORGE B. (1867–1933)
American painter and cartoonist who originated the comic strip "Hogan's Alley." His painting identified him as a member of the so-called Ashcan School. See Nathan's profile of Dreiser.

LUNT, ALFRED (1893–1977) AND LYNN FONTANNE (1887–1983)
American stage, screen, and television celebrities. In 1919 Alfred scored his first triumph in *Clarence* by Booth Tarkington (q.v.). Alfred married Lynn Fontanne in 1922. Thereafter the Lunts starred together in many plays, movies, and television productions—among them, *Sweet Nell of Old Drury* (1923), *The Guardsman* (1924), *Design for Living* (1933), *Idiot's Delight* (1936), *Amphitryon 38* (1938), *Oh Mistress Mine* (1945), and *The Visit* (1958ff.) See Maurice Zolotow, *Stage Struck* (New York: Harcourt Brace Jovanovich, 1965) and Jared Brown, *The Fabulous Lunts* (New York: Atheneum, 1986).

LUNT-FONTANNE THEATRE
1555 Broadway, between 46th and 47th Streets; it opened May 1948; previously the Globe Theatre, which had opened in January 1910.

LYCEUM THEATRE
The English Lyceum was popularized by Henry Irving (q.v.) and Ellen Terry (q.v.). The American Lyceum Theatre, at 149–157 West 45th Street between Broadway and Avenue of the Americas (6th Avenue) in New York, opened on 1 November 1903. It was opened by Daniel Frohman, the brother of Charles Frohman (q.v.).
Originally the Lyceum, near Athens, Greece, was a gymnasium where Aristotle (q.v.) taught (peripatetically—that is, walking back and forth). During the 19th century in England and America, a lyceum was a program of lectures popularized by adult education organizations.

LYONS, LEONARD (1906–1976)
Free-lancer New York newspaper columnist.

LYTTON, BULWER
See Bulwer-Lytton

MACARTHUR, CHARLES (1895–1956)
American journalist, playwright, and screenwriter. In 1928 he married the actress Helen Hayes (q.v.). See Hecht, Ben.

MCCLINTIC, GUTHRIE (1893–1961)
American director and producer in whose honor the Guthrie Theatre of Minneapolis was named. In 1921 he married the American actress Katharine Cornell (q.v.). See Nathan's *Encyclopedia of the Theatre* (New York: Knopf, 1940), p. 378.

MCCUTCHEON, GEORGE BARR (1866–1928)
American journalist, novelist, and frustrated playwright. After leaving Purdue University at the end of his sophomore year because he had devoted himself to too much unassigned writing, he worked as a reporter on the *Lafayette* (Ind.) *Journal* and later became City Editor of the *Lafayette Courier*. For both newspapers he was unofficially the drama reviewer. His reviews of major performers (including Modjeska, the Booths, and Minnie Maddern) were made possible as the Lafayette Opera House provided a one-night stand on a railroad stop between Chicago and Indianapolis. Among his Purdue lifelong friends were George Ade (q.v.) and Booth Tarkington (q.v.) before the latter transferred to Princeton.
In 1893 McCutcheon moved to Chicago, where he at first roomed with his brother John T. McCutcheon (q.v.) and with George Ade. According to *The Bookman,* George Barr McCutcheon's first two novels, *Graustark* and *Brewster's Millions,* at the turn of the century sold more than 5 million copies each. These were the first of 40 novels published mostly by Dodd, Mead and Co., New York. A few of these were dramatized by "play doctors" and were also sold to the movies. Early on, he became a millionaire, but he died broken-hearted, a frustrated and failed playwright. Several of his plays—among them *Brood House* and *The Man Who Loved Children*—were found in manuscript in a carton in the attic of the Purdue Library. For further details, see A. L. Lazarus and Victor H. Jones, *Beyond Graustark: George Barr McCutcheon, Playwright Discovered* (Port Washington and London: Kennikat Press, 1981).

MCCUTCHEON, JOHN T. (1870–1949)
Pulitzer Prize winning cartoonist; brother of George Barr McCutcheon (q.v.). His autobiography *Drawn from Memory* (Indianapolis: Bobbs-Merrill, 1950), was published posthumously.

MCFADDEN, BERNARR (1868–1955)
American physical culturist and publisher.

MACGOWAN, KENNETH (1888–1963)
American playwright, teacher, and producer. As a student at Harvard, he participated in the 47 Workshop of George Pierce Baker (q.v.). Upon graduation he became associated with the Provincetown Players (q.v.), of which he was a charter member, along with Robert Edmond Jones, Susan Glaspell, and her husband, George Cram Cook. Later Macgowan was associated with Guthrie McClintic (q.v.) in Minneapolis. Much later, Macgowan taught playwriting at UCLA. He was the author of *A Primer of Playwriting* (New York: Random House, 1951) and editor of *Famous American Plays of the 1920s* (New York: Dell, 1959).

MACK, JOHN ALFRED, SR. (CA. 1800–1891)
British playwright; author of *March Hares* (1879), a farce to be distinguished from a comedy of the same name by Harry Gribble (q.v.), produced in 1921.

MACKELLER, HELEN (b. 1891)
American actress who played the leading role in the first New York production of *Beyond the Horizon* by Eugene O'Neill (q.v.).

MACKEY, MARIE
See Corelli, Marie.

MACKLEN, CHARLES (1699–1797)
English playwright.

MCLAGLIN, VICTOR (1886–1959)
Anglo-American movie actor.

MACLEISH, ARCHIBALD (1892–1982)
American poet, playwright, and critic. From 1939 to 1944 he was Librarian of Congress and represented the United States at UNESCO (United Nations Educational, Scientific, and Cultural Organization). In 1949 he was appointed Boyleston Professor of Literature at Harvard University. He was the author of the verse play *Nobodaddy* (1926); and of such other works as *Conquistador* (1932); *Active and Other Poems* (1948); *The Trojan Horse* (1950); the play *J.B.* (1958), which was inspired by the ever enigmatic Biblical Book of Job; and a book of literary criticism, *Poetry and Experience* (1961). One of his most frequently quoted lines is from his poem "Ars Poetica" ("A poem should not mean but be").

MCLURE, S. S. (1857–1949)
Irish-American editor and publisher. He came to the United States in 1866. In 1884, in New York, he founded the first U.S. newspaper syndicate. In 1893 he acquired a magazine that came to be known as *McLure's* and which until its demise in the depression of 1929 competed with such other popular magazines as *Munsey's* and *The Saturday Evening Post*. Editors that McLure employed included Hamlin Garland (q.v.) and Willa Cather (q.v.). These editors succeeded in attracting a few prominent authors but not many of the calibre who published in such quality magazines as the *Atlantic, Harper's, Scribner's, Putnam's, The Century,* and *North American Review*. In 1929 *McLure's* merged with the *New Smart Set*. McLure's *My Autobiography* (New York: Frederick Stokes, 1914) was ghostwritten by Willa Cather.

MCRAE, BRUCE (1867–1927)
American actor and playwright.

MACY, JOHN (1877–1932)
American feminist critic.

"MADAME BUTTERFLY" (1898)
A short-story by John Luther Long (1861–1927); it was dramatized in 1900 by Long and David Belasco (q.v.) and in 1906 was made into an opera by Giacomo Puccini (1858–1924).

MADAME X (1910)
    A play by Alexandre Bisson (1848–1912).

MAD WOMAN OF CHAILLOT (1946)
    A play by Jean Giraudoux (q.v.).

MAETERLINCK, MAURICE (1862–1949)
    Major Belgian playwright, symbolist, and naturalist who wrote all his works in French. In 1911 he was awarded the Nobel Prize for Literature. He was the author of *Pelleas et Melisande* (1892), basis for the opera by Debussy; and *The Blue Bird* (1909; tr. 1911). He also wrote the well-known treatise *The Life of the Bee* (1907). Nathan made an unfavorable assessment of Maeterlinck in *The Theatre of the Moment* (New York: Knopf, 1936), pp. 231–32.

MAGELLAN, FERDINAND (1480–1521)
    Portuguese seaman; he was first to circumnavigate the world.

MAID OF THE OZARKS (1946)
    A play by Claire Parrish (fl. early 1900s). See Nathan's profile of O'Neill.

MAJOR BARBARA (1907)
    An anti-war play by George Bernard Shaw (q.v.).

MALAPROP, MRS.
    A character in the play *The Rivals* by Richard Brinsley Sheridan (q.v.). She was continually using near-miss words and expressions that sounded almost like the appropriate ones—for example, for allegation, "alligator"; for anecdote, "antidote"; for epithet "epitaph." In naming this character, Sheridan was informed by the French *mal à propos*, meaning "inappropriate." See, further, A. L. Lazarus and H. Wendell Smith, *The NCTE Glossary of Literature & Composition* (Urbana: National Council of Teachers of English, 1983).

MALVOLIO
    A conceited male character in Shakespeare's *Twelfth Night*.

MAN AND SUPERMAN (1903)
    A play by George Bernard Shaw (q.v.).

MAN OF MODE, THE (1676)
    A play by George Etherege (1635–1692).

MAN WITH A LOAD OF MISCHIEF, THE (1924)
    A play by S. Ashley Dukes (1885–1959).

MANN, HEINRICH (1871–1950)
    German novelist; brother of Thomas Mann (q.v.). Heinrich Mann was the author of *Professor Unrat* (1905), which was filmed as *The Blue Angel* (1930), starring Marlene Dietrich.

MANN, HORACE (1796–1859)
    American educator; "father of public education." He was a champion of higher education for women and became the first president of Antioch College.

MANN, LOUIS (1865–1931)
American actor and playwright.

MANN, THOMAS (1875–1955)
German novelist who in 1929 won the Nobel Prize for Literature. He escaped Nazi Germany and in 1944 became a naturalized American citizen. He was the author of *Buddenbrooks* (1901), *Death in Venice* (1912), and *The Magic Mountain* (1924). His short novel *Mario and the Magician* (1930) attacks fascism.

MANNERS, T. HARTLEY (1870–1928)
English actor and playwright who often played opposite Lily Langtry (q.v.). See Nathan's profile of Ferenc Molnar.

MANSFIELD, RICHARD (1854–1907)
Anglo-American actor of immense popularity. He began his career as a monologuist in England and later took roles in operettas by Gilbert and Sullivan (q.v.). Mansfield played Cyrano in Rostand's play and was even more successful in the leading role of Clyde Fitch's *Beau Brummel* (1890), the role that first made him a matinée idol. He climaxed his career in America by touring the country in Shakespearian roles. See Nathan's profile of Walter Hampden.

MANSHIP, PAUL (1885–1966)
American sculptor who created the *Prometheus* at Rockefeller Center, New York.

MANTELL, ROBERT (1854–1928)
Scottish actor and producer.

MANUEL I (1469–1521)
King of Portugal from 1495 to 1521.

MAN WHO ATE THE POPOMACK, THE (1924)
A play by J. W. Turner (fl. early 1900s).

MANTLE, BURNS (1873–1948)
American journalist. From 1919 until his death he edited an annual series of play synopses—"Best Plays of . . ."

MARCH HARES (1921)
A comedy by Harry Gribble (q.v.); to be distinguished from the comedy with the same name, that was produced in 1879 by John Alfred Mack Sr., (q.v.).

MARCH, IRIS
A character in *The Green Hat* (1924) by Michael Arlen (q.v.). In the movie version the role was played by Greta Garbo.

MARCO MILLIONS (1925)
A play by Eugene O'Neill (q.v.). O'Neill protested that all too many journalists were garbling the title as "Marco's." See Nathan's profile of O'Neill.

MARK HELLINGER THEATRE
1655 Broadway at the northwest corner near 51st Street. It opened in January

1949. It had originally been the Hollywood Theatre, which had opened in April 1930.

MARK TWAIN.
See Twain, Mark

MARQUIS, DON (1878–1937)
American journalist, humorist, poet, and playwright. He remains best known as the author of *archy and mehitabel* (1927), about the cockroach archy and the cat mehitabel. The cockroach was afflicted with literary ambitions but could not reach the shift key on the typewriter and hence could not make capital letters. The jazz opera *archy and mehitabel* by George Kleininger and Joe Danon was produced in 1954. Marquis's own plays include *The Old Soak* (1916).

MARS, ANTHONY (1861–1915)
English playwright.

MARS, LILY (1779–1847)
French comedienne born Anne Francoise Boutet. She made her reputation at the Theatre Français for her excellent interpretations of the plays of Moliere (q.v.).

MARTIN BECK THEATRE
302 West 45th Street between 8th and 9th Avenues, New York. It opened 11 November 1924.

MARX, KARL (1815–1883)
German political philosopher; best known for his treatise *Das Kapital* (1867), which denounces the capitalistic system. He wrote *The Communist Manifesto* (1848) in collaboration with Friedrich Engels (1820–1895). In 1849 Marx was expelled from Prussia and settled in England. A statue of him still stands in London's Highgate Cemetery.

MASK
See Dramatis Personae.

MASK
An English theatre-magazine edited from 1908 to 1929 by Gordon Craig (q.v.). This is to be distinguished from the play *The Mask* (1924) by H. M. Harwood and F. T. Jesse. See Craig's 9 January 1916 letter to Nathan, p. 199.

MASON, JOHN (1857–1919)
American actor; to be distinguished from the critic John Mason Brown (q.v.).

MASQUE
Sometimes a drama but always an aristocratic and allegorical entertainment using music, singing, dancing, elaborate stage sets and costumes. The earliest masques were essentially pantomimes, the speaking parts added later. Masques are also called court masques because they were almost always performed for royalty. For example, Samuel Daniel's *Vision of the Twelve Goddesses* (1604) was performed at the court of James I. It was an allegorical celebration of the blessings that that monarch had bestowed on England. For most of the Jacobean masques (during the era of the two Jameses until the closing of the theatres in 1642) the

chief staging designer was Inigo Jones (q.v.). Often a masque was given at a garden party, weather permitting, and involved audience participation (for example, in dance sequences). A prominent convention was the antimasque, which was a playful parody of the theme or story line of the main masque.

MASSEY, RAYMOND (b. 1896)
Canadian-American stage and screen actor and director who performed brilliantly in *Captain Brassbound's Conversion* (1923), *Abe Lincoln in Illinois* (1938), and *Pygmalion* (1945). In 1926 Massey directed O'Neill's *Beyond the Horizon;* and in 1949 he produced Strindberg's *The Father.* Since 1930 Massey has appeared in many films, with memorable roles as Abe Lincoln and as Sherlock Holmes. See Nathan's profile of Strindberg.

MASTERS, EDGAR LEE (1869–1950)
American poet best known as the author of *Spoon River Anthology* (1915). See Nathan's profile of H. L. Mencken.

MATERIA CRITICA (1924)
A book by George Jean Nathan.

"MATRON OF EPHESUS, THE"
A story by Petronius (q.v.). See Nathan's profile of Christopher Fry.

MATTHEWS, BRANDER (1852–1929)
American critic and teacher, long associated with Columbia University, to which he left his personal library, the nucleus of the Brander Matthews Dramatic Museum. His books include *Development of the Drama* (1903) and *Principles of Playmaking* (1919).

MATURIN, ERIC (1883–1957)
Anglo-Indian actor.

MAUGHAM, W. SOMERSET (1874–1965)
English fiction writer and playwright. Although trained as a physician, he left that profession for a career first as an artist, ultimately as a writer. His short story "Miss Thompson" was first published by Nathan in *Smart Set* and was later dramatized as *Rain* (1922). Maugham was also the author of *Of Human Bondage* (1915), *The Moon and Sixpence* (1919), *The Painted Veil* (1925), *Cakes and Ale* (1930), and *The Razor's Edge* (1944). His plays include *The Circle* (1921) and—his best known—*The Constant Wife* (1926). See Nathan's letter of 12 August 1953 to August Mencken, p. 232, and his profile of Maugham, p. 170.

MAYERLING
An Austrian village in the Vienna Woods. It was the site of a hunting-lodge where in 1889 Crown Prince Rudolf and Baroness Maria Vetsera died mysteriously. That event was the subject of the play *Masque of Kings* (1936) by Maxwell Anderson (q.v.). See Nathan's profile of Maxwell Anderson.

MEDEA
A legendary Greek princess who fell in love with Jason and helped him acquire the Golden Fleece, after which she married him and bore him two children. When Jason left her for a new love, Creusa, Medea killed her two children. This legend is

the subject of the play *Medea* by Euripides (q.v.). See Nathan's profile of Maxwell Anderson.

MELODRAMA
Literally, a play with music, although the only musical background during the 1800s was a tinny piano in the orchestra pit. Melodrama came to be a type of play using contrived situations and stereotyped characters (the drunken father, the lecherous landlord or mortgage holder, the innocent heroine's handsome but penniless fiancé). Popular during the 1800s in London music halls and American "opera houses," melodramas competed with Shakespearian plays on tour. The most popular melodramas included *East Lynne* (1884) and *M'Liss* (1887) Conventionally the audience indulged in hissing the villain. Several modern books about melodrama include the following; Frank Rahill, *The World of Melodrama* (Philadelphia: University of Pennsylvania Press, 1967); Peter Brooks, *The Melodramatic Imagination* (New Haven: Yale University Press, 1976); and David Grimsted, *Melodrama Revisited* (Berkeley: University of California Press, 1988). See Nathan's essay "On Melodrama," p. 70.

MENCKEN, AUGUST (FL. 1900S)
Brother of H.L. Mencken (q.v.).

MENCKEN, H. L. (1880–1956)
American editor and essayist who was co-editor with Nathan of the magazines *Smart Set* (1914–23) and the *American Mercury* (1924–33). Mencken's books include *Prejudices* (in six series, 1919–27); *The American Language* (1918), a monumental work of lexicography comparable with Samuel Johnson's (q.v.) *Dictionary;* and the autobiographical *Newspaper Days* (1941). Notable biographies of Mencken include those by William Manchester *Disturber of the Peace* (New York: Harper, 1951) and by Carl Bode *Mencken* (Carbondale: Southern Illinois Univ. Press, 1969). See profile of Mencken.

MEPHISTOPHELES
The devil in several literary works, notably in *Faust* by Goethe (q.v.).

MERIVALE, HERMAN (1839–1906)
American playwright.

METROPOLITAN OPERA HOUSE
Broadway to 7th Avenue; 39th and 40th Streets, New York. It opened on 22 October 1983.

MILLAY, EDNA ST. VINCENT (1892–1950)
American poet and playwright. In 1912, when she was barely out of her teens, her prize-winning poem "Renascence" was published in *The Lyric Year.* She lived in Greenwich Village and acted with the Provincetown Players (q.v.). She published several books of poetry, excelling in the sonnet form. *A Few Figs From Thistles* appeared in 1920. *The Harp Weaver & Other Poems* (1923) won a Pulitzer Prize. Among her often quoted lines: "My candle burns at both ends/It will not last the night/But ah, my foes, and oh, my friends, it gives a lovely light." Her plays include *Aria da Capo* (1919), *The Lamp and the Bell* (1921), and *Two Slatterns and a King* (1921). She also wrote the libretto for *The King's Henchmen* (1927), an opera composed by Deems Taylor (q.v.).

MILLER, ARTHUR (b. 1915)
American playwright whom Nathan encouraged. During the early 1930s Miller was a member of Kenneth Rowe's playwriting workshop at the University of Michigan, where Miller won a major Hopwood Award. It was in this workshop that he wrote the first draft of the play that would be produced several years later as *All My Sons* (1947). From 1956 to 1962 Miller was married to the actress Marilyn Monroe. Besides *All My Sons,* Miller's plays include *Death of a Salesman* (1949), *The Crucible* (1953), *A View from the Bridge* (1955), and *After the Fall* (1964). He also wrote the scenario for the film *The Misfits* (1961). In *Theatre of the Fifties* (New York: Knopf, 1953), p. 105, Nathan praised Miller for *Death of a Salesman* but derogated *The Crucible* for paying less attention to characterization than to propagandistic theme. See Miller's autobiography, *Time Bends* (New York: Grove Press, 1987).

MILLER, GILBERT (1884–1969)
Broadway producer; one of the theatre managers employed by the Frohman Syndicate (q.v.). Miller produced plays not only in New York but also in London, principally at the St. James Theatre. His productions—a long list of triumphs—include *Monsieur Beaucaire* (1919), *Peter Pan* (1920; 1922), *Berkeley Square* (1929), *Journey's End* (1929), *Strange Interlude* (1931), *The Petrified Forest* (1935), *Murder in the Cathedral* (1936), *Victoria Regina* (1938), *The Cocktail Party* (1950), *Caesar and Cleopatra* (1951), and *The Caine Mutiny* (1956).

MILLER, HENRY (1860–1926)
English actor and manager (to be distinguished from the Big Sur American novelist). See Nathan's profile of Winthrop Ames.

MILNE, ALAN ALEXANDER (1882–1956)
English writer best known as the author of books for children, including *When We Were Very Young* (1924), *Winnie the Pooh* (1926), *Now We Are Six* (1927), and *The House on Pooh Corner* (1928). He created the characters Pooh Bear, Piglet, Christopher Robin, and Eeyore. His plays include *Mr. Pim Passes By* (1920) and *The Dover Road* (1921). See Nathan's profile of Shaw.

MILTERN, JOHN (1870–1937)
American actor.

MILTON, JOHN (1608–1674)
English poet and tract writer. Among his numerous works, best known remain "L'Allegro and Il Penseroso" (1632), *Comus, a Masque* (1637), *The Doctrine and Discipline of Divorce* (1643), *Areopagitica* (1644), *Paradise Lost* (1667), *Paradise Regained* (1671), and *Samson Agonistes* (1672).

MIMES.
See Pantomime.

MINSKY, ABRAHAM (1881–1949)
New York theatrical manager who, along with his brothers Harold and Howard, produced popular burlesque shows.

MIRACLE PLAYS
Medieval plays based on the lives of saints and on Biblical themes and episodes. Cf. Morality Plays.

MISE EN SCÈNE
1. On stage and screen the set and properties.
2. The configuration or arrangement of actors in relation to the set and properties. See Nathan's profile of Dreiser.

"MISS THOMPSON"
A short story by W. Somerset Maugham (q.v.).

MITCHELL, LANGDON (1862–1935)
American playwright.

MIZENER, ARTHUR (b. 1907)
Cornell University professor and biographer; author of *This Side of Paradise*
(1951), a biography of F. Scott Figtgerald (q.v.). See Nathan's profile of Fitzgerald.

MODJESKA, HELENA (1844–1909)
Polish actress who achieved fame for her Shakespearian roles both in the United
States and abroad. She also triumphed in her portrayal of Nora in Ibsen's *A Doll's
House*. Both in New York and on tour she played opposite such celebrities as
Edwin Booth, Maurice Barrymore, and Otis Skinner. See Antoni Gronowicz,
Modjeska, Her Life and Loves (New York: Thomas Yoseloff, 1956).

MOLIÈRE, JEAN BAPTISTE POUQUELIN (1622–1673)
French actor and playwright, a giant figure in the history of drama. He was
influenced in part by the commedia dell'arte (q.v.). Initially working with a touring
company, he ultimately settled in Paris, where his company became the forerun-
ners of the Comèdie Française (q.v.). Moliere wrote satirical comedies and farces,
often on short notice from his patron, King Louis XIV. Moliere's best known plays
include *Les Precieuses Ridicules* (1659); *Tartuffe* (1664, tr. *The Hyprocrite*); *Don
Juan ou Le Festin de Pierre* (1665); *Le Physician Malgre Lui* (1666, tr. *The Doctor
in Spite of Himself*); *L'Avare* (1668, tr. *The Miser*); *Le Bourgeois Gentilhomme*
(1672, tr. *The Would-Be Gentleman*); and *The Imaginary Malady* (1673, concerning hypocondriacs). See the biography of Molière by Wyndham Lewis *The
Comic Mask* (New York: Coward McCann, 1959). See Nathan's profile of Rostand.

MOLNAR, FERENC (1878–1952)
Hungarian playwright and novelist. He was the author of *Liliom* (1909; tr. 1921)
which was made into the musical comedy *Carousel* (1944); *The Guardsman* (1910;
tr. 1924); *The Swan* (1920; tr. 1922); and *The Play's the Thing* (1928), adapted by
P. G. Wodehouse (q.v.). During the Nazi regime, Molnar fled to the United States.
Among Molnar's novels, *The Paul Street Boys* (1927) depicts Budapest boys
playing "war games." See David Belasco, "Foreword," *All the Plays of Molnar*
(New York: Vanguard Press, 1929).

MONKS ARE MONKS (1929)
Nathan's only novel. It contains a fictionalized profile of George Bernard Shaw.

MONTEZ, LOLA (1818–1861)
Irish-American dancer and adventuress, born Marie Gilbert. From 1847 to 1848
she was the mistress of Louis I of Bavaria. In 1851 she performed in the United
States: and, in 1855–56, in the music halls of Australia. She was the author of the
autobiographical *Anecdotes of Love* (1858). See Nathan's profile of Strindberg.

MOODY, WILLIAM VAUGHN (1869–1910)
American poet, teacher, and playwright. He was the author of *The Masque of Judgment* (1900), *The Fire Bringer* (1904), *The Sabine Women* (1906), *The Great Divide* (1909), and *The Faith Healer* (1909).

MOON FOR THE MISBEGOTTEN, A (1957)
A play by O'Neill (q.v.).

MOON IN THE YELLOW RIVER, THE (1931)
A play by Denis Johnston (fl. 1900s).

"MOON OF THE CARIBBEES, THE"
A play by O'Neill (q.v.).

MOONEY, THOMAS (1883–1942)
American labor agitator. See Nathan's profile of Dreiser.

MOORE, GEORGE (1852–1933)
Irish writer associated with William Butler Yeats and George Russell in the Irish literary renaissance (see Abbey Theatre). Moore remains best known for his novel *Esther Waters* (1894). Nathan called him "a scoffer at drama."; see his profile of Dreiser.

MOORE, THOMAS (1779–1852)
Irish poet and composer best remembered for *Irish Melodies* (1807–35), which contains the songs "Believe Me If All Those Endearing Young Charms" and "Oft in the Stilly Night." Several of Moore's songs were sung by characters in stories by James Joyce (q.v.). Moore was also the author of the novel *The Epicurean* (1827), the biography *A Life of Byron* (1830), and a *History of Ireland* (1846).

MORALITY PLAYS
Medieval verse plays in which virtues and vices—for example, temperance and greed—were personified. One of the best known morality plays remains *Everyman* (ca. 1500). Morality plays tended to be cruder than miracle plays (q.v.) especially when biblical morality plays were performed by players from crafts and guilds, a series that came to be known as "craft cycles." In York, for example, between 1350 and 1400, *Noah's Ark* was performed by shipwrights; *The Last Supper*, by cooks and bakers; *The Creation*, by plasterers; and *The Kings*, by goldsmiths. Cf. Interludes

MORGAN, CHARLES L. (1894–1958)
English playwright and critic. See Nathan's profile of Behrman.

MORLEY, CHRISTOPHER (1890–1957)
American editor, essayist, and playwright. He served as an editor at the Doubleday, Page publishing company and on the editorial board of the *Ladies' Home Journal*. From 1924 to 1941 he was a contributing editor to the *Saturday Review*. As reflected in two of his books, *Parnassus on Wheels* (1917) and *The Haunted Bookshop* (1919), he was an ardent bibliophile, as were his Dutch Treat Club friends Booth Tarkington and George Barr McCutcheon (q.v.). Morley's plays include *Three's a Crowd* (1920), which he wrote in collaboration with Earl Biggers (q.v.).

In 1928, unaware that his friend McCutcheon had been writing melodramas, Morley joined Cleon Throckmorton in founding the Hoboken (N.J.) Theatrical Company, which produced play revivals, mostly melodramas. Morley's novels include *Kitty Foyle* (1939), which was made into a successful movie. See Morley's autobiography, *John Mistletoe* (New York: Doubleday, 1952).

MORLEY, ROBERT (b. 1908)

English actor and playwright, the author of *Edward, My Son* (1947). In 1947 at the Old Vic in London (q.v.) he starred as Henry Higgins in Shaw's *Pygmalion*. He has also performed in several films.

MOROSCO, OLIVER (1876–1945)

American theatrical producer.

MORRIS, GOUVERNEUR (1752–1816)

American statesman who in 1792 served as U.S. Minister to France.

MOSCOW ART THEATRE

Russian national theatre; it was founded in 1898 by Vladimir Danchenko (1858–1943) and Konstantin Stanislavsky (1863–1938). It was devoted to realistic drama and to realistic (as opposed to stylized) acting. This theatre was the first to produce the plays of Anton Chekhov (q.v.). See Stanislavsky.

MOSTEL, ZERO (b. 1915)

American comic actor. He has performed as Shu Fu in *The Good Woman of Setzuan* (1956), as John in *Rhinoceros* (1961), and as Prologue in *A Funny Thing Happened on the Way to the Forum* (1962). He has also appeared in several movies, including *Waiting for Godot* (1961). See Jared Brown, *Zero Mostel: A Biography* (New York: Atheneum, 1989).

MOURNING BECOMES ELECTRA (1931)

A play by Eugene O'Neill (q.v.).

MOZART, WOLFGANG AMADEUS (1756–1791)

Precocious and prolific Austrian composer. He was the subject of the movie *Amadeus* (1985).

MR. GEORGE JEAN NATHAN PRESENTS (1917)

A book by Nathan.

MRS. WARREN'S PROFESSION (1893)

a play by George Bernard Shaw (q.v.).

MUMFORD, LEWIS (b. 1895)

American architect; author of *Utopia* (1922) and *The Brown Decades* (1931). See Wilfred McClay, "From the Belly of the Whale," *American Scholar* (Winter 1983) pp. 111; 198–205.

MUMMERS

Performers of dances and pantomimes in "mumming plays," a form of entertainment developed in England during the early 1600s. These skits were based on the legend of St. George and the Dragon and on the medieval sword dance that symbolized the earth's reawakening in the spring from the death of winter. See Alan Brody, *English Mummers and Their Plays* (Philadelphia: University of Pennsylvania Press, 1970). See Nathan's profile of Maurice Evans.

MURDER IN THE CATHEDRAL (1935)
A play by T. S. Eliot (q.v.) about the life and death of Thomas à Beckett (1118–1170). See Nathan's profile of Eliot.

MURPHY, ARTHUR (1727–1805)
Irish playwright.

MURRAY, JOHN (b. 1906)
American playwright and lyricist, born John Pfeferstein. Early in his career he contributed songs to several Ziegfeld Follies (q.v.). He collaborated with Allen Boretz (q.v.) on the play *Room Service* (1937) and on several of the Hallmark Hall of Fame television productions.

MUSIC BOX, THE
239-247 West 45th Street; owned by Irving Berlin and Sam Harris.

MUSIC MASTER, THE (1927)
A play by Charles Klein (1867–1915).

MY HEART'S IN THE HIGHLANDS (1939)
a play by William Saroyan (q.v.). See Nathan's profile of Saroyan.

NATHAN'S FAMILY
Frederick Nördlinger (fl. late 1700s), Nathan's maternal grandfather; pioneer and pillar of Fort Wayne, Indiana.
Hannah Nördlinger (fl. early 1800s), Nathan's maternal grandmother.
Charles Narat-Nathan (fl. late 1800s), Nathan's father.
Ella Nördlinger Nathan (fl. early 1900s), Nathan's mother.
Paul Nathan (fl. early 1900s), Nathan's uncle; a professor of history at Brussells University.
Charles Nördlinger (1863–1940), Nathan's uncle; a drama critic for the *New York Herald*.
Fred Nördlinger-Nixon (1837–1935), Nathan's uncle; an owner of theatres in Cleveland, Ohio.
Julie Haydon Nathan (b. 1910), Nathan's wife (married 1955).

NATION, THE
A weekly periodical founded in 1865 by E. L. Godkin. It has emphasized politics, literature, and the arts.

NATION, CARRY (1846–1911)
American temperance crusader.

NATIONAL THEATRE
208 West 41st Street between 7th and 8th Avenues, New York. It opened 1 September 1921 and re-opened 18 October 1959 as the Billy Rose Theatre.

NATIONAL THEATRE
Pennsylvania Avenue, Washington D.C. Founded in 1836, its stage has hosted such celebrities as Edwin Booth, James O'Neill, Sarah Bernhardt, Jenny Lind, Lillian Gish, George M. Cohan, Helen Hayes, John Gielgud, Judith Anderson. See *Stage for a Nation* ed., Douglas B. Lee et al (Lanham, Md.: University Press of America, 1986).

NATURALISM
In philosophy, a system that seeks to explain all phenomena in scientific and natural (as opposed to supernatural) terms; hence, a deistic and sometimes atheistic position. It is the opposite of idealism. Well known naturalistic philosophers include Aristotle (q.v.), Spinoza (q.v.), Nietzsche (q.v.), Darwin (q.v.), and William James (q.v.). In literature, a movement akin to realism (q.v.) but even more pessimistic. Naturalistic novels and plays emphasize the devastating forces of nature, the environment, and industry as they control the characters' behavior. *Nana* (1880), for example, by Emile Zola (q.v.) is a well known example of naturalism in French fiction. *Sister Carrie* (1900) by Theodore Dreiser (q.v.) is an example in American fiction. An example of a naturalistic play is *The Iceman Cometh* (1939) by Eugene O'Neill (q.v.), which is said to have been influenced by *The Lower Depths* (1903) by Maxim Gorki (q.v.). Regarding naturalism in novels and plays, an idealist has quipped that for the reader or spectator the experience is little more elevating than riding a glass-bottomed boat through a sewer.

"NEARER MY GOD TO THEE"
Refrain of a hymn by Sarah Flower Adams (1805–1898).

NEGATIVE CAPABILITY
This expression does not pertain to a lack of capability. Rather, it connotes a desirable quality that the poet John Keats introduced and described in a letter (21 December 1817) to his brothers George and Tom: ". . .At once it struck me what quality went to form a Man of Achievement, especially in Literature, and which Shakespeare possessed so enormously. . . . I mean Negative Capability; that is, when a man is capable of being in uncertainties, mysteries, doubts, without any irritable reaching after fact and reason . . ." Keats thus wished "to let one's mind be a thoroughfare for all thoughts; to let the subconscious do its work." In a letter to his friend Richard Woodhouse (27 October 1818) Keats wrote: "A poet . . . has no identity . . . he is continually filling some other body." See Aileen Ward, *John Keats, the Making of a Poet* (New York: Viking Press, 1963).
    Almost surely, Nathan rejected out of hand the idea of negative capability for playwrights; he expected playwrights to know quite specifically what they were about. Still, he did not subscribe to any such ideology as the power of positive thinking. In his essay "Intelligence and the Drama" (p. 76) he wrote, "Nothing is so corruptive of drama as hard logic. What the drama calls for is not mental intelligence but only emotional intelligence."

"NEGROES IN AMERICAN DRAMA"
An essay by Nathan, p. 77. See Leslie Catherine Sanders, *The Development of Black Theatre in America* (Baton Rouge: Louisiana University Press, 1988).

NEW AMSTERDAM THEATRE
214 West 42nd Street, between 7th and 8th Avenues, New York. It opened in October, 1903, with a production of Shakespeare's *A Midsummer Night's Dream*

(short run) and shortly thereafter with a long run of Winchell Smith's dramatization of *Brewster's Millions* by George Barr McCutcheon (q.v.). Ironically, the New Amsterdam was owned by Klaw and Erlanger, the lawyers associated with the Frohman Syndicate (q.v.), an enemy of McCutcheon and the Fiskes (q.v.).

NEWMAN, GREATEX (b. 1892)

Anglo-American lyricist and playwright; author of *The Optimists* (1929) and *Stop the Press* (1935). See Zelda Fitzgerald's letter of fall 1930 to her husband, p. 216.

NEWSWEEK

A weekly periodical founded in 1933 by Samuel Williamson.

NEW YORKER, THE

A sophisticated weekly magazine (to be distinguished from Horace Greeley's nineteenth century magazine of the same name) founded in 1925 by Harold Ross (1892–1951), q.v., who edited it until his death. He initiated the one-line cartoon; The "Goings on About Town" section, a directory of current stage and screen fare; and reviews of plays and movies. He cultivated such writers as James Thurber, Ogden Nash, Robert Benchley, Dorothy Parker, and Edmund Wilson. Under Ross's successor, editor William Shawn (b. 1907), the magazine underwent little change. On Shawn's retirement in 1987, Robert A. Gottlieb became the editor.

NEW YORK TIMES, THE

A daily newspaper founded in 1851 by Henry Raymond, George Jones, and Edward Wesley. In 1896 the paper was purchased by Adolph Ochs (1858–1925), who developed it into a major periodical boasting it prints "all the news that's fit to print." Ochs made the Sunday edition especially into a much sought-after source of reviews of stage and screen fare.

NEW YORK TRIBUNE, THE

A daily newspaper founded in 1841 as a weekly by Horace Greeley (q.v.).

NIEBELUNGEN, RING OF THE

See Richard Wagner.

NICCODEMI, DARIO (1874–1934)

Italian playwright and translator who wrote not only in Italian but also in French and Spanish. His own plays include *The Shadow* (tr. 1915) and *The Little Teacher* (tr. 1918).

NIETZSCHE, FRIEDRICH WILHELM (1844–1900)

German philosopher and classical scholar who rejected Christianity for naturalism (q.v.) that would go beyond good and evil. In 1889 he became blind and insane. He was the author of several prominent works, including *The Birth of Tragedy* (1872), *Thus Spake Zarathustra* (1883), (q.v.) and *Beyond Good and Evil* (1886), all of which strongly influenced Eugene O'Neill (q.v.). Nietzsche also unwittingly influenced the Nazis, who perverted his idea of Superman. See *Also Sprach Zarathustra*, p. 348. See Nathan's profile of H. L. Mencken.

NŌ (ALSO NOH) PLAYS

Oldest of Japanese dramatic forms, these date from the middle of the 1300s.

More than 500 of these plays have survived. They are performed by schools and companies using masks and elaborate costumes. The performers dance in deliberately slow rhythms against an obbligato of drums, flutes, and a chorus that chants the text. In the Western world, interest in these plays was stimulated by William Butler Yeats (q.v.) and Bertold Brecht (q.v.). See Arthur Waley, ed., *The Nō Plays of Japan* (New York: Grove Press, 1921; revised 1957).

NOVELLO, IVOR (1893–1951)
   Anglo-American actor, born David Ivor Davies. He was also a playwright, composer, and producer. He composed 60 songs, including "Keep the Home Fires Burning" (1915). His plays include *The Truth Game* (1928) and *Symphony in Two Flats* (1929). He became a matinée idol, not only in the movies but also when he starred in the musical comedies that he wrote: *Glamour Night* (1935), *Careless Rapture* (1936), *Crest of the Wave* (1937), *Perchance to Dream* (1945), and *King's Rhapsody* (1949). See Nathan's profile of Strindberg.

OBEY, ANDRÉ (1892–1975)
   French playwright.

O'CASEY, SEAN (1884–1964)
   Irish playwright who was admired and aided by Nathan. O'Casey grew up in the midst of poverty and violence, as reflected in the tragic irony of his plays. He was one of the leaders in the Irish Renaissance (*see* Abbey Theatre). His best known plays include *The Shadow of the Gunman* (1925); *Juno and the Paycock* (1925); *The Plough and the Stars* (1926), which touched off a riot in the Abbey Theatre; *The Silver Tassle* (1928); *Within the Gates* (1933), which Nathan helped bring to New York; *Red Roses For Me* (1942); *Cock-a-Doodle Dandy* (1949); and *The Bishop's Bonfire* (1955). Among his six biographical works, best known remains *Sunset and Evening Star* (London: Macmillan, 1959). See Nathan's profile of O'Casey.

ODETS, CLIFFORD (1906–1963)
   American playwright associated with the Theatre Guild (q.v.), the Group Theatre, and the Hollywood movie industry. He was the author of *Waiting for Lefty* (1935), *Awake and Sing* (1935), *Golden Boy* (1937), *The Flowering Peach* (1954) and other plays and movies. See Nathan's profile of Odets in *Passing Judgments* (New York: Knopf, 1935), pp. 163–65.

OEDIPUS REX (CA. 429 B.C.)
   A tragedy by Sophocles (q.v.).

O'FLAHERTY, LIAM (1897–1984)
   Irish novelist and playwright; author of *The Informer* (1925), *Mr. Gilhooley* (1926), *The Assassin* (1928), *Famine* (1937), *Land* (1946), and *Insurrection* (1951), most of which are set in nineteenth century Ireland and are good examples of naturalism (q.v.). Several have been made into films. See his autobiography, *Shame the Devil* (Dublin: Wolfhound Press, 1934). See also Nathan's profile of Helen Hayes.

O. HENRY (1862–1910)
   Pen-name of William Sidney Porter. American journalist and short-story writer who was the author of such story collections as *Cabbages and Kings* (1904), *The*

Four Million (1906), and *Rolling Stones* (1912). His best known short stories include "Gift of the Magi," "Ransom of Red Chief," "A Retrieved Reformation," and "Alias Jimmy Valentine." Most of his stories draw on his own adventuresome career. In writing plays, O. Henry collaborated with the well known columnist Franklin P. Adams (1881–1960). The annual O. Henry awards for best short stories were named in his honor. See Karen Blansfield, *Cheap Rooms and Restless Hearts* (Bowling Green, Ohio: Bowling Green State University Press, 1988). See Nathan's profile of Theodore Dreiser.

O'KEEFE, JOHN (1747–1833)
Irish playwright.

OLCOTT, CHAUNCEY (1860–1932)
American minstrel, librettist, and song-writer, best known for his song "My Wild Irish Rose."

OLDCASTLE, SIR JOHN, LORD COBHAM (?1378–1417)
A leader of the Lollards, a group of religious heretics and activists against materialism and war. In 1414 Oldcastle was imprisoned in the London Tower, escaped, was recaptured, hanged, and burned at the stake. See Nathan's profile of Maurice Evans.

OLD HOMESTEAD, THE (1915)
A play by Denman Thompson (1833–1911).

OLD MAID, THE (1924)
A novelette by Edith Wharton (q.v.), which was dramatized in 1935 by Zoë Aikens (1886–1958). See Nathan's profile of Helen Hayes.

OLD VIC THEATRE, LONDON
It opened in 1818 as the Coburg Theatre; re-opened as the Victorian Theatre in 1833. Although it featured melodramas and popular music-hall fare, it was condemned as a brothel and closed in 1880. In the same year, it was bought by Emma Cons (fl. 1800s) and re-opened as a temperance amusement palace called the Royal Victoria Hall and Coffee Tavern. In 1912 Cons's niece Lillian Bayliss (1874–1917), a theatrical producer, took it over to produce classical dramas and operas. In 1931 the production of operas moved to the Sadler's Wells Theatre, the Old Vic concentrating on classics, including Shakespeare. A renovated Old Vic re-opened in 1950. In 1963 the Old Vic became the home of the National Theatre Company, under the direction of Sir Lawrence Olivier (q.v.). See Ronald Bergan, *The Great Theatres of London* (San Francisco and London: Chronicle Books, 1988), pp. 110–14.

OLIN LIBRARY, CORNELL UNIVERSITY.
Home of the major Nathan collections; they were bequeathed by Nathan to Cornell, his alma mater. Curator is Donald Eddy (b. 1929).

OLIVER, EDNA MAY (1885–1942)
American stage and screen actress.

OLIVIER, SIR LAWRENCE (1907–1989)
English stage and screen actor.

O'NEILL, NANCE (1874–1974)
American actress, born Gertrude Lamson.

O'NEILL, CARLOTTA MONTEREY (1888–1970)
Third wife of Eugene O'Neill (q.v.).

O'NEILL, EUGENE (1888–1953)
American playwright, Nobel Laureate of 1936. Son of the celebrated Irish actor James O'Neill and a drug-addicted mother, Ella Quinlan O'Neill, who had been a convent classmate of Nathan's mother. Eugene traveled as a boy all over the country before he was sent to a Catholic boarding school. During some of the summers when James was not on tour the family managed to re-unite in New London, Connecticut. In 1903 the 15-year-old Eugene was shocked by his mother's attempt to drown herself in the Thames River.

In 1906, on the strength of his father's reputation, Eugene was accepted into Princeton University but was expelled the next year because of disorderly conduct. Renouncing his Catholic upbringing, Eugene began to frequent saloons and brothels. At age 21, during a brief marriage to Kathleen Jenkins, he fathered a son, who would one day commit suicide. Eugene and Kathleen were divorced in 1910.

An avid reader, Eugene was especially influenced by Baudelaire, Nietzsche (q.v.), Ibsen (q.v.), and Strindberg (q.v.). He was also attracted to sea life. About 1912 he shipped out to Honduras, where he contracted but survived malaria; shipped to Argentina and worked his way back on a freighter to New York. Once back in the United States, he lived in a flophouse above a saloon in lower Manhattan, barely surviving by doing menial work, but writing assiduously when not working. After a six months' bout with tuberculosis, he obtained a job as a reporter on the *New London Telegraph* but realized he needed to complete his education. In 1913 he was accepted at Harvard where he enrolled in the playwriting workshop under George Pierce Baker (q.v.). Here O'Neill wrote and rewrote many one-act plays, one of which, "Bound East for Cardiff," was produced in Cape Cod by the Provincetown Players, which he had joined, along with classmate Kenneth Macgowan in 1915.

In 1918 O'Neill married the short-story writer Agnes Boulton. They had two children, Shane and Oona, but were divorced in 1928. In 1929 Eugene married the actress Carlotta Monterey, who was to nurse him through many afflictions, including his fatal Parkinson's disease. O'Neill renounced his daughter Oona, who at 18 married the actor Charles Chaplin.

As early as 1917 O'Neill's promise as a genius was recognized by the drama critic George Jean Nathan, his senior by only six years. But it was not until May 1919 that they met in person. In *Smart Set* Nathan had published three of O'Neill's one-act plays—"The Long Voyage Home" (October, 1917), "Ile" (May, 1918), and "The Moon of the Caribbees" (August, 1918). Nathan had also brought O'Neill's full-length play *Beyond the Horizon* to the attention of the Broadway producer John Williams (q.v.).

O'Neill was the prolific author of successful, intermingled with unsuccessful, plays: *Bound East for Cardiff and Other Plays* (1916); *The Moon of the Caribbees and Other One-Act Plays of the Sea* (1919); *Exorcism* (1919); *Gold* (1920); the Pulitzer Prize play *Beyond the Horizon* (1920); *Diff'rent* (1920); *The Emperor Jones* (1921); the Pulitzer Prize play *Anna Christie* (1922); *The Hairy Ape* (1922); *Welded* (1923); *Desire Under the Elms* (1924); *All God's Chillun Got Wings* (1924), in which a white woman is married to a black man; *The Great God Brown* (1925); *Lazarus Laughed* (1926); the 9-act play *Strange Interlude* (1928), which used a technique akin to stream of consciousness (q.v.); *Marco Millions* (1928); *Dynamo* (1929); *Mourning Becomes Electra* (1931); *Ah, Wilderness!* (1933); *Days Without End* (1934); *The Iceman Cometh* (1946); the posthumously published *Long Day's Journey Into Night* (1956); *A Moon for the Misbegotten* (1957); *Touch of the Poet* (1958); and *More Stately Mansions* (1959). See O'Neill, *The Complete Plays* (New York: Library of America, 1988); Arthur and Barbara Gelb, *O'Neill* (New York: Harper, 1962); Nancy and Arthur Roberts, eds. *As Ever Gene: The Letters of Eugene O'Neill to George Jean Nathan* (Madison, N.J.: Fairleigh Dickinson University Press, 1987); Travis Bogard and Jackson Bryer, eds. *Selected Letters of Eugene O'Neill* (New Haven: Yale University Press, 1988).

See also Nathan's profile of O'Neill.

O'NEILL, JAMES (1847–1920)

Father of Eugene O'Neill (q.v.), he was best known for his leading role in Dumas' *The Count of Monte Cristo* (adapted in 1883 for the stage by G. H. Andrews). With very few interruptions, James appeared in over 6,000 performances.

ON THE PHONE (1917)

A play by George Broadhurst (q.v.), adapted from the Hungarian play *Hallo* by Imre Földes.

OPPENHEIM, E. PHILLIPS (1866–1946)

English author of over 150 novels. See Nathan's profile of Pirandello.

OUR TOWN (1938)

Best known play by Thornton Wilder (q.v.) It opened on 4 February 1938 at the Henry Miller Theatre and remains one of the most popular productions in American schools and colleges. One of its leading characters is the Stage Manager, who, from one end of the stage, comments as a kind of author-mouthpiece. See Edith Oliver, "Whose Town?" *The New Yorker* (19 December 1988), p. 82.

OUTRAGEOUS FORTUNE (1942)

A farce by Ben Travers (1886–1953). See Nathan's essay "Myself," p. 33.

OUTSIDER, THE

A play (1924) by H. D. Saddler; a play (1928) by Evelyn Neurenburg. See Nathan's profile of Katharine Cornell.

PANTOMIME

The art of acting by means of gestures and facial expressions with no speech, as in charades. A comic art, it originated in antiquity in several cultures. It was popular in ancient Rome, in the medieval *commedia dell'arte* (q.v.), and in the *Grand Guignol* (q.v.) In modern times the star pantomimist, after Charles Chaplin, is Marcel Marceau (b. 1923).

PARADOX

A seeming inconsistency; for example, "The first shall be last." Cf. Chesterton's *Tremendous Trifles*. See Bert States, *The Shape of Paradox* (Berkeley: University of California Press, 1978).

PARIS, UNIVERSITY OF
Also known as the Sorbonne, although the latter is only one of the colleges; it is on the left bank (Latin Quarter) of the River Seine. The University of Paris, founded in 1250, originally trained theology students.

PARKER, DOROTHY (1893–1967)
American humorist and screenwriter, born Dorothy Rothschild. Early in her career she was encouraged by Harold Ross, editor of *The New Yorker* (q.v.), who published many of her humorous pieces. She is probably best remembered for her quip "Men do not make passes at women who wear glasses."

PASTICHE
A literary work that pieces together imitations from a variety of sources. Examples include *The Waste Land* by Eliot and Nathan's *The Avon Flows*.

PASTOR, TONY (1837–1908)
American actor, theatre manager, and developer of vaudeville (q.v.). In the Bowery, he opened in 1865 Tony Pastor's Opera House, which, like most other so-called opera houses of those times, was devoted less to opera than to vaudeville.

PAVLOVA, ANNA (1882–1931)
Famous Russian ballerina. See Paul Magriel, *Pavlova, an Illustrated Album* (New York: Holt, 1947).

PAXINOU, KATINA (b. 1900)
Greek actress, translator, and theatrical producer. In Athens she translated and directed English-language plays, including *Volpone* by Ben Jonson (q.v.), *Anna Christie* by Eugene O'Neill (q.v.), and *Ghosts* by Henrik Ibsen (q.v.). In 1939 she toured England and Germany, playing the role of Ruth Atkins in O'Neill's *Beyond the Horizon*. Her film roles include those of Pilar in *For Whom the Bell Tolls*.

PEABODY, JOSEPHINE (FL. EARLY 1900S)
American playwright; author of *The Piper* (1911).

PEARN, VIOLET (FL. EARLY 1900S)
American playwright; author of *Hush!* (1916).

PEG O' MY HEART (1913)
A play by J. Hartley Manners (1870–1928). See Nathan's profile of Molnar.

PELOPONNESIAN WARS
The wars (431–404 B.C.) between Athens and Sparta resulting in the defeat of Athens and its ultimate decline.

PENNINGTON, ANN (1893–1970)
Popular American dancer and actress.

PERIPETY
In a plot, usually in tragedy, a reversal or an ironic complication, twist, or turn of events.

PERKINS, MAXWELL (1884–1947)
American editor at Scribner's who helped develop the talents of such writers as Fitzgerald, Hemingway, and Thomas Wolfe chiefly through the techniques of tightening their writing. See M. S. Burt, ed., *Editor to Author: Letters of Maxwell Perkins* (New York: Grosset & Dunlap, 1950).

PETER I ("THE GREAT" 1672–1725)
Russian czar who strove to westernize the institutions and manners of his times. In 1725 he founded the Russian Academy of Sciences, transferred the capital from Moscow to St. Petersburg (now Leningrad), and moved most of his previously collected treasures to the Leningrad Hermitage, one of the world's foremost art museums. One of his celebrated biographers was Voltaire (q.v.).

PETRONIUS, TITUS (D. 66 A.D.)
Roman official and writer; he was the author of *The Satyricon,* including the story "The Matron of Ephesus," which formed the basis for a one-act play by Gotthold Lessing (q.v.); and for the play *The Lady's Not for Burning* by Christopher Fry (q.v.). See Nathan's profile of Christopher Fry.

PHANTOM OF THE OPERA (1925)
A silent-screen play by Elliot Clawson (fl. 1900s), based on the novel of the same name by Gaston Leraux (fl. late 1800s). The role of Erik (the phantom) was played by Lon Chaney (1883–1930). This silent film influenced many other horror films including the 1946 sound film *Beauty and the Beast* by Jean Cocteau (1869–1963). The popularity and durability of *Phantom of the Opera* are reflected in its 1988 revival by Andrew Lloyd Weber (b. 1948)

PHI BETA KAPPA
An honorary academic society founded in 1776 at the College of William and Mary. The Greek letters stand for Philosophia, Biou, Kubernetes—philosophy the guide of life. A perusal of *Who's Who in America* reveals that many men and women of achievement (including Nathan) were as undergraduates elected to Phi Beta Kappa. The society's quarterly journal is *The American Scholar,* which is published at its headquarters in Washington, D.C.

PHILANDERER, THE (1914)
A play by George Bernard Shaw (q.v.).

PHILLIPS, DAVID GRAHAM (1867–1911)
American feminist novelist and playwright. His novels include *Susan Lennox* (1917), and his plays include *The Worth of a Woman* (1908). That play is reprinted in A. L. Lazarus, ed., *The Indiana Experience* (Bloomington: Indiana University Press, 1977). See Nathan's profile of Theodore Dreiser.

PHILIPPOTEAUX, HENRI (1815–1884)
French artist who specialized in historical and battle scenes.

PHOENIX TOO FREQUENT, A (1946)
A play by Christopher Fry (q.v.).

PHYRONISM
An alternate form of pyronism or arson. See Nathan's profile of O'Neill.

PICARESQUE
Pertaining to a picaro or rascal; fewer plays than novels have been built around this type of character. See Ulrich Wicks, "The Nature of Picaresque Narrative," *PMLA* (March 1974) pp. 240–49.

PICON, JACINTO (1852–1923)
Anti-clerical Spanish novelist and critic. Picon is also a beverage.

PINERO, SIR ARTHUR WING (1855–1934)
English playwright and essayist; his best known plays include *The Second Mrs. Tanqueray* (1893) and *Trelawney of the Wells* (1898). See Nathan's profile of Katharine Cornell.

PIPER, THE (1911)
A play by Josephine Preston Peabody (fl. early 1900s). See Nathan's profile of Winthrop Ames.

PIRANDELLO, LUIGI (1867–1936)
Major Italian poet, fiction writer, and playwright. In 1934 he received the Nobel Prize for Literature. Early in his career, when he was a literature teacher in a girls' school, he established his own theatre in Rome. His earliest works, especially his fiction, reflect his interest in Sicilian folklore. He wrote more than 40 plays, of which the best known include *Cosi è se vi pare (Right You Are If You Think You Are,* 1918), *Six Characters in Search of an Author* (1922), *The Pleasure of Honesty* (1922), and *As You Desire Me* (1931). In most of his plays the theme centers in the search for distinction between illusion and reality. See Lander MacClintock, *The Age of Pirandello* (Bloomington: Indiana University Press, 1951). See also Nathan's profile of Pirandello.

PISA AND LUCA, BATTLES OF (1200S, ITALY)
Battles betwen Guelphs and Ghibellines.

PISCATOR, ERWIN (1893–1966)
German theatrical producer noted for his staging innovations (for example, use of news reels in competition with actors' dialogue or movements); he was very much interested in expressionism (q.v.).

PITKIN, WALTER (1878–1953)
American journalist; author of *Life Begins at Forty* (1932). See Nathan's profile of Oscar Wilde.

PITOËFF, GEORGES (1886–1939)
French actor and director admired by Eugene O'Neill. See Nathan's profile of Max Reinhardt.

PIXÉRECOURT, RENÉ (1773–1844)
"Father of melodrama."

PLAY-WITHIN-A-PLAY
A brief scene (a kind of parenthesis) within a main action, usually with the major character(s) looking on. Example: the Players' scene in *Hamlet*. In Elizabethan

plays such an episode if used at all often came at the beginning and was called an induction.

PLEASURE MAN, THE (1928)
A play by Mae West (q.v.). See Nathan's essay "Myself," p. 33.

PLESSIS, LE
The O'Neills' chateau in France.

PLOT
Rising suspensive action toward a goal; action in which the protagonist overcomes (as in comedy) or fails to overcome (as in tragedy) successive obstacles of mounting intensity. Encountering the most intense obstacle constitutes the climax (q.v.), the Greek word for "ladder". From there to the end of the play, the action is said to be falling. The falling action in comedies is called the denouement (q.v.). Most scenes of a plot are related by a cause-and-effect action.

PLOUGH AND THE STARS, THE (1925)
A play by Sean O'Casey (q.v.).

PLYMOUTH THEATRE
226–240 West 45th Street between Broadway and 8th Avenue, New York. It opened on 10 October 1917 and was owned by the Shuberts (q.v.).

POETIC JUSTICE
In any play—especially in melodramas and operettas—poetic justice is said to be served when the villain gets his due, as in the operettas of Gilbert and Sullivan (q.v.). Poetic justice may also pertain to the just reward earned by a good person.

POLICHINELLE
Obsolete form of Punchinello (q.v.). *See* Commedia Dell'arte.

POLLOCK, CHANNING (1880–1946)
American playwright, composer, and critic. He began his career as a drama critic for the *Washington Post,* where he attacked both pornography and censorship. He also contributed drama reviews to *Smart Set* (q.v.). For Fanny Brice (q.v.), Pollock wrote the popular song "My Man." His 30 plays include *The Pit* (1904) and—in collaboration with Avery Hopwood (q.v.)—*Clothes* (1906).

POLLOCK, JACKSON (1912–1956)
American painter devoted to the abstract.

PONCE DE LEON (1460–1521)
Spanish explorer in search of a fountain of youth; an associate of Christopher Columbus. De Leon's search is the subject of *The Fountain* (1926) by Eugene O'Neill (q.v.).

PONTOPPIDAN, HENRIK (1859–1943)
Danish novelist and playwright who in 1917 shared the Nobel Prize for Literature with Karl Giellerup. Pontoppidan was the author of such realist works as *Clipped Wings* (1881) and *The Promised Land* (1896).

POOR LITTLE RICH GIRL (1913)
A play by Eleanor Gates (1874–1951).

POPE, ALEXANDER (1688–1744)
Major English poet and satirist. His best known works include *Essay in Criticism* (1711), *Rape of the Lock* (1714), and *The Dunciad* (1728).

POPULAR THEATRE, THE (1918)
A book by Nathan.

PORTER, COLE (1893–1964)
Major American popular lyricist; one of the many Hoosier natives (among them Lew Wallace, George Ade, Theodore Dreiser, Booth Tarkington, and George Barr McCutcheon) who became prominent in the world of literature and theatre arts. Porter was author or co-author of such stage successes as *Greenwich Follies of 1925, 50 Million Frenchmen* (1928), *Anything Goes* (1934), *Red Hot and Blue* (1936), *Panama Hattie* (1940), *Something for the Boys* (1943), *Kiss Me, Kate* (1948), *Can-Can* (1953), and *Silk Stockings* (1958), several of which were adapted to the cinema. His best known films include *Night and Day* (1946), *High Society* (1956), and *Les Girls* (1957). His best known songs include "Night and Day," "Begin the Beguine," "In the Still of the Night," "I've Got You Under My Skin," and "You'd Be So Nice to Come Home to." (In 1954 Random House published *103 Lyrics by Cole Porter.*)
Most of the originals of Cole Porter's works as well as many of his sound-recordings are in the Beinecke Library of Americana, Yale University. For a profile of Porter see Brendan Gill, "Wouldn't It Be Fun?" *The New Yorker* (18 September 1971) pp. 48–64.

PORTER, KATHERINE ANNE (1890–1980)
Major American fiction writer who was the author of the novel *Ship of Fools* (1962), which in 1963 was adapted to the cinema. Her short-story collections include *Flowering Judas* (1930) and *Pale Horse, Pale Rider* (1934). In 1935 her *Collected Short Stories* won a Pulitzer Prize.

PORTO-RICHE, GEORGES DE (1849–1930)
French playwright; author of *L'amoureuse* (1891) and othe psychological dramas dealing with marital triangles. See Nathan's profile of T. S. Eliot.

POTTER, PAUL (1853–1921)
American playwright.

POWER, TYRONE (1914–1958)
American movie actor and matinée idol.

POWYS, LLEWELYN (1884–1939)
English essayist; brother of the better known John Cowper Powys (1872–1960). See Nathan's profile of T. S. Eliot.

PREJUDICES, FIRST SERIES (1919)
First of a series by Mencken (q.v.).

PRE-RAPHAELITES

A school of Victorian artists and writers including Dante Rossetti, John Millais, Holman Hunt, Edward Burne-Jones, and William Morris. The Pre-Raphaelite Brotherhood ("PRB") published the periodical *The Germ* (fl. late 1800s), which contained their manifestos. In revolt against Victorian academism, they advocated a return to art as they regarded it to be before the time of Raphael (1483–1520). They admired hedonistic realism and sensuous details. A contemporary critic, Robert Buchanan, attacked their eroticism in his essay "The Fleshly School." But the eminent essayist John Ruskin (1819–1900) came to their defense in his letters to the *London Times* and in his book *Pre-Raphaelitism* (1851). See also Jerome Buckley, ed., *The Pre-Raphaelites* (Cambridge: Harvard University Press, 1968)

PROBLEM PLAY

Any play that deals with a serious issue—for example, emancipation of women as in *A Doll's House* (1879) by Henrik Ibsen (q.v.). The term is also a private joke among producers and script doctors.

PROPERTIES (PROPS)

Stage furniture (main props) and artifacts that are not just ornaments but are actually used by the characters as part of their "stage business"—for example, exercise equipment, tea servers, knitting materials, and periodicals. O'Neill's producers chided him for not having any character use (shout from) the men's room, stage left, although this "THIS IS IT" was technically less a prop than part of the *mise en scene* (q.v.).

PROTAGONIST

Chief character; hero or heroine.

PROVINCETOWN PLAYERS, THE (FL. EARLY 1900S)

A little-theatre group founded by Susan Glaspell (q.v.) and her husband, Ralph Adams Cram, in Provincetown, Mass. They produced several one-act plays by Eugene O'Neill (q.v.). *See* Provincetown Playhouse.

PROVINCETOWN PLAYHOUSE

135 MacDougal Street between 3rd and 4th Avenues, New York. It opened in November 1918 with a program of one-act plays including "Where the Cross Is Made" by Eugene O'Neill (q.v.).

PULITZER, JOSEPH (1847–1911)

American journalist and newspaper publisher. In 1883 he bought *The New York World*. In 1912 he founded the School of Journalism at Columbia University and established the annual Pulitzer Prizes. See William Stuckey, *The Pulitzer Prizes* (Norman: Oklahoma University Press, 1966).

PUNCH MAGAZINE

See Taylor, Tom.

PUNIC WARS, THE

Between Rome and Carthage; the first occurred between 264 and 241 B.C., the second, between 218 and 201 B.C., and the third, between 149 and 146 B.C. They ended in the defeat and destruction of Carthage, the ancient city near the present site of Tunis, northern Africa. In ancient times Carthage was the home of Queen

Dido, who was enamored of Aeneas. See *The Aeneid* by Virgil (70–19 B.C.) in Robert Fitzgerald's translation (New York: Random House, 1984).

PUSHKIN, ALEKSANDR (1799–1837)
Major Russian poet, novelist, short-story writer, and playwright. He remains best known for *Eugene Onegin* (1831), a novel in verse; it was the basis for Tchaikovsky's opera of the same name (1879).

"QUEM QUAERITIS TROPE, THE" (NINTH CENTURY)
One of the first religious playlets; a dialogue between the three Marys and the guardian angels at the tomb of Jesus.

> *Interrogatio (of the angels).* Quem quaeritis (whom are you seeking) in sepulchro, O Christicolae?
> *Responsio (of the Marys).* Jesum Nazarenum crucifixum.
> *Angels.* Non est hic; surrexit (he has risen), sicut praedixerat (even as he had predicted). Ite (Go) nunciate quia surrexit de sepulchra.

Ever since the early 800s this dialogue has been incorporated into the Catholic Easter mass. See Michal Kobialka, "The Quem Quaeritis: Theatre History Displacement," *Theatre History Studies,* vol. 8, 1988. (Grand Forks: University of North Dakota).

QUINLAN, ELLA (FL. 1800S)
A classmate of Nathan's mother at St. Mary's Convent Academy, which is associated with the University of Notre Dame, South Bend, Indiana. Ella Quinlan married James O'Neill (q.v.), the father of Eugene O'Neill and became the latter's mother.

RACINE, JEAN (1639–1699)
Major French playwright who, like Corneille (q.v.), specialized in classical tragedy, although with more psychological introspection. Racine's plays include *Andromache* (1667), *Berenice* 1671), *Iphigenia en Aulide* (1674), *Phèdre* (1677), and *Esther* (1689). John Masefield and Robert Lowell have been among Racine's translators. The definitive biography is by Geoffrey Brereton (London: Cassell, 1974). See also Lytton Strachey, *Books and Characters* (London: Chatto and Windus, 1922). See Nathan's profile of Max Reinhardt.

RAFFLES (1930)
A popular play by E. W. Horning (1866–1921).

RAIN (1922)
A film based on W. Somerset Maugham's short story "Miss Thompson," which Nathan had published in *Smart Set*. The story was adapted to the screen by Clemence Randolph (1899?–1970) and J. Colton (1886–1946). See Nathan's profile of Maugham.

RAIN FROM HEAVEN (1934)
A play by Elmer Rice (q.v.).

RALEIGH, CECIL (1856–1914)
English playwright.

RANDOLPH, CLEMENCE (1899?–1970)
English actress and playwright who, with J. Colton (1886–1946), adapted Somerset Maugham's short story "Miss Thompson" into the play and movie *Rain* (1922).

RAPHAEL SANZIO (1483–1520)
Renaissance Italian painter. In 1514 he was appointed chief architect of St. Peter's Cathedral, Rome. Raphael's many paintings include *Saint Michael* (ca. 1501), *Portrait of Balthazar Castiglione* (1516), and *Victory of Leo IV at Ostia* (ca. 1520). In Victorian England the Pre-Raphaelite Brotherhood (q.v.) espoused the conviction that most artists since the times of Raphael left all too much to be desired.

RASCOE, BURTON (1892–1957)
American journalist.

RATTIGAN, TERENCE (1911–1977)
English playwright and screenwriter. His best known works include *The Winslow Boy* (1947) and *The Browning Version* (1948).

REESE, LIZETTE WOODWORTH (1856–1935)
American poet best remembered for her poem "Tears." See Nathan's letter of 1924 to H. L. Mencken, p. 209.

REHAN, ADA (1860–1916)
Popular Irish-American actress. Born Ada Crehan in Ireland, she came to the United States when she was very young. From 1879 to 1899 she was a member of a touring company headed by Augustin Daly (q.v.), in which she starred in his adaptations of French and German comedies.

REHEARSAL, THE (1672)
A comedy attributed to George Villiers, second Duke of Buckingham (1628–1687).

REID, HAL (1860–1920)
American melodramatist, born James Hallock. See Nathan's profile of Strindberg.

REINHARDT, MAX (1873–1943)
Austrian-American director and producer, born Max Goldman. His major productions included *Oedipus Rex, Faust, A Midsummer Night's Dream,* and Gorki's *The Lower Depths.* See Nathan's profile of Reinhardt.

RENNIE, JAMES (b. 1890)
Canadian actor and writer.

REPARTEE
Witty exchange of short explosive lines; stichomythy; conversational ping-pong.

REVELLE, ARTHUR HAMILTON (1873–1858)
European actor.

RICE, ELMER (1892–1967)
American novelist, playwright, and screenwriter. Early on, he abandoned a career in law. His play *On the Trail* (1914) was one of the first to incorporate cinematic effects. His play *The Adding Machine* (1923) reflected the influence of German expressionism (q.v.). *Street Scene* (1929) won a Pulitzer Prize. *The Left Bank* (1931) satirized American expatriates in Paris. His other plays include *Counselor at Law* (1931), *We, the People* (1933), *Judgment Day* (1934), *Between Two Worlds* (1935), *Two on an Island* (1940), and *Dream Girl* (1945). See his autobiography, *Minority Report* (New York: Simon and Schuster, 1963). See Nathan's negative appraisal (probably premature) in *Passing Judgments* (New York: Knopf, 1935), pp. 163–65.

RICHMAN, ARTHUR (1886–1944)
American playwright.

RILEY, JAMES WHITCOMB (1849–1916)
Hoosier poet.

RING OF THE NIBELUNG
See Richard Wagner.

"RIP VAN WINKLE" (1819)
A story by Washington Irving (1783–1859), it was dramatized (1859 and 1865) by Dion Boucicault (q.v.) and provided for Joseph Jefferson (q.v.) a lifelong role. See Nathan's profile of Jefferson.

RISE OF SILAS LAPHAM, THE (1885)
A novel by W. D. Howells (q.v.). See O'Neill's letter of 4 November 1919 to Nathan, p. 201.

RISTORI, MADAME ADELAIDE (1822–1906)
Italian actress.

RITTNER, THADDEUS (TADEUSZ) (1873–1921)
Polish playwright and novelist. See Nathan's profile of Rostand.

RIVALS, THE (1775)
A play by Richard Brinsley Sheridan (q.v.).

ROBARDS, JASON, JR. (b. 1922)
American stage and screen actor.

ROBESON, PAUL (1898–1976)
American actor and singer who starred in O'Neill's *The Emperor Jones* (1920) and *All God's Chillun Got Wings* (1924). Robeson is also remembered for his rendition of the song "Ole Man River" in Jerome Kern's *Show Boat* (1928; film, 1936). See Leslie Catherine Sanders, *The Development of Black Theatre in America* (Baton Rouge: Louisiana University Press, 1988); also Nathan's essay "Negroes in American Drama," p. 77.

ROBINSON, LENNOX (1886–1958)
Manager of the Abbey Theatre (q.v.).

ROCKEFELLER CENTER
A complex of buildings and recreation areas in central Manhattan between 48th and 51st Streets, 5th Avenue, and Avenue of the Americas (6th Avenue). The Center embraces the 70-story RCA building, Radio City Music Hall, the Time-Life building, and an outdoor skating rink.

RODGERS, RICHARD (1902–1979)
American composer who collaborated with the lyricist Lorenz Hart (1895–1943) in writing musical comedies. Their best known include *Babes in Arms* (1937), with its songs "Where Or When" and "The Lady is a Tramp"; *The Boys From Syracuse* (1938) with its song "Falling in Love with Love"; and *Pal Joey* (1940), with its song "Bewitched, Bothered and Bewildered." Rodgers also collaborated with the lyricist Oscar Hammerstein II (q.v.) in writing *Oklahoma* (1943), with its songs "Oh, What a Beautiful Morning," "The Surrey with the Fringe On Top," and "People Will Say We're in Love"; *Carousel* (1945), with its song "You'll Never Walk Alone"; *South Pacific* (1949), with its songs "Younger than Springtime," "Some Enchanted Evening," and "I'm Gonna Wash That Man Right Outa My Hair"; *The King and I* (1951), with its song "Getting to Know You"; and *The Sound of Music* (1959), with its songs "My Favorite Things" and "Climb Every Mountain." See Deems Taylor, *Some Enchanted Evenings, The Story of Rodgers and Hammerstein* (New York: Harper, 1953).

ROGERS, WILL (1879–1935)
American humorist and actor. See Homer Croy *Our Will Rogers* (New York: Duell, Sloan, and Pearce, 1953).

ROOM SERVICE (1936)
A comedy by Allen Boretz (1909–   ) and John Murray (1906–   ) produced in 1937 by George Abbott (q.v.) at the Cort Theatre and later made into the screen musical *Step Lively.*

ROOSEVELT, THEODORE (1858–1919)
Twenty-sixth President of the United States.

"ROPE, THE" (CA. 1917)
a one-act play by O'Neill (q.v.).

ROSE MONDAY (1900)
A play by Otto Hartleben (1864–1905).

ROSS, HAROLD (1892–1951)
Editor of *The New Yorker* (q.v.) from 1925 to 1951. Aside from his astute choices of what went into that magazine, Ross is well remembered as being a meticulous grammarian. For example, he would not tolerate indefinite references of pronouns: in marking up an otherwise publishable manuscript, he would ask, in the margins, such questions as "Who he?" or "Who she?" or "What does which refer to?" See James Thurber, *The Years with Ross* (Boston: Atlantic/Little, Brown, 1957; reprinted 1981). See also Nathan's letter of 17 August 1950, to August Mencken, p. 230.

ROSTAND, EDMOND (1864–1918)
Romantic French poet and playwright best remembered for his poignant comedy

Cyrano de Bergerac (1897), with a leading role ensuring the successful careers of many an actor in several countries. Rostand was also the author of *Les Romanesques* (1894, tr. *The Fantastics,* 1900); *The Princess Far Away* (1895), which he wrote for Sarah Bernhardt (q.v.); *L'Aiglon* (1900, tr. *The Eaglet*), a six-act play about Napoleon's son, a role glamorized by Sarah Bernhardt; and *Chantecler* (1910), a role popularized by Maude Adams (q.v.) in the United States. See Nathan's profile of Rostand.

ROUSSEAU, JEAN JACQUES (1712–1778)
Major Swiss-French philosopher and writer. He contributed articles on music—he had been an amateur composer—to the *Encyclopedie* edited by Denis Diderot (1713–1784). In 1749 Rousseau won first prize in the Dijon Academy essay contest. In this essay he contended that man is by nature good but is corrupted by so-called civilization—a theme that was to permeate most of his subsequent writing. Besides his novel *Julie; or the New Heloise* (1761), his best known philosophical works include *The Social Contract* (1762) and *Emile* (1762), a treatise on ideal education. His writings were so controversial, and his love affairs so anti-social, he was compelled to flee to England. Here he was befriended as a guest by the philosopher David Hume (1711–1776). At Hume's residence, Rousseau wrote the first part of his *Confessions* (1781), revealing details of his many love affairs. In 1749 Rousseau had married a young serving-girl, Therese Levasseur. Rousseau's doctrines influenced Wordsworth, Shelley, and other romanticists. See a well known sceptical appraisal entitled *Rousseau and Romanticism* by Irving Babbitt (1865–1933) (Boston: Houghton Mifflin, 1919). Nathan appears to have agreed with Babbitt on at least the issue mentioned above.

ROWE, NICHOLAS (1674–1718)
English playwright and editor. His plays include *The Ambitious Stepmother* (1700). *Tamerlane* (1710), and—his best—*The Fair Penitent* (1703). But above all, Rowe remains celebrated for his edition of Shakespeare (1709), which was the first published edition to divide the plays into acts and scenes.

ROYALTON HOTEL
44th Street, New York; Nathan's residence from 1907 to 1958.

RUBENS, PETER PAUL (1577–1640)
Flemish painter. His best known works include *Elevation of the Cross* (1610), *The Last Judgment* (1616), *Marie de Medici* (ca. 1624), *Rape of the Sabines* (1634), *Venus and Adonis* (1635), and *The Judgment of Paris* (1638).

RUNNYMEDE
A meadow in England, south of the Thames River, where in 1215 King John accepted the Magna Carta. In Runnymede, too, there stands a memorial to John F. Kennedy.

RUSSELL, BERTRAND (1872–1970)
English mathematician and philosopher. In 1918 he was imprisoned because of his pacifist pronouncements. In 1950 he won the Nobel Prize for Literature. Earlier, he had collaborated with Alfred North Whitehead (1861–1947) on *Principia Mathematica* (1910). Russell was also the author of *A History of Western Philosophy* (1945) and the controversial *Marriage and Morals* (1929). See his *Autobiography* (Boston: Little, Brown, 1967).

RUSSELL, LILLIAN (1861–1922)
American singer and actress, born Helen Louise Leonard. In New York, early in her career, she was introduced as "The American Beauty" by Tony Pastor (q.v.). She later became a close friend of Diamond Jim Brady (q.v.). She performed often at Weber and Fields' Music Hall (q.v.) and for the McCaull Opera Company. See Parker Morrell, *Lillian Russell, the Era of Plush* (New York: Random House, 1940). See also Nathan's letter of 1 July 1953 to August Mencken, p. 231.

SACRÉ COEUR (SACRED HEART)
The cathedral that crowns the Montmartre, Paris.

SACRED NINE (THE MUSES)
Calliope, epic poetry; Clio, history; Erato, love poetry; Euterpe, lyric poetry; Melpomene, tragedy; Polyhymnia, sacred poetry; Terpsichore, choral song and dance; Thalia, comedy; and Urania, astronomy.

ST. JAMES THEATRE
246–256 West 44th Street between Broadway and 8th Avenue, New York. It opened in December 1932. It had previously opened in December 1927 as the Erlanger Theatre. There is also a St. James Theatre in London.

SAINT JOAN (1934)
A play by George Bernard Shaw (q.v.). See Nathan's profile of Katharine Cornell.

SALVATION NELL (1908)
A melodrama by Edward Sheldon (q.v.), a first draft of which he wrote when he was a student at Harvard in George Pierce Baker's Workshop 47. (q.v.). The heroine, Nell Sanders, upon losing her job as a bar girl, turns to the Salvation Army for work and rehabilitation. She succeeds with the help of Lieutenant Maggie O'Sullivan. Apparently not all melodrama was to be condemned: see Nathan's essay "On Melodrama," p. 70. *Salvation Nell* premiered on 17 November 1908, at the Hackett Theatre, which Harrison Grey Fiske (q.v.) had rented. Starring in the play was of course his wife, Minnie Maddern Fiske (q.v.). There were hundreds of performances. A reviewer wrote "Mrs. Fiske, in the manner of a slender ribbon of pale light, brings to the part of Nell, the saved girl of the slums, a little strange face with the look of dawn upon it and a voice of spring . . ." See P. C. Griffith, *Mrs. Fiske* (New York: Neale Publishing Co., 1912) p. 38.

SAM HARRIS THEATRE
226 West 42nd Street between 7th and 8th Avenues, New York. It opened in February 1921. It had originally opened in May 1914 as the Candler Theatre.

SAM SHUBERT THEATRE
225–233 West 44th Street between Broadway and 8th Avenue, New York. It opened 9 October 1913 with a production of *Hamlet*.

SANDBURG, CARL (1878–1967)
American poet and biographer, best remembered for his "Chicago" poems and for his biography of Abraham Lincoln.

SANDOW, EUGENE (1867–1928)
German-American physical culturist; see Nathan's profile of Sinclair Lewis.

SANTA ROSA, S. S.
The Grace Line cruiser on which Nathan and Julie Haydon were married in 1955.

SAPOLIO
A soap advertised in song during the early days of radio; see Nathan's profile of Walter Hampden.

SARDOU, VICTORIEN (1831–1908)
French melodramatist prominent in the late 1800s; he was also the author of the historical melodrama *Fedora* (1882). He and Sarah Bernhardt were close friends. See Nathan's profile of Theodore Dreiser.

SAROYAN, WILLIAM (1908–1981)
American playwright and novelist who was encouraged by Nathan. Saroyan's novels include *The Human Comedy* (1942). His plays include *The Daring Young Man on the Flying Trapeze* (1934); *Inhale and Exhale* (1936); *Little Children* (1937); *The Trouble with Tigers* (1938); *My Heart's in the Highlands* (1939); *The Time of Your Life* (1939), for which he declined to accept a Pulitzer Prize; *Love's Old Sweet Song* (1940); *The Beautiful People* (1941); and *The Bicycle Rider of Beverly Hills* (1952). See his autobiography, *My Name is Aram,* (New York: Harcourt Brace Jovanovich) 1940). See Lawrence Lee and Barry Gifford, *Saroyan* (New York: Paragon House, 1987). See also Nathan's profile of Saroyan.

SARTRE, JEAN PAUL (1905–1980)
French existentialist philosopher and playwright. In his essay *Being and Nothingness* (1943) he expounded his conviction that man is a responsible but lonely being who has been set adrift in a meaningless universe. During World War II he was a member of the anti-fascist resistance, and during the Nazi occupation of France, he wrote such plays as *The Flies* (1943) and *No Exit* (1944). His later plays include *The Respectful Prostitute* (1947), *Dirty Hands* (1948), *The Devil and the Good Lord* (1951), and *The Condemned of Altorea* (1956). His works of literary criticism include *What is Literature?* (1948). In 1946, with Simone de Beauvoir (q.v.), his lifelong friend, he founded and edited the periodical *Les Temps Modernes*. In 1964 he declined the Nobel Prize for Literature on the rationale that it exerts too much influence that is often unjustifiable. See Existentialism.

SATURDAY REVIEW
A weekly literary review founded in 1924 by Henry Seidel Canby (1878–1961) of Yale, Christopher Morley (q.v.), Amy Loveman, and William Rose Benet (q.v.). Originally named *Saturday Review of Literature*, it shortened its name to *Saturday Review* in 1952. Besides addressing readers interested in literature, music, and theatre arts, it discussed political, economic, educational, and other cultural issues. One of its most prominent editors was Norman Cousins (q.v.). This American *Saturday Review* is to be distinguished from the much older British *Saturday Review*, on which George Bernard Shaw (q.v.) served as drama critic.

SCALA
See La Scala.

SCARLET PIMPERNAL, THE (1905)
A popular romantic novel by the Hungarian-British Baroness Magdalena Orczy (1865–1947). This book was many times adapted to stage and screen.

SCENARIO
Outline or detailed synopsis of a movie; an even more condensed version is known as a "treatment."

SCENE
1. In old long plays, divisions within an act, with or without curtain-dropping, to indicate change of time and/or place of the action.
2. A synonym for set or stage set. For purposes of economy, most modern plays use a single set for the entire play. Set or setting is also known as *mise en scène*, although that French term connotes a certain aesthetic effect created by set, props, lighting, costumes, etc. in reciprocal configuration.

SCHELLING, ERNEST (1876–1939)
American composer and conductor.

SCHLEGEL, FRIEDRICH (1772–1829)
German critic and philosopher.

SCHMITZ, ETTURE
See Svevo, Italo.

SCHNITZLER, ARTHUR (1862–1931)
Austrian novelist and playwright who gave up a career as a physician, devoting himself to literature and theatre arts. Schnitzler's fiction, much of which uses the stream of consciousness technique (q.v.), includes *Leutnant Gasti* (1901), (tr *None But the Brave* 1931); *Die Toten Schweigen* (1897), tr *The Dead Are Silent* (1947); and *Flight Into Darkness* (1931). His plays include *Anatol* (1893), (tr. by Harley Granville-Barker) (q.v.); *Liebelei* (1895); *The Green Cockatoo* (1899); *The Reckoning* (1907); *Light O'Love* (1912); and *Professor Bernhardt* (1912). Schnitzler's best known plays remain the Anatol series (1900s), which depict sophisticated Viennese marriage. Schnitzler was one of Nathan's favorites. See R. Urbach, *Arthur Schnitzler*. (New York: Ungar, 1971). Nathan's profile of Schnitzler is combined with that of Rostand, p. 122.

SCHÖNBERG, ARNOLD (1874–1951)
German-American composer.

SCHOPENHAUER, ARTHUR (1788–1860)
German misogynist philosopher; his best known work remains *The World as Will and Idea* (1819), which influenced Nietzsche (q.v.) See Nathan's profile of Florenz Ziegfeld.

SCHORER, MARK (1908–1977)
American biographer and essayist, author of *Sinclair Lewis, An American Life* (New York: McGraw-Hill, 1961).

SCHOOL FOR SCANDAL (1771)
A play by Richard Brinsley Sheridan (q.v.).

SCRIBNER'S MAGAZINE
A literary monthly founded in 1870 by Charles Scribner Sr. (1821–1871). In 1881 that periodical became *The Century Magazine*. In 1887 Charles Scribner Jr. (1854–1930) founded a new *Scribner's*. He also donated to Princeton University the Princeton University Press building.

SEA GULL, THE (1896)
A play by Chekhov (q.v.).

SEDGWICK, ELLERY (1872–1960)
Editor of the *Atlantic Monthly* from 1908 to 1938. See his autobiography, *The Happy Profession* (Boston: Little, Brown, 1946). See Nathan's letter of 1924 to H. L. Mencken, p. 209.

SELWYN, ARCHIBALD (1877–1959)
American theatrical producer.

SELWYN, EDGAR (1875–1944)
Actor, playwright, and producer.

SELWYN, RUTH (1905–1954)
American actress and producer.

SELWYN THEATRE
229–231 West 42nd Street between 7th and 8th Avenues; it opened 3 October 1918. See O'Neill's letter of 4 November 1919 to Nathan, p. 201.

SERRANO, VINCENT (1870–1935)
American actor; on tour, an idol.

SET TO MUSIC (1939)
A musical revue by Noel Coward (q.v.)

SEVEN DEADLY SINS, THE
Pride, lechery, envy, anger, covetousness, gluttony, and sloth; these were often personified in medieval literature, especially in morality plays (q.v.).

SEVEN KEYS TO BALDPATE (1913)
A novel by Earl Biggers (q.v.); in 1913 it was melodramatized by George M. Cohan (q.v.). It ran for many performances on Broadway, and in 1935 it was made into a movie.

SEVENTH HEAVEN (1920)
A play by Austin Strong (1881–1952). It had a long run both at the Booth Theatre in 1922 and at the ANTA Theatre in 1955, and was later made into a successful movie, starring Janet Gaynor.

SEYMOUR, JOHN D. (b. 1897).
American actor; see Nathan's profile of Strindberg.

SHAKESPEARE, WILLIAM (1564–1616)
England's greatest dramatist. See Marchette Chute, *Shakespeare of London* (New York: Dutton, 1949).

SHAW, ALBERT (1857–1947)
American editor.

SHAW, GEORGE BERNARD (1856–1950)
Major Anglo-Irish playwright and critic. In 1925 he won the Nobel Prize for Literature. For a long time he was a member of the (socialist) Fabian Society. In 1895 he became the drama critic of the English *Saturday Review*. Aside from his pamphlets, treatises, and play prefaces, he remains best known for his plays. These include *Candida* (1893); *Arms and the Man* (1894), the title echoing the first line "arma virumque cano" of Virgil's epic poem *The Aeneid; The Devil's Disciple* (1897); *Mrs. Warren's Profession,* which appeared in his collection *Plays Pleasant and Unpleasant* (1898); *Caesar and Cleopatra* (1898); *Major Barbara* (1905); *Man and Superman* (1905); *The Doctor's Dilemma* (1906); *Androcles and the Lion* (1912); *Heartbreak House* (1913); *Pygmalion* (1913), which in 1956 was adapted to the musical *My Fair Lady; Back to Methuselah* (1921); and *Saint Joan* (1923). The definitive biography remains that by Hesketh Pearson (London: Collins, 1942). See Nathan's fictionalized profile of Shaw.

SHELDON, EDWARD (1866–1946)
American playwright; a member of Workshop 47 (q.v.). At the age of only 22, he was the author of *Salvation Nell* (q.v.). See Eric Barnes, *The Man Who Lived Time* (New York: Scribner's, 1958).

SHERIDAN, FRANK (1869–1943)
American actor.

SHERIDAN, RICHARD BRINSLEY (1751–1816)
English playwright best known for his comedies *School for Scandal* (1771) and *The Rivals* (1775). See Alice Glasgow, *Sheridan of Drury Lane* (New York: Frederick Stokes, 1940).

SHERMAN, LOWELL (1885–1934)
American actor and film director.

SHERMAN, STUART (1881–1926)
American teacher and critic.

SHERWOOD, ROBERT (1896–1955)
American playwright and critic. In the 1919–20 season he served as drama critic for *Vanity Fair* and shortly thereafter as movie critic for the old *Life Magazine*. His best known plays include *The Petrified Forest* (1935); the anti-war *Idiot's Delight* (1936), the hero-worshipping *Abe Lincoln of Illinois* (1938), and *There Shall Be No Night* (1940).

SHIPMAN, SAMUEL (1883–1937)
American playwright; see Nathan's profile of Katharine Cornell.

SHORE ACRES (1912)
A play by James A. Hearne (1839–1901).

SHUBERT, THE BROTHERS SAM (1876–1905), JACOB (1880–1963) AND LEE (1875–1953)
Theatrical producers and theatre managers; see Nathan's profile of George Abbott.

SIDDONS, SARAH (1755–1831)
Celebrated English actress, born Sarah Kemble.

SIDNEY, SYLVIA (b. 1910)
American actress, born Sophia Koson. See Nathan's profile of Katharine Cornell.

SIENKIEWICZ, HENRYK (1846–1916)
Polish fiction writer best known for his novel *Quo Vadis?* (1896), which was made into a popular movie.

SIERRA, GREGORIO MARTINEZ (1881–1947)
Spanish playwright and director; see Nathan's profile of Max Reinhardt.

SIGNIFICANT PAUSE
An actor's deliberate pause in stream and tempo of speech in order to emphasize the word or phrase that will follow. Audiences, almost always aware of what will follow, enjoy the anticipation and affirmation or the pleasant disappointment of expectation.

SIMONSON, LEE (1888–1967)
American stage and set designer for the Washington Square Players (q.v.), The Theatre Guild (q.v.), and the Metropolitan Opera Company; his books include *The Art of Scenic Design* (Westport, Ct.: Greenwood Press, 1950).

SINCE IBSEN (1933)
A book by Nathan. Cf. George Bernard Shaw's *Quintessence of Ibsen* (1891).

SIROVICH, WILLIAM (1882–1939)
New York state congressman who in January, 1932, blamed drama critics for depression in the theatres.

SITWELL, EDITH (1887–1964)
English poet noted for her originality in the use of exotic and onomatopoetic words and images, as demonstrated in her collection *Façade and Other Poems* (1950). Her phonograph album of that collection was set to music composed by William Walton (fl. early 1900s) and produced by an amateur group in a London fire station.

SITWELL, OSBERT (1892–1969)
English author and light versifier; his *Collected Poems and Satires* appeared in 1931. He was the brother of Edith Sitwell (q.v.).

SKINNER, CORNELIA OTIS (1901–1979)
American actress and writer; daughter of Otis Skinner. See Emily Kimbrough, *Our Hearts Were Young and Gay* (New York: Dodd, Mead, 1942).

SKINNER, OTIS (1858–1942)
American actor on stage and screen whose best known roles include those in *Kismet* (1911), *Merry Wives of Windsor* (1927), and *The Merchant of Venice* (1931). See Cornelia Otis Skinner, *Family Circle* (Boston: Houghton Mifflin, 1948).

SKINNER, RICHARD DANA (1893–1945)
American critic; see Nathan's profile of Eugene O'Neill.

SLAPSTICK
In vaudeville (q.v.), farce (q.v.), and vulgar comedy since medieval interludes (q.v.), the use of nonsensical, often physical actions—for example, pratfalls or beatings with sticks. See Buster Keaton, *My Wonderful World of Slapstick* (Garden City: Doubleday, 1960).

SMART SET
Best remembered as the magazine brilliantly edited by Nathan and H. L. Mencken between 1914 and 1923 (with offices at 34th Street and 8th Avenue), although a periodical by the same name had been founded in 1890 by "Colonel" William D'Alton. D'Alton's periodical, touted "A Magazine of Cleverness," proved a failure within ten years. He sold it to J. A. Thayer, who in 1912 hired as editor the capable W. H. Wright (q.v.). For details of the handing over of the editorship to Nathan and Mencken, see the introduction, p. 16. See, also, Fitzgerald's letter of December, 1923, to Bernard Vaughan, p. 208.

SMITH, NEWMAN (FL. EARLY 1900S)
Husband of Zelda Fitzgerald's sister Rosalind; see Zelda's letter of fall 1930 to Scott, p. 216.

SMITH, T. R. (1860–1933)
Managing editor of *The Century* magazine; see Nathan's profile of Sinclair Lewis, p. 180.

SMITH, WINCHELL (1871–1933)
American actor, playwright, and director; in 1906 he staged his dramatization of *Brewster's Millions* by George Barr McCutcheon (q.v.). It enjoyed a long run at the New Amsterdam Theatre, New York. Smith's even bigger success came with his play *Lightnin'* (1918), which he wrote in collaboration with Frank Bacon (1864–1922); it ran for 1,291 performances.

SOAP OPERA
1. Serialized ephemeral play aired on radio and television under the sponsorship of soap companies and other commercial enterprises.
2. In general, a derogatory term applied by critics to any play which resembles such a play.

SOCK
See Buskin.

SOLILOQUY
Thinking out loud; a character's speech addressed to the audience, usually when he or she is alone on stage. For example: Hamlet's "To be or not to be, that is the question" speech in act 3, scene 1 of the Shakespeare play.

SOPHOCLES (CA. 496 B.C.–406 B.C.)
Major Greek playwright of numerous tragedies; of those that have survived, the best known include *Antigone* (ca. 441 B.C.); *Oedipus Rex* (ca. 429 B.C.), which Aristotle (q.v.) called the perfect example of a tragedy; *Philoctetes* (409 B.C.); and *Oedipus of Colonus* (407 B.C.)

SOTHERN, EDWARD HUGH (1859–1933)
American actor and matinée idol whom Charles Frohman (q.v.) chauvinistically introduced as "from England." Sothern starred in many Shakespearian roles opposite Julia Marlowe (q.v.), whom he married in 1911. In 1908 at the Hackett Theatre, Sothern starred in *The Prisoner of Zenda,* a dramatization of Anthony Hope's swashbuckling novel. The play, one of the most popular of its time, had a long run. In 1915 at the Booth Theatre he played in *Our American Cousin* by Tom Taylor (q.v.). This was the play President Lincoln attended in Ford's Theatre in Washington, D.C., the night he was assassinated by John Wilkes Booth in 1865.

SOUND OF HUNTING, A (1945)
A play by Harry Brown (fl. 1900s).

SOUTH PACIFIC (1943)
A musical by Richard Rodgers (q.v.); see Nathan's profile of Strindberg.

SPENDER, STEPHEN (b. 1909)
English poet and critic.

SPINOZA, BARUCH (1632–1677)
Major Dutch-Jewish philosopher. By trade a lens grinder, he had fled from the Inquisition of Spain. In 1673 he declined the offer of a professorship at Heidelberg University (q.v.). A devotee of Descartes, Spinoza edited several of Descartes' works. Spinoza's own works include *On the Improvement of Understanding* (ca. 1670) and *Ethics* (1675). Like Descartes, Spinoza was a pantheist of sorts and influenced such idealists as Goethe (q.v.) and Lessing (q.v.). See S. P. Kashap, *Studies in Spinoza* (Berkeley: University of California Press, 1972).

SPOOK SONATA, THE (1907)
Also known as *The Ghost Sonata,* a play by Strindberg (q.v.).

SQUIRE, J.C. (1884–1958)
An English playwright.

STAGE BUSINESS
Characters' use of properties (q.v.); also a character's physical actions.

STALLINGS, LAURENCE (1894–1968)
American novelist, playwright, and screenwriter; he was the author of the novel *Plumes* (1924) and of the play *What Price Glory* (1924) in collaboration with Maxwell Anderson (q.v.). His best known films include *The Big Parade* (1925) and *A Farewell to Arms* (1930), his adaptation of Hemingway's novel. In 1933 Stallings published *The First World War,* photographic essays against war.

STANDING, SIR GUY (1873–1937)
English actor.

STANDING, HERBERT (1884–1955)
English actor.

STANISLAVSKY, CONSTANTIN (1863–1938)
Major Russian director, teacher, producer; born Constantin Aleyseyev. In 1938, with Vladimir Danchenko (q.v.) he founded the Moscow Art Theatre, where he directed and produced several plays by Chekhov (q.v.). Echoing the tenets of Lessing's *Hamburgishche Dramaturgie* (q.v.), Stanislavsky strove to eliminate mechanical gestures in acting. He emphasized, rather, the importance of the actor's "becoming the role" and using natural voice and gestures—the heart of the celebrated Stanislavsky Method. His books include *An Actor Prepares* (1936), *Making a Character* (1950), *Creating a Role* (1951), and *My Life in Art* (1924). See Christine Edwards, *The Stanislavsky Heritage* (NY: NY University Press, 1965); Nikolas Gorchakov, *Stanislavsky Directs* (NY: Funk & Wagnalls, 1968); and David R. Jones, *Great Directors at Work* (Berkeley: University of California Press, 1986).

STANLAWS, PENRYHN (1877–1957)
Penname of Penryhn Adamson.

STAPLETON, MAUREEN (b. 1925)
American actress.

STEELE, RICHARD (1672–1729)
Major English essayist and playwright who collaborated with Joseph Addison (q.v.) on contributing essays to the periodicals *The Tatler* (1709–11) and *The Spectator* (1711–12). Steele's plays include *The Funeral* (1701), a sentimental comedy; *The Lying Lover* (1703); *The Tender Husband* (1705); and—his last and best—*The Conscious Lovers* (1722). In 1720 Steele founded *The Theatre,* one of the first periodicals of theatre criticism. See Nathan's profile of Shaw.

STEFFENS, LINCOLN (1866–1936)
American journalist; see Nathan's profile of Theodore Dreiser.

STEINBECK, JOHN (1902–1968)
American novelist who won the Nobel Prize for Literature in 1962. His works include *Pastures of Heaven* (1932); *To a God Unknown* (1933); *Tortilla Flat* (1935); *In Dubious Battle* (1936); *Of Mice and Men* (1937), a play that was made into a movie; *The Grapes of Wrath* (1939), a Pulitzer Prize novel that was made into a movie; *Sea of Cortez* (1941): *The Red Pony* (1945); *The Wayward Bus* (1947); *The Pearl* (1947); *East of Eden* (1952), which was made into a movie starring James Dean; *The Short Reign of Pippin IV* (1957); *The Winter of Our Discontent* (1961); and *Travels with Charley* (1962). He was also the author of several screen plays including *Viva Zapata!* (1952). See Nathan's profile of Steinbeck in *The Theatre Book of the Year 1950–51* (New York: Knopf, 1951), pp. 209–12.

STELOFF, FRANCES
See Gotham Book Mart.

"STENDHAL" (1783–1842)
Pen-name of Marie Henri Beyle. French novelist who served as a soldier in

Napoleon's army, Stendhal remains best known for his novel *The Red and the Black* (1830).

STERN, PHILIP VAN DOREN (b. 1900)
American novelist and anthologist; his books include *The Man Who Killed Lincoln* (1929), *The Drums of Morning* (1942), *Lola* (1949), and *A Pictorial History of the Automobile* (1935). See Nathan's profile of Strindberg.

STERNBERG, JOSEF VON (1894–1969)
Austrian-American film director.

STEVENSON, ROBERT LOUIS (1850–1894)
Major Scottish novelist, poet, and essayist whose best known books include *Treasure Island* (1883), *A Child's Garden of Verses* (1885), *Kidnapped* (1886), and *The Strange Case of Dr. Jekyll and Mr. Hyde* (1886). Despite his enchanting prose and his verse for children, he remained a failed playwright. See James Hart, *From Scotland to Silverado* (Cambridge: Harvard University Press, 1966).

STEWART, DONALD OGDEN (1894–1980)
American actor, humorist, and scenario writer; see Nathan's profile of the Fitzgeralds.

STICHOMYTHY
See repartee.

STOCK CHARACTER
A traditional, conventional role—for example, the pretty, young ingenue; the governess; the nurse; the upstairs maid; the cantankerous uncle or grandfather; the sidekick friend.

STOCK, SUMMER
1. A company of actors, usually including one or two celebrities, who perform in or near a summer resort
2. The repertoire of plays performed by such a company.

STOICISM
A dogged coping with hardships; indifference to pleasure or pain; the teachings of Zeno (fourth century B.C.), "porch philosopher" popularized in the works of Seneca the Younger (48–65 A.D.)

STRACHEY, LYTTON (1880–1932)
English essayist and biographer; author of *Eminent Victorians* (1918); see Nathan's profile of T. S. Eliot.

STRANGE INTERLUDE (1927)
A play in nine acts by Eugene O'Neill (q.v.); it was performed in two parts (before and after dinner). This play objectifies the stream of consciousness technique (q.v.) by means of hidden audio devices airing asides (that is, what the characters are thinking as opposed to what they say). See Nathan's profile of O'Neill.

STRASBERG, LEE (1901–1982)
Austrian-American actor, director, and theatre manager; father of the actress Susan Strasberg. He was a drama teacher at the Actors' Studio, New York, and lectured at Harvard, Brown, Brandeis, and Northwestern universities. He co-founded, with Harold Clurman (q.v.), the Group Theatre, New York.

STRAUS, OSCAR (1870–1954)
Austrian composer whose operetta *The Chocolate Soldier* (1908) was based on Shaw's play *Arms and the Man* (1894).

STRAUSS, JOHANN (1804–1849)
Patriarch of the Viennese family of waltz composers; see Nathan's profile of Lillian Gish.

STRAUSS, RICHARD (1864–1949)
German composer; he was the author of several works of "program music" based on such literary figures as Til Eulenspiegel, Don Quixote, and Zarathustra.

STRAW, THE (1919)
A play by Eugene O'Neill (q.v.); see O'Neill's letter of 4 November 1919 to Nathan, p. 201.

STREAM OF CONSCIOUSNESS
A narrative and dramatic technique in which a character seems to be thinking out loud and revealing symptoms of subconscious experience. In creating this illusion, the writer abandons normal sentence structure; he may run words, images, feelings, and past experiences, together in one continuous stream. The technique is also known as "interior monologue." Examples include Molly Bloom's monologue (the Penelope passage) at the end of *Ulysses* by James Joyce (q.v.). Other users of this technique have been Virginia Woolf in *The Waves,* William Faulkner in *The Sound and the Fury,* and Dorothy Richardson in *Pilgrimage.* The phrase was first published by the psychologist William James in his book *Principles of Psychology* (1890).

STREET, JULIAN (1879–1947)
Popular American writer; a collaborator of Booth Tarkington's (q.v.).

STREETCAR NAMED DESIRE, A (1947)
A play by Tennessee Williams (q.v.); it was denigrated by Nathan in a review of 3 December 1947.

STREET SCENE (1929)
A play by Elmer Rice (q.v.).

STRIFE (1909)
A play by John Galsworthy (q.v.).

STRINDBERG, JOHAN AUGUST (1849–1912)
Major Swedish playwright; although he also wrote novels, he is best remembered for the plays *The Father* (1887), *Miss Julie* (1888), *Creditors* (1888), and *The Ghost Sonata* (1907), also known as *The Spook Sonata.* His bitter autobiography,

Son of a Servant, appeared in 1886 (tr. 1913). Harry Carlson has edited *Strindberg; Five Plays* (Berkeley: University of California Press, 1983). One of the best biographies is by Michael Meyer (New York: Oxford University Press, 1967). See Nathan's profile of Strindberg.

STROHEIM, ERICH VON (1885–1957)
Austrian-American film director; early in his career he was an actor and assistant under D. W. Griffith (q.v.).

STRONG, AUSTIN (1881–1952)
American architect and playwright; he was the author of such plays as *Rip Van Winkle* (1911), based on the story by Washington Irving (q.v.); and *Seventh Heaven* (1920), which was made into a popular movie.

STURM UND DRANG (STORM AND STRESS)
A literary movement that began in Germany in the late eighteenth century and was similar to romanticism (q.v.). The name originated in the play *Sturm und Drang* (1776) by Friedrich Klinger (1752–1831), but the substance of the movement got its impetus from the play *Götz von Berlichingen* (1773) by Goethe (q.v.). The protagonist, a romantic figure, is full of angst and inner conflict between natural desire and the duties that a strait-laced society burdens him with. Even his *thoughts* about wishing to rebel elicited for Goethe some harsh criticism by ultra-conservative patriots. Among other works in the movement, the play *Die Rauber* (*The Robbers,* 1781) by Friedrich von Schiller (1759–1805) attacks political tyranny and reiterates that the individual needs more space—more freedom from Establishment rules and expectations. These themes permeated Sturm und Drang literature through the last of the eighteenth and the beginning of the nineteenth centuries and no doubt encouraged the 1848 uprisings in Berlin, Paris, Vienna, and Milan.

Although the postures in the Sturm and Drang literature were sincere and genuinely human, certain aspects of their self-centeredness lay vulnerable to satire and generated a kind of backlash. One of the most notable and scholarly criticisms of the movement, along with Rousseauean romanticism, its analogue, is Irving Babbitt's *Rousseau and Romanticism* (Boston: Houghton Mifflin, 1919).

SUDERMANN, HERMANN (1857–1928)
German novelist and playwright devoted to naturalism (q.v.). In 1891 two of his best known plays were produced in New York: *Sodom's End* and *Maggda.* The latter provided a starring role for Sarah Bernhardt (q.v.). Sudermann was also the author of the plays *Honor* (1915) and *The Three Heron Feathers* (1916).

SULLAVAN, MARGARET (1911–1960)
American stage and screen actress.

SULLIVAN, SIR ARTHUR (1842–1900)
Popular English composer, well known for his collaboration with Sir William Gilbert (q.v.) in creating celebrated comic operas including *The Pirates of Penzance* (1978), *Iolanthe* (1882), *The Mikado* (1885), and *The Gondoliers* (1889).

SURREALISM
An effect, or effects, of images and scenes that go beyond what is normal or realistic. Just as in the anti-rational paintings of the Spanish artist Salvador Dali

(1904–1989), in which legs grow out of ears and fingers out of furniture, so, in certain contemporary poetry, fiction, and drama there may appear similarly incongruous images and scenes. These have been called sub-realistic and surrealistic, a term coined in 1917 by the French poet Guillaume Apollinaire (1880–1918). Although more poets and novelists use surrealism than do playwrights, an example of a surrealistic play is *Under Milk Wood* (1953) by the Welsh poet Dylan Thomas (1914–1953). See Roger Shattuck, "Apollinaire," *The Banquet Years* (New York: Doubleday, 1958).

SUTRO, ALFRED (1863–1933)
English playwright; see Nathan's profile of S. N. Behrman.

SVENGALI
The mesmeric seducer of Trilby. See Du Maurier.

SVEVO, ITALO (1861–1928)
Pen-name of Ettore Schmitz. Italian fiction writer and playwright. In 1907, in Trieste, he was befriended by James Joyce (q.v.). Svevo's best known work remains *Confessions of Zeno* (1933). That book and most of his others were championed by Eugenio Montale (1896–1981), the Italian poet, critic, and Nobel Laureate.

SWINNERTON, FRANK (FL. EARLY 1900S)
American newspaperman who collaborated with F. Scott Fitzgerald (q.v.) on "The St. Paul Daily Dirge," a parody news sheet that Fitzgerald distributed at a dance in 1922. See Fitzgerald's letter of December 1923 to Bernard Vaughan.

SYMBOL
A literary device in which a given image stands for something beyond itself; for example, a pen standing for communication; in the adage "The pen is mightier than the sword," the sword standing for war or violence. A symbol may also suggest multiple meanings. For example, in *Moby Dick,* the white whale may stand for several concepts beyond itself. See Kenneth Burke, "Symbolic Action," *The Philosophy of Literary Form* (Baton Rouge: Louisiana University Press, 1967).

SYMBOLISTES
In France, shortly before the turn of the century, a group of writers who wished to turn away from philosophic and literary naturalism (q.v.) came to be called by this name. This group included the poets Paul Verlaine (1844–1896), Stephen Mallarmé (1842–1898), Arthur Rimbaud (1854–1891); and the playwright Maurice Maeterlinck (q.v.). Maeterlinck's play *The Bluebird* (1909) symbolically denies the reality of death. See Edmund Wilson, *Axel's Castle* (NY: Scribner's, 1936); Kate Flores, ed., *The Anchor Anthology of French Poetry* (New York: Anchor Books, 1958): and Anna Balakian, *The Symbolist Movement* (New York: New York University Press, 1967).

SYNGE, JOHN MILLINGTON (1871–1909)
Irish playwright associated with William Butler Yeats (q.v.), Lady Gregory (q.v.), and the Abbey Theatre (q.v.). Synge's plays include the one-act "Riders to the Sea" (1904) and the full-length *Playboy of the Western World* (1907).

TALLEY METHOD, THE (1904)
A play by S. N. Behrman (q.v.); see Nathan's profile of Helen Hayes.

TAMMANY HALL
See Tweed, "Boss."

TANDY, JESSICA (b. 1909)
English-American actress whose earliest performances in England were under the auspices of the Birmingham Repertory Company. In her Broadway, New York, debut she played Toni in *The Matriarch* (1930). During the 1930s and 1940s, both in New York and in London she performed in scores of plays. In 1942, after divorcing her first husband, she married Hume Cronyn (q.v.). He wrote and directed many of the plays she starred in, including *Portrait of a Madonna* (1946). She also played Blanche du Bois in *A Streetcar Named Desire* (1947), Cassandra in *Troilus and Cressida* (1961), Olga in *Three Sisters* (1963), and Linda in *Death of a Salesman* (1963). Her film appearances included those in *The Seventh Cross* (1944), *Forever Amber* (1945), *The Desert Fox* (1951), and *The Birds* (1963). On television, she has performed with her husband in several productions, including *The Marriage* (1953), *The Moon and Sixpence* (1959), the CBS Alfred Hitchcock Hour, and the Hallmark Hall of Fame *Foxfire* series (1987).

TANGUAY, EVA (1878–1947)
Anglo-American popular entertainer; see Nathan's profile of Maurice Evans.

TARKINGTON, BOOTH (1869–1946)
American novelist and playwright. Scion of a wealthy Indianapolis family, he was educated at Purdue and Princeton. His fiction is best known for its sympathetic treatment of adolescence—for example, in *Penrod* (1914), *Seventeen* (1916), and *Alice Adams* (1921). His best known plays include *Monsieur Beaucaire* (1901); *The Man From Home* (1907); *The Country Cousin* (1916), which he wrote in collaboration with Julian Street (q.v.); and *Clarence* (1921), which he wrote in collaboration with Harry Leon Wilson (q.v.). In New York City, at the Dutch Treat Club (q.v.) and also during the summers in Kennebunkport, Me., Tarkington fraternized with Julian Street, Harry Leon Wilson, and George Barr McCutcheon (q.v.). Tarkington, Street, and Wilson spent many of their play-collaborating sessions on the Isle of Capri.

TAYLOR, DEEMS (1885–1966)
American composer and music critic

TAYLOR, JEREMY (1613–1667)
English prelate and critic; see Nathan's profile of Christopher Fry.

TAYLOR, LAURETTE (1884–1946)
American actress, born Laurette Cooney.

TAYLOR, SAMUEL (1896–1958)
American playwright who wrote *The Happy Time* (1949), a 1950 hit at the Plymouth Theatre.

TAYLOR, ZACHARY (1784–1850)
Twelfth president of the United States and maternal grandfather of Lillian Gish (q.v.)

TAYLOR, TOM (1817–1880)

English editor and playwright, the manager of *Punch* magazine from 1874 to his death in 1880. He was better known as a playwright, having written over 100 plays, mostly melodramas. He was the author of *Our American Cousin* (1853), a performance of which President Lincoln attended at Ford's Theatre in Washington, D.C. the night in 1865 when he was assassinated. Taylor collaborated with the novelist Charles Reade (1814–1884) on the successful play *The Ticket-of-Leave Man* (i.e, the parollee) 1863.

In 1884, during a summer road show, George Barr McCutcheon (q.v.) helped produce his adaptation of Tom Taylor's melodrama *The Fool's Revenge* (1859). The exigencies of weather and terrain necessitated some radical doctoring. "Poor Tom Taylor . . ." wrote McCutcheon, "If he could have lived forty years longer than he did and could have managed to visit any one of a number of small Indiana towns during the summer of 1884 he might have seen a play that would have given him the pleasure of laughing himself to death. But fortunately he was already dead and buried in England." *Beyond Graustark* (Port Washington and London: Kennikat Press, 1981), p. 32.

TCHAIKOVSKY, PETER ILYICH (1840–1893)

Major Russian composer celebrated for his symphonies, operas, concertos, and ballets (including the "Nutcracker Suite").

TÉLLEZ, GABRIEL (1580–1648)

Spanish playwright whose *El Burlador de Sevilla* (1634) introduced Don Juan into dramatic literature.

TERRY, ELLEN (1847–1928)

Celebrated English actress; mother of Gordon Craig (q.v.). She made her debut at the age of eight as Mamillius in *The Winter's Tale* produced by Charles Kean (q.v.). In 1878 she joined Henry Irving (q.v.) as his leading lady in several productions at the London Lyceum Theatre. After 1902, under the management of the Frohman Syndicate (q.v.), she toured the United States, lecturing as well as acting. Her most successful roles included those as Portia, Olivia, and Beatrice. In 1925 she was made a Dame of the British Empire. See Nina Auerbach, *Ellen Terry, Player in Her Time* (New York: Norton, 1987).

TESTAMENT OF A CRITIC, THE (1931)

A book by Nathan.

THEATRE BOOK(S) OF THE YEAR (1943–51)

A series of books by Nathan.

THEATRE, THE DRAMA, AND THE CRITIC, THE (1921)

A book by Nathan.

THEATRE GUILD, THE

A New York organization devoted to excellence in theatre arts. With financing mostly by the philanthropist Otto Kahn (q.v.), the guild was first established in 1919 under the direction of Lawrence Langner (q.v.) and other members of the Washington Square Players (q.v.). In 1925 the Guild took over the theatre it had built on 52nd Street. The Guild gave its initial support to plays by Eugene O'Neill and George Bernard Shaw. It also produced musicals by George Gershwin and others. It was the first to produce *Oklahoma* by Rodgers and Hammerstein (q.v.).

THEATRE IN THE FIFTIES, THE (1953)
A book by Nathan.

THEATRE OF THE ABSURD
A movement started off Broadway in the early 1950s by playwrights devoted to existentialism (q.v.), dadaism (q.v.), and similar movements. Among the best known plays of this genre are *Waiting for Godot* (1953) by Samuel Beckett (q.v.) and *Rhinoceros* (1959) by Eugene Ionesco (q.v.). The label was first used by the drama critic Martin Esslin (b. 1918).

THEATRE ROYAL
See Drury Lane Theatre.

THERE SHALL BE NO NIGHT (1940)
A play by Robert E. Sherwood (q.v.); see Nathan's profile of Helen Hayes.

THOMA, LUDWIG (1867–1923)
German playwright; author of *The Orphanage* (1913).

THOMAS, AUGUSTUS (1857–1934)
American playwright; author of more than 50 plays, of which the best known remain *The Burglar* (1889) and *The Witching Hour* (1907). At the Madison Square Theatre, Thomas succeeded Dion Boucicault (q.v.) as translator and adapter of foreign plays. See Nathan's profile of O'Neill.

THOMAS, BRANDON (1856–1914)
American playwright; author of the farce *Charlie's Aunt* (1892).

THOMPSON, DENMAN, AKA JOSHUA WHITCOMB (1833–1911)
American actor.

THREE MEN ON A HORSE (1935)
A play by George Abbott (q.v.); see Nathan's profile of George Abbott.

THUNDERBOLT, THE (1910)
A play by Pinero (q.v.); see Nathan's profile of Lillian Hellman.

TIFFANY'S
A celebrated New York jewelry store, 5th Avenue at 57th Street.

TIGER AT THE GATES (1955)
A play by Anouilh (q.v.).

TIGER CATS (1924)
A play by Karen Bramson (d. 1936) and Michael Orme, born Alice Greeven (1894–1944); Nathan called this play "a dose of Scandinavian Minsky." See his profile of Katharine Cornell.

TIME OF YOUR LIFE, THE (1939)
A play by Saroyan (q.v.)

TINTORETTO (1518–1594)
Born Jacopo Robusti; Venetian painter whose works include *Adam and Eve, Miracle of St. Mark, The Last Supper, Bacchus and Ariadne, The Three Graces, Minerva and Mars, Miracle of the Loaves and the Fishes.*

TITAN, THE (1914)
A novel by Dreiser (q.v.).

TOBACCO ROAD (1932)
A novel by Erskine Caldwell (1903–1989); the dramatization by Jack Kirkland (1933) ran for 3,182 performances.

TODD, MICHAEL (1895–1940)
American producer born Michael Goldbogen.

TOLLER, ERNST (1893–1939)
German expressionist playwright; author of *The Machine Wreckers* (1922).

TOLSTOI (ALSO TOLSTOY), COUNT LEO (1828–1910)
Major Russian novelist best known for his masterpieces *War and Peace* (1862) and *Anna Karenina* (1873); his other works include the novel *The Kreutzer Sonata* (1889), the short story "Death of Ivan Ilyitch" (1884), and the play *The Living Corpse* (1910). Tolstoi's conversion from youthful libertinism to Christianity is described in his *Confession* (1879) and *What I Believe* (1882). One of Tolstoi's best friends was Maxim Gorki (q.v.). See Nathan's profile of O'Neill.

TORQUEMADA, TOMÀS DE (1420–1498)
Spanish churchman and leader of the (medieval) Spanish Inquisition; see Nathan's profile of Maxwell Anderson, p. 144. See also Benito Galdós, *Torquemada* (New York: Columbia University Press, 1986).

TOUCH OF THE POET, A (1958)
A play by Eugene O'Neill (q.v.).

TRAGI-COMEDY
A tragedy with a happy ending; a serious play with an admixture of comic moments. Cf. Theatre of the Absurd.

TRAVERS, BEN (1886–1953)
English playwright and novelist; before his career in the theatre, he worked at the Bodley Head with publisher John Lane. Travers was the author of several farces, including *Outrageous Fortune* (1942), produced at the Aldwych Theatre, London.

TRILBY (1894)
A novel by George du Maurier (q.v.). It is the story of a lovely young Parisian model who is hypnotized by the mesmeric Svengali and who later becomes a celebrated singer. It was first dramatized in 1905 and produced at the New Amsterdam Theatre, New York.

TRUMBO, DALTON (b. 1905)
American novelist and screen writer best known for his novel *Johnny Got His Gun* (1939). For ten years after World War II, he was black-listed by the movie companies because he had refused to cooperate with the congressional Committee on Un-American Activities. Nevertheless, he was the author of 40 screenplays—among them, *Kitty Foyle, 30 Seconds Over Tokyo, Spartacus,* and *Exodus.*

TUSSAUD, MADAME MARIE (1760–1850)
Born Marie Grosholtz; Swiss modeler in wax. In 1802 she founded her Baker Street, London, museum with its Chamber of Horrors.

TWAIN, MARK (1835–1910)
Pen-name of Samuel Langhorne Clemens, novelist and America's most cele-brated humorist. He was brought up in Hannibal, Missouri, on the Mississippi River, a locale depicted in several of his works, including the autobiographical *Life on the Mississippi* (1883) and the novels *The Adventures of Tom Sawyer* (1876) and *The Adventures of Huckleberry Finn* (1884). From 1857 to 1861 he worked as a river pilot on the Mississippi. In 1861 he engaged in prospecting for gold near Carson City, Nev. In 1862 he worked as a reporter for the Virginia City (Nev.) *Territorial Enterprise* and, during the following year, as a reporter in San Fran-cisco. After his first book, *The Celebrated Jumping Frog of Calaveras County and Other Sketches* (1867) he started his lecture tours, which were celebrated for their humorous cynicism. These tours did not prosper until 1896, when he sought to clear tremendous debts incurred in the failure of his venture in publishing a biography of Ulysses S. Grant. Mark Twain's other books include *The Prince and the Pauper* (1882); *A Connecticut Yankee in King Arthur's Court* (1889); *The Gilded Age* (1873), written in collaboration with Charles Dudley Warner (q.v.); and the posthumous *The Mysterious Stranger* (1916), edited by John Tuckey.

TWEED, "BOSS" WILLIAM M. (1823–1878)
New York City Democrat politician; a power ("Grand Sachem") in Tammany Hall, who controlled nominations and appointments. The "Tweed Ring" consisted of Boss Tweed and his henchmen.

TYLER, GEORGE CROUSE (1867–1946)
New York theatrical producer.

TZPZYZPK
A town in Hungary; see Nathan's essay "Mysteries," p. 76.

UNCLE VANYA (1899)
A play by Chekhov (q.v.). The 1930 production at the Booth Theatre in New York starred Lillian Gish (q.v.) as Helena and elicited Nathan's rave notice. See his profile of Lillian Gish.

UNDER THE GASLIGHT (1867)
A popular melodrama by Augustin Daly (q.v.).

UNITIES, THE
In his treatise on poetry *(Poetica)* Aristotle (384–322 B.C.) inductively described (that is, he did not prescribe, but only reported) how the great Greek playwrights (Aeschylus, Sophocles, Euripides, Aristophanes) had treated in their plays the

problems of time, space, and action. Aristotle observed that these masters of their art form had limited, in most of their plays, the time to one day; the space, to one city-state or palace; and the action to one unified story-line or plot (with a beginning, a middle or climax, and an end or resolution). These three boundaries came to be called "the three unities." Given these Aristotelian observations as guidelines, however, very few playwrights through the ages have followed them. Even the so-called classicists Corneille and Racine (q.v.) were taken to task by Lessing (q.v.) for *not* adhering to the classical unities.

UNIVERSITY WITS, THE
Sixteenth century graduates of Oxford and Cambridge universities who became popular playwrights; these included Robert Greene (1558–1592), George Peele (1558–1597), Thomas Nashe (1567–1601), Thomas Kyd (1558–1594), Christopher Marlowe (1564–1593), John Lyly (1554–1606), and—the master of them all—Ben Jonson (q.v.). In the epithet, "wit" (close to its roots *witan* and *wissen*) suggests sophistication.

UNTERMEYER, LOUIS (1885–1977)
American anthologist.

UP IN MABEL'S ROOM (1919)
A popular play by Otto Harbach (1873–1963) and Wilson Collison (1893–1941).

UREY, HAROLD (1893–1981)
American scientist; in 1934 he was awarded the Nobel Prize in Chemistry. See Nathan's letter of 1 July 1953 to August Mencken, p. 231.

USPENSKY (ALSO OUSPENSKY), PETER D. (1878–1947)
Russian writer, best remembered for novels of peasant life.

VALENCY, MAURICE (b. 1903)
American writer who translated *The Mad Woman of Chaillot* by Giraudoux (q.v.) and *The Visit* (1958) by Friedrich Duerrenmatt (1921–   ). See Nathan's profile of Giraudoux, p. 131.

VALENTINA
A costume-designing company of the 1920s and 1930s.

VAN DINE, S. S.
See Wright, Willard.

VAN DOREN, CARL (1885–1950)
American educator and editor.

VAN DOREN, MARK (1894–1973)
American poet, critic, and educator.

VAN DRUTEN, JOHN (1901–1957)
English novelist and playwright whose plays include *The Voice of the Turtle* (1943), *I Remember Mama* (1944), and *Bell, Book, and Candle* (1950).

VAN LOON, HENDRICK (1882–1944)

Dutch-American writer and illustrator; best known for *The Story of Mankind* (1921), *Van Loon's Geography* (1932), and *Van Loon's Lives* (1942). His droll drawings were addressed primarily to children but also won the admiration of adults. He was also a designer of play posters.

VARIETY

A weekly periodical devoted to show business; it was founded in 1905 by Sime Silverman.

VAUDEVILLE

A pre-television era, music-hall entertainment performed by singers, dancers, and comedians; big-city theatres presented vaudeville acts before or after screen presentations of main features. One of the most popular New York vaudeville bills could be enjoyed at the Weber and Fields Music Hall (q.v.). With the advent of television (ca. 1950s), vaudeville all but vanished, although from time to time attempts to revive it can be seen on television.

VAUGHAN, BERNARD (FL. EARLY 1900S)

The St. Paul (Minnesota) journalist who collaborated with F. Scott Fitzgerald on a parody newsheet, "The St. Paul Daily Dirge" (1922), which Fitzgerald distributed at a *haute monde* dance; see Fitzgerald's letter of December 1923, to Vaughan, p. 208.

VEBER, PIERRE (1869–1942)

French playwright and novelist.

VEGETABLE, THE: OR, FROM PRESIDENT TO POSTMAN (1923)

An abortive play by F. Scott Fitzgerald (q.v.) intended as a spoof on the Harding administration. According to Charles Scribner III in his introduction to the 1983 paperback edition of *The Great Gatsby,* this play, which opened and closed disastrously in Atlantic City in 1923, was "a dry run for Gatsby" but proved to be a closet drama (q.v.). See Fitzgerald's letter of December 1923 to Bernard Vaughan.

VERONESE, PAOLO (1523–1588)

Italian painter associated with the Venetian school of Titian (fl. 1500s). Paolo's best known paintings include *Age and Youth, Marriage at Cana,* and *The Rape of Europa.* See Jacob Burckhardt, *The Civilization of the Renaissance in Italy* (New York: Oxford, 1937). See Nathan's essay "Intelligence and the Drama."

VERSE DRAMA

Plays written in verse as distinguished from prose; from ancient times through the 1600s many plays were written in verse (Shakespeare's iambic pentameter, for example). In modern times verse drama has been the exception. Nevertheless, certain well-known dramatists have attempted it—among them, Maxwell Anderson (q.v.), T. S. Eliot (q.v.), and Christopher Fry (q.v.). See T. S. Eliot's convictions concerning verse drama, p. 189.

VICTORIA REGINA (1935)

A play by Laurence Housman (1865–1959), whose 1935 production starred Helen Hayes (q.v.). See Nathan's essay "Myself," p. 36.

VIGNY, ALFRED VICTOR DE (1797–1863)
French romantic poet, novelist, and playwright acclaimed by Victor Hugo. De Vigny's plays include *Chatterton* (1835; tr. 1908)). His novels include *The Spider and the Fly* (1826), *Stella* (1832), and *The Military Necessity* (1835). See Nathan's profile of George Bernard Shaw.

VILLIERS, GEORGE, SECOND DUKE OF BUCKINGHAM (1628–1687)
Prominent during the reign of King Charles II, Buckingham was probably the author of *The Rehearsal* (1671).

VOLLMER, LULA (1898–1955)
American playwright; see Nathan's profile of Lillian Hellman.

VOLSTEAD ACT, THE
The Volstead Act, enacted in 1919, also known as the Prohibition Act, prohibited the sale and purchase of beverages with an alcoholic content over 5 percent by volume. This act passed over the veto of President Woodrow Wilson, although it was modified in 1933 to permit the sale of 3.2 percent beer and wine. But it became void and irrelevant after the Twenty-First Amendment (1933) repealed the Eighteenth (or Prohibition) Amendment. Meanwhile many a compulsive drinker had patronized "speak-easies" and other "bootleg" liquor dealers, and much racketeering and crime occurred as concomitants of the unpopular law. Nathan and his partner H. L. Mencken were hardly ever, if at any time, drunk; Nathan liked cocktails in moderation while Mencken drank beer in moderation. Miss Gish was also a moderate. Not so Eugene O'Neill, F. Scott and Zelda Fitzgerald, and Sinclair Lewis. In a desperate attempt to regain his health when he was on the verge of death, Eugene O'Neill became a teetotaler. Lewis often *feigned* drunkenness. The Fitzgeralds persisted with intermittent drunkenness during the 1920s and 1930s before they tapered off in the 1940s and after.

VOLTAIRE, FRANCOIS MARIE AROUET DE (1694–1778)
Major French writer and one of the chief figures in the eighteenth century Enlightenment; a deistic philosopher, he remains best known for his romance *Candide* (1759), which pokes fun at the optimism of the German idealist philosopher Leibniz (1646–1716). Voltaire contributed to the *Encyclopedie* of Denis Diderot (1713–1784) and wrote a brilliant biography of Charles XII of Sweden. See Nathan's profile of Lillian Hellman.

VON TILZER, ALBERT (1878–1956)
American author of the song "Take Me Out to the Ball Game."

VON TILZER, HARRY (1872–1946)
American composer who wrote such popular songs as "A Bird in a Gilded Cage," "Wait Till the Sun Shines, Nellie," and "I Want a Girl Just Like the Girl That Married Dear Old Dad." Nathan played the Von Tilzers's pieces, among others, on the piano.

WAGNER, RICHARD (1813–1883)
Major German composer and originator of the music drama. Born into a theatrical family, he used folk themes and strove for a harmonious blend of several art forms. In 1843 he was made director of the Dresden Theatre. He was the author of

such operas as *The Flying Dutchman* (1841), which was based on a version by Heinrich Heine (q.v.); *Tannhäuser* (1843); *Lohengrin* (1846); *Der Ring des Niebelungen* (1853; 1876), which embraced *Das Rheingold, Die Walküre,* and *Siegfried; Tristan und Isolde* (1857); *Die Meistersinger* (1862), his only comic opera; *Die Götterdämmerung* (1874); and *Parsifal* (1877), a religious drama. In 1870 he married Liszt's daughter Cosima, who helped found the Wagner Theatre and, in 1872, The Bayreuth Festival.

WAITING FOR GODOT (1952)
A play by Samuel Beckett (b. 1906), Anglo-French novelist and playwright.

WATKINS, MAUREEN (b. 1902?)
American playwright, author of *Chicago* (1926); she had been a student at George Pierce Baker's (q.v.) Workshop 47.

WALKLEY, ARTHUR (1855–1926)
British essayist and drama critic.

WALKER, STANLEY (1898–1962)
American journalist.

WALLACE, DEREK
The pseudonym used by Nathan for his play-pastiche *The Avon Flows* (1937).

WALLACE, LEW (1827–1905)
Hoosier soldier, statesman, and novelist who remains best known for his novel *Ben Hur: A Tale of the Christ* (1880); in 1899 this was dramatized by William Young (1847–1920). It was later produced in the movies, both in 1925 and 1959.

WALLACK'S THEATRE
Broadway and 30th Street, New York; it opened 4 January 1882 and re-opened 8 October 1888 as the Palace Theatre, with the presentation of *Les Precieuses Ridicules* by Moliere (q.v.). The theatre was demolished in 1915.

WALPOLE, HUGH (1884–1941)
Born in New Zealand, he moved to England, where he became a popular novelist. His best remembered novel remains *Rogue Herries* (1930). See Nathan's profile of Sinclair Lewis.

WALTER, EUGENE (1874–1941)
American theatrical press representative.

WARD, MRS. HUMPHREY (1851–1920)
Novelist and suffragist, she was born Mary Augusta Arnold, the niece of Matthew Arnold (q.v.).

WARFIELD, DAVID (1866–1951)
Major American actor celebrated for his Jewish character roles, notably Shylock in *The Merchant of Venice* (1922) produced by David Belasco (q.v.). Warfield had also starred in *The Auctioneer* (1901) and *The Music Maker* (1904).

WARNER, CHARLES DUDLEY (1829–1903)
American essayist whose "A-Hunting of the Deer" (1871) aroused keen interest among hunters and anti-hunters alike. Warner is also remembered as the writer who collaborated with Mark Twain (q.v.) on *The Gilded Age* (1873). In his unproduced play *Brood House* George Barr McCutcheon satirizes the hunting of animals. See A. L. Lazarus and Victor Jones, *Beyond Graustark* (Port Washington and London: Kennikat Press, 1981), p. 103.

WARNER, ELTINGE F. (FL. EARLY 1900S)
Owner of *Smart Set* who offered its editorship to Nathan.

WEBER AND FIELDS VAUDEVILLE
See Weber, Joseph and Fields, Lew.

WEBER AND FIELDS MUSIC HALL
216–230 West 44th Street between Broadway and 8th Avenue, New York; it opened 5 June 1913 and re-opened several times with and without its roof garden until its demolition in July 1945.

WEBER, JOSEPH (1867–1942)
Partner of Lew Fields (q.v.) in one of the most popular comedy and vaudeville teams of the times (1895–1904).

WEBSTER, DAME MARGARET (1905–1972)
Anglo-American actress and director, primarily of plays by Shakespeare. See Nathan's profile of Maurice Evans.

WEDEKIND, FRANK (1864–1918)
German playwright, an important exponent of expressionism (q.v.). His plays *Earth Spirit* (1914) and *Pandora's Box* (1918) use grotesque fantasy. In his essay "On Eroticism," the preface to his book *Fireworks* (1905), he anticipated Freud in the conviction that "sex is both the chief force and chief problem of humanity." Wedekind's plays include, besides the two cited above, *Karl Hetmann* (1904); *Totentang* (tr. *Death and the Devil,* 1906); and the *Lulu* plays (tr. 1972), which are laced with eroticism and attack Philistine hypocrisy. Politically anti-Bismarck and anti-Prussianism, the satirical poems he published in the periodical *Simplissimus* led to his imprisonment as a subversive. See Günter Seehaus, *Frank Wedekind und das Theatre* (Munich: Laokoön Verlag, 1964). See also Nathan's profile of Strindberg.

WELDED (1921)
A play by Eugene O'Neill (q.v.), which ran for only 24 performances.

WELL-MADE PLAY, THE
A conventional formula play; a play with predictable plot outcome and character behavior. Well-known playwrights criticized for this shortcoming include Henry James (q.v.), Arthur Pinero (q.v.), and Victorien Sardou (q.v.).

WELLS, CAROLYN (1862–1942)
American parodist and author of humorous sketches and mystery stories, including *Spooky Hollow* (1923) and *The Skeleton at the Feast* (1931).

WELLS, HERBERT GEORGE (1866–1946)
English novelist, science fiction writer, and popularizer of history and the social sciences. His best known books include *The Time Machine* (1895), *The War of the Worlds* (1898), *Tono Bungay* (1909), *History of Mr. Polly* (1910), *Outline of History* (1920), *The Science of Life* (with Julian Huxley, 1929), and *Experiment in Autobiography* (1934). His best known short story, "The Country of the Blind" (1911), is reprinted in Robert Freier et al., eds., *Adventures in Modern Literature, 5th Edition* (New York: Harcourt Brace Jovanovich 1962). See Gordon Ray, *H. G. Wells and Rebbecca West* (New Haven: Yale University Press, 1974). See also Nathan's profile of Theodore Dreiser.

WERLEAN
Pertaining to a werle, a kind of costume.

WEST, MAE (1892?–1979)
American movie actress and playwright; author of *The Pleasure Man* (1928) and *Diamond Lil* (1928). See her autobiography *Goodness Had Nothing to Do With It* (Englewood Cliffs, N.J.: Prentice-Hall, 1959).

WEST, DAME REBECCA (1892–1983)
British novelist and critic, born Cicily Fairfield. She is best known for her travel book *Black Lamb and Grey Falcon* (1942). For her relationship with H. G. Wells (q.v.) see Gordon Ray, *H. G. Wells and Rebecca West* (New Haven: Yale, 1974). See also Fitzgerald's letter of December 1923, to B. Vaughan, p. 208.

WESTLY, JOHN (1878–1948)
American actor.

WEYMAN, STANLEY (1878–1928)
American playwright.

WHARTON, EDITH (1862–1937)
American novelist noted for her depiction of New York society at the turn of the century. Her best known works include *The House of Mirth* (1905), *The Age of Innocence* (1920), and *Ethan Frome* (1911), which was adapted for the stage, as were several other of her novels. See R. W. and Nancy Lewis, eds., *Letters of Edith Wharton* (New York: Charles Scribner's Sons, 1988).

WHAT A LIFE! (1938)
A play by Clifford Goldsmith (1899–1971).

WHAT EVERY WOMAN KNOWS (1918)
A play by James M. Barrie (q.v.).

WHAT'S IN A NAME? (1920)
A play by John Murray Anderson (q.v.). See Nathan's profile of Florenz Ziegfeld.

"WHERE THE CROSS IS MADE"
A one-act play by Eugene O'Neill (q.v.) that was expanded into the full-length play *Gold*.

WHITE CARGO (1924)
A play by A. E. Anson (1879–1936) and Leon Gordon (1884–1960). See Nathan's essay "Myself," p. 33.

WHITE, DR. WILLIAM ALANSON (1870–1937)
Superintendent of St. Elizabeth's Hospital, Washington D. C.; and co-founder of the *Psychoanalytic Review*. Dr. White was one of Freud's earliest supporters in the United States.

WHITE, WILLIAM ALLEN (1868–1944)
American editor and essayist, the "sage of Emporia"; he was the editor of the *Emporia (Kansas) Gazette* and author of *A Certain Rich Man* (1910). He was also the author of "Mary White," a widely reprinted essay about his teen-age daughter who was killed in a horse-riding accident.

WHITE-HEADED BOY, THE (1916)
A play by Lennox Robinson (1886–1938), director and manager of the Abbey Theatre (q.v.).

WHITEOAKS (1938)
A play by Mazo de la Roche (1879–1961), Canadian novelist and playwright. It was based on her novel *Whiteoaks of Jalna* (1929). The 1938 production of the play starred Ethel Barrymore (q.v.). See Nathan's profile of Helen Hayes.

WHYTAL, RUSS (1860–1934)
American actor and playwright.

WILD DUCK, THE (1884)
A play by Ibsen (q.v.).

WILDE, OSCAR (1854–1900)
Anglo-Irish poet, playwright, and novelist, born Oscar Fingall O'Flahertie; he was educated at Trinity College, Dublin, and at Magdalen College, Oxford. In 1895 he was sentenced to a two years' term of imprisonment at hard labor because of his homosexual relationship with young Lord Alfred Douglas. Wilde's experience in prison inspired his poem *The Ballad of Reading Gaol* (1898) and a posthumous apology in *De Profundis* (1905). His novels include *The Picture of Dorian Gray* (1891). But Wilde is best remembered for his witty plays, especially *Lady Windermere's Fan* (1892) and *The Importance of Being Earnest* (1895), his masterpiece. See Hesketh Pearson, *Oscar Wilde: His Life and Works* (New York: Harper & Brothers, 1946); Peter Ruby, *Oscar Wilde* (New York: Cambridge University Press, 1989); and Nathan's profile of Wilde.

WILDER, THORNTON (1897–1975)
American novelist and playwright. His best known novel remains *The Bridge of San Luis Rey* (1927). His best known plays include *Our Town* (1938) and *The Matchmaker* (1954), which was made into the popular musical *Hello, Dolly!* (1964). See Donald Gallup, ed., *The Journals of Thornton Wilder* (New Haven: Yale University Press, 1985).

WILLARD, EDWARD SMITH (1853–1915)
English actor.

WILLIAMS, EMLYN (1905–1987)
Welsh actor and playwright whose plays include *Night Must Fall* (1936) and *The Corn is Green* (1940). During the 1950s he toured in solo readings of Charles Dickens and Dylan Thomas.

WILLIAMS, HERSCHEL (b. 1909)
American playwright and director who in 1960 produced a stage version of *John Brown's Body* by Stephen Vincent Benet (q.v.).

WILLIAMS, JOHN D. (1886–1941)
Broadway producer associated with the Frohman Syndicate (q.v.). See O'Neill's letter of 19 June 1920, to Nathan, p. 203.

WILLIAMS, TENNESSEE (1911–1983)
Major American playwright to whose play *The Glass Menagerie* (1944) Nathan contributed the drunkard episode at the beginning of scene 4. See Williams' *Memoirs* (N.Y.: Doubleday 1975), pp. 81–82. Nathan saw Julie Haydon, who was to become his wife in 1955, perform as Laura in the world premiere of this play in Chicago. Other plays by Williams include *A Streetcar Named Desire* (1947), *Summer and Smoke* (1948), *The Rose Tattoo* (1951), *Camino Real* (1953), *Cat on a Hot Tin Roof* (1955), *Suddenly Last Summer* (1958), *Sweet Bird of Youth* (1959), and *The Night of the Iguana* (1961). Nathan derogated Williams' use of sex in *The Rose Tattoo*. See Nathan's *The Theatre Book of the Year, 1950–1951* (New York: Knopf, 1951), pp. 209–12. Nathan's criticism may have been rooted in a more or less subconscious prejudice against homosexuals like Williams.

WILLIS, NATHANIEL PARKER (1806–1867)
American journalist and poet. He was the author of *Tortesa or the Usurer* (1839), a play in blank verse admired by Edgar Allan Poe. See Nathan's profile of George Bernard Shaw.

WILSON, EDMUND (1895–1972)
Major American critic; a Princetonian, he was a friend of F. Scott Fitzgerald (q.v.) and edited his *The Crackup and Journals* (1945). From 1920 to 1921 Wilson was managing editor of *Vanity Fair*. From 1926 to 1931 he was on the staff of the *New Republic;* and from 1944 to 1948, on the staff of *The New Yorker* (q.v.), to which before and after he contributed frequently. Wilson wrote a couple of novels—*I Thought of Daisy* (1920) and the erotic *Memoirs of Hecate County* (1946). He also wrote a few plays, including *The Little Blue Light* (1950) and *Cyprian's Prayer* (1954), but his fiction and plays now seem negligible when compared with his critical essays: *Axel's Castle* (1931), *To the Finland Station* (1940), *Classics and Commercials* (1950), *The Shores of Light* (1952), *The Dead Sea Scrolls* (1958), *Apologies to the Iroquois* (1960), and *Patriotic Gore* (1962). See Nathan's profile of Fitzgerald, p. 156; also his complimentary assessment of Wilson in *Theatre Book of the Year, 1950–1951* (New York: Knopf, 1951), pp. 289–92.

WILSON, HARRY LEON (1867–1939)
American playwright, humorist, and novelist; from 1892 to 1902 he contributed humourous pieces to the old *Puck* magazine. Two of his novels—*Ruggles of Red Gap* (1915) and *Merton of the Movies* (1922)—were adapted to stage and screen. Wilson also collaborated with Booth Tarkington (q.v.) on *The Man from Home* (1907), which ran on Broadway for five years.

WILSON, WOODROW (1856–1924)
A president of Princeton University and the twenty-eighth president of the United States (1913–21).

WINGLESS VICTORY, THE (1926)
A play by Maxwell Anderson (q.v.).

WINSOR, KATHLEEN (b. 1919)
American novelist; author of *Forever Amber* (q.v.)

WITHIN THE GATES (1933)
A play by Sean O'Casey (q.v.).

WINTERSET (1935)
A tragedy by Maxwell Anderson (q.v.).

WITCHING HOUR, THE (1907)
A play by Augustus Thomas (q.v.).

WODEHOUSE, P. G. (1881–1975)
English humorist and novelist; creator of the characters Jeeves and Bertie Wooster in *The Invincible Jeeves* (1924).

WOFFINGTON, PEG (CA. 1714–1760)
Anglo-Irish actress. See Sheila Stowell, "Actors as Dramatic Personae . . . ," *Theatre History Studies,* vol. 8 (Grand Forks, N.D.: University of North Dakota Dept. of Theatre Arts, 1988).

WOOD, ELLEN, AKA MRS. HENRY WOOD (1814–1887)
English novelist; author of the immensely popular *East Lynne* (1861), which was dramatized by Clifton Tayleure (fl. 1800s). A melodrama, *East Lynne* toured the United States in the late 1800s. At one time, it starred Minnie Maddern (q.v.).

WOODRUFF, HARRY (1869–1916)
American actor.

WOODWARD, W. E. (1874–1950)
American banker, editor, and biographer; his works include *George Washington* (1926), *Meet General Grant* (1928), *Tom Paine* (1945), and *The Gift of Life* (1947).

WOOLLCOTT, ALEXANDER (1887–1943)
New York drama critic; at various times he worked on (and/or contributed to) the *New York Times,* the *New York Sun,* the *New York World, Vanity Fair,* and *The New Yorker* (q.v.).

WORKSHOP 47, HARVARD
See Baker, George Pierce.

WORLD IN FALSEFACE, THE (1923)
A book by Nathan.

WORTHING, FRANK (1866–1910)
British actor.

WRIGHT, HAROLD BELL (1872–1944)
American clergyman and popular novelist, he was the author of *Barbara Worth* (1911), which was later made into a syndicated cartoon.

WRIGHT, WILLARD (1888–1936)
The *Smart Set* Editor who preceded Nathan and Mencken. Under the pen-name of S. S. Van Dine, Wright created novels whose hero was the detective Philo Vance.

WYLIE, ELINOR (1885–1928)
American poet. Author of *Nets to Catch the Wind* (1921) and *Collected Poems* (1922), she excelled in sonnet sequences and sensuous imagery. Her third husband was William Rose Benet (q.v.).

XANTHIPPE
The shrewish wife of Socrates (q.v.).

YEATS, WILLIAM BUTLER (1865–1939)
Major Irish poet and playwright who won the Nobel Prize for Literature in 1923, he led the revival of interest in Irish folklore, legends, and culture. With Lady Augusta Gregory (q.v.) he founded the Abbey Theatre (q.v.), where he produced several of their plays. His unrequited love for Maud Gonne, a beautiful activist in the Irish Uprising of 1916, inspired several of his poems and plays. In 1917 he married Georgie Hyde-Lees, who was interested in seances and "automatic writing." She is said to have inspired his theories of symbolism expounded in his long critical essay *A Vision* (1925). His best known plays include *On Baile's Strand* (1904) and *Deirdre* (1907). He published numerous volumes of poetry, including *The Wild Swans at Coole* (1917), *The Winding Stair* (1929), *Wheels and Butterflies* (1934), and *New Poems* (1938). His best remembered individual poems include "Down by the Sally Gardens" (1892), "The Lake Isle of Innisfree" (1893), "Land of Heart's Desire" (1894), "A Coat" (1914), "After Long Silence" (1933), and "Sailing to Byzantium" (1933)—his most celebrated. Other works of Yeats that were popular when he was alive include *The Wanderings of Oisin* (1889), *The Celtic Twilight* (1893), and *Cathleen ni Houlihan* (1902). See Peter Ure, *Yeats the Playwright* (New York: Barnes & Noble, 1963).

YELLOW BOOK, THE (1894–1897)
An English quarterly magazine, whose contributors included Henry James (q.v.), Max Beerbohm (q.v.), and the art nouveau illustrator Aubrey Beardsley (1872–1898).

YOUNG, BRIGHAM (1801–1877)
Leader of Mormon settlers to Salt Lake City, Utah, in 1846

YOUNG, STARK (1881–1963)
American playwright, novelist, and critic. From 1921 to 1957 he served as drama critic on the *New Republic,* and later as contributor of drama criticism to various New York periodicals. His best known work remains his novel *So Red the Rose* (1934), although he also wrote several (lesser known) plays. In 1938 his adaptation of *The Sea Gull* (1896) by Chekhov (q.v.) had a successful run on Broadway.

ZIEGFELD, FLORENZ (1869–1932)
Popular American producer of the annual "Ziegfeld Follies" from 1907 until his

death; he also produced *Show Boat* (1927) and *Bittersweet* (1929). Among his close friends: Anna Held (q.v.) the "flapper" model and singer whom he married in 1896 and divorced in 1912. In 1914 he married Billie Burke (q.v.).

ZIEGFELD THEATRE
Northwest corner of 54th Street and Avenue of the Americas (6th Avenue); it opened in February 1927. After changing hands and names several times, it reopened in January 1963, with "An Evening with Maurice Chevalier" (1888–1972).

ZOLA, EMILE (1840–1902)
Major French novelist and critic. His best known novel remains *Nana* (1880), often cited as a classic example of naturalism (q.v.); and his influential essay *The Experimental Novel* appeared in 1889. In 1894 his widely circulated letter "J'accuse!" championed Alfred Dreyfus (1859–1935), the French Army officer prejudiciously treated because of his religion. See Nathan's profile of Theodore Dreiser.

ZUCKMAYER, CARL (1896–1977)
German playwright and screen writer. Early on, he abandoned a career in the sciences he had studied at Heidelberg. He was the author of the *Merry Vineyard* (1925) and the *Captain of Koepenick* (1932), which satirized the rising Nazis. During Hitler's regime Zuckmayer fled to Vermont. His other plays include *The Devil's General* (1946) and *The Gold Light* (1955). He also contributed to the screenplay for *The Blue Angel* (q.v.). In 1987, his autobiography *A Part of Myself* (1966) was translated posthumously in *The Reader's Digest*.

Selected Bibliography

Angelin, Patricia, and Robert G. Lowery, eds. *My Very Dear Sean: George Jean Nathan on Sean O'Casey*. Rutherford, N. J.: Fairleigh Dickinson University Press, 1985.

Amory, Cleveland and Frederic Bradlee, eds. *Vanity Fair: A Cavalcade of the 1920s and 1930s*. New York: Viking Press, 1960.

Angoff, Charles. *The Bitter Spring*. New York: Thomas Yoseloff, 1961. (This novel contains a portrait of Nathan.)

———. "Mencken, Nathan, and God," chapter 5 in *H. L. Mencken: a Portrait from Memory*. New York: Thomas Yoseloff, 1956.

Atkinson, Brooks. "Account Closed: Death of George Jean Nathan Finishes an Era," *New York Times* (Sunday, 27 April 1958, section 2, part I): p. 1.

Bergan, Ronald. *The Great Theatres of London*. San Francisco and London: Chronicle Books, 1988.

Bode, Carl. *Mencken*. Carbondale: Southern Illinois University Press, 1969.

Bogard, Travis. *Contour in Time: the Plays of Eugene O'Neill*. New York: Oxford University Press, 1987.

——— and Jackson Bryer, eds. *Selected Letters of Eugene O'Neill*. New Haven: Yale University Press, 1988.

Brook, Peter B., "The Immediate Theatre," *The Atlantic* (November, 1968) pp. 82–94.

Brooks, Peter. *The Melodramatic Imagination*. New Haven: Yale University Press, 1976.

Brown, John Mason, "Critic's View of a Critic: The Late George Jean Nathan, Wizard of Verbal Cactus," *New York Times*, Drama section 2 (13 April 1958): p3.

Bruccoli, Matthew, and Margaret Duggan, eds. *Correspondence of F. Scott Fitzgerald*. New York: Random House, 1980.

Carlson, Harry, ed. *Strindberg: Five Plays*. Berkeley: University of California Press, 1983.

Commins, Dorothy, ed. *Love and Admiration and Respect: The O'Neill-Commins Correspondence*. Durham, N. C.: Duke University Press, 1986.

Cooke, Alistair. *The Vintage Mencken*. New York: Vintage Books, 1955.

Deutsch, Helen, and Stella Hanau eds. *The Provincetown: a Story of the Theatre*. New York: Farrar and Rinehart, 1931.

Dolmetsch, Carl. *The Smart Set: a History and Anthology*. New York: Dial, 1966.

Donaldson, Scott. *Fool for Love: F. Scott Fitzgerald*. New York: Condon and Weed, 1981.

Downer, Alan, ed. *American Drama and Its Critics*. Chicago: University of Chicago Press, 1965.

Elias, Robert H., ed. *Letters of Theodore Dreiser: a Selection.* Philadelphia: University of Pennsylvania Press, 1959.

Fitzgerald, F. Scott. "A Short Autobiography," (with homage to Nathan) *The New Yorker* (25 May 1929): pp. 22–23.

———. *The Beautiful and Damned.* New York: Charles Scribner's Sons, 1950. (Character Maury Noble is a caricature of Nathan.)

Frick, Constance. *The Drama Criticism of George Jean Nathan.* Ithaca: Cornell University Press, 1943.

Gallup, Donald, ed., *The Journals of Thornton Wilder.* (New Haven: Yale University Press, 1985.

Gelb, Arthur and Barbara. *O'Neill.* New York: Harper & Brothers, 1967.

Gish, Lillian, with Ann Pinchot. *The Movies, Mr. Griffith and Me.* Englewood Cliffs, New Jersey: Prentice-Hall, 1969.

——— with James Frasher. *Dorothy and Lillian Gish.* New York: Charles Scribner's Sons, 1973.

Goldberg, Isaac. *The Theatre of George Jean Nathan.* New York: Simon & Schuster, 1926.

Graham, Sheila. *The Real F. Scott Fitzgerald.* New York: Grosset & Dunlap, 1976.

Grimsted, David. *Melodrama Unveiled.* Berkeley: University of California Press, 1987.

Gropper, William. "George Jean Nathan," *The Bookman* (August 1924): pp. 695–700.

Hatteras, Owen (pseudonym for Nathan and Mencken). *Pistols for Two.* New York: Alfred Knopf, 1917.

Hergescheimer, Joseph. "Lillian Gish," *The American Mercury* (April 1924): pp. 397–402.

Isaacs, Edith. "The Critical Arena, The Theatre of George Jean Nathan," *Theatre Arts* (February 1942): pp. 191–96.

Jones, David Richard. *Great Directors at Work.* Berkeley: University of California Press, 1987.

Knopf, Alfred. "The Mencken-Nathan Breakup," *The Baltimore Evening Sun* (22 June 1981) p. A9.

Kozlenko, Vladimir. *The Quintessence of Nathanism.* New York: Vrest Orton, 1930.

Lazarus, A. L. *The Best of George Ade.* Bloomington: Indiana University Press, 1985.

——— and Victor H. Jones. *Beyond Graustark: George Barr McCutcheon, Playwright Discovered.* Port Washington and London: Kennikat Press, 1981.

——— and H. Wendell Smith. *A Glossary of Literature and Composition.* Urbana, Illinois: National Council of Teachers of English, 1983.

——— et al., *Modern English.* New York: Grosset & Dunlap, 1971.

Lingemann, Richard. *Theodore Dreiser: At the Gates of the City.* New York: G. P. Putnam's Sons, 1986.

Manchester, William. *Disturber of the Peace: The Life of H. L. Mencken.* New York: Harper & Brothers, 1951.

Mencken, H. L. *Prejudices: First Series.* New York: Alfred Knopf, 1919.

Milford, Nancy. *Zelda, a Biography.* New York: Harper & Row, 1970.

Mitchell, Sally, ed., *East Lynne*. New Brunswick, N.J.: Rutgers University Press, 1984. (Reissue of a hitherto out-of-print book)

Mizener, Arthur. *The Far Side of Paradise*. Boston: Houghton Mifflin, 1965.

Morell, Parker. *Diamond Jim, the Life and Times of James Buchanan Brady*. New York: Simon and Schuster, 1934.

———. *Lillian Russell, the Era of Plush*. New York: Random House, 1940.

Nathan, George Jean. "American Drama," *Encyclopaedia Britannica*, 1943.

———. *Another Book of the Theatre*. New York: Alfred Knopf, 1915.

———. *Art of the Night*. New York: Alfred Knopf, 1928.

———. *Autobiography of an Attitude*. New York: Alfred Knopf, 1925.

———. *The Avon Flows*. New York: Random House, 1937.

———. *The Bachelor Life*. New York: Reynal & Hitchcock, 1941.

———. *Beware of Parents*. New York: Alfred Knopf, 1943.

———. *A Book Without a Title*. New York: Philip Goodman, 1918.

———. *Bottoms Up*. New York: Philip Goodman, 1917.

———. *Comedians All*. New York: Alfred Knopf, 1919.

———. *The Critic and the Drama*. New York: Alfred Knopf, 1922. Reprinted by Fairleigh Dickinson University Press, 1972.

———. "Critics Behind Bars," *Vanity Fair* (30 April 1931).

———. *Encyclopedia of the Theatre*. New York: Alfred Knopf, 1940. Reprinted by Fairleigh Dickinson University Press, 1970.

———. *Entertainment of a Nation*. New York: Alfred Knopf, 1942.

———. *The Eternal Mystery*. New York: Alfred Knopf, 1913.

———. *Europe After 8:15*. London: John Lane, 1914.

———. "Happiest Days of H. L. Mencken," *Esquire* (October 1957): pp. 146–150.

———. *The House of Satan*. New York: Alfred Knopf, 1926.

———. *I Believe*. New York: Alfred Knopf, 1939.

———. *The Intimate Notebooks of George Jean Nathan*. New York: Knopf, 1932.

———. *Land of the Pilgrims' Pride*. New York: Alfred Knopf, 1927.

———. Letters to August Mencken. The Mencken Room, Enoch Pratt Free Library, Baltimore, Md.

———. *Materia Critica*. New York: Alfred Knopf, 1924.

———. "Memories of Mencken," *Esquire* (October 1957), pp. 146–150.

———. "Memories of Fitzgerald, Lewis, and Dreiser," *Esquire* (October 1958): pp. 148–51.

———. *Monks Are Monks*. New York: Knopf, 1929.

———. *The Morning After the First Night*. New York: Knopf, 1938.

———. *Mr. George Jean Nathan Presents*. New York: Knopf, 1917.

———. *The New American Credo*. New York: Knopf, 1927.

———. *Passing Judgments*. New York: Knopf, 1934.

———. *The Popular Theatre*. New York: Knopf, 1918.

———. *Since Ibsen*. New York: Knopf, 1933.

———. *Testament of a Critic*. New York: Knopf, 1931.

———. *Theatre Book of the Year, 1942–43*. New York: Knopf, 1943.

———. *Theatre Book of the Year, 1943–44*. New York: Knopf, 1944.

———. *Theatre Book of the Year, 1944–45*. New York: Knopf, 1945.

———. *Theatre Book of the Year, 1945–46*. New York: Knopf, 1946.

———. *Theatre Book of the Year, 1946–47*. New York: Knopf, 1947.

———. *Theatre Book of the Year, 1947–48*. New York: Knopf, 1948.

———. *Theatre Book of the Year, 1948–49*. New York: Knopf, 1949.

———. *Theatre in the Fifties*. New York: Knopf, 1953.

———. *The Theatre of the Moment*. New York: Knopf, 1936.

———. *The Theatre, The Drama, The Girls*. New York, Knopf, 1921.

———. "Why Are Manuscripts Rejected by *Smart Set?*" *The Bookman* (May 1916): pp. 280–83.

———. "Why I Am Giving Up Bacherlorhood," *The American Weekly* (20 February 1955).

———. *The World in Falseface*. New York: Knopf, 1923.

Nathan, George Jean and H. L. Mencken. *The American Credo*. New York: Alfred Knopf, 1920.

———. (with H. L. Mencken) *Heliogabulus, a Buffoonery in Three Acts*. New York: Alfred Knopf, 1920.

O'Neill, Eugene. *The Complete Plays*. New York: Library of the Americas, 1988.

———. *The Moon of the Caribbees and Six Other Plays of the Sea*. New York: Boni and Liveright, 1923.

Ortolani, B. Ed., *Interntl Bibliography of Theatre*. Brooklyn College, 1988.

Rascoe, Burton. "Mencken, Nathan, and Cabell," *The American Mercury* (March 1940).

——— and Groff Conklin, eds. *The Smart Set Anthology*. New York: Reynal & Hitchcock, 1934.

Reynolds, R. C. *Stage Left: Development of the American Social Drama in the Thirties*. Troy, New York: Whitston Publishing Company, 1987.

Rigdon, Walter, ed. *The Biographical Encyclopaedia & Who's Who of the American Theatre*. New York: James Heineman, Inc. 1966.

Roberts, Nancy, and Arthur Roberts, eds. *As Ever Gene: The Letters of Eugene O'Neill to George Nathan*. Rutherford, N.J.: Fairleigh Dickinson University Press, 1987.

Roberts, Roderick. *The Friendship of Eugene O'Neill and George Jean Nathan*. Ann Arbor, Mich.: University Microfilms, 1970.

Schorer, Mark. *Sinclair Lewis: An American Life*. New York: McGraw-Hill, 1961.

Torrence, Bruce. *Hollywood: The First Hundred Years*. New York: Zoetrope, 1982.

Williams, Richard. "The Gallant Gish Girls," *Life* (August 1951): pp. 115–127.

Williams, Tennessee. *Memoirs*. New York: Doubleday, 1975.

Wilson, Edmund. *The Crackup and Journals*. New York: James Laughlin, 1945.

Index